# THOMAS HARDY'S ENGLISH

# THE LANGUAGE LIBRARY

EDITED BY DAVID CRYSTAL

RALPH W. V. ELLIOTT

# Thomas Hardy's English

BASIL BLACKWELL
in association with
ANDRÉ DEUTSCH

First published 1984
Reprinted and first published in paperback 1986

Basil Blackwell Ltd
108 Cowley Road, Oxford OX4 1JF, UK
in association with André Deutsch Limited
105 Great Russell Street, London WC1B 3LJ, England

Basil Blackwell Inc.
432 Park Avenue South, Suite 1505,
New York, NY 10016, USA

*British Library Cataloguing in Publication Data*

Elliott, Ralph W. V.
Thomas Hardy's English.—(The Language Library)
1. Hardy, Thomas, *1840 – 1928*—Language
I. Title    II. Series
823'.8    PR4758
ISBN 0-631-13659-2
ISBN 0-631-14922-8


*Library of Congress Cataloging in Publication Data*

Elliott, Ralph Warren Victor.
Thomas Hardy's English.

Bibliography: p.
Includes index.
1. Hardy, Thomas, *1840 – 1928*—Language. 2. Hardy,
Thomas, *1840 – 1928*—Style. I. Title.
[PR4758.E4   1986]   823'.8   85-26738
ISBN 0-631-13659-2
ISBN 0-631-14922-8 (pbk.)


Printed in Great Britain
by Billing and Sons Ltd, Worcester.

# Contents

🐚🐚🐚🐚🐚🐚

*For Margaret*

# Phonemic Symbols

🌀🌀🌀🌀🌀🌀

The following letters are used as phonemic symbols with their usual English values: p, b, t, d, k, g, f, v, s, z, h, l, r, m, n, w. Other symbols are used with the values indicated by the italicized letters in the keywords which follow:

### CONSONANTS

| ʃ | *sh*ip | Θ | *th*in |
|---|---|---|---|
| dʒ | *j*u*dg*e | j | *y*es |
| ŋ | lo*ng* | | |

### VOWELS

| ɪ | s*i*t | ʌ | c*u*b |
|---|---|---|---|
| iː | s*ee* | uː | s*oo*n |
| ɛ | s*e*t | ʊ | p*u*t |
| æ | s*a*t | ɔː | b*ou*ght |
| ɜː | *ea*rth | ɒ | n*o*t |
| ə | *a*bout | ɑː | c*a*lm |

### DIPHTHONGS

| ɪə | h*ere* | ʊə | g*our*d |
|---|---|---|---|
| eɪ | pl*ay* | oʊ | *oa*k |
| ɛə | th*ere* | ɔɪ | b*oy* |
| aɪ | fl*y* | aʊ | n*ow* |

Slant lines enclose phonemic symbols. A colon after a phonemic symbol indicates length.

# Preface

🌀🌀🌀🌀🌀🌀

EVERY reader of Thomas Hardy's novels, stories, and poems has had to come to terms with the singularities of his language, especially its vocabulary. This book represents one reader's attempt to do so. Eschewing both the abstractions of literary theories and the technical terminology of linguistics, I have concentrated on the raw materials of Hardy's English, his words, where he found them and how he used them. Largely self-educated, Hardy fashioned his language from many sources, prominent among them the dialect of his native Dorset, his early familiarity with the English Bible, and his wide reading. His architectural training taught him form, his studious visits to galleries made him aware of colours, his love of music inculcated rhythms; all brought enrichment to his English. But through all Hardy's linguistic schooling and practice ran a deep, persistent awareness of the past of the English language and its present heritage. This he exploited to the full, reviving obsolete words, using archaic words, coining new words according to traditional modes of word-formation.

To study Hardy's English closely is to become aware of a thousand years of linguistic history; his works are a place, to quote his own words in the first chapter of the final book of *A Laodicean*, 'for a mediaevalist to revel in, toss up his hat and shout hurrah in, send for his luggage, come and live in, die and be buried in'. I make no apology for repeatedly drawing the reader's attention to what I believe to be the key to an understanding of the often idiosyncratic character of Hardy's English, its timelessness. It is both ancient and modern, one moment stilted archaic and the next contemporary colloquial. It manages to be Anglo-Saxon Wessex and Victorian Dorset rolled into one, sometimes uneasily, at other times superbly so. But it is always unmistakably his English.

In the dialect with which Hardy was familiar from childhood, ancient words long since abandoned by the standard language sur-

9

vived in current usage. Grammatical forms and aspects of syntax as well as regional pronunciation, puzzling to the reader, were part of Hardy's mother tongue, certainly of his father's tongue and of the tongues of all those humble kinsfolk of whom in later life he so often felt ashamed. But for his early introduction to the speech of Wessex, seconded by the example of William Barnes, the Dorset poet, schoolmaster and philologist, Hardy's English could not have developed as it did. Nor would the Wessex novels and poems have acquired their unique music, the cadences of modern English reverberating insistently with echoes of the past.

Many of the echoes are literary; some inhere in the Wessex names which Hardy shaped out of real places. And just as rustic words and phrases force themselves into narrative and dialogue, so does the life of the countryside form itself into simile and metaphor. Moreover, there is a continuity of themes and attitudes in Hardy's work which links the earliest novels and poems unmistakably with the rest and makes increasing demands upon his linguistic resourcefulness. Hence a study of Hardy's English must embrace his verse as well as his prose, for they are all of a piece – 'this demonstrably coherent *oeuvre*', as a recent reviewer called it, a description that is also chronologically appropriate, for 'Hap' and *Desperate Remedies* are as demonstrably products of the same pen as *Tess of the d'Urbervilles* and 'We Are Getting to the End'.

Since the expiry of Hardy's copyright, editions of his works have multiplied, and I have therefore quoted poems invariably by their titles, the texts being those of *The Complete Poems* edited by James Gibson. Hardy's short stories are similarly identified by their titles, accompanied by the title of the collection of which they form part in Macmillan's Wessex Edition. The texts used are those of The New Wessex Edition. All longer quotations and, where appropriate, some of the shorter illustrations are accompanied by references to chapters, or books and chapters, and in *The Dynasts* to part, act, and scene. This should facilitate consultation by the reader without restriction to a given edition.

I have refrained from the barbarous practice of referring to Hardy's novels by abbreviated titles like *Tess* or *The Mayor*, or by initials, preferring to spell them out in full as Hardy entitled them. As Hardy gave much thought to the titles of his books they deserve to be respected. Footnotes have been kept to a minimum, and full details of books or articles to which reference is made in the text will be found in the Select Bibliography.

## Preface

All labourers in the Hardy vineyard are greatly indebted to their many precursors among whom Richard Little Purdy, Michael Millgate, and F.B. Pinion merit special mention. I am conscious of numerous debts to other scholars, critics and students, and gratefully acknowledge them herewith. I owe a special debt to Professors Claude Abrahams, Cleanth Brooks, J.T. Laird, and Gordon Williams, and to Mr. Gregory Hill for invaluable research assistance. Thanks are also due to Paul and Margaret Williams of Winterbourne Abbas; to the Curator and staff of the Dorset County Museum; to Mr Charles Pettit and his colleagues at the Dorset County Library; to the Librarian and staff of the Australian National University Library and of the State Library of South Australia; to the Director and staff of the Humanities Research Centre in Canberra; and to the Trustees of the National Humanities Center in North Carolina for awarding me a Visiting Fellowship, and to the Director and staff of the Center for making my visit such a fruitful and pleasant one. I also wish to thank the Editor of The Language Library, Professor David Crystal, for helpful advice and Mrs. Sara Menguc for skilfully steering the book through the press.

I gratefully acknowledge financial assistance from the Australian Research Grants Committee, the Australian National University, and the National Humanities Center. To my wife and family I am permanently indebted for being ever considerate and long-suffering.

Ralph W.V. Elliott
*University House*,
*Canberra*

# Acknowledgements

🈁🈁🈁🈁🈁🈁

I am grateful for permission to quote passages from the following works to:

Macmillan, London and Basingstoke: *The Life of Thomas Hardy, 1840–1920*, by F.E. Hardy; *Thomas Hardy's Personal Writings*, ed. Harold Orel; *The Complete Poems* and *The Variorum Edition of The Complete Poems*, ed. James Gibson; The New Wessex Edition of the Novels and Stories of Thomas Hardy.

Oxford University Press: *Our Exploits at West Poley*, ed. R.L. Purdy, 1978; *The Woodlanders*, ed. Dale Kramer; *The Collected Letters of Thomas Hardy*, ed. R.L. Purdy and Michael Millgate.

Hutchinson Publishing Group Ltd: *An Indiscretion in the Life of an Heiress*, ed. T. Coleman.

Columbia University Press: *The Personal Notebooks of Thomas Hardy*, ed. R.H. Taylor.

The Trustees of the Thomas Hardy Memorial Collection in the Dorset County Museum, Dorchester, Dorset: *The Architectural Notebook of Thomas Hardy*.

Professor Lennart A. Björk: *The Literary Notes of Thomas Hardy*.

Centaur Press Ltd: *The Poems of William Barnes*, ed. Bernard Jones.

I apologize for any inadvertent omissions of acknowledgement for passages quoted from any other copyright source.

# CHAPTER I

# The Charm of a Muddy Country Road

🦢🦢🦢🦢🦢🦢

'SIGHING about Hardy's style is a fairly old game among critics', remarks Robert B. Heilman, 'and one could make quite an anthology of despairing and witty observations about Hardy's verbal manners.' Since style, at its most basic, is 'proper words in proper places', in Swift's phrase, and since the present book is concerned with Hardy's words, such an anthology may serve as an appropriate introduction to a study of Hardy's English. Responding to Heilman's hint, Norman Page has recently given us the skeleton of such an anthology in his excellent essay 'Hardy and the English Language', a skeleton that deserves to be furnished with some flesh in the more leisurely context of the present study.

*   *   *

There are a few faults of style and grammar, but very few. 'Whomsoever's' is an odd formation, and 'factitiously pervasive' is a clumsy expression. A lawyer, too, might find fault with a deed full of stops, and containing the phrase 'on the determination of this demise', and a surgeon with '*os femoris*', but these technical errors are few. On the whole, the chief blemish of the book will be found in the occasional coarseness to which we have alluded, and which we can hardly further particularize, but which, startling as it once or twice is, is confined wholly to expressions, and does not affect the main character of the story. If the author will purge himself of this, though even this is better than the prurient sentimentality with which we are so often nauseated, we see no reason why he should not write novels only a little, if at all, inferior to the best of the present generation.
Review of *Desperate Remedies*, in *The Athenaeum* 1 April 1871

We have found it hard to read, but its shortcomings are easier to summarise than to encounter in order. Mr. Hardy's novel is very long, but his subject is very short and simple, and the work has been distended to its rather formidable dimensions by the infusion of a large amount of conversational and descriptive padding and the use of an ingeniously verbose and redundant style. It is inordinately diffuse, and, as a piece of narrative, singularly inartistic. The author has little sense of proportion, and almost none of composition.

Review of *Far from the Madding Crowd* by Henry James, in *The Nation* (New York), 24 December 1874

The style is pellucid, as a rule, but there are exceptions. 'Human mutuality' seems, to myself, an ill phrase. 'There, behind the blue narcotic haze, sat "the tragic mischief" of her drama, he who was to be the blood-red ray in the spectrum of her young life'. Here is an odd mixture of science and literature. A face is, or rather is not, 'furrowed with incarnated memories representing in hieroglyphic the centuries of her family's and England's history'. . . . Why people who are drinking beer should be said to 'seek vinous bliss' is not apparent. A woman, at the public-house in the evening, finds her troubles 'sinking to minor cerebral phenomena for quiet contemplation, in place of standing as pressing concretions which chafe body and soul'. Here is the very reef on which George Eliot was wrecked. However, tastes differ so much that the blemishes, as they appear to one reader, of Mr. Hardy's works may seem beauty-spots in the eyes of another reader. He does but give us of his best, and if his best be too good for us, or good in the wrong way, if, in short, we are not *en rapport* with him, why, there are plenty of other novelists, alive and dead, and the fault may be on our side, not on his.

Review of *Tess of the d'Urbervilles* by Andrew Lang, in *New Review*, February 1892

As the naturalist with a bone, so Mr. Hardy with a word can construct for us the whole manner of a man, the whole aspect of a place. Not the looks of definite objects only, but their surrounding and intervening atmospheres, become plain to us; the blue mists, or dusty gold lights, or thin gray breaths of air: once familiarised with one of his places, we know all about it . . . But if we search Mr. Hardy's books, to discover why we know this so surely, we are hard put to it for a reason: so delicate has been his manner, so natural and unobtrusive his 'mental tactility', that we have learned it all from his pages, as we should learn it by experience: our certainty and familiarity have grown upon us . . . It is no small task, to set whole spheres of life and work in a light so true, that all must own its truth. Patience and loving study alone can do it: no brilliant epigram, nor biting phrase, can make us understand the slowly prevailing, gently lingering, charm of all those rural lives and ways. It is the province of a deeper art: an art, patient, studious, and sure.

Lionel Johnson, *The Art of Thomas Hardy*, 1894

I mention this singular inaptness of expression, because I regard it as a sign of the general slackening of attention, the vagueness showing itself in the casual distribution of the subject-matter; showing itself, as we shall see in lack of masterful treatment of the Reader's attention, in utter deficiency of logical arrangement. These are the co-related deficiencies due to the same inactivity and confusion of thought.

I will not go over the subsequent passages again; my Reader can verify at a glance this lack of coherence, of sense of direction, particularly if he will bear in mind, for comparison, Stevenson's marvellously constructed account of his descent from one Cévennes valley into another, and of their respective physical and moral characteristics. The two passages – Hardy's and Stevenson's – represent, within the limit of endurable writing, the two extremes of intellectual slackness and intellectual activity.

'Vernon Lee' (Violet Paget), *The Handling of Words and Other Studies in Literary Psychology*, 1923

Do we insist that a great novelist shall be a master of melodious prose? Hardy was no such thing. He feels his way by dint of sagacity and uncompromising sincerity to the phrase he wants, and it is often of unforgettable pungency. Failing it, he will make do with any homely or clumsy or old-fashioned turn of speech, now of the utmost angularity, now of a bookish elaboration. No style in literature, save Scott's, is so difficult to analyse; it is on the face of it so bad, yet it achieves its aim so unmistakably. As well might one attempt to rationalise the charm of a muddy country road, or of a plain field of roots in winter. And then, like Dorsetshire itself, out of these very elements of stiffness and angularity his prose will put on greatness; will roll with a Latin sonority; will shape itself in a massive and monumental symmetry like that of his own bare downs.

Virginia Woolf, 'The Novels of Thomas Hardy', *The Second Common Reader*, 1932 (written in January 1928)

The work of the late Thomas Hardy represents an interesting example of a powerful personality uncurbed by any institutional attachment or by submission to any objective beliefs; unhampered by any ideas, or even by what sometimes acts as a partial restraint upon inferior writers, the desire to please a large public. He seems to me to have written as nearly for the sake of 'self-expression' as a man well can; and the self which he had to express does not strike me as a particularly wholesome or edifying matter of communication. He was indifferent even to the prescripts of good writing: he wrote sometimes overpoweringly well, but always very carelessly; at times his style touches sublimity without ever having passed through the stage of being good.

T.S. Eliot, *After Strange Gods*, 1934

Though I shouldn't think of calling Hardy a great poet, I do believe that he wrote a certain amount of major poetry. And this major poetry is hardly ever represented in the anthologies that bring him in. It is a very small amount, though he wrote a great deal of verse: there are nine hundred and fifty pages in the collected volume, and to go through them again, as I did before writing this note, was to be, if possible, still more convinced of the need for a strictly discriminating justice. The judicious admirer wishing to ensure proper attention for Hardy would select a very small proportion indeed of that mass.

The best things are lost in it, and prolonged exploration is discouraging and blunting. Never did a writer of good poems show less promise and distinction in the common run of his work . . . In saying that his characteristic verse has no distinction one is not intending to deny that it is characteristic: it is positively, even aggressively, so. Lack of distinction in Hardy becomes a positive quality. If one says that he seems to have no sensitiveness for words, one recognises at the same time that he has made a style out of stylelessness. There is something extremely personal about the gauche, unshrinking mismarriages – group-mismarriages – of his diction, in which, with naïf aplomb, he takes as they come the romantic-poetical, the prosaic banal, the stilted literary, the colloquial, the archaistic, the erudite, the technical, the dialect word, the brand-new Hardy coinage . . .

These [examples quoted] are representative; they give a fair idea of what one may expect to find at any opening of the collected Hardy. They scarcely, however, suggest how the assertive oddity of the Character can begin to look like the strength of a poet. He who handles words in this way, it might reasonably be concluded on such evidence (which could be multiplied indefinitely), couldn't possibly be a distinguished writer of any kind. Nevertheless, it is an unusually dull patch when half-a-dozen pages don't yield instances in which the same assertively characteristic hand achieves a decided expressive strength or vivacity.

F.R. Leavis, 'Hardy the Poet', *Southern Review*, Summer 1940

Hardy was not a careless writer. The difference between his first and last editions proves this, in matters of style aside from his painful reconstruction of his manuscripts mutilated for serial publication. He wrote and wrote again, and he never found it easy. He lacked elegance, he never learned the trick of the whip-lash phrase, the complicated lariat twirling of the professed stylists. His prose lumbers along, it jogs, it creaks, it hesitates, it is as dull as certain long passages in the Tolstoy of *War and Peace*, for example. That celebrated first scene on Egdon Heath, in *The Return of the Native*. Who does not remember it? And in actual re-reading, what could be duller? What could be more labored than his introduction of the widow Yeobright at the heath fire among the dancers, or more unconvincing than the fears of the timid boy that the assembly are literally raising the Devil? Except for this in my memory of that episode, as in dozens of others in many of Hardy's novels, I have seen it, I was there. When I read it, it almost disappears from view, and afterwards comes back, phraseless, living in its somber clearness, as Hardy meant it to do. I feel certain. This to my view is the chief quality of good prose as distinguished from poetry. By his own testimony, he limited his territory by choice, set boundaries to his material, focused his point of view like a burning glass down on a definite aspect of things. He practiced a stringent discipline, severely excised and eliminated all that seemed to him not useful or appropriate to his plan. In the end his work was the sum of his experience, he arrived at his particular true testimony; along the way, sometimes, many times, he wrote sublimely.

Katherine Anne Porter, 'Notes on a Criticism of Thomas Hardy', *Southern Review*, Summer 1940

The parodist may fairly indulge his humour on some prevalent weaknesses of the Muse of Hardy . . . the style, like the substance, has its oddities, tempting to the cheerful lover of a little burlesque. Hardy's poetic language is sometimes a peculiar compound of the high-flown and the dull. If he means 'I asked' he is liable to say 'I queried' or rather 'Queried I'; he is liable to 'opine' instead of think, and if it be a crime to exclaim 'God wot' he commits it more than once. No admirer of the Wordsworthian

Spade, with which Wilkinson hath tilled his lands

can go far unrewarded in Hardy's poems; they have their share of stuffed-owl simplicities, such as the observation in the railway waiting-room,

The table bore a Testament
For travellers' reading, if suchwise bent.

But Hardy risks all that. He goes his road in the matter of expression, unworried about grinning faces, and in this spirit he arrives at numberless decisive ways of putting things, offered him and accepted from an open love of life . . .

Such is his independence in saying what he means in his verse, such his strength founded in a constant principle of doing the work thoroughly. The result is to be a translation of the actual, and the terms must therefore have as much of the shrewdness and particularity of life, according to our senses' report, as words can have; it does not matter to Hardy whether others would have given these words a ticket of admission or not. So long as they are words that strike, bite in, caress, disturb, unveil the truth, quicken the curiosity, they will suit him . . . Hardy's respect for and reliance upon the intellectual resources of the fully developed English tongue are obvious; he was entirely receptive of that eloquence also, and can employ it; yet in many of his poems the immediate, physical, substantial effect of local experience, the word formed with primitive intensity upon the thing indicated, is his mark and his command.

Edmund Blunden, *Thomas Hardy*, 1924

One of the advantages of being a largely self-taught writer and of coming out of an old-fashioned society is that one may be less inhibited and constrained and more open and creative in his handling of language . . .

Hardy will yield plenty of problem cases of the sort with which I am here concerned. Indeed, I was at first tempted to draw all of my illustrations, the successes as well as the failures, from Hardy's poetry. For Hardy, in his diction, constantly violates nineteenth-century literary decorum. He was not in conscious revolt. He was quite happy with Victorian poetic diction and used it as a matter of course. But he uses along with it Dorsetshire dialect words, technical terms taken from science and philosophy, occasional grotesque coinages of his own, and sometimes something very close to slang. For example, the ghosts that he describes in 'Wessex Heights' have 'weird detective ways'. A look of love is *thorough-sped*, a woman *lips* a reply, a cave has the character of *stillicide*, one man tells another that he will meet him tonight or tomorrow night or *anywhen*, light *illumes* a page. Shadrach with his companions Meshoch and Abednego stood in the firey furnace *unshent*.

These words drawn from such different levels of diction often jangle together most unfortunately. And yet the liberties which Hardy allowed himself – even though not because of any consciously held theory – even if only through some sort of inspired bungling – constitute the basis of his characteristic successes. What is too often an inept dissonance finds resolution, from time to time, in harmonies much richer than the music of some of Hardy's contemporaries who never depart from a limiting decorum. No wonder T.S. Eliot once remarked that as a poet Hardy on occasion attained to greatness without first having gone through the prior state of being simply good.

Cleanth Brooks, 'The Language of Poetry: Some Problem Cases', *Archiv für das Studium der Neueren Sprachen*, 1967

The critics who have written on Hardy's poetry spend an inordinate time in complaining about the badness of his bad poems. The bad poems are certainly there, but though they may be boring or ridiculous they are never pretentious. By contrast, if you take the collected Yeats, you feel the strain of all that rhetorical striving in the minor poems, and it is only in the best of Yeats, and not always then, that he is able to free himself from the rhetoric. Rhetoric is a form of pretence, of making something appear bigger or more important than you know it is. Well, you never feel, even in Hardy's most boring and ridiculous poetry, that he is pretending – he is never rhetorical. And there are not many poets of whom this can be said. If the price paid for his fifty best poems is some hundreds of bad ones, it is well paid. And throughout, there is always the feeling that he is trying to see things as they are, whether it is an abstract term like Pity or a physical thing like the way the heat of noon breathes out from old walls at midnight; he is never trying to falsify either them or his emotion about them – and so much the worse if the poem ends up in bathos or flatness. Ezra Pound more than once praises Hardy for his insistence on immersing himself in his subject. And this is well said, for the immersion leaves him no room for pretence, or for anything other than honesty. Much of what sustains me through the flatter parts of the *Collected Poems* is this feeling of contact with an honest man who will never lie to me.

Thom Gunn, 'Hardy and the Ballads', *Agenda*, 1972

A contrast of a different kind between the major and the minor fiction is stylistic: no major novelist's language absents itself from felicity more quickly than Hardy's when the quickening impulse grows feeble or dies altogether. Even the best novels are not altogether free from lapses into ponderousness or banality, and some of the minor novels contain fine passages; but the different degree to which novels as close in time as *Tess* and *The Well-Beloved* utilize the resources of the language is a matter for astonishment: the contrast between the seen and felt in one and the cerebral and mechanical in the other is very evident on the stylistic level.

Norman Page, *Thomas Hardy*, 1977

&ast; &ast; &ast;

The most striking impression of such critical observations as the foregoing, which could easily be multiplied beyond any reader's patience, is that many of them contradict one another. Hardy wrote 'always very carelessly', says Eliot; 'Hardy was not a careless writer', says Katherine Anne Porter. One reviewer finds 'coarseness', another critic describes Hardy's manner as 'delicate'. One reader finds 'singular inaptness of expression', another discovers 'number-less decisive ways of putting things'. One speaks of Hardy's 'sombre clearness', another criticizes his 'ingeniously verbose and redundant style'. Hardy is taxed with practically every linguistic and stylistic offence which a writer of English is capable of committing: oddity, clumsiness, indifference to the prescripts of good writing, lack of elegance, ponderousness, banality, lumbering prose, stuffed-owl simplicities, stylelessness.

And yet at the same time practically all his critics, and presumably the countless readers whom his works continue to attract, pay tribute to his strengths as a writer of English: his pungency, his natural and unobtrusive 'mental tactility', his reliance upon the vast resources of the English language, the rich harmonies of his 'music', the fact that he could write 'overpoweringly well'.

There is truth in both camps, and the most reliable critics of Hardy are those who recognize that what are so easily spotted as Hardy's weaknesses are often the sources of his strength. F.R. Leavis acknowledges this most succinctly: 'He has made a style out of stylelessness.' The present study will try to argue the same case for Hardy's language: that his peculiar mixture of the archaic and the modern, of dialect and received standard English, of grammatical quirks, syntactic idiosyncrasies, of 'the odd mixture of science and literature' noted by Andrew Lang, are not the results of carelessness or intellectual slackness or indifference to the precepts of good writing, but represent a deliberate forging of a linguistic instrument suited to Hardy's purposes as storyteller and poet. Edmund Blunden and Norman Page both draw attention to Hardy's respect for, his reliance upon, and his utilization of the resources of the English language. Herein lies the key to Hardy's English and to our understanding of the style which it shaped. Not content with the Victorian English of his time, Hardy sought colour in dialect, as William Barnes did, and truth of expression in words and forms as far back as the language would take him, as Gerard Manley Hopkins did. Hardy was quite explicit on this point, as he made clear to William Archer:

> I have no sympathy with the criticism which would treat English as a dead language – a thing crystallized at an arbitrarily selected stage of its existence, and bidden to forget that it has a past and deny that it has a future. Purism, whether in grammar or in vocabulary, almost always means ignorance. Language was made before grammar, not grammar before language. And as for the people who make it their business to insist on the utmost possible impoverishment of our English vocabulary, they seem to me to ignore the lessons of history, science, and common-sense.

Hardy's practice bears out the theoretical stance here adopted. He never forgot that English has a past, a long and colourful past, nor that grammar is an instrument of language, not a law unto itself. The accident of his birth in a part of England in which much traditional speech was still alive provided Hardy with invaluable insight into chapters of English linguistic history not so readily accessible to other writers. His search for education wherever he could find it after the limited resources of country schooling were exhausted brought further insight and continuing linguistic enrichment. The fruits of such a background and such an education were, on the one hand, the angularities and janglings and oddities noticed by the critics. But more importantly, as in the case of Faulkner, they were an unfettered, uninhibited creativity of language and a receptiveness to linguistic promptings from whatever source offered itself: dialect, literature, science, painting, music, architecture, even jargon and slang. To trace the shaping influences of these and other sources of Hardy's English and relate them to Hardy's art in prose and verse is the main business of the following pages.

# CHAPTER II

# Three Strands

𝕲𝕲𝕲𝕲𝕲𝕲

IN the words of W.H. Auden:

> The properties of Hardy's world were the properties of my own child-
> hood: it was unsophisticated and provincial, and it was the England of the
> professional classes, clergymen, doctors, lawyers, and architects. A world
> still largely Victorian, in which one went to church twice on Sundays and
> had daily family prayers before breakfast, did not know divorced persons
> or artists, rode in pony traps or on bicycles to rub brasses or collect fossils,
> and relied for amusement on family resources, reading aloud, gardening,
> walks, piano duets, and dumb crambo; above all a world which had
> nothing to do with London, the stage, or French literature.

Hardy's world certainly acquired many of the 'properties' here
enumerated, and indeed London, the stage, and French literature as
well, and much else besides. But his childhood was a good deal less
well furnished than Auden's, and even as a young man the transition
into the milieu of the professional classes was a gradual and painstaking process. Whether Hardy ever played dumb crambo does not
appear to have been recorded; if he did, his unorthodox rhymes
probably astonished his family as much as they later did his critics.

As Hardy's English is unmistakably the product of his formative
years, a look at his background and the influences shaping his youth
will help to account in some measure for the quirks of language and
oddities of style so persistently remarked upon in the passages cited
in the preceding anthology.

Speaking of himself as he entered upon the third decade of his life,
Hardy refers to

> a triple existence unusual for a young man – what he used to call, in looking
> back, a life twisted of three strands – the professional life, the scholar's life,
> and the rustic life.

The first of these 'lives', in linguistic terms, denotes the acquisition of a considerable technical vocabulary, not confined to the architectural profession to which he was apprenticed on leaving school. That his architectural training influenced his prose and more especially his verse in other ways as well, has long been remarked. 'The scholar's life' embraces that propensity for 'omnivorous' reading which Hardy ascribes to his mother and his grandmother and which may well have been prompted by their example as well as by his own innate curiosity and natural talent. 'The rustic life' is his childhood and adolescent background of Dorsetshire countryside, customs, and speech. All three strands, and the latter in particular, had a profound effect upon the shaping of Hardy's English.

Hardy's professional life as a student and practising architect was a relatively short one. His training with John Hicks in Dorchester extended from 1856 to 1862. This was followed by five years in Arthur Blomfield's office in London and by further professional work in Dorset, Cornwall, and London, until Hardy finally gave up architecture as a profession in favour of literature in 1872. But he never lost interest in it, and as late as 1927 was reminiscing about mudwall and thatch cottages and their mode of construction. This continuing interest also permeates his fiction and influenced the shaping of his poetry. Hardy knew, as he wrote in his autobiography,*

> that in architecture cunning irregularity is of enormous worth, and it is obvious that he carried on into his verse, perhaps in part unconsciously, the Gothic art-principle in which he had been trained – the principle of spontaneity, found in mouldings, tracery, and such like – resulting in the 'unforeseen' (as it has been called) character of his metres and stanzas, that of stress rather than of syllable, poetic texture rather than poetic veneer; the latter kind of thing, under the name of 'constructed ornament', being what he, in common with every Gothic student, had been taught to avoid as the plague.
>
> (*Life*, p. 301)

---

* As *The Life of Thomas Hardy* by Florence Emily Hardy, comprising *The Early Life of Thomas Hardy* and *The Later Years of Thomas Hardy*, was largely written by Hardy himself, it is now generally referred to as his autobiography, although written in the third person. I have referred to it throughout as the *Life*.

In the novels several of Hardy's characters are architects: Springrove and Manston, Ambrose and Owen Graye in *Desperate Remedies*; Stephen Smith in *A Pair of Blue Eyes*; George Somerset and Havill in *A Laodicean*, in which novel the villain Dare also claims 'some knowledge' of architectural draughtsmanship and is engaged as Somerset's assistant. There are numerous instances of buildings described with an architect's trained eye mellowed by the poet's vision of what, in his description of Oxwell Hall in *The Trumpet-Major*, Hardy called 'the marks of human wear and tear'; that interplay between people and places, especially buildings, to which he repeatedly draws attention in his 'Memories of Church Restoration' of 1906.

Hardy's architectural training entailed the acquisition of a considerable technical vocabulary, to which we shall return; but it was also a period of intellectual growth in other fields. Apart from his reading, the years in London were by no means concerned solely with 'Coloured Bricks and Terra Cotta', with Gothic designs and iron girders. Hardy went to dances, to the theatre, the opera, the galleries, and the museums. In his first year in London, he wrote to his sister Mary:

> I generally run down to the Exhibition for an hour in the evening two or three times a week, after I come out I go to the reading room of the Kensington Museum.

He systematically studied the masters at the National Gallery and took French classes at King's College. Inevitably, his vocabulary was greatly enlarged by these activities, and we shall find his fiction and his verse having recourse to the language of music and of the pictorial and theatrical arts, while of the foreign words and expressions interspersed in his writing, those from French are in the majority.

Hardy's 'scholar's life' is summed up, echoing Hardy's own words, in Philip Collins's description, 'He was a "born bookworm" – like Jude, "crazy for books",' and much patient scholarship has traced for us the influences of Hardy's reading on his thought and art: from William R. Rutland's invaluable pioneering study of 1938 to Lennart A. Björk's work on Hardy's literary notes and his informative essay of 1980. The early influences are many and diverse and have left their mark on Hardy's language: the English Bible and Shakespeare, ballads, romantic fiction, poetry, even literary periodicals. While still in his teens, Hardy was introduced to *The Saturday*

*Review* by his friend and mentor Horace Moule who exerted considerable influence on the shaping of Hardy's intellectual interests. Before he was twenty-five he had read, among others, Darwin, Bagehot, Ruskin, and Fourier's *The Passions of the Human Soul*.

In a letter to Edmund Gosse, written on 2 November 1883, Hardy makes the interesting comment that Gosse's

> study on Lodge reminds me that Lodge's poem to Rosaline was one of the first two or three which awakened in me a true, or mature, consciousness of what poetry consists in – after a Dark Age of five or six years which followed that vague sense, in childhood, of the charms of verse that most young people experience.

Some of his earliest reading is mentioned in the autobiography, and it is not too hard a task to seek the inspiration for some of Hardy's later 'stilted literary' moments or his 'Latin sonority' in his early acquaintance with Dryden and Johnson, or in the classical writers themselves whom he read 'from six to eight in the morning', while apprenticed to John Hicks in Dorchester.

By this time, according to the *Life*, Hardy had been studying Latin for some eight years, since he was twelve, adding Greek while studying architecture. At times the atmosphere in Hicks's office must have resembled an undergraduate seminar when Hicks, Hardy, and his fellow-pupil Henry Robert Bastow (who later had a notable career as an architect in Tasmania and Victoria) debated 'some knotty point' of Latin or Greek grammar.

The fruits of the young 'scholar's life' are evident in Hardy's earliest verse and prose. Wordsworth clearly fathered Hardy's 'Domicilium'; and in his poems written in his twenties there appear words which were unlikely to have been in common use in Bockhampton: the first of those lexical heavyweights, the 'dictionary words' encountered in his eclectic reading which were to become such a marked feature of his style: 'these purblind Doomsters' ('Hap'); 'The Great Dame whence incarnation flows' ('At a Bridal'); 'it cuts like contumely' ('Revulsion'); 'deeply skilled/In every intervolve of high and wide' ('Heiress and Architect'), with its substantival use of *intervolve*, probably triggered by the corresponding verb used by Milton and Shelley.

Into his first published piece, 'How I Built Myself a House' (1865), there creeps a biblical allusion, a reference to Euclid, and a mention of the leading articles in *The Times* which Hardy considered valuable reading 'in a study of style'. So he did Defoe, whose 'affected simplicity' he tried to emulate in *An Indiscretion in the Life of an Heiress* – the remnant of that first novel *The Poor Man and the Lady* 'which never saw the light', as Hardy wrote to Macmillans in 1871, and which also has its share of quotations from the Bible as well as the marks of Shelley and Browning.

*Desperate Remedies*, his first published novel (1871), bears ample witness to young Hardy's scholarly endeavours. Not only are there the first literary forays into dialect ('here's a caddle', 'an outstep place', 'no 'tidn' ', 'avore night'), but here are literary echoes, notably of Shelley and Virgil, also of Wordsworth, Terence, Dante, and others, and above all the Bible, with verbal echoes as frequent as direct quotations. Here, as in the early verse, are the 'sonorities' which Hardy presumably introduced because, as F.B. Pinion surmises, 'Hardy assumed from the start that a writer was expected to be cultured'. And so we find 'bread-and-butter cut into diaphanous slices'; 'the subjoined facts sprang, as it were, into juxtaposition in his brain'; the coachman 'panting from his exertions in pedestrianism'. Not at all untypical is the collocation of a foreign idiom, a classical allusion, and an echo of Hardy's scientific reading:

> Manston was utterly at fault now. His previous experience of the effect of his form and features upon womankind *en masse*, had taught him to flatter himself that he could account by the same law of natural selection for the extraordinary interest Miss Aldclyffe had hitherto taken in him, as an unmarried man; an interest he did not at all object to, seeing that it kept him near Cytherea, and enabled him, a man of no wealth, to rule on the estate as if he were its lawful owner. Like Curius at his Sabine farm, he had counted it his glory not to possess gold himself, but to have power over her who did.
>
> (*Desperate Remedies*, Ch. 9)

The linguistic seminars in Hicks's office in Dorchester led to an occasional impasse, whereupon Hardy would run next door to seek an authoritative resolution from the Dorset sage, the 'Poet Barnes', who kept school there and whose contribution to Hardy's development, linguistic and literary, extended far beyond questions of Latin or Greek grammar. William Barnes, so Samuel Hynes has claimed,

> is the only poet, with the obvious exception of Shakespeare, whose influence is demonstrable; and the direction of his influence is the direction taken by English poetry in the transitional period between High Victorianism and the twentieth century.

Barnes made Hardy aware of poetic forms – Welsh, Persian, Italian –
which he might never have encountered in his own reading and which
he used in his poems. There were natural affinities as well as temper-
amental differences between the two men. For one thing, Barnes was
much older: he was fifty-five when Hardy, at sixteen, began his
pupillage with Hicks; for another, Hardy did not share Barnes's
'zunny' idealization of the countryside and its people and the
younger poet's vision took on a more sombre hue.

Nor, as is plain from Hardy's style, did he share Barnes's passion
for linguistic purity, a phenomenon not unfamiliar among philologists of that period, like the redoubtable George Stephens; but he
was strongly impressed by Barnes's use of dialect. The immediate
effect was to reinforce Hardy's native speech and to make him aware
of the resources of Dorset English for poetry, as the first of Barnes's
collections of Dorset dialect poems had appeared by the time Hardy
began his apprenticeship in Dorchester: *Poems of Rural Life in the
Dorset Dialect* (1844). The impact of these poems, and of those yet to
come, remained with Hardy all his life. He learned them by heart,
recited them to his friends, and eventually published his own selection of them, in 1908, with a preface in which his views on the
employment of dialect in poetry were clearly articulated. Hardy
visited Barnes on a number of occasions until the latter's death in
1886, and there is much justice in Harold Orel's description of
Barnes as 'the hero of [Hardy's] youth, indeed of his entire life'. That
this hero was a living embodiment of Hardy's native speech, whose
voice could be heard, duly supported by appropriate spellings and
diacritics, in his poems, was a fact of great importance in the shaping
of Thomas Hardy's English.

Hardy's early years were spent in intimate contact with the 'world
of shepherds and ploughmen' of which he speaks in his autobiography, and whose speech was the Dorset dialect upon which both
the poet and the novelist were to draw readily and fruitfully throughout his long creative career. That Hardy persistently belittled this
dialectal background is thoroughly in accord with his obfuscating
tendency to conceal his humble origins amid 'the rustic life' of which
his family formed part.

The point is not unimportant; for if we are to believe his protestations, his early linguistic influences were much more those of what
in *Tess of the d'Urbervilles* he calls 'ordinary English' than those
of the majority of the neighbours in Bockhampton and Stinsford,
Puddletown and even Dorchester, who spoke the local dialect. But we

do not have to believe his protestations. It is now widely recognized that when it came to his personal affairs (and the word is applicable in its several connotations), Hardy was quite capable of deception. J.I.M. Stewart describes the autobiography as 'full of fibs, and of fibs which Hardy clearly enjoyed fabricating', and more recently Richard H. Taylor bluntly states that Hardy 'in later years falsified the record of his humble origins'.

Hardy's ambivalence towards his native dialect as man and as artist is succinctly described in his authorial comment upon Elizabeth-Jane's speech in *The Mayor of Casterbridge*:

> One grievous failing of Elizabeth's was her occasional pretty and pictur-esque use of dialect words – those terrible marks of the beast to the truly genteel.
> (Ch. 20)

Within his own immediate family the marks of the beast were prominent enough: his father spoke dialect to his labourers, and presumably to others as well; and Hardy's brother Henry retained his broad Dorset accent throughout his life. Whether his mother Jemima Hardy, as seems less likely, 'habitually spoke the dialect', as Mrs. Durbeyfield did, although she too sprang from a long line of Dorset folk, is not known for certain. In the *Life* hers is an idealized portrayal, although we need not doubt her inclination for reading and the influence this had upon her son, nor the fund of local stories and legends with which she regaled him. According to Hardy, reminiscing at the age of eighty-two, as reported by Vere Collins, Mrs. Hardy used dialect only when speaking to the cottagers. Per-haps it is not irrelevant to recall that in *A Pair of Blue Eyes* Stephen Smith's master-mason father and his mother both speak dialect to their architect son.

When Hardy says of Tess that 'the dialect was on her tongue to some extent, despite the village school' (Ch. 2), he is close to des-cribing his own boyhood speech, especially if we leave the 'extent' unquantified. That even in his thirtieth year his speech suggested the Dorset pronunciation of his youth is probably the import of Emma Lavinia Hardy's 'recollection' of 'his slightly different accent' when they first met at St. Juliot. But for his anxiety to conceal his humble origins, Hardy might well have been as ready as young Joey in *The Hand of Ethelberta* to acknowledge rather than to deny his native speech:

If I talk the Wessex way 'tisn't for want of knowing better; 'tis because my staunch nater makes me bide faithful to our old ancient institutions.
(Ch. 18).

Mrs. Garland, in *The Trumpet-Major*, might have profited from this attitude, whenever she grieved over Anne's catching up 'some dialect-word or accent from the miller and his friends' (Ch. 1).

At the same time, Hardy's appreciation of the value of dialect words, especially, as he said to William Archer, 'if they express an idea which cannot otherwise be so accurately or so briefly expressed', steadily increased, helped along by the example of Barnes, and more especially as the destructive inroads of 'ordinary' English grew ever more insistent. It is worth recalling that in the passage from *The Mayor of Casterbridge* quoted earlier the words 'pretty and picturesque' did not appear in the serial version; they were included from the first edition onwards. Already into his earliest known poem, the Wordsworthian lines entitled 'Domicilium', there creeps the southern dialectal word *efts*, elsewhere spelt *effets*,* which standard English replaced by *newts*, and which looks oddly out of place amid the 'variegated box' and 'yonder garden-plots' diction of this stylized youthful composition. When such a word reappears later in Hardy's work, its integration is generally much more unobtrusive:

> Choosing her path amid the efts that were basking upon the outer slopes of the plantation she wound her way up the tree-shrouded camp to the wooden cabin in the centre.
> (*Two on a Tower*, Ch. 34)

It is important to form a true picture of Dorsetshire rusticity and its language. Hardy's father-in-law, John Attersoll Gifford, is reputed to have referred to his daughter's husband as a 'low-born churl who has presumed to marry into my family'. Hardy was certainly of humble origin, but the word 'churl' carries disparaging connotations of ill-breeding which are wholly inappropriate. 'Their reasonings and emotions are as complicated as ours', exclaims Christine in 'The Waiting Supper' (*A Changed Man*), retorting to Bellston's 'It does one's heart good . . . to see these simple peasants enjoying themselves.' Hardy refers to the music-hall image of the countryman as

---

* See the interesting map showing words for 'newt' reproduced from the Leeds *Survey of English Dialects* in G.L. Brook, *English Dialects*. (The Language Library) London, 1963, p. 82

'Hodge' in his essay 'The Dorsetshire Labourer', deliberately drawing a caricature, 'the pitiable dummy', as he calls it in *Tess of the d'Urbervilles*, Ch. 18, in order to demolish it. The true picture of the rustic family is sympathetic and authentic and includes this sketch of their language:

> [The visitor] would, for one thing, find that the language, instead of being a vile corruption of cultivated speech, was a tongue with grammatical inflection rarely disregarded by his entertainer, though his entertainer's children would occasionally make a sad hash of their talk. Having attended the National School they would mix the printed tongue as taught therein with the unwritten, dying, Wessex English that they had learnt of their parents, the result of this transitional state of theirs being a composite language without rule or harmony.
>
> ('The Dorsetshire Labourer')

Hardy's father, whom his wife described as 'rather amusingly old-fashioned', is not untypical, in manner of speech, of the 'entertainer', the Dorsetshire countryman, of this sketch, although Hardy was ever at pains to emphasize his social standing. He wrote to C. Kegan Paul on 18 April 1881:

> From time immemorial – I can speak from certain knowledge of four generations – my direct ancestors have all been master-masons, with a set of journeymen masons under them: though they have never risen above this level they have *never* sunk below it – i.e. they have never been journeymen themselves.

William Barnes's linguistic background was similarly local: both his father and his grandfather had been farmers.

The 'composite language' of the younger, Hardy's, generation, which Hardy so expressively describes as 'hash', is exemplified most consistently in the speech of Tess whose bilingualism is primarily social: 'the dialect at home, more or less; ordinary English abroad and to persons of quality' (Ch. 3). The latter was the product of school and 'a London-trained mistress'; in *The Well-Beloved* Hardy calls it 'the governess-tongue of no country at all' (I, Ch. 2). The change to more general education, for all the benefits it conferred, was bound to have deleterious effects upon local dialects in which, as Hardy claims in *Far from the Madding Crowd*, Ch. 22, 'ten generations failed to alter the turn of a single phrase'. The misgivings about sending country children to school are voiced with particular vehemence by Eustacia's grandfather in *The Return of the Native*, II, Ch. 1:

> 'They say, too, that Clym Yeobright is become a real perusing man, with the strangest notions about things. There, that's because he went to school early, such as the school was.'
>
> 'Strange notions, has he?' said the old man. 'Ah, there's too much of that sending to school in these days! It only does harm. Every gatepost and barn's door you come to is sure to have some bad word or other chalked upon it by the young rascals: a woman can hardly pass for shame sometimes. If they'd never been taught how to write they wouldn't have been able to scribble such villainy. Their fathers couldn't do it, and the country was all the better for it.'

And yet, even with having passed 'the Sixth Standard in the National School', Tess's dialect remains 'on her tongue', and in moments of emotional tension she instinctively slips into it, very audibly, for example, in Chapter 38. We are reminded that in the manuscript of the novel, Tess used dialect 'only when excited by joy, surprise, or grief' (f. 19), which Hardy changed in 1892 to the version quoted above. Similarly, Elizabeth-Jane in *The Mayor of Caster-bridge*: 'But I can't help using rural words sometimes, when I don't mean to' (Ch. 20). So do those much better educated men in *Jude the Obscure*, Phillotson and Gillingham, of whom Hardy observes: 'Though well-trained and even proficient masters, they occasionally used a dialect-word of their boyhood to each other in private' (IV, Ch. 4). So, too, does Thomas Hardy himself. In his autobiography and in his letters he now and then employs a dialectal word or phrase, usually in quotation marks or accompanied by an extenuating or explanatory comment: 'Her husband *is what we call* a "yopping, or yapping" man'; 'they are wild hyacinths, or *as we call them*, graegles\*. Then a sheet of red; they are ragged robins, or *as they are called here*, robin-hoods'; 'I was at her house some time ago, but "my pride was sick" (*as they say here*) that I would not allude to it.'

At times the hash is of a different kind, as the dialect-speaker employs a word or expression learnt at school or acquired from 'persons of quality'. We have noted how readily Hardy himself

---

\* In the *Mayor of Casterbridge*, Ch. 20, we are told that Elizabeth-Jane 'grew to talk of "greggles" as "wild hyacinths" '. Barnes, in his poem 'The Spring', speaks of 'the wood-screen'd graegle's bell', and in 'Lindenore' of 'graegle bells in beds o' blue'.

enriched his own vocabulary in this way and how this affected even his earliest poems and prose. It is a device which he uses with humorous effect in his fiction, but beneath the humour is the awareness that the hitherto unchanged phrases of rustic generations are altering, not necessarily for the better:

> 'I'd as soon miss the great peep-show that comes every year to Greenhill Fair as a sight of such an immortal spectacle as this!' said Amos Fry.
> ' "Immortal spectacle", – where did ye get that choice mossel, Hay-moss?' inquired Sammy Blore. 'Well, well, the Lord save good scholars – and take just a bit o' care of them that bain't!'
> (*Two on a Tower*, Ch. 13)

The three strands of Hardy's early life, which this brief survey has endeavoured to follow some way along, provided Hardy with linguistic advantages not enjoyed by writers of more conventional backgrounds and education. Cleanth Brooks was writing of Faulkner in the sentence which opens the passage quoted in the previous chapter, but the words are wholly applicable to Hardy, as are these: 'I think that some of Faulkner's triumphs in the handling of language as well as his mistakes are to be ascribed to his special kind of literary education.' Hardy's special kind of literary education brought together elements of language not unlike Shakespeare's, whose dialectal background of a Warwickshire village can be glimpsed at times through the rich tapestry of Renaissance English, much as Hardy's native Dorsetshire woodnotes are heard throughout his writings, in accord or discord (according to the reader's point of view) with the total diapason of his professional, social, and other interests. Inevitably, there are moments when such eclectic elements fail to fuse satisfactorily: we may have grown accustomed to the scientific diction and imagery of *Two on a Tower* by Chapter 41, but we may still baulk at 'poor old Mrs. Martin, to whose earthly course death stood rather as the asymptote than as the end'. The long learned word protrudes awkwardly and self-consciously from a sentence comtposed almost wholly of monosyllables, and more especially in a reference to one whose Dorset modulation of 'poor jimcracks and trangleys as he left 'em' still echoes in the mind from some twenty-odd pages before.

One almost wishes now and then that Hardy had not read and studied and observed and note-taken as much as he did, for it led him at intervals into an almost medieval display of 'auctoritees', as

Chaucer called them, with consequent failure of artistic discretion. Michael Millgate rightly notes that

> Hardy was, as a young man, fascinated with technical terminology and eager to display his mastery not only of architecture but also of the kind of knowledge to be found in encyclopaedias and in educational works of the self-help variety.

But the fascination continued throughout his life: there are architectural lists in *Jude the Obscure* as well as in *Desperate Remedies*, and all the other technicalities acquired during his life continue to surface in his writings.

The crux of Hardy's problem of making the best of his special kind of literary education ultimately resolves into one of method. The single moment of memorable incisiveness is worth all the rhetoric of medieval 'enumeratio', and this can be illustrated as well from Hardy's memoirs, with their occasionally astonishing failures of tact, as from his fiction. Here are two typical catalogue passages, dear to the admirer of well-bred and beautiful women and to the eager exhibitor of acquired skills:

> He found himself continually invited hither and thither to see famous beauties of the time – some of whom disappointed him; but some he owned to be very beautiful, such as Lady Powis, Lady Yarborough, Lady de Grey – 'handsome, tall, glance-giving, arch, friendly' – the Duchess of Montrose, Mrs. John Hanbury, Lady Cynthia Graham, Amélie Rives, and many others.
>
> (*Life*, p. 266)

> His suggestion to Paula of her belonging to a worthy strain of engineers had been based on his content with his own intellectual line of descent through Pheidias, Ictinus and Callicrates, Chersiphron, Vitruvius, Wilars of Cambray, William of Wykeham, and the rest of that long and illustrious roll.
>
> (*A Laodicean* III, Ch. 5)

And here, by contrast, is the skilful, discreet hint of the rich private associations or connotative force of a single name, the artistic exercising of sensitive discrimination:

> Lady Carnarvon went about the room weaving little webs of sympathy between her guests.
>
> (*Life*, p. 185)

The face that confronted Barnet had a beautiful outline; the Raffaelesque oval of its contour was remarkable for an English countenance, and that countenance housed in a remote country-road to an unheard-of harbour.
(*Wessex Tales*: 'Fellow-Townsmen', II)

The roll-call of names, like the apologetic quotation marks and glosses, are symptoms of a form of linguistic self-consciousness, perhaps not uncommon among autodidacts. They are the counterparts to Hardy's social self-consciousness as evinced by the denial of his humble origins, by his seeking out the crushes and fashionable assemblies in the London season and in country houses, and not least by the iteration of the poor man and the lady motif in his writings.

The resources of Hardy's English, which the following chapters will examine more fully, were indeed varied and plentiful. His home life, his schooling, his professional training, his reading, his widening social contacts, all equipped him with appropriate language. He learnt what had once been King Alfred's English in the heart of the West Saxon countryside and was able in several subtle ways, as we shall see, to revivify some of its strengths; he spoke Queen Victoria's English in the salons of London and frequently raised the 'common English' of his day to heights of excellence in prose and verse. He consciously drew into his writing the language of painting and other arts; he instinctively drew upon the inimitable heritage of the English Bible. The verses of other poets echoed in his memory. The expressions of philosophers and scientific writers, as he remarked after reading Comte, 'passed into his vocabulary'. The unending jottings from newspapers and magazines, anecdotes, snatches of folklore, songs and ballads, created phrases and images as well as incidents and stories in his work. And when all these failed to provide the word he needed, he made it up, coining, compounding, altering, enriching the language as few English writers had found it necessary to do, or, to give Hardy full credit, had ventured to do.

It is not surprising that in the face of all this linguistic abundance and fertility Hardy's sense of discrimination should occasionally falter, especially when we recall the long-enduring pressure of the demands of serialization and publishers' deadlines. What is surprising is how often he did scale the heights of excellence in his work, how often, in Virginia Woolf's phrase, his writing 'put on greatness'. In Hardy's case, more patently so than with many another English writer's, the language is the man: they are all there – the stonemason's son from Higher Bockhampton, the architectural apprentice, the self-taught classical scholar, the frequenter of galleries, the habitué of clubs and country houses, the friend and admirer of William Barnes, the intensely private man who became a public figure, the rustic poet with his corner in Westminster Abbey, the teller of tales known to millions, the owner of that 'fragile frame' whose heart is buried where it began to beat, in Stinsford parish.

# CHAPTER III

# Ancient and Legitimate

🔲🔲🔲🔲🔲🔲

THE 'Wessex' dialect which Hardy introduces into his fiction is a literary compromise. He observed two guiding principles: not to court incomprehensibility by over-use, and not to make his rustic characters appear ridiculous by caricaturing their speech as Dickens was prone to do with his lexical corruptions and comic popular etymologies.* Hardy's use of dialectal features, whether lexical, grammatical, or phonological, is studiously selective, 'deliberately and carefully impressionistic' Patricia Ingham calls it; nor is it confined as strictly to Dorset as Barnes's is. Hardy clearly knew what he wished to achieve in creating his rustics, and he knew the local dialect 'thoroughly', as he records in an interview published in 1892 in *The Pall Mall Gazette*, although thirty years later he still vigorously denied to Vere Collins that he learnt to speak it at home.

In his poems the use of dialect words and forms is more obviously a part of the poet's exploitation of every register of speech with which Hardy was familiar. Only in a handful of poems and an occasional scene in *The Dynasts* does dialect assume the function it has in the prose fiction, to characterize speakers and to lend verisimilitude to scenes of country life. Hardy's first published poem, written in 1866, 'The Bride-Night Fire', originally called 'The Fire at Tranter Sweatley's', and the Wessex scene, III.v.6, in *The Dynasts* are notable examples.

Hardy does not confine dialect to dialogue. When dialect words are used in narrative or description, however, they are often placed in quotation marks and in many instances a gloss is provided by the author, either in the text itself or, as in 'The Bride-Night Fire', in footnotes:

---

* Occasionally a Dickensian note enters, as in David Heddegan's reiterated 'mee deer' in 'A Mere Interlude' (*A Changed Man*).

'Take up the God-forgive-me, Jacob. See if 'tis warm, Jacob.'
Jacob stooped to the God-forgive-me, which was a two-handled tall
mug standing in the ashes, cracked and charred with heat.
(*Far from the Madding Crowd*, Ch. 8)

The quarryman 'pitched his nitch', and explained to the seeming stranger
that there had been three families thereabouts in the stone trade.
(*The Well-Beloved*, II, Ch. 4)

Sometimes the process is reversed and a standard English word is
accompanied by its corresponding dialect word as a 'local' embell-
ishment:

He began lopping off – 'shrouding' as they called it at Hintock – the lowest
boughs.
(*The Woodlanders*, Ch. 13)

Although, as Hardy said in his Preface of 1898 to *Wessex Poems*, such
dialect words as he used were both 'ancient and legitimate', he fully
realized that they might still create difficulties for many of his
readers. His Russian correspondent and translator Vera Spasskaia
complained in a letter of 14 September 1892 that there were words in
*Tess of the d'Urbervilles* 'which even a well cultivated English
gentleman, with whom I lately happened to meet, was unable to
explain to me'. The reader undoubtedly has occasional problems in
Hardy's dialect passages, but the context is usually clear enough.
Other writers who used dialect, like George Eliot or D.H. Lawrence, faced similar problems, although their attitudes to its function
in their novels may have differed from Hardy's.

Hardy's dialect contains many elements found outside Dorset,
and extending even beyond the original Anglo-Saxon kingdom of
Wessex, whose name he made so much his own, and by which he
meant 'the six counties, whose area he traverses in his scenes' (*Life*, p.
122). His principal dialect resources stretched from Devon in the
south-west to Surrey, and even into the south-eastern English of
Kent at times, which had distinctive dialectal features going back
to Jutish settlements. The word *dumbledores*, 'bumble-bees', for
example, was a Wessex word in its widest sense, current from Devon
to Kent and north into Gloucestershire and Berkshire. Hardy uses it
figuratively in *Under the Greenwood Tree* as a word of rustic
opprobrium to describe the new-fangled musical instruments threat-
ening the ancient traditions, notably 'harmonions and barrel-
organs':

'Miserable dumbledores!'

'Right, William, and so they be – miserable dumbledores!' said the choir with unanimity.

(I, Ch. 4)

The word reappears in the list of dialect words in *The Mayor of Casterbridge* which Elizabeth-Jane is endeavouring to unlearn in response to Henchard's painful insistence that dialect is socially inferior: 'she no longer spoke of "dumbledores" but of "humble bees" ' (Ch. 20).

In Middle English dialects a major dividing line separated the eastern and western halves of England, giving rise, for example, to the distinctive dialectal characteristics of the west midland and northwest midland alliterative poems of the fourteenth century. This division survives in the dialect of Hardy's prose and verse, so that the greater part of his dialect vocabulary, as well as certain grammatical and phonological features, are predominantly western and south-western.

To this region belongs Dorset, whose dialect had recently been accorded contemporary literary status by the poems of William Barnes, three of whose collections had appeared by the time Hardy wrote 'The Bride-Night Fire'. Hardy himself conferred literary distinction on a goodly number of Dorset words, although it must be remembered that in about ten per cent of cases recorded as Dorset-shire by the *English Dialect Dictionary*, Hardy is the only source cited. Some of these words have since been confirmed as current in Dorset by the work of Bertil Widén in Hilton parish and from other evidence.

Even within his own county Hardy was aware of local variations. An interesting example is one to which he draws attention in a letter to Edmund Gosse of 26 October 1888:

"Ich". This & kindred words – e.g. – "Ich woll", "er woll", "er war", &c, are still used by old people in N.W. Dorset & Somerset. (*vide* Grammer Oliver's conversation in *The Woodlanders* which is an attempted repro-duction.) I heard "Ich" only last Sunday; but it is dying rapidly. I know nobody under seventy who speaks so, & those above it use the form only in impulsive moments when they forget themselves.

Grammer Oliver's speech is clearly distinguished by this survival of the Old English *ic*, pronounced /ɪtʃ/: ' 'Ch woll not have him!';

'because 'ch have something on my mind'; ' 'Ch have been going to ask him' (*The Woodlanders*, Ch. 17). The puzzling refrain in 'Vagrant's Song' – '*Che-hane, mother; che-hane, mother*' – which Hardy calls an 'Old Wessex Refrain', contains the same form of the pronoun. Grammer Oliver's usage helps to localize *The Woodlanders* in the vicinity of Yeovil where Hardy and his wife lived for some months in 1876. That forms with *ch* were originally more widely used is apparent from their inclusion in John Haynes's *Dorsetshire Vocabulary* of about 1730.

Another example of patois occurs in *The Well-Beloved* where Hardy uses words distinctive of Portland speech: *kimberlin*, a local variant of *comeling*, denotes an outsider, as Hardy glosses: ' "kimberlins", or "foreigners" (as strangers from the mainland of Wessex were called)' (I, Ch. 2); and *lerret*, which is explained as 'one of the local boats' (I, Ch. 4) and even more definitely assigned to Portland in *The Dynasts*: 'These be inland men who, I warrant 'ee, don't know a lerret from a lighter!' (I.ii.5). Appropriately enough, the word is used by John Loveday, speaking to Anne Garland from the cliff at Portland Bill, in Chapter 34 of *The Trumpet-Major*, while both are gazing after the *Victory* across the Channel.

Although the majority of Hardy's dialect features are characteristic of the western and southern regions of England, he uses many words which are also recorded in other parts of the British Isles and even beyond, in North America and Australia. A year after the word *chevy* occurred in *The Woodlanders*, for example, where Grammer Oliver says 'If you only knew how he do chevy me round the chimmer in my dreams you'd pity me' (Ch. 17), it was recorded in Rolf Boldrewood's *Robbery Under Arms* (1888) in Australia. The word is found in many parts of England from Cumbria to East Anglia and as far south-west as Cornwall; what gives it a more local colour in this instance is its association with the form *chimmer*, Hardy's spelling of the distinctive south-western pronunciation of *chamber*. Such contextual localization is not uncommon in Hardy, and there are many instances where a dialect word of countrywide currency is given a more local flavour phonetically or grammatically or by its collocation with a characteristic Dorset word or phrase. One of Hardy's regional trademarks, as it were, is *home-along*, which is quite often employed to add local colour to another word of wider dialectal usage, like *clink*: 'He've clinked off home-along, depend upon 't' (*Under the Greenwood Tree*, I, Ch. 5).

In the following survey, which is indebted especially to the works of William Barnes, to the *English Dialect Dictionary*, and to Martha Döll's and Ulla Baugner's studies of Hardy's dialect in his novels and short stories, no attempt has been made to treat the vocabulary, the grammar, and the pronunciation exhaustively. My aim is to illustrate the various dialectal characteristics which Hardy used in order to create the impression of Wessex speech and to add local colour to his rustic scenes and descriptions of country life, and to indicate wherever possible the antiquity of Hardy's dialect usages.

Readers of *The Mayor of Casterbridge* will remember that Wessex is not the only dialect Hardy is concerned with. Farfrae's Scottish speech is Hardy's declared attempt, as stated in his Preface, to represent a Scotsman as he would appear to a Southerner, and that would-be phonetic spellings like *warrld*, *cannet*, *advairrtisment* seemed to him exact representations of Scottish sounds as heard by 'people of outer regions'. Farfrae's dialect is as selective, as much a literary compromise, as the speech of the Wessex rustics, but whereas the latter is based on Hardy's thorough knowledge of local speech, he obviously came rather closer to something like caricature in the case of Farfrae. By portraying Farfrae as speaking a kind of music-hall Scots, Hardy was running the risk of turning him into a stock comic character, a risk which the novel avoided, however, in his case as successfully as in the portrayal of the worthies of Wessex.

Another dialect which makes occasional brief appearances is that of London, with which Hardy's several extended residences in that city had made him familiar. Here, too, there is a risk of caricature, as in this snippet from a letter to his sister Katharine of 8 May 1898, quoting a London bus conductor:

> 'Oh, nao; their sex pertects them. We dares not drive over them, wotever they do; & they do jist wot they likes. 'Tis their sex, yer see; & its wot I coll takin' a mean adventage. No man dares to go where they go.'

Baugner has indicated the major classes of dialect words Hardy used in his novels and short stories. To these we need to add examples found in his poems, in *The Dynasts*, and occasionally in other writings where such occurrences can elucidate or corroborate. In what follows here our concern is to survey and illustrate rather than to evaluate Hardy's use of dialect: critical appraisal belongs elsewhere.

# Ancient and Legitimate

## I. VOCABULARY

The majority of dialect words occurs in the dialogue of Hardy's rustics and denotes aspects of rural life, work, pastimes, and the natural environment. There are nouns denoting food, garments, local customs, terms of endearment and of abuse, and so on; there are adjectives denoting states of mind, habits, physical characteristics; verbs denoting movement, rural and domestic activities, physical actions of various kinds. Hardy uses a number of idiomatic expressions current in dialect, as well as variations or modifications of standard English forms and dialectal corruptions of words from other languages reminiscent of some of Dickens's memorable distortions. To do full justice to such a rich and varied collection of words would require a comprehensive glossary with explanatory notes, which is beyond the scope of this chapter. I shall therefore follow Hardy's own example of judicious selection, classifying my samples of words not by grammatical categories or meaning, but by dialectal distribution, as follows: (i) words of wider dialectal currency, particularly in the north, west, and south-west of England; (ii) words of restricted dialectal currency, mainly occurring in Hardy's Wessex; and (iii) words principally confined to Dorset. A fourth section (iv) gathers a number of phrases and dialectal corruptions which Hardy uses to add further dialectal verisimilitude.

Dialects are not watertight compartments, however, strictly following contours or county boundaries, and my divisions should be regarded as approximate rather than as absolute. Nevertheless, this method may help to establish the character of Hardy's fictional dialect more clearly than has been done hitherto.

In every case, one or more examples are given to illustrate Hardy's usage and its distribution in his prose and verse. As Hardy's use of dialect owes, unmistakably and from the beginning, a strong debt to the example of William Barnes, the latter's *Glossary* and poems have been drawn upon freely to illuminate Hardy's usage or to elucidate meanings.

(i) *Words of wider dialectal currency, particularly in the north, west, and south-west of England.*

### bivering

> Crooping from sight
> In the lewth of a codlin-tree, bivering wi' fright.
> ('The Bride-Night Fire')

Hardy's footnote glosses 'with chattering teeth'. To Barnes's 'an' cry wi' biv'ren chin' (which appears as *bibb'ren* in the 1893 edition and thus in Jones's edition) from 'I'm out o'Door', Hardy adds the gloss 'shaking'; while Barnes in his *Glossary* equates the two forms and defines the word as 'to shake or quiver, as with cold or fear'. The origin is Old English *bifian*, *beofian* 'to tremble', pronounced with medial [v].

## caddle

'Here's a caddle wi' these letters! Guide my soul, what will Billy do!' (*Desperate Remedies*, Ch. 17)

Who, half shrammed to death, stood and cried on a chair
At the caddle she found herself in.
('The Bride-Night Fire')

Hardy adds the gloss 'quandary' to the poem. This is one of several colourful dialect words denoting a 'dilemma', or a 'pickle' in current colloquial English usage, and represents one of Hardy's earliest uses of dialect both in fiction and in verse, possibly prompted by Barnes who uses the phrase 'Oh! Here's a caddle' in 'The Waggon A-stooded'. The word derives from Middle English *ca(u)del* 'mess', of Anglo-French origin, as used in Langland's *Piers Plowman*.

## deedy

'There! don't ye look so deedy!' (*Jude the Obscure*, I, Ch. 2)

'That you'll never be told', said she deedily. (*Jude the Obscure*, I, Ch. 6)

She rolled round her face, remained a moment looking deedily aslant at him. (*Jude the Obscure*, I, Ch. 8)

Instead of a Baron there stood Jim, white-waistcoated, demure, every hair in place, and, if she mistook not, even a deedy spark in his eye. (*A Changed Man*: 'The Romantic Adventures of a Milkmaid', XII)

The moon was at the window-square,
Deedily brooding in deformed decay –
('Honeymoon Time at an Inn')

'Serious, earnest, intent'. The word is a late medieval derivative of the substantive *deed*.

## fay

> 'It must be because his suit don't fay', said Captain Bob.
> (*The Trumpet-Major*, Ch. 29)

> The sharp reprimand was not lost upon her, and in time it came to pass that for 'fay' she said 'succeed'.
> (*The Mayor of Casterbridge*, Ch. 20)

> 'Then things don't fay with her any more than with we!'
> (*The Woodlanders*, Ch. 5)

'To fit; to succeed; to answer; or go on favourably' (Barnes, *Glossary*). From Old English *fēgan* 'to join'.

## glutch

> 'And now Robert Creedle will be nailed up in parish boards 'a b'lieve; and nobody will glutch down a sigh for he!'
> (*The Woodlanders*, Ch. 43)

'To gulp, to swallow with difficulty, hence to stifle a sob or sigh'. The noun *glutchpipe*, 'throat', denotes the passage down which food makes its way, as distinct from the trachea:

> 'I'd move every man's wyndpipe a good span away from his glutchpipe, so that at harvest time he could fetch breath in 's drinking, without being choked and strangled as he is now.'
> (*Two on a Tower*, Ch. 2)

The word is recorded in the thirteenth century as *gulchen* and *gluchen* 'to drink greedily'.

## hatch

> At the foot of an incline the church became visible through the north gate, or 'church hatch', as it was called here.
> (*Under the Greenwood Tree*, I, Ch. 6).

A country word, meaning a 'gate', as above, or a sluice, as in the description of Shadwater Weir with its 'ten huge hatches' in *The Return of the Native*, V, Ch. 9. The root is Old English *hæc(c)*, 'a

half-door, wicket, grating'. Dorchester's Ten Hatches Weir is just
north of Grey's Bridge. Barnes makes a neat distinction in 'Our
Be'thpleace':

> How dear's the door a latch do shut,
> An' geärden that a hatch do shut.

## hele

> 'Well, if you don't mind, we'll have the beaker, and pass 'en round; 'tis
> better then heling it out in dribbles.'
> (*The Return of the Native*, I, Ch. 5)

'To pour'. The Dorset currency is attested by Barnes, who cites the
sentence: 'Shall I hële out another cup?' (*Glossary*). The word is of
Scandinavian origin, from Old Norse *hella* 'to pour'.

## jonnick

> 'And his jonnick face, as white as his clothes with keeping late hours.'
> (*A Laodicean*, I, Ch. 5)

'Honest, genuine, jolly' generally appears as *jonnock*, or *jannock* in
other dialects, and derived from Old Norse *jafn*, *jamn* 'equal, even,
even-tempered'.

## kex

> 'My throat's as dry as a kex.'
> (*The Woodlanders*, Ch. 48)

> 'I'm as dry as a kex with biding up here in the wind.'
> (*The Return of the Native*, I, Ch. 3)

'The dry hollow stalk of a hollow-stemmed umbeliferous plant like
the cow parsnip, cow parsley, or chervil'. Hence particularly common in the phrase 'dry as a kex', as in Hardy's examples. Barnes, in
'The Veäiries', has 'a little pipe/A-meäde o' kexes or o' straws'. The
word is widely distributed in English dialects and occurs in place-
names of Scandinavian origin. It may be of Celtic origin, however.
Shakespeare, in *Henry V*, has the line: 'But hateful docks, rough
thistles, kecksies, burs.'

## lammocken

'He's a cheat, and that in the eye of the law is ayless a rogue, and that is ayless a lammocken vagabond; and that's a punishable situation.'
(*Far from the Madding Crowd*, Ch. 52)

'He'll adorn it better than a poor lammicken feller like myself can.'
(*Tess of the d'Urbervilles*, I, Ch. 7)

This is the present participle of *lammock* 'to slouch', with various related meanings 'slouching, ungainly, clumsy', also recorded in some eastern counties. The word may be related to *lammiger* 'cripple', which is listed below, and which derives from *lame*.

## larry

'And my brain is all in a spin, wi' being rafted up in such a larry!'
(*The Hand of Ethelberta*, Ch. 44)

'Oh, please, ma'am, 'tis this larry about Mr. Henchard.'
(*The Mayor of Casterbridge*, Ch. 28)

'For what's all the world if yer mind is always in a larry, Miss Henchet?'
(*The Mayor of Casterbridge*, Ch. 31)

'I've seen such larries before.'
(*The Woodlanders*, Ch. 20)

'That wer all a part of the larry!'
(*Tess of the d'Urbervilles*, Ch. 3)

'And my counsel to 'ee is to carry this larry no further.'
(*A Changed Man*: 'The Romantic Adventures of a Milkmaid', XVI)

'Disturbance, commotion, frolic'. A dialectal form of *larum*, a variant of *alarm*, this is a favourite with Hardy, who has a considerable stock of dialect words with similar meanings.

## leer, leery

'I've been strolling in the Walks and churchyard, father, till I feel quite leery.'
(*The Mayor of Casterbridge*, Ch. 20)

'And 'a knowed that nobody would come that way for hours, and he so leery and tired that 'a didn't know what to do.'
(*Tess of the d'Urbervilles*, Ch. 17)

The lover Tim Tankens mourned heart-sick and leer
To be thus of his darling deprived.
('The Bride-Night Fire')

Hardy's gloss to the poem is 'empty-stomached', *leery* being a later
variant of *leer*, 'empty, hungry, faint', Middle English *lere*, cognate
with German *leer*, 'empty'.

## lewth

'I warrant that whether we were going with the sun or against the sun,
uphill or downhill, in wind or in lewth, that wart of hers was always
towards the edge, and that dimple towards me.'
(*The Woodlanders*, Ch. 48)

'Fear-filled, I stayed me till summer-tide,
In lewth of leaves to throne her bride.'
('Postponement')

In the lewth of a codlin-tree.
('The Bride-Night Fire')

Hardy glosses 'shelter' in the last quotation given; cp. Barnes: 'In
lewth ageän the northern storm' ('Brookwell'). Derived from Old
English *hléowð* 'shelter'.

## limber

'Martin has been tolling ever since, almost. There, 'twas expected. She was
very limber.'
(*A Pair of Blue Eyes*, Ch. 26)

'I should be inclined to think it was from general neshness of constitution.
She was such a limber maid that 'a could stand no hardship, even when I
knowed her, and 'a went like a candle-snoff, so 'tis said.'
(*Far from the Madding Crowd*, Ch. 41)

So savage winter catches
The breath of limber things.
('The Farm-Woman's Winter')

The usual dialectal meaning is 'supple, flexible, nimble', but these
examples suggest a sense of 'frail, infirm'. Barnes (*Glossary*) defines
as 'very limp, flaccid', and in 'The Carter' writes of 'my limber whip'.
The word is known in English from the sixteenth century, but its

origin is obscure; it may be related to *limb*. Hardy uses the derivative *limberish* in *Two on a Tower*, Ch. 1.

### mommet, mammet

'Lord's sake, I thought, whatever fiery mommet is this come to trouble us?'
(*The Return of the Native*, I, Ch. 3)

'Had it anything to do with father's making such a mommet of himself in thik carriage this afternoon?'
(*Tess of the d'Urbervilles*, Ch. 3)

'What a mommet of a maid!' said the next man who met her to a companion.
(*Tess of the d'Urbervilles*, Ch. 42)

Then the play . . . But how unfitted
Was *this* Rosalind! – a mammet quite to me, in memories nurst.
('The Two Rosalinds')

'This is only a mommet they've made of him, that's got neither chine nor chitlings. His innerds be only a lock of straw from Bridle's barton.'
(*The Dynasts*, III. v. 6)

'A guy, an effigy' (Barnes, *Glossary*); also 'a puppet, a scarecrow'. The word is recorded in English from the thirteenth century; its more usual form *maumet* reveals its derivation from Old French *mahumet* 'idol', derived from *Mahomet*, *Mohammed*, whom the Middle Ages believed to be worshipped as a god. The meaning of 'image, puppet, doll' is found from the late fifteenth century in literary English. By Hardy's time it was restricted to dialect usage in the north country, the west midlands and the south-west of England. The ancient custom of Christmas mumming in which St. George fights with a Mohammedan leader, usually a Turkish knight as in *The Return of the Native*, II, Ch. 5, may have helped to keep the word alive in dialect.

### nammet-time

'I haven't seen the colour of drink since nammet-time to-day.'
(*The Return of the Native*, I, Ch. 3)

It was not till 'nammet'-time, about three o'clock, that Tess raised her eyes and gave a momentary glance round.
(*Tess of the d'Urbervilles*, Ch. 48)

This is a corruption of *noon-meat*, Old English *nōn-mete*. *Nammet* has various dialectal forms, e.g. *nummet*, *nummock*, the latter also recorded in Dorset. The word denotes a luncheon, especially one eaten in the field by farm-labourers, as in Barnes's 'To have woone's nammet down below / A tree where primrwosen do grow'.

### nesh, neshness

'She was such a childlike, nesh young thing that her spirit couldn't appear to anyone if it tried, I'm quite sure.'
(*Far from the Madding Crowd*, Ch. 43)

'I should be inclined to think it was from general neshness of constitution. She was such a limber maid.'
(*Far from the Madding Crowd*, Ch. 41)

'And if he keeps the daughter so long at boarding-school he'll make her as nesh as her mother was.'
(*The Woodlanders*, Ch. 4)

The adjective (from Old English *hnesce* 'soft') means 'delicate, weak, sickly'; whence the noun 'weakness, delicacy'. Barnes glosses 'tender', and writes of 'nesh young leaves o' yollow green' ('Hope in Spring'). According to G.L. Brook (*English Dialects*, p. 31), nesh 'is a north-country word to describe anyone who is too fond of sitting in front of the fire and who is consequently unduly sensitive to cold', but its dialectal distribution extends into the south-western counties as well.

### night-rail

'A poor twanking woman like her – 'tis a godsend for her, and hardly a pair of jumps or night-rail to her name.'
(*The Mayor of Casterbridge*, Ch. 13)

'Just when we was packing your few traps and your Mis'ess's night-rail and dressing things into the cart.'
(*Tess of the d'Urbervilles*, Ch. 34)

'Not that ornamental night-rails can be much use to a' ould 'ooman like I.'
(*Jude the Obscure*, VI, Ch. 5)

Wi' on'y her night-rail to cover her plight.
('The Bride-Night Fire')

'I love you still, would kiss you now,
But blood would stain your nighty-rail!'
('At Shag's Heath')

'A night-dress, or dressing-gown', from Old English *hrægl*, 'garment'.


## rantipole

'I don't care a curse what the words be', said Henchard. 'Hymns, ballets, or rantipole rubbish; the Rogue's March or the cherubim's warble – 'tis all the same to me if 'tis good harmony.'
(*The Mayor of Casterbridge*, Ch. 33)

'Wild, noisy, rough'; probably connected with to *rant* and the noun *ranter* denoting a primitive Methodist, a Dissenter, as used by Hardy:

'O no. 'Tis a ranter pa'son who's been sniffing after her lately.'
(*Tess of the d'Urbervilles*, Ch. 47)

Similarly, in the *Life* there is reference to one who ' "turned ranter" – *i.e.* street-preacher', and the *English Dialect Dictionary* records this quotation from West Sussex (1897): 'They Ranters makes a deal of noise and talks a deal of rubbish.'


## squail

'These easterly rains, when they do come, which is not often, come wi' might enough to squail a man into his grave.'
(*The Hand of Ethelberta*, Ch. 44)

Recorded in various related senses, 'to hit, strike, throw, etc.', and attested for Dorset by Barnes, who defines it in his *Glossary*: 'To throw stones or any missiles at birds or other things'. The word is probably a dialectal variant of the verb *quail* in its transitive sense 'to overpower, destroy', recorded since the sixteenth century.


## steer, stoor

'Owing to your coming a day sooner than we first expected', said John, 'you'll find us in a turk of a mess, sir . . . Never were such a steer, 'a b'lieve.'
(*A Pair of Blue Eyes*, Ch. 23)

'Ay, and the house were all in a stoor with her and the old woman, and their boxes and camp-kettles.'
(*The Hand of Ethelberta*, Ch. 1)

'O, there's such a stoor, Mrs Newberry and Mr Stockdale! The king's officers can't get the carts ready nohow at all!'
(*Wessex Tales*: 'The Distracted Preacher', 7)

The two words both mean 'tumult, commotion, stir', and are probably derived from the same root, Old English *styrian* 'to stir'. Barnes characterizes *steer* as East Dorset, and for *stoor* only has this gloss: 'To stir, as a liquid'.

**tallet**

> In the tallet he stowed her; there huddied she lay.
> ('The Bride-Night Fire')

'Now up in the tallet with 'ee, there's a good boy, and down with another lock or two of hay.'
(*The Hand of Ethelberta*, Ch. 44)

Hardy glosses 'loft' in the poem; the general dialectal meaning is 'a hay-loft, especially one over a stable'. Adopted from medieval Latin *tabulatum* 'flooring' into Celtic, whence into western English dialects from Cheshire to Cornwall.

**teave**

'At that very moment up comes John Woodward, weeping and teaving, "I've lost my brother! I've lost my brother!" '
(*Under the Greenwood Tree*, I, Ch. 3)

'See how I've got to teave and slave, and your poor weak father with his heart clogged like a dripping-pan.'
(*Tess of the d'Urbervilles*, Ch. 12)

' 'Tis like your brazen impudence to teave and wail when you be another woman's husband.'
(*A Changed Man*: 'The Romantic Adventures of a Milkmaid', XVI)

A variant spelling of *tave*, from Old Norse *tava* 'to foil, struggle, fumble'; the phrasal link with 'weep' or 'wail' suggests a meaning 'toss, throw oneself about, be agitated'; cp. Barnes's: 'he drow'd / Hizzelf about, an' teäv'd, an' blow'd,' ('Polly Be-en Upzides Wi'

Tom'.) The phrase 'to tew and teave', to toss about as in a fever, is recorded in the north country and in Lincolnshire, as well as in Dorset and Somerset.

## tole

> The old woman suggested to the wood-girl that she should walk forward at the heels of Grace, and 'tole' her down the required way.
> (*The Woodlanders*, Ch. 20)

> 'Yes', said Latimer musingly. 'Unless 'tis all done to tole us the wrong way.'
> (*Wessex Tales*: 'The Distracted Preacher', 5)

> 'His having won her once makes all the difference in the world. 'Twould be a thousand pities if he were to tole her away again.'
> (*Tess of the d'Urbervilles*, Ch. 52)

> 'She was a pupil-teacher under me, as you know, and I took advantage of her inexperience, and toled her out for walks.'
> (*Jude the Obscure*, IV, Ch. 4)

'To entice, allure, draw'. The word was in English literary usage until the end of the seventeenth century, but survives as such in America. The more usual form is *toll*; Middle English *tullen*, *tollen* is found in Chaucer's *Reeve's Tale*.

## wamble

> 'Ay, 'a will sit studding and thinking as if 'a were going to turn chapel-member, and then do nothing but traypse and wamble about.'
> (*Under the Greenwood Tree*, IV, Ch. 4)

> 'I know I am only a poor wambling man that 'ill never pay the Lord for my making, sir.'
> (*A Pair of Blue Eyes*, Ch. 2)

> 'It is a mercy that your grammer were not killed, sitting by the hearth, poor old soul, and soon to walk wi' God, – for 'a 's getting wambling on her pins, Mr Swithin, as aged folks do.'
> (*Two on a Tower*, Ch. 16)

> 'She was wambling about quite dangerous to the thoroughfare, and when I approached to draw near she committed the nuisance, and insulted me.'
> (*The Mayor of Casterbridge*, Ch. 28)

> 'Fancy her white hands getting redder every day, and her tongue losing its

pretty up-country curl in talking, and her bounding walk becoming the regular Hintock shail-and-wamble.'

'She may shail; but she'll never wamble', replied his wife decisively.
(*The Woodlanders*, Ch. 11)

> Towards the west
> Bertrand keeps open the retreating-way,
> Along which wambling waggons since the noon
> Have crept in closening file.
> (*The Dynasts*, III. iii. 3)

A favourite word with Hardy, *wamble* is attested in various senses from the fourteenth century. Probably of Scandinavian origin, related to Norwegian *vamla*, *vamra* 'to stagger', the general sense, as Hardy uses the word, is 'to roll, turn, twist, totter, wriggle about', the participial adjective meaning 'shaky, unsteady'.

Hardy also used the noun *wambler*; thus William Worm describes himself in Chapter 4 of *A Pair of Blue Eyes*.

The word *shail* implies a somewhat different motion, as its use in *The Woodlanders* suggests: 'to shuffle, drag the feet, walk awkwardly', rather than 'totter and walk unsteadily'. It occurs in the fourteenth-century north-west midland alliterative poem *Morte Arthure* as the present participle *schaylande* 'walking awkwardly'.

(ii) *Words of restricted dialectal currency, mainly occurring in Hardy's Wessex.*

### black-hearts

'I was picking black-hearts, and went further than I meant.'
(*The Return of the Native*, V, Ch. 2)

The element *heart* represents dialectal *hurt*, found in Middle English *hurtilberi*, which is used in southern and south-western counties for the 'bilberry'. Baugner notes that the phrase 'to go harting', current in Hampshire, is preserved as 'arts' in Dorset. The element survives in the modern name *whortleberry*.

### bleachy

'When we have to sink 'em for long it makes the stuff taste bleachy, and folks don't like it so well.'
(*Wessex Tales*: 'The Distracted Preacher', 5)

The reference is to contraband liquor, and the word means 'saltish, brackish', or as we might say today, 'off'. Derived from *bleach*.

## blooth

'A few stripling boys and maidens have busted into blooth.'
(*Two on a Tower*, Ch. 41)

A common Wessex word for 'bloom, blossom', as in the refrain to Barnes's poem 'The Zummer Hedge':

How cool's the sheäde, or warm's the lewth,
Bezide a zummer hedge in blooth.

The word derives from the verb *blow* and the suffix *-th*, as in *growth*.

## blue-vinnied

'My scram blue-vinnied gallicrow of an uncle'.
(*The Trumpet-Major*, Ch. 9)

'They felt 'twould be a thousand pities to let such good things get blue-vinnied for want of a ceremony to use 'em upon.'
(*The Trumpet-Major*, Ch. 20)

'Blue-vinny' is a blue-mouldy Dorset cheese, whence the adjective 'covered with blue mould, mouldy, mildewed'. 'Vinny cheese' is mentioned in Barnes's poem 'Praise o' Do'set' as one of the special delights of the county, along with ale, cider, brown bread, butter, and cream. John Haynes's *Dorsetshire Vocabulary* of about 1730 lists *vinny* 'mouldy', and J. Maskell records 'Vinny-Cross, so called from a (now departed) decayed old cross at the corner of a road'. The word occurs in Old English *fynig* 'mouldy' and is thus used by Ælfric.

## boam

'She was about the figure of two or three-and-twenty when a' got off the carriage last night, tired out wi' boaming about the country.'
(*The Hand of Ethelberta*, Ch. 1)

The word is recorded in nineteenth-century Somerset with the meaning of 'to draggle, to trail along'. It may represent a coalescence of *roam* and *boom* in the sense of 'to move along like a ship under sail'.

## chimp

> 'You've said that a few stripling boys and maidens have busted into blooth, and a few married women have plimmed and chimped.'
> (*Two on a Tower*, Ch. 41)

Barnes defines the substantive *chimp* as 'a young shoot, as of a potatoe [*sic*]', and the verb is also commonly applied to sprouting potatoes, i.e. 'to germinate, sprout'. As *plim* (used, for example, of doors swelling with damp) means 'to swell', the sense of Hezzy's phrase in *Two on a Tower* is obvious. The word *chimp* may be connected with Old English *cinan* 'to burst open, germinate'.

## clitch

> 'I assure 'ee, Pa'son Tarkenham, that in the clitch o' my knees, where the rain used to come through when I was cutting clots for the new lawn in old my lady's time, 'tis as if rats wez gnawing every now and then.'
> (*Two on a Tower*, Ch. 2)

> 'The clitches of my arms are burning like fire from the cords those two strapping women tied round 'em.'
> (*Wessex Tales*: 'The Distracted Preacher', 7)

Probably derived from the same root as Old English *clyccean* 'to bend', the word denotes 'the fork of leg or arm, crook, groin'. The corresponding verb is recorded in the south-west, meaning 'to clutch, grasp tightly, stick, make fast'.

## coll

> 'It was just as if they had one and all caught Dick kissing and coling [*sic*] ye to death, wasn't it, Mrs Dewy?'
> (*Under the Greenwood Tree*, V, Ch. 1)

> 'The woman walks and laughs somewhere at this very moment whose neck he'll be coling [*sic*] next year as he does hers to-night.'
> (*The Woodlanders*, Ch. 48)

> ' 'Tis melancholy work facing and footing it to one of your own sort, and no clipsing and colling at all.'
> (*Tess of the d'Urbervilles*, Ch. 2)

'You couldn't expect her to throw her arms round 'ee, an' to kiss and coll 'ee all at once.'
(*Tess of the d'Urbervilles*, Ch. 6)

'No, no, no! I merely did it not to be clipsed or colled, Marian.'
(*Tess of the d'Urbervilles*, Ch. 42)

> You'll see none's looking; put your lip
> Up like a tulip, so;
> And he will coll you, bend, and sip:
> Yes, Carrey, yes; I know!
> ('To Carrey Clavel')

'To embrace, to hug', derived from French *coler* 'to embrace', and current in literary English until the seventeenth century.

## coomb

Among the few features of agricultural England which retain an appearance but little modified by the lapse of centuries, may be reckoned the long, grassy and furzy downs, coombs, or ewe-leases, as they are called according to their kind, that fill a large area of certain counties in the south and south-west.
(*Wessex Tales*: 'The Three Strangers')

He had passed an hour of relaxation in the lonely house on the slope of the coomb.
(*Ibid.*)

> 'Come; see the oxen kneel
> In the lonely barton by yonder coomb.'
> ('The Oxen')

A topographical term, found in many south-western place-names where it denotes 'a steep, short valley running up from the sea coast', as well as 'a deep valley or hollow on the side of a hill'. The old maltster in *Far from the Madding Crowd* was married 'at Norcombe Church', and the village of 'Overcombe', below Bincombe Down, is the setting for Loveday's mill in *The Trumpet-Major*. The word is an Old English adoption from Celtic *cumbo*, 'valley'.

## daps

'Yes, good-now; she's the very daps of her mother – that's what everybody says.'
(*The Well-Beloved*, II, Ch. 4)

And now this 'daps' of her mother (as they called her in the dialect here), this perfect copy, why did she turn away?
(*The Well-Beloved*, II, Ch. 6)

'A perfect copy', as Hardy says; or 'a likeness as if a cast from the same mould', as Barnes says (*Glossary*), and in his poem 'What John were A-tellen his Mis'ess out in the Corn Ground':

> An' now your little maïd, a dear,
> Your childhood's very daps, is here.

The origin of the word is uncertain, but it may be the same as in *dabchick*, which occurs as *dapchicke* in the sixteenth century and is used by Ben Jonson in *The Alchemist* to mean 'a girl'; while *dab* occurs in the eighteenth century with the meaning of 'a small child'.

## drave

'  'Tis wrong for a man of such a high family as his to slave and drave at common labouring work.'
(*Tess of the d'Urbervilles*, Ch. 49)

'To toil', especially as in the above phrase. The word is recorded in Wiltshire and Dorset, and may be a variant of *drive*.

## draw-latching

'Come along to bed, do, you draw-latching rogue – keeping a body awake like this!'
(*Far from the Madding Crowd*, Ch. 36)

'She seed thee to be a drawlacheting rogue, and 'twas her wisdom to go off that morning and get rid o' thee.'
(*A Changed Man*: 'The Romantic Adventures of a Milkmaid', XIII)

Barnes (*Glossary*) writes: 'DRAWLATCHET. Walking lazily and slowly'; thus 'to dawdle, idle'. Literally, a *drawlatch* is one who draws a latch, a thief, a sneaking rogue, whence the verb meaning 'to sneak, idle, lag behind'.

## drong

'The first time I met en was in a drong.'
(*Under the Greenwood Tree*, II, Ch. 2)

Soon to turn into the lane leading out of the highway and then into the 'drong' which led to the house.
(*The Woodlanders*, Ch. 40)

At the back was a dairy barton, accessible for vehicles and live-stock by a side 'drong'.
(*Wessex Tales*: 'Interlopers at the Knap', II)

By the 'Hart' and Grey's Bridge into byways and 'drongs',
  Or across the ridged loam.
('At Casterbridge Fair'. VII. 'After the Fair')

'A narrow way between two hedges or walls' (Barnes, *Glossary*), as in his 'down the dusky drong' in 'The Linden on the Lawn'. The form *drong* is the Dorset variant of the more common *drang*, derived from the Old English verb *þringan* 'to press, crowd upon, throng'.

## eltrot

'I used to make trumpets of paper, eldersticks, eltrot stems, and even stinging-nettle stalks, you know.'
(*The Trumpet-Major*, Ch. 9)

Hardy, glossing Barnes's use of the word in 'Meaken up a Miff', defines it as 'wild parsnip'; Barnes himself applies it to the 'cow-parsley'. The word appears to have been used of several umbelliferous plants, including cow-parsley, cow-parsnip, water-parsley, water-parsnip, wild parsley, and wild parsnip. The word derives from Late Old English *gilte*, which survives in dialectal *yelt*, *hilt*, 'sow', and root.

## fess

'Well, what a fess little bonfire that one is, out by Cap'n Vye's!'
(*The Return of the Native*, I, Ch. 5)

'Y'll be fess enough, my poppet, when th'st know!'
(*Tess of the d'Urbervilles*, Ch. 3)

The word has several meanings in the dialects of Wessex, two of which, 'lively, vigorous' and 'proud, conceited', are illustrated in the above quotations. Barnes defines the word in his *Glossary*, thus: 'Fussy, meddling, and eager in what is going on. "There's a fess feller." ' The word may have developed from a south-eastern form of Old English *fȳsan* 'to impel, hasten, incite, stimulate', or it may be a variant of *fussy*.

## gallicrow

'And what ghastly gallicrow might the poor fellow have been like, Master Fairway?' asked the turf-cutter.
(*The Return of the Native*, I, Ch. 3)

'My scram blue-vinnied gallicrow of an uncle.'
(*The Trumpet-Major*, Ch. 9)

'Captain de Stancy, who is as poor as a gallicrow, is in full cry a'ter her.'
(*A Laodicean*, III, Ch. 9)

'A scarecrow'; derived from the dialectal verb *gally* which follows below.

## gally

'He said that if we didn't hear from him for six months we were not to be gallied at all.'
(*Two on a Tower*, Ch. 38)

'We've all been gallied at the dairy at what might ha' been a most terrible affliction.'
(*Tess of the d'Urbervilles*, Ch. 34)

'Read ye this, sir. It was left in her bedroom, and we be fairly gallied out of our senses!'
(*The Well-Beloved*, III, Ch. 6)

While her great gallied eyes through her hair hanging loose
    Shone as stars through a tardle o' trees.
    ('The Bride-Night Fire')

'Everybody however was fairly gallied this week when the King went out yachting.'
(*The Dynasts*, I. ii. 4)

'To frighten, alarm, scare'; the word, from Old English *ā-gǣlwan* 'to alarm', is widely recorded in Wessex dialects, as well as in America and Australia. Shakespeare knew it as *gallow*, and John Haynes's *Vocabulary* lists it as *galley* 'fright'.

## gawk-hammer

'He's a poor gawk-hammer. Look at his sermon yesterday.'
(*Under the Greenwood Tree*, II, Ch. 2)

'O Lord, not he, ma'am! A simple tool. Well enough, but a poor

gawkhammer mortal,' the wife replied.
(*Far from the Madding Crowd*, Ch. 10)

'If ye'd been minding your business instead of zwailing along in such a gawk-hammer way, you would have zeed me!' retorted the wroth representative of Henchard.
(*The Mayor of Casterbridge*, Ch. 27)

Middle English *goky* 'fool' occurs in *Piers Plowman* and may be connected with Old Norse *gaukr* 'cuckoo'. The noun *gawk* 'a stupid person, fool' is probably related. The element *hammer* is found from the sixteenth century in such compounds as *hammer-headed* 'dull, stupid'.

## giltycups

'I can walk among the high grass and giltycups – they will not yellow my stockings as they will yours.'
(*The Trumpet-Major*, Ch. 7)

'Buttercups' – the word appears in Barnes's poems as *gil'cups*, i.e. 'gilt cups', as in 'May':

> An' gil'cups, wi' the deäisy bed,
> Be under ev'ry step you tread.

Barnes notes: 'So called from the gold-like gloss of its petals.'

## glane

'How they'll squint and glane, and say, "This is yer mighty match is it!"'
(*Tess of the d'Urbervilles*, Ch. 38)

' 'Tis well for 'ee to stand there and glane!' said Arabella. 'Owing to your being late the meat is blooded and half spoiled!'
(*Jude the Obscure*, I, Ch. 10)

'To smile sneeringly' is Barnes's gloss; he uses it thus, in 'Wold Friends A-Met':

> If other vo'ks do gleen to zee
> How loven an' how glad we be.

The derivation is obscure, but the word has persisted into the twentieth century in Dorset and Somerset with the more general meaning 'to laugh'. Haynes lists it in his *Vocabulary* as 'to gleam, to jear' (jeer). The word also occurs in Northamptonshire dialect and may be of Scandinavian origin.

## good-now

'He's very clever for a silly chap, good-now, sir.'
(*Under the Greenwood Tree*, II, Ch. 4)

'We shall form a very striking object walking along in rotation, good-now, neighbours?'
(*Under the Greenwood Tree*, V, Ch. 1)

'I've heard what I've heard, good-now.'
(*Tess of the d'Urbervilles*, Ch. 5)

'She'll get over it, good-now?'
(*Jude the Obscure*, IV, Ch. 4)

'Yes, good-now; she's the very daps of her mother.'
(*The Well-Beloved*, II, Ch. 4)

Hardy, writing to John Hales, on 19 July 1892, explains as follows:

> The expression "good-now" is still much in use in the interior of this county though it is dying away hereabout. Its tone is one of conjectural assurance, its precise meaning being "you may be sure": and such phrases as 'I'll warrant', 'methinks', 'sure enough', would be used as alternatives. The American 'I guess' is near it.
>
> Though I should know exactly how & when to say it I have never thought about its root-meaning. As the people who use it are those who pronounce "enough" in the old way "enow", it is possible that "good-now" means "good enow" – i.e. "true enow", "sure enough".
>
> The commentators are quite in error in taking 'good' to be vocative – meaning "good man", "my good fellow" – as is proved by the frequency of such a sentence as this "You won't do it my lad, good-now", which would otherwise be redundant.

Barnes was one of the erring commentators on this occasion, according to Hardy, with his explanation 'Good neighbour; my good fellow', although this is how it is used in his poem 'Eclogue: The 'Lotments'. The expression is recorded from the sixteenth century, was used by Shakespeare and Dryden, and was recorded not only in Dorset but also in Wiltshire in the late nineteenth century. It could convey a variety of interjectional tones, as Hardy's usage illustrates: affirmation, questioning, astonishment, entreaty, and so on. The modern English use of the auxiliary plus negative and pronoun as question ('isn't he?', 'won't she?' etc.) is able to express similar nuances of meaning. The German dialectal *gell* or *gelt* serves much the same function.

## ho

> 'I cannot understand Farmer Boldwood being such a fool at his time of life as to ho and hanker after thik woman in the way 'a do.'
> (*Far from the Madding Crowd*, Ch. 53)

Barnes, who often uses the word, glosses it 'anxious care'; while Hardy himself, glossing Barnes's line 'An' I do little ho vor goold or pride', defines it simply as 'wish'. The strength of the word clearly depends upon its context, as the phrase 'to ho and hanker' indicates. It derives, through Middle English *howe*, from Old English *hogian* 'to think, intend'.

## huffle

> 'Egdon Heth is a bad place to get lost in, and the winds do huffle queerer to-night than ever I heard 'em afore.'
> (*The Return of the Native*, I, Ch. 3)

This is another of Barnes's favourite words, which, in the line 'The hufflen winds be music all' in the poem 'Ivy Hall', Hardy glosses 'blustering'. Probably a diminutive of *huff*, an onomatopoeic verb, it denotes 'wind blowing in gusts'.

## husbird

> 'The husbird of a feller Sam Lawson – that ever I should call'n such, now he's dead and gone, poor heart!'
> (*Under the Greenwood Tree*, I, Ch. 2)

> 'But O, to be slave to thik husbird, for bread!'
> ('The Bride-Night Fire')

Hardy's gloss is 'rascal'. Barnes's definition in his *Glossary* is worth quoting in full: 'HUZ-BIRD, Whore's-bird. Bird meaning child, a naughty name by which anger sometimes calls a child. It does not seem that the becaller, sometimes a mother! always knows the meaning of it.' In *Tess of the d'Urbervilles* Hardy uses the more explicit form *'hore's-bird*, as a more obvious term of abuse:

> 'Jack Dollop, a 'hore's-bird of a fellow we had here as milker at one time, sir.' (Ch. 21)

> 'Well', said the dairyman, ' 'tis that slack-twisted 'hore's-bird of a feller, Jack Dollop.' (Ch. 29)

## keacorn

> 'I'd go, and 'a might call, and call, till his keacorn was raw; but I'd never come back-no, not till the great trumpet, would I!'
> (*The Mayor of Casterbridge*, Ch. 1)

'The gullet, throat, windpipe'. This is a Dorset form of *kecker* 'gullet', related to *kex* 'dry hollow stalk', discussed earlier. The echoic verb *keck* 'to retch' is recorded from the early seventeenth century.

## lammiger

> 'When you take away from among us the fools and the rogues, and the lammigers, and the wanton hussies, and the slatterns, and such like, there's cust few left to ornament a song with in Casterbridge, or the country round.'
> (*The Mayor of Casterbridge*, Ch. 8)

> 'What can we two poor lammigers do against such a multitude!' expostulated Stubberd.
> (*The Mayor of Casterbridge*, Ch. 39)

Barnes (*Glossary*) prints *laminger* and glosses 'One become lame', thus 'a cripple', although Hardy's usage suggests more pejorative connotations. A derivative of *lame*.

## linhay

> She went to the 'linhay' or lean-to shed, which formed the root-store of their dwelling and abutted on the fuel-house.
> (*The Return of the Native*, II, Ch. 4)

> Owing to the slope of the ground the roof-eaves of the linhay were here within touch.
> (*The Woodlanders*, Ch. 46)

> The bridegroom yet laitered a beaker to drain,
> Then reeled to the linhay for more.
> ('The Bride-Night Fire')

And then among the crocks and things, and stores for winter junket-
ings,

> In linhay, loft, and dairy.
> ('The Rash Bride')

Hardy glosses 'lean-to building' in 'The Bride-Night Fire', corresponding to Barnes's 'LINHAY, Linnedge. A low-roofed shed attached
to a house; a penthouse' (*Glossary*). The origin of the word, also spelt
*linny*, is not known, but a connection with Old English *hlinian* 'to
lean' seems likely.


## mandy

> 'I'll crack thy numskull for thee, you mandy chap!' said Mrs Nunsuch.
> (*The Return of the Native*, I, Ch. 3)

'Saucy, insolent'. The word is also applied to horses being restive. It
is perhaps related to the verb *maunder*, 'to grumble, mutter, growl',
in common use in seventeenth-century English. Haynes's *Vocabulary* lists it as *maundy*.


## mouster

> 'We've to mouster by half-past three to-morrow.'
> (*The Woodlanders*, Ch. 46)

A dialectal variant of *muster*, meaning 'to stir, to be on the move, to
move quickly'. The verb was adopted into Middle English from Old
French *moustrer*. With the spelling *ou*, cp. Barnes's *doust* 'dust',
representing a diphthongal pronunciation /au/.


## nott

> 'But as nott cows will keep it back as well as the horned ones.'
> (*Tess of the d'Urbervilles*, Ch. 17)

Old English *hnot* 'bare, bald'; thus used by Chaucer ('a not-heed
hadde he'), and used in the south-west of hornless cows and sheep.
Barnes puns on the word in his poem 'Riddles':

Oh! *horns*! but no, I'll tell ye what,
My cow is hornless, an' she's *knot*.

## nunnywatch

'You see, after kicking up such a nunny-watch and forbidding the banns
'twould have made Mis'ess Yeobright seem foolish-like to have a banging
wedding in the same parish all as if she'd never gainsaid it.'
   (*The Return of the Native*, I, Ch. 3)

'What a nunnywatch we were in, to be sure, when we heard they weren't
married at all.'
   (*The Return of the Native*, II, Ch. 1)

'Yes, the truth is, father, I've got rather into a nunnywatch, I'm afeard!'
   (*Life's Little Ironies*: 'Tony Kytes, the Arch-Deceiver')

A variant form of *ninnywatch*, literally 'a "ninny's" view of things',
*ninny* being a corruption of *innocent*, 'a simpleton'. The sense of
*ninnywatch*, *nunnywatch* is thus: looking like a fool, not knowing
what to do; being in a quandary; whence 'a fix, a dilemma, a fuss, a
disturbance'. Barnes (*Glossary*) relates a lengthy anecdote about the
meaning of the word, concluding with 'Ninnywatch is most likely a
"ninny's outlook" as for he knows not what'.

## ooser

'What have made you so down? Have you seen a ooser?'
   (*The Return of the Native*, IV, Ch. 6)

'O, if you was sickening for the plague itself, and going to be as ugly as the
Ooser in the church-vestry, I wouldn't –'
   (*A Group of Noble Dames*: 'The First Countess of Wessex')

'A grotesque mask worn to frighten people'. The mask was made of
wood, with a movable jaw pulled by a string, surmounted with a
cow's horns and hair. The word *ooser* probably represents Middle
English *wurse*, literally 'worse', which is recorded in some early
thirteenth-century sources used as a substantive to denote the Devil.
Firor suggests that the Hooset- or Wooset-Hunting, in some counties corresponding to the Dorset skimmington ride, contains the
same word.

## outstep

'You see, Mr Manston, an outstep place like this is not like a city, and there is nobody to busy himself for the good of the community.'
(*Desperate Remedies*, Ch. 14)

'I don't think Fifth-of-Novembers ought to be kept up by night except in towns. It should be by day in outstep, ill-accounted places like this!'
(*The Return of the Native*, I, Ch. 3)

'Out of the way, lonely. Applied to a village or house' (Barnes, *Glossary*). The meaning is clear; the word has a parallel in the Australian *outback*, used by Rolf Boldrewood in *The Squatter's Dream* in 1875.

## raft

'They should ha' stuck to strings. Your brass-man is a rafting dog – well and good.'
(*Under the Greenwood Tree*, I, Ch. 4)

'My brain is all in a spin, wi' being rafted up in such a larry!'
(*The Hand of Ethelberta*, Ch. 44)

'Refrain yourself, my dear woman, refrain!' she said hastily to Mrs Martin, 'don't ye see how it do raft my lady?'
(*Two on a Tower*, Ch. 38)

'Don't raft yourself without good need, George', she replied.
(*The Woodlanders*, Ch. 29)

'The poor man – he felt so rafted after his uplifting by the pa'son's news – that he went up to Rolliver's half an hour ago.'
(*Tess of the d'Urbervilles*, Ch. 3)

'I think you are rafted, and not yourself', he continued.
(*Jude the Obscure*, IV, ch. 4)

> Young Tim away yond, rafted up by the light,
> Through brimbles and underwood tears.
> ('The Bride-Night Fire')

'Roused' is Hardy's gloss to the poem, where Barnes (*Glossary*) is more explicit: 'To rouse one as when going to sleep or dying, or to raft a beast'. Also 'to disturb, alarm, irritate, upset', as the above contexts require. The word may be a dialectal variant of *ruff* 'a state of excitement', recorded in the sixteenth and seventeenth century, or of the verb *ruffle*.

**rozum**

> 'And yet he's a projick, a real projick, and says the oddest of rozums.'
> (*The Woodlanders*, Ch. 6)

> 'Mr Clare', said the dairyman emphatically, 'is one of the most rebellest rozums you ever knowed – not a bit like the rest of his family.'
> (*Tess of the d'Urbervilles*, Ch. 19)

The primary meaning is 'an odd or quaint saying', whence 'a saw or proverb' (thus Barnes, *Glossary*). Hardy's extension of this, in *Tess of the d'Urbervilles*, to denote 'an odd person, an eccentric' is not otherwise recorded. The origin of the word is unknown.

**rozum away**

> 'And then, when they got to church-door he'd throw down the clarinet, mount the gallery, snatch up the bass-viol, and rozum away as if he'd never played anything but a bass-viol.'
> (*The Return of the Native*, I, Ch. 5)

This word appears as *rozzen* in the west midlands and is thus not strictly a Wessex word. It is included here, as it may be connected with the preceding word, as Hardy used it. The meaning is 'to set to work in a vigorous manner', possibly (as Hardy may be suggesting) in a somewhat eccentric manner. It is, however, just possible that this is the verb *rosin* 'to rub a violin bow or string with rosin (resin)' which is recorded in a variety of spellings, and may be used figuratively by Hardy to describe vigorous playing.

**scammish**

> 'And even as 'tis we all look a little scammish beside him.'
> (*The Return of the Native*, II, Ch. 6)

'Awkward, untidy'. Possibly related to *scram*, *shram*. Barnes gives *scram* as a synonym. This is presumably the same word as *chammish*, 'awkward' in Haynes's *Dorsetshire Vocabulary*.

**scram, shram**

> 'There's sure to be some poor little scram reason for 't staring us in the face all the while.'
> (*Under the Greenwood Tree*, I, Ch. 5)

'Just flashed her haughty eyes upon my poor scram body.'
(*Far from the Madding Crowd*, Ch. 52)

'And on a frosty winter night he'll keep me there while he tweedles upon the Dulcianner till my arms be scrammed for want of motion.'
(*The Hand of Ethelberta*, Ch. 40)

'My scram blue-vinnied gallicrow of an uncle.'
(*The Trumpet-Major*, Ch. 9)

'My arm.' She reluctantly showed the withered skin.
'Ah! – 'tis all a-scram!' said the hangman, examining it.
(*Wessex Tales*: 'The Withered Arm', 8)

'I'd ha' knocked him down wi' the rolling-pin – a scram little feller like he! Any woman could do it.'
(*Tess of the d'Urbervilles*, Ch. 29)

'Do 'ee get on to bed, ma'am. You must be shrammed to death!'
(*A Changed Man*: 'The Waiting Supper', VII)

He had nothing quite seemly for Barbree to wear,
Who, half shrammed to death, stood and cried on a chair
   At the caddle she found herself in.
     ('The Bride-Night Fire')

Both words derive from Old English *scrimman* 'to shrink, shrivel', whence the several related meanings in Hardy's usage: as an adjective, 'puny, awkward, insignificant, shrunken, withered'; as a verb, 'to shrink, shrivel, become numb'. Barnes, in his idiosyncratic manner, glosses *scram* 'screwy grown, dwarfish', and *shram* 'a screwing up or out of the body and limbs from keen cold'. In 'The Bridge-Night Fire', Hardy's original manuscript reading was *scrammed*: he clearly equated the two forms.

## scroff

'Sergeant, I was no more to her than a morsel of scroff in the fuel-house!'
(*Far from the Madding Crowd*, Ch. 52)

'We who have stayed at home shall seem no more than scroff in his eyes.'
(*The Return of the Native*, II, Ch. 1)

'If you can't get the cork out of the jar, David, bore a hole in the tub of Hollands that's buried under the scroff in the fuel-house.'
(*The Trumpet-Major*, Ch. 15)

When she came close and looked in she beheld indistinct forms racing up and down to the figure of the dance, the silence of their footfalls arising

from their being overshoe in 'scroff' – that is to say, the powdery residuum from the storage of peat and other products, the stirring of which by their turbulent feet created the nebulosity that involved the scene.
(*Tess of the d'Urbervilles*, Ch. 10)

Barnes has a whole poem about this, 'Picken o' Scroff', and, too, the lines from 'The Stwonen Bwoy upon the Pillar':

> An' there the while the rooks do bring
> Their scroff to build their nest in Spring,

Hardy provides the gloss 'light fragments of wood-refuse'. The word can be applied to any odds and ends, rubbish, refuse, as well as being used specifically as defined in *Tess of the d'Urbervilles*. The word was current as *scruff* (from Late Old English *scurf*) 'worthless things, litter' in sixteenth- and seventeenth-century English;\ it appears as *shroff* in Hardy's poem 'The Wood Fire'.

## skimmer-cake

The motive of his return was shown by his helping himself to a cut piece of skimmer-cake that lay on a ledge beside where he had sat.
(*Wessex Tales*: 'The Three Strangers')

One of her leather gloves, which she had taken off to eat her skimmer-cake, lay in her lap.
(*Tess of the d'Urbervilles*, Ch. 47)

> 'Here's a skimmer-cake for supper, peckled onions,
>    and some pears.'
>    ('The Homecoming')

'A small pudding made up from the remnants of another, and cooked upon a "skimmer", the dish with which the milk is skimmed.'

## souls

'Well so's', said the clerk modestly. 'I do know a little. It comes to me.'
(*Desperate Remedies*, Ch. 8)

'Why, souls, what's the use o' the ancients spending scores of pounds to build galleries if people down in the lowest depths of the church sing like that at a moment's notice?'
(*Under the Greenwood Tree*, I, Ch. 6)

'Come in, souls, and have something to eat and drink wi' me and my wife.'
(*Far from the Madding Crowd*, Ch. 57)

'And I don't think Hezzy and Nat had, either, – had ye, souls?'
(*Two on a Tower*, Ch. 2)

And her father said: 'Souls, for God's sake be steady!'
('The Country Wedding')

The shorter form, *so's*, appears mainly in the earlier novels. This was a common form of address, equivalent to 'friends', in south-western Wessex. Barnes (*Glossary*) writes: 'Souls, meaning folks or men in distinction from brutes. "O so's", "O folks!".' In his poem 'The Stage Coach' he uses the same pair: 'good so's' and 'good vo'k'.

Elsewhere, Hardy uses *sonnies* or *my sonnies* in the same way, for example:

'That's the question, my sonnies.'
(*Under the Greenwood Tree*, I, Ch. 6)

This is followed immediately by Mr. Penny's 'souls'. On the other hand, there is the comic use of 'my sonnies' as a mode of address by the tranter to his wife, which underlines the irrelevance of the literal meaning:

'Well, now, look here, my sonnies', he argued to his wife, whom he often addressed in the plural masculine for economy of epithet merely.
(*Under the Greenwood Tree*, I, Ch. 8)

Such usage, as a mode of address to wives, or by sons to their fathers, is recorded elsewhere in the south-west.

Yet another variant is *hearties*, as used by Bob Loveday in *The Trumpet-Major*, Ch. 40.

## sprawl

'But, O no – poor or'nary child – there never was any sprawl on thy side of the family, and never will be!'
(*Jude the Obscure*, I, Ch. 2)

'Oh that I hadn't married a fiery sojer, to make me bring fatherless children into the world, all through his dreadful calling! Why didn't a man of no sprawl content me!'
(*The Dynasts*, I. ii. 5)

'Energy, strength, agility'. Also found as *sproil* and in other spell-ings, and probably derived from the same source, Old English *sprēawlian*, as the verb 'to sprawl'.

## stitch

> Henchard crossed the shaded avenue on the walls, slid down the green rampart, and stood amongst the stubble. The 'stitches' or shocks rose like tents about the yellow expanse.
> (*The Mayor of Casterbridge*, Ch. 27)

> Every one placing her sheaf on end against those of the rest, till a shock, or 'stitch' as it was here called, of ten or a dozen was formed.
> (*Tess of the d'Urbervilles*, Ch. 14)

'A set of sheaves stuck up in the field, top to top' (Barnes, *Glossary*). This is possibly the same word as *stitch* 'a strip or ridge of ploughed land', recorded from the fifteenth century.

## strawmote

> 'Then Gabe brought her some of the new cider, and she must needs go drinking it through a strawmote, and not in a nateral way at all.'
> (*Far from the Madding Crowd*, Ch. 52)

'A single straw, a stalk of straw', also 'a stalk of grass' (Barnes, *Glossary*) as in Barnes's 'Hallowed Pleaces':

> Light strawmotes rose in flaggen flight,
> A-floated by the winds o' night.

Standard English *mote* derives from Old English *mot* 'a speck'.

## strent

> 'My breeches were tore into a long strent by getting through a copse of thorns and brimbles for a short cut home-along.'
> (*Under the Greenwood Tree*, II, Ch. 2)

'A tear, rent, slit'. The word may be connected with *strand*, 'a thread or strip of material', which is of obscure origin. The meaning of *strent* is the same as that of dialectal *slent*, both of which Barnes defines in his *Glossary* as 'to tear as linen. Also a slit'. Barnes uses the latter word in 'Out A-Nutten': 'wi' clothes in slents', while Hardy, in his poem 'Valenciennes', extends the meaning from ripping cloth to an explosion in his line 'A shell was slent to shards anighst my ears'.

### stud

'And you see', continued Reuben, 'at the very beginning it put me in a stud as to how to quarrel wi' en.'
(*Under the Greenwood Tree*, II, Ch. 5)

'Ay, 'a will sit studding and thinking as if 'a were going to turn chapel-member.'
(*Under the Greenwood Tree*, IV, Ch. 4)

The noun is defined by Barnes (*Glossary*) as 'a steadfast stillness of body, as of one in thought', and can mean 'a dilemma' or 'a reverie'. The verb means 'to think, contemplate' as well as 'to daydream'. The word is a dialectal form of *study*.

### stunpoll

'Then she's a bigger stunpoll than I took her for', said Mr Springrove. 'Why, she's old enough to be his mother.'
(*Desperate Remedies*, Ch. 8)

'The little stunpoll of a fellow.'
(*Desperate Remedies*, Ch. 9)

'You stun-poll! What will ye say next?' said Coggan.
(*Far from the Madding Crowd*, Ch. 33)

'And I zid myself as the next poor stunpoll to get into the same mess.'
(*The Return of the Native*, I, Ch. 3)

'A man must be a headstrong stunpoll to think folk would go up to that bleak place to-day.'
(*The Mayor of Casterbridge*, Ch. 16)

' 'Tisn't a mo'sel o' good for thee to cry out against Wessex folk, when 'twas all thy own stunpoll ignorance.'
(*The Dynasts*, III. v. 6)

'A stupid fellow, a dunce'. Used, and glossed 'stonehead, stunhead. A blockhead', by Barnes, which suggests its literal meaning 'stone-head'; *poll*, Middle English *polle*, means 'head'.

## thirtover

'Dear, what a thirtover place this world is!' continued Mrs Coggan.
(*Far from the Madding Crowd*, Ch. 9)

'I have been living on in a thirtover, lackaday way, and have not seen what it may lead to!'
(*Tess of the d'Urbervilles*, Ch. 43)

But she bode wi' a thirtover uncle.
('The Bride-Night Fire')

Hardy provides the gloss 'cross' in the poem, his other uses requiring the meanings 'perverse, contrary, obstinate, ill-tempered'. Literally, 'thwart over', *thirt* is the Wessex equivalent of standard English *thwart*; the adverb 'athwart' having its dialectal counterpart in *athirt*, frequent in Barnes's poems.

A variant form, also meaning 'perverse, wrong-headed', is *thirtingill* in *Under the Greenwood Tree*, I, Ch. 3: 'scatter-brained and thirtingill as a chiel', not recorded outside Dorset.

## three-cunning

'Don't be so three-cunning.'
(*Desperate Remedies*, Ch. 13)

Defined by Barnes (*Glossary*) as 'over sharp'; literally, having the knowledge or cunning of three people.

## tisty-tosty

'They say she's a rosy-cheeked, tisty-tosty little body enough.'
(*Wessex Tales*: 'The Withered Arm', 1)

'Round like a ball, plump and comely, pleasant'. The *tisty-tosty* is the ball of cowslips made yearly by the children of Dorset and Somerset on Cowslip Sunday, the first Sunday in May, and used in a game to foretell the occupation of a girl's future husband, with the help of this verse:

Tisty-Tosty, tell me true,
Who shall I be married to?
Tinker, tailor, soldier, sailor, etc.

(See N. Rogers, *Wessex Dialect*, p. 66). Udal, in *Dorsetshire Folk-*

*Lore*, p. 190, gives a slightly different version, in which names of girls or boys, depending on who is playing, are called out instead of trades. The word is probably derived from the verb *toss*.

## unray

> 'He had un'rayed for a dip, but not being able to pitch it just there had gone in flop over his head.'
> (*Under the Greenwood Tree*, I, Ch. 3)

> 'I be old and low, and it takes me a long while to un-ray. I han't unlaced my jumps yet.'
> (*Jude the Obscure*, VI, Ch. 9)

'To undress'. The verb *ray* is an aphetic form of *array* 'dress', first recorded in the fourteenth century.

## vlankers

> She helplessly danced round with him, her feet playing like drumsticks among the sparks. 'My ankles were all in a fever before, from walking through that prickly furze, and now you must make 'em worse with these vlankers!'
> (*The Return of the Native*, I, Ch. 3)

> Flames spread, and red vlankers wi' might
> and wi' main
> Around beams, thatch, and chimley-tun roar.
> ('The Bride-Night Fire')

'Fire-flakes' is Hardy's gloss in the poem, and 'spark' is his gloss to Barnes's use in 'Gruffmoody Grim'. The word occurs in the north-west midland alliterative poetry, as 'flaunkes of fyr', and may represent a nasalized variant of *flake*; in the case of *vlankers* with dialectal voicing of the initial /f/.

## withywind

> 'He is a man who notices the looks of women, and you could twist him to your will like withywind, if you only had the mind.'
> (*The Return of the Native*, I, Ch. 10)

'The bindweed'; in Barnes also *withwind*:

> That roun' the risen tow'r do wind,
> Like withwind roun' the saplen's rind.

73

('The Leady's Tower'). The element *withy* derives from Old English *wīþig* 'willow'.

## workfolk

> The labourers – or 'workfolk', as they used to call themselves immemor-
> ially till the other word was introduced from without – who wish to
> remain no longer in old places are removing to the new farms.
> (*Tess of the d'Urbervilles*, Ch. 51)

Hardy makes the same comment in his autobiography: 'The
workfolk (they always used to be called "workfolk" hereabout –
"labourers" is an imported word)', and he glosses Barnes's use of the
word in 'Trees Be Company' with 'field-labourers as distinguished
from artisans, &c.' For Barnes 'workvo'k' was the regular word.
Another distinction is drawn by Hardy in 'The Dorsetshire
Labourer': on the one hand, 'the regular farmer's labourers –
"workfolk" as they call themselves – '; on the other, 'the adjoining
class, the unattached labourers, approximating to the free labourers
of the middle ages, who are to be found in the larger villages and small
towns of the county – many of them, no doubt, descendants of the
old copyholders who were ousted from their little plots when the
system of leasing large farms grew general.'

## wropper

> An old milkman near, in a long white pinafore or 'wropper', and with the
> brim of his hat tied down, so that he looked like a woman.
> (*Wessex Tales*: 'The Withered Arm', 1)

> And others, older, in the brown-rough 'wropper' or over-all – the old-
> established and most appropriate dress of the field-woman, which the
> young ones were abandoning.
> (*Tess of the d'Urbervilles*, Ch. 14)

> Their forms standing enshrouded in Hessian 'wroppers' – sleeved brown
> pinafores, tied behind to the bottom, to keep their gowns from blowing
> about.
> (*Tess of the d'Urbervilles*, Ch. 43)

A variant of 'wrapper', it corresponds less to the British than to the
American usage of 'pinafore', that is an overall, fastened at the back.

## zwailing

'If ye'd been minding your business instead of zwailing along in such a
gawk-hammer way, you would have zeed me!'
(*The Mayor of Casterbridge*, Ch. 27)

Barnes's definition, in his *Glossary*, is 'to sway about from side to
side. To swagger'. The word denotes 'a rolling, lazy gait', with arms
swinging. A south-western form of *swail* or *swale*, possibly derived
from *sway*.

(iii) *Words principally confined to Dorset.*

## borus-snorus

'Still, for my part', said old William, 'though he's arrayed against us, I like
the hearty borus-snorus ways of the new pa'son.'
(*Under the Greenwood Tree*, II, Ch. 2)

Barnes (*Glossary*) has this entry: 'BORIS-NORIS. Going on blindly,
without any thought of risk or decency.' The form used by Hardy is
apparently confined to Dorset, although, as Baugner notes, similar
forms have been recorded in Wiltshire: *nolus-bolus*, *snorus-vorus*,
*vorus-norus*, all of them probably corruptions of Latin *nolens volens*
'willy-nilly'.

## cappel-faced

'Dick, that thou beest a white-lyvered chap I don't say, but if thou beestn't
as mad as a cappel-faced bull let me smile no more.'
(*Under the Greenwood Tree*, II, Ch. 8)

According to Barnes (*Glossary*), a 'capple cow' is 'a cow with a white
muzzle', from Old English *ceafl* 'jaw, cheek, muzzle'. The *English
Dialect Dictionary* defines *cappel-faced* as 'white-faced with red or
dun speckles'.

## clipse

'Why don't he clipse her to his side, like a man?' said the biggest and rudest
boy.
(*The Trumpet-Major*, Ch. 38)

' 'Tis melancholy work facing and footing it to one of your own sort, and no clipsing and colling at all.'
(*Tess of the d'Urbervilles*, Ch. 2)

'No, no, no! I merely did it not to be clipsed or colled, Marian.'
(*Tess of the d'Urbervilles*, Ch. 42)

Barnes (*Glossary*) defines: 'To clasp between the thumb and fingers, or to fathom between the two arms.' He uses it thus in 'The Sky a-Clearen':

> 'Tis wrong vor women's han's to clips
> The zull an' reap-hook, speädes an' whips.

The common meaning 'to embrace, hug' is as in Hardy's usage. The root is Old English *clyppan* 'to embrace', with *s* from the adjectival ending *sum*, as in *clipsome* 'fit to be embraced'.

### ewe-lease

The next clue was furnished them by a shepherd. He said that wherever a clear space three or four yards wide ran in a line through a flock of sheep lying about a ewe-lease, it was a proof that somebody had passed there not more than half-an-hour earlier.
(*Desperate Remedies*, Ch. 20)

Over the snowy down or ewe-lease on Weatherbury Upper Farm.
(*Far from the Madding Crowd*, Ch. 14)

The long, grassy and furzy downs, coombs, or ewe-leases, as they are called according to their kind.
(*Wessex Tales*: 'The Three Strangers')

One of the poems in *Wessex Poems* is entitled 'In a Eweleaze near Weatherbury'. The word, important in Hardy's countryside, denotes 'a grass field or down stocked with sheep', and derives from Old English *lǣs*, *lǣse* 'pasture, meadow-land'.

### home-along

'Every man home-along straight as a line.'
(*Desperate Remedies*, Sequel)

'Through a copse of thorns and brimbles for a short cut home-along.'
(*Under the Greenwood Tree*, II, Ch. 2)

'And now we'll move these two, and home-along', interposed John Smith.
(*A Pair of Blue Eyes*, Ch. 26)

'So I'll take myself off home-along, Mrs Hurst.'
(*Far from the Madding Crowd*, Ch. 4)

'And, please God, here's for home-along.'
(*Wessex Tales*: 'The Distracted Preacher', 7)

> Some miles homealong.
> ('The Fight on Durnover Moor')

> The sun was set when home-along
> You ambled in the gray.
> ('At the Mill')

A favourite term with Hardy, as the above examples illustrate. The suffix *-along* is found added to other words as well, in south-western Wessex, e.g.: 'And when, on my way backalong, I saw you waiting . . .' (*The Well-Beloved*, II, Ch. 8), or in the line from 'Widecombe Fair' 'All along, down along, out along lea', quoted in K.C. Phillipps, *Westcountry Words and Ways*, p. 24. The suffix *-along* is the equivalent of standard English *-wards*.

### hontish

'She's akin to that hontish fellow Henchard.'
(*The Mayor of Casterbridge*, Ch. 37)

'I thought if I spoke of his fond feelings and what they might lead to, you would be hontish wi' him and lose your chance', she murmured.
(*Tess of the d'Urbervilles*, Ch. 12)

'Bashful, ashamed' is the primary meaning, as the word derives from the same French root as Middle English *hontous* 'full of shame', and this is the likely sense in *Tess of the d'Urbervilles*. The editorial gloss 'haughty' is less appropriate in either instance, and the meaning 'boorish, unmannerly' recorded for this word by Widén, suits the context of Henchard's rude behaviour in the incident where it is used in *The Mayor of Casterbridge*. Whereas *hontish* is Dorsetshire, the form *hountish* has been recorded in neighbouring Somerset.

### house-ridding

The four breakfasted by the thin light, and the 'house-ridding' was taken in hand.
(*Tess of the d'Urbervilles*, Ch. 52)

The annual migration on Lady Day, Old Style, – 6 April – from one farm to the next, was called 'house-ridding', and is described in detail in 'The Dorsetshire Labourer'. So it is in Barnes's poem 'Leady-Day, an' Ridden House', and in one of his finest poems, 'Woak Hill', occur the lines:

> Zoo – lest she should tell me hereafter
> I stole off 'ithout her,
> An' left her, uncall'd at house-ridden,
> To bide at Woak Hill.

## huddied

'When you was following me to Street o' Wells, two hours ago, I looked round and saw you, and huddied behind a stone!'
(*The Well-Beloved*, II, Ch. 8)

> In the tallet he stowed her; there huddied
> she lay,
> Shortening sleeves, legs, and tails to her limbs.
> ('The Bride-Night Fire')

This may represent a distinctive Dorsetshire word, related to standard English *hood* 'covering' and to the verb *hide*, Old English *hȳdan*, and to the dialectal *huddick*, *huddock*, defined by Barnes (*Glossary*) as 'a bag or case for a sore finger'; or it may represent the Dorset pronunciation of *hidded*, i.e. hid, as in Dorset *wull* for 'will'. As the form *hud* for 'hid' is recorded in Wiltshire, the latter is the more likely alternative. John Haynes's *Vocabulary* records 'To ly in huddy-box, in ambush'. The original manuscript reading in 'The Bride-Night Fire' was *hidied*.

## lanchets

'A large bed of flints called locally a "lanch" or "lanchet".'
(*Desperate Remedies*, Ch. 10)

The 'lanchets', or flint slopes, which belted the escarpment at intervals of a dozen yards, took the less cautious ones unawares.
(*Wessex Tales*; 'The Three Strangers')

A stretch of a hundred odd acres, in one patch, on the highest ground of the farm, rising above stony lanchets or lynchets – the outcrop of siliceous veins in the chalk formation, composed of myriads of loose white flints in bulbous, cusped, and phallic shapes.
(*Tess of the d'Urbervilles*, Ch. 43)

And still sadly onward I followed
That Highway the Icen,
Which trails its pale riband down Wessex
By lynchet and lea.
('My Cicely')

Of the three forms Hardy uses, – *lanch*, *lanchet*, *lynchet*, – the first
two are dialectal variants of *landshard*, synonymous with *lynchet*
which derives from Old English *hlinc* 'a ridge'. The words have
related meanings: 'an unploughed ridge or strip between ploughed
fields' and 'a slope or terrace along the face of a chalk down'.

## mampus

'You have been looking out, like the rest o' us, no doubt, Mrs Garland, at
the mampus of soldiers that have come upon the down?'
(*The Trumpet-Major*, Ch. 2)

'No doubt a mampus of volk of our own rank will be down here in their
carriages as soon as 'tis known.'
(*Tess of the d'Urbervilles*, Ch. 3)

'What a mampus o' folk it is here to-day!'
(*The Dynasts*, I. ii. 4)

Barnes (*Glossary*) defines thus: 'MAMPUS, mumpus. A great number;
a crowd. "A mampus o' volk".' The etymology of *mampus* is not
known, but the word may be a corruption of *magnum posse*,
analogous to that of *borus-snorus*. The noun *posse*, derived, via
Medieval Latin, from the Latin verb meaning 'to be able', was current
in English from the sixteenth century, denoting a quantity of things,
or a group, collection, assemblage, or crowd of animals or persons.
The word stands for the legal term *posse comitatus*, 'the force, or
manpower, of a county', and is still used in a similar sense in the
United States. A *mampus* is thus, literally, 'a large assemblage or
crowd'. John Haynes gives *mampus* in his *Vocabulary* with the
meaning 'multitude'.

## market-nitch

'Bless thy simplicity, Tess', said her companions. 'He's got his market-
nitch. Haw-haw!'
(*Tess of the d'Urbervilles*, Ch. 2)

*Nitch* is a common western dialect word, from Cumbria to Devon, denoting 'a bundle, a load', and is thus used by Hardy in *Two on a Tower* and in *The Well-Beloved* in the phrase 'pitch my (his) nitch', to set down one's bundle or load. In *Tess of the d'Urbervilles*, *market-nitch* denotes the amount of liquor consumed on market days, as Barnes notes in his definition of *nitch*: 'A burthen; as much as one can carry of wood, hay, or straw, and sometimes of drink.' The origin of *nitch* is Old English *gecnycc* 'bond'.

## maul down

> 'Christian, maul down the victuals from corner-cupboard if canst reach, man, and I'll draw a drap o' sommat to wet it with.
> (*The Return of the Native*, VI, Ch. 4)

The meaning, 'to lift down, to grab', is clear enough; the peculiar usage of *maul* appears to be confined to Dorset and is only recorded in Hardy.

## mollyhorning

> 'We were wondering what could keep you home here mollyhorning about when you have made such a world-wide name for yourself in the nick-nack trade – now, that's the truth o't.'
> (*The Return of the Native*, III, Ch. 1)

Barnes does not record this word. A contextual meaning of 'idling', 'wasting one's time' seems appropriate. Pinion glosses 'gallivanting'. The context suggests that this may be a Dorsetshire variant of the western dialectal *mullocking* 'idling, wasting time', whereas the form Hardy uses recalls southern and south-midland forms like *molly-hern* and *mollyheron*, which denote the 'heron', especially the female bird. The allusion may be to the fact that some herons do not migrate with the rest but remain in England during the winter, *mollyhorning* about at home.

## mumbudgeting

> 'Ay, there was this to be said for he, that you were quite sure he'd never come mumbudgeting to see ye, just as you were in the middle of your work, and put you out with his fuss and trouble about ye.'
> (*Under the Greenwood Tree*, II, Ch. 2)

She searched in the corner-cupboard, produced the bottle and began to dust the cork, the rim, and every other part very carefully, Dick's hand and Shiner's hand waiting side by side.

'Which is head man?' said Mrs Day. 'Now, don't come mumbudgeting so close again. Which is head man?'

(*Under the Greenwood Tree*, IV, Ch. 2)

On this word Geoffrey Grigson (in his Introduction to the novel in the New Wessex Edition (1974) ) writes:

The dialect may at times be a little forced or *voulu* (did the 'mumbud-geting' of page 90 ever sound in a Dorset mouth? Consult the *Oxford English Dictionary* on 'mumbudget'). The touches of folklore are out of books rather than the recesses of the Dorset mind or the practices of Stinsford.

This is a curious judgement, especially if one notes the possibility, mooted by the *OED*, that the word may derive from a children's game in which silence was required. There are other such words, like *tisty-tosty*, noted earlier, and a considerable 'mampus' of words, which like *mumbudgeting* were once found in colloquial English, and then survived as good 'mouth-filling' dialect words. One recalls *nunnywatch* or the expressive *mollyhorning about* in *The Return of the Native*, III, Ch. 1.

'To come mumbudgeting' means to creep up silently, secretly on someone, as in the children's game variously called 'Creeping Up', 'Red Light' or 'Red Letter', which Hardy is more likely to have played as a boy at Stinsford than, say, dumb crambo. That Hardy knew about children's games is clear from such allusions as the mention of 'a game o' dibs' in *Jude the Obscure*, V, Ch. 4. This and other Dorsetshire games are mentioned in Chapter XII of Udal's *Dorsetshire Folk-Lore*.

### no'thern, Northern

'Don't be a no'thern simpleton!' said Henchard drily.
(*The Mayor of Casterbridge*, Ch. 27)

'If I had done such a thing you would have sworn I was a curst no'thern fool to be drawn off the scent by such a red-herring doll-oll-oll.'
(*Wessex Tales*: 'Interlopers at the Knap', IV)

The bride sought her chamber so calm and so pale
That a Northern had thought her resigned.
('The Bride-Night Fire')

The apostrophe suggests 'northern', implying the southerner's disparaging view of anyone from the north; but the word may represent a local variant of *noddering* 'trembling from cold or age', which may be the origin of the Somerset *nothering* meaning 'stupid'. 'To nodder' is recorded elsewhere and is presumably related to *noddy* 'foolish, drowsy' and the verb *nod*. In 'The Bride-Night Fire', Hardy explicitly contrasts 'a Northern', as being unaware of what is known to the locals, with 'eyes that had seen her in tidetimes of weal': the word thus suggests ignorance.

### sniche

> 'H'm, not a large quantity of cattle. The old rascal!'
> 'No, 'tis not a large quantity. Old what did you say, sir?'
> 'O nothing. He's within there . . . 'He's a regular sniche one.'
>     (*The Trumpet-Major*, Ch. 6)

'Grasping, greedy, eager'. This corresponds to the Devon word *sneechy* 'greedy', both presumably local variants of 'snatch(ing)'. In Middle English the verb 'snatch' occurs as *snecchen* as well as *snacchen*, and the raising of /ɛ/ to /ɪ/ is not uncommon in Dorset, as in *hidge*, 'hedge'.

### stooded

> 'Her mind can no more be heaved from that one place where it do bide than a stooded waggon from the hole he's in.'
>     (*Tess of the d'Urbervilles*, Ch. 47)

Barnes (*Glossary*) defines the word *a-stooded* as 'sunk (as waggon wheels) into the ground' and has a whole poem about it, 'The Waggon A-Stooded', in which the vehicle 'is here a-stooded in theäse bed o' clay'. The word is a Dorset form of *stood* and, according to Widén, survives in the phrase 'to get stooded', i.e. to stop a horse.

### tardle

> While her great gallied eyes through her hair hanging loose
>     Shone as stars through a tardle o' trees.
>         ('The Bride-Night Fire')

Hardy's gloss is 'entanglement'; Barnes (*Glossary*) simply has 'to tangle much'. The word may be a local variant of 'tangle'.

**teuny**

> 'I can mind her mother', said the hollow-turner. 'Always a teuny, delicate piece; her touch upon your hand was like the passing of wind.'
> (*The Woodlanders*, Ch. 4)

'Weak, sickly, undersized' (*English Dialect Dictionary*, adding Hardy's comment: 'Mostly used of children'). This is presumably the same word as *tewly*, listed in Barnes's *Glossary* and defined as 'Small and weakly, spoken of a child or a plant', although *teuny* is phonetically closer to *tiny* or *teeny* of which it is probably a variant form.

**trangleys**

> 'When he comes back he may find all his poor jim-cracks and trangleys as he left 'em, and not feel that I have betrayed his trust.'
> (*Two on a Tower*, Ch. 38)

While *jim-cracks* or *gimcracks*, 'cheap trifles or gadgets', is found in many dialect areas as well as in standard English, *trangleys* appears to be confined to Dorset. It is a variant of *trangle*, *tringle*, from Old French *tringle* 'beam', and denotes pieces of ironmongery and pieces of wood such as children use as toys.

**twanking, twanky**

> 'Only Mr Wildeve is twanky because 'tisn't a boy – that's what they say in the kitchen.'
> (*The Return of the Native*, V, Ch. 2)
> 'A poor twanking woman like her – 'tis a godsend for her, and hardly a pair of jumps or night-rail to her name.'
> (*The Mayor of Casterbridge*, Ch. 13)

The basic meaning is 'complaining'. Hardy is reported in the *English Dialect Dictionary* as writing: 'To "querk" is to complain without good cause; to "twank" is to complain with real cause.' The verb *twank* is a dialectal variant of *twang*, an echoic word, denoting various sounds made by instruments or by a speaker.

**vell**

> 'Yes, this morning at six o'clock they went up the country to do the job, and neither vell nor mark have been seen of 'em since.'
> (*The Return of the Native*, I, Ch. 3)

*Vell*, Old English *fell*, means 'hide, skin', and 'neither vell nor mark', i.e. no trace, originally applied to lost cattle, is a Dorset expression, also recorded by Barnes: 'I can't zee vell or mark o't' (*Glossary*), and included in John Haynes's *Vocabulary* with the definition 'no sign or token'.

## wanzing

> Not as one wanzing weak
> From life's roar and reek,
> His rest still to seek.
>> ('He Revisits his First School')

> But do for ever softly say:
>> 'From now unto the end
> Come weal, come wanzing, come what may,
>> Dear, I will be your friend.'
>> ('The Beauty')

'To wither, waste, decay'. The word is recorded in the Middle Ages, and in East Anglia in the early nineteenth century. It derives from Old English *wansian* 'to diminish'. It is not recorded by Barnes.

## whickered

> The harts that had been hunted here, the witches that had been pricked and ducked, the green-spangled fairies that 'whickered' at you as you passed; – the place teemed with beliefs in them still, and they formed an impish multitude now.
> (*Tess of the d'Urbervilles*, Ch. 50)

Applied to horses, *whicker* is 'to whinny, to neigh'; thus Barnes in his *Glossary* and, for example, in 'Gammony Gay':

> An' the ho'ses do look over raïls,
> An' do whicker to zee'n at the pleäce.

Applied to people, or to fairies, *whicker* is 'to laugh, in a tittering, whinnying manner', recorded in this sense in Dorset from the eighteenth century. Haynes glosses simply 'to laugh'. The word corresponds to Middle High German *wiheren*, German *wiehern* 'to neigh'.

(iv) *Dialectal phrases and corruptions.*

Among the words discussed above are some which tend to occur mainly in idiomatic phrases, like 'to hele out', 'dry as a kex', 'kiss and coll', 'clipse and coll', 'slave and drave', 'neither vell nor mark'; yet these words are by themselves sufficiently unfamiliar to most readers of Hardy to convey the desired effect of dialect speech when sprinkled selectively in rustic dialogue, and are therefore sedulously annotated by modern editors. Like obsolete words in an Elizabethan play, the reader is immediately aware of a linguistic hurdle and reaches for his glossary.

On the other hand, there are phrases in Hardy's dialogue which do not thus immediately declare themselves. The reader of the nineteen-eighties coming across the tranter's words 'we new-married folk went a-gaying round the parish behind 'em' (*Under the Greenwood Tree*, V, Ch. 1), may perhaps need a moment's reminder that 'to go a-gaying' does not connote the recent semantic development of the word *gay*, but means 'to gad about, have a pleasant time'. But he or she might have been more genuinely puzzled by Izz Huett's remark to Tess 'You was not called home this morning', in *Tess of the d'Urbervilles*, Ch. 32, if Hardy himself had not seen fit to annotate this in his footnote: 'local phrase for publication of banns'. There is no such footnote in *Under the Greenwood Tree*, V, 1, where the phrase also occurs, but Hardy's meaning is made clear by an appropriate authorial comment a few lines previously:

> The conversation just now going on was concerning the banns, the last publication of which had been on the Sunday previous.

The same notion is expressed rather more forcefully in 'The Bride-Night Fire':

> The pa'son was told, as the season drew near,
> To throw over pu'pit the names of the pair
> As fitting one flesh to be made.

And again, in *Far from the Madding Crowd*, Ch. 20, in Oak's words:

> 'That Farmer Boldwood's name and your own were likely to be flung over pulpit together before the year was out.'

There are many such phrases in Hardy's dialect, often of no less robustness. Thus in *Tess of the d'Urbervilles* 'one of the elderly boozers' observes, referring to Tess, 'But Joan Durbeyfield must mind that she don't get green malt in floor' (Ch. 4). The phrase refers to the germination by moisture of a cereal grain, such as barley, in the production of malt, and simply means 'to become pregnant'. Perhaps a little less enigmatic for most readers is Laban Tall's remark, in *Far from the Madding Crowd*, Ch. 22: 'Well, better wed over the mixen than over the moor', a proverb meaning that it is better to marry a neighbour from across the mixen (dunghill), than a stranger from further away. Mrs Dewy and grandfather James offer other homely proverbs: 'Well, if you make songs about yourself, my dear, you can't blame other people for singing 'em', says the one; and 'When they be'n't too poor to have time to sing', says the other (*Under the Greenwood Tree*, V, Ch. 1 and 2).

Equally picturesque is Jonathan Kail's phrase in *Tess of the d'Urbervilles*, Ch. 34:

'And as there is not much doing now, being New Year's Eve, and folks mops and brooms from what's inside 'em.'

A domestic image connoting the uselessness of people who have had too much to drink, the phrase 'to be mops and brooms' has been recorded with this meaning in Devon, as well as here by Hardy. In *Far from the Madding Crowd*, Ch. 36, the hair of the heads of the drunken revellers is 'suggestive of mops and brooms', which suggests the origin of the phrase.

In *Tess of the d'Urbervilles*, Ch. 21, occurs this passage: 'I don't believe in en; though he do cast folks' waters very true.' The dairyman's reference here is to Conjuror Trendle's ability to diagnose diseases or to interpret the future by examining the *cast* or appearance of a person's urine. The meaning 'appearance' is recorded by the *English Dialect Dictionary* for north Lincolnshire. In *Two on a Tower*, Ch. 2, occurs the sentence: 'The child was sure to chaw high, like his father!', the phrase 'chaw high' recurring in *Jude the Obscure*, V, Ch. 8: 'That's the only way with these fanciful women that chaw high – innocent or guilty.' Hardy explained the phrase in a letter of 26 June 1897 to Joseph Wright, the editor of the *English Dialect Dictionary*, in these words:

'To chaw high' = to eat mincingly & fastidiously. Hence, fig. to be nice-stomached; scornful of the commonplace; genteel . . . Only used by a few old people, but in common use 20 or 30 years ago.

Literally, *chaw* is 'chew', as in the phrase 'chaw up well wi' a dab o' mustard' (*A Pair of Blue Eyes*, Ch. 23), and elsewhere, so that 'to chaw high' is to be, as Hardy explained, fastidious, hence genteel, looking for higher things.

Grammer Oliver's 'no chick nor chiel' (*The Woodlanders*, Ch. 6), literally 'neither chicken nor child', juxtaposes *chick*, found in the sense of 'child' in colloquial as well as in dialectal usage, and the Dorset pronunciation of *child* /tʃi:l/ containing a long vowel which Hardy spells either *ie* as here, or *ee*, as in *vlee* 'fly', i.e. carriage (*Tess of the d'Urbervilles*, Ch. 3). Mrs Wright quotes the rustic proverb 'a child and a chicken should always be pickin' '.

Similar pairs occur in other phrases. The tranter in *Under the Greenwood Tree* favours the expression 'neck and crop' to describe utter extinction, and in the same novel, Mrs Penny avers that ' 'tis humps and hollers with the best of us', ups and downs, that is. Hardy, or rather his characters, play variations on the phrase 'Jack Straw or Tom Rig', which, describing any ordinary man or woman, simply means 'anyone'. In *The Hand of Ethelberta*, Ch. 12, a countryman says 'there isn't a Tom-rig or Jack-straw in these parts', while in *Two on a Tower*, Ch. 22, Hezekiah Biles refers to 'every Jack-rag and Tom-straw', as does Henchard with his mention of 'any Jack Rag or Tom Straw' in Ch. 1 of *The Mayor of Casterbridge*. While Jack Straw is a familiar enough figure since the fourteenth century, the word *rig*, known since the sixteenth century, is a distinctive dialectal term in the south-west for 'a wanton girl, a strumpet', thence for any loose character.

The phrase 'to kick up Bob's-a-dying' is used by Geoffrey Day in *Under the Greenwood Tree*, II, Ch. 6, and by the coachman in the final chapter of *The Hand of Ethelberta*. A similar phrase, also recorded in the nineteenth century, is 'to kick up a bobbery', which was popular in British India and apparently derived from Hindustani. Its meaning, 'to make a commotion, to kick up a shindy', is the same as that of Hardy's phrase. On the other hand, the latter may have derived from the nursery rhyme 'Who killed Cock Robin?', recorded from the mid-eighteenth century, in which the death of Robin (or Bob) causes all the birds of the air to fall a-sighing and a-sobbing, a hubbub comparable to that denoted by 'to kick up Bob's-a-dying'.

No more certain is the origin of Granny Martin's phrase in *Two on a Tower*, Ch. 2: 'Hardly a soul would be left alive to say to me, dog how art!' The use of *dog* in a playful, informal manner applied to persons, as in 'old dog', 'lucky dog', is recorded from the seventeenth century; here the reference is to the lack of notice being taken of a person wandering, like a dog, among strangers none of whom has a greeting or kind word to say to the lonely soul.

In both *Under the Greenwood Tree*, II, Ch. 4, and *The Return of the Native*, III, Ch. 7, occurs the phrase 'chips in porridge', on which, in the former instance, Hardy comments in a footnote: 'This, a local expression, must be a corruption of something less questionable.' In the first case, the tranter is addressing Thomas Leaf: 'You'll be like chips in porridge, Leaf – neither good nor hurt.' In the other example, Wildeve is addressing the distraught Christian Cantle: 'Poor chips-in-porridge, you are very unmannerly.' The proverbial 'chip in porridge' is a thing of no importance or a harmless, useless person, and as 'pottage' or 'broth' are also found in place of 'porridge', there is presumably nothing very 'questionable' about a 'chip' (of whatever consistency) being occasionally found therein. According to Ruth Firor, the 'chip' may be an innocuous herb, which had no effect on the cooking, but was believed to have magical properties.

The phrase 'Mellstock Club walked the same day' in *Under the Greenwood Tree*, V, Ch. 1, is not elucidated by Hardy, although its association with Whitsuntide is spelt out. Nor is it in the reference to 'Weatherbury club-walking on White Tuesdays' in *Far from the Madding Crowd*, Ch. 33. But there is authorial comment in *Tess of the d'Urbervilles*, Ch. 2:

> The May-Day dance, for instance, was to be discerned on the afternoon under notice, in the guise of the club revel, or 'club-walking', as it was there called.

Barnes testifies to the same Whitsuntide tradition in his poem 'Whitsuntide an' Club Walken', and in another poem, 'Woodley', writes:

> As all the club, wi' dousty lags,
> Do walk wi' poles an' flappen flags,
> An' wind, to music, roun' between
> A zwarm o' vo'k upon the green!

The 'club' is a village or parish friendly society, known as a benefit society in the United States, an association of contributing members for ensuring benefits in sickness or old age. The 'club walking' is the annual festival as Barnes's poem vividly describes it. In *Two on a Tower*, Ch. 2, 'club-walking' is mentioned as similar to a fair or a feast. Ruth Firor sees the Whitsuntide club-walking as a Christianized survival of May rites, 'a sort of local Cerealia'. Udal records that at Symondsbury, in West Dorset, the old club day was the second Tuesday in May.

The phrase 'to go snacks with', meaning to share, and, specifically, to get married, is used by Mrs Penny in *Under the Greenwood Tree*, I, Ch. 8: 'Penny asked me if I'd go snacks with him, and afore I knew what I was about a'most, the thing was done'; and by Coney in *The Mayor of Casterbridge*, Ch. 37: ' 'Tis wonderful how he could get a lady of her quality to go snacks wi' en in such quick time.' The word *snack* meaning 'a share, portion' occurs in literary English from the seventeenth century, as does the phrase 'to go snacks' in the sense 'to have a share in something, to divide the profits'. Hardy's matrimonial connotations belong to dialect.

'If her ear is as fine as her face, we shall have enough to do to be upsides with her', says grandfather William in *Under the Greenwood Tree*, I, Ch. 3. Barnes, in his *Glossary*, provides an appropriate definition of 'upsides with': 'Even with. Having given another tit for tat'. In *The Return of the Native*, Hardy uses the expression 'to be in mangling' a couple of times; both times it is Timothy Fairway speaking:

> 'Yes, it will do. I didn't know the two had walked together since last fall, when her aunt forbad the banns. How long has this new set-to been in mangling then?'
> (I, Ch. 3)

> 'Never mind that question, Grandfer. Stir your stumps and get some more sticks. 'Tis very nonsense of an old man to prattle so when life and death's in mangling.'
> (IV, Ch. 7)

Although it is tempting to associate 'in mangling' with a machine also known as a 'wringer' which tends to smash buttons, according to Jocelyn Pierston in *The Well-Beloved*, the word *mangling* may here be a variant of *mingling*, as in the word *mingle-mangle*. The verb *mingle* derives from a late Middle English *mengel*. A variant occurs in the form *monglung* in a western text of the thirteenth century. The sense is of something being compounded, blended, in the balance, at stake.

Some phrases occurring in the dialect of Hardy's country folk are also familiar in more general colloquial English: 'She'll fetch round' (*The Return of the Native*, IV, Ch. 7), for example, meaning 'she will recover'; or the use of *hit* in the sense of 'to traverse', as in these examples:

'First we het across to Great Hintock, then back to here.'
(*The Woodlanders*, Ch. 45)

'You hit athwart the grounds of Mount Lodge, Miss Margery, or you wouldn't ha' met me here.'
(*A Changed Man*: 'The Romantic Adventures of a Milkmaid', II)

The south-western dialects preserve the sense of 'to say, speak, reckon' for *tell*, and it is thus used by one of the smugglers in 'The Distracted Preacher' (*Wessex Tales*): 'And d'ye tell o't!', of which the modern equivalent is the colloquial 'you don't say!' Barnes's *Glossary* defines 'TELL. To reckon'.

Some other dialect phrases require little glossing: 'By-long and by-late', meaning 'in due course, eventually', is used, for example, by Mrs Penny and by the witch Endorfield in *Under the Greenwood Tree*. One of the passengers in *The Dynasts* I. i. 1 concludes a sentence with 'at all at all', as does Mrs Smith in Ch. 36 of *A Pair of Blue Eyes*: 'I can't think what's coming to these St. Launce's people at all at all.' Squire Dornell's 'You shan't have her till she's dree sixes full', that is, eighteen years of age, in 'The First Countess of Wessex' (*A Group of Noble Dames*), is also self-explanatory, if it is remembered that /-r/ frequently becomes /dr/ in Dorset dialects. The use of *over-right*, which Barnes glosses 'Right over, against, opposite', is found in several dialects, mainly in southern counties. Hardy uses it, for example, in the lime-burner's phrase 'straight over-right him' in 'The Romantic Adventures of a Milkmaid' (*A Changed Man*).

Various exclamations and expletives are used by Hardy's dialect speakers, and these are for the most part easily understood. Not surprisingly, they hardly figure in the writings of the Rev. William Barnes. For example: 'Sakes', for Heaven's sake; 'daze it!'; 'chok' it all!'; 'be jowned!'; ' 'nation', damnation; ' 'mighty I!', God Almighty. Barnes does record 'by gum' in one of his rustic Eclogues, and his ' 'dhang my buttons' from the same poem parallels Hardy's 'dang my old sides!'.

Corruptions of standard English or of foreign words are not necessarily a mark of dialect speakers, although Hardy tends to assign them to these. Some are obviously intended for comic effect rather than to add local colour. Of this kind are the London citizen's *compass-mentas* in *The Dynasts* I. v. 5; the soldier's *forty-whory* in *The Dynasts* II. iii. 3; the head blower's *dulcianner* in *The Hand of Ethelberta*, Ch. 40; and Christian Cantle's *maphrotight* in *The Return of the Native*, I, Ch. 3.

There are local pronunciations which look like corruptions, like *mischty* for 'mischief' in *Jude the Obscure*, for example, or *plannards* for 'planets' in *Two on a Tower*. Grammer Oliver's description of Fitzpiers in *The Woodlanders* as 'a projick, a real projick, and says the oddest of rozums' has caused some debate. Baugner notes that *projick* and its adjectival derivative *projicky* (with the meaning of 'ingenious scheming') have been recorded in Somerset, but can find no dialectal evidence for Pinion's explanation of *projick* as a corruption of 'prodigy'. Yet context and meaning favour this suggestion: in the simple world of Grammer Oliver's experience, Fitzpiers is certainly a 'prodigy' capable of uttering 'rozums'. And even in Joan Durbeyfield's use of the word in *Tess of the d'Urbervilles*, Ch. 4, there is an element of the prodigious in her *projick*.

Apocopated forms are not uncommon among dialect speakers. Some of these merely represent local pronunciation, like Robert Penny's *empt* for 'empty' in *Under the Greenwood Tree*, but occasionally they represent distinctive dialect words, like *dand* ('dandy'), which is used by a variety of speakers: Gad Weedy in *Desperate Remedies*, Liddy Smallbury and Susan Tall in *Far from the Madding Crowd*, Mrs Smith in *A Pair of Blue Eyes*, and Joan Durbeyfield in *Tess of the d'Urbervilles*.

Finally, there is the occasional foreign word, comfortably adapted to the speech habits of Hardy's countryside. Miller Loveday, in *The Trumpet-Major*, says *bagnet* for 'bayonet'; the milkman in *The Hand of Ethelberta* and the landlord in *A Laodicean* respectively turn 'equipage' into *ekkypage* and *ikkipage*; and Jude's great-aunt refers to him as a *harlican*, that is 'harlequin', thus 'a rascal'. The word *randy* is a widely distributed dialect word, denoting 'a party, merrymaking, celebration', and Hardy uses it frequently, also in the compound *wedding-randy*, as in the opening sentence of 'The History of the Hardcomes' in *Life's Little Ironies*. In *The Trumpet-Major*, Miller Loveday adds an appropriate qualification: 'I can do no less than have a bit of a randy, as the saying is' (Ch. 2), but for most of Hardy's dialect speakers who use it, as for Barnes, it is a commonplace word, a shortening of 'rendezvous', which is more audibly preserved in George Melbury's *randyvoo* in *The Wood-landers*, a form found in the south-west as far as Cornwall.

When, in *The Well-Beloved*, II, Ch. 6, Hardy is looking through Pierston's eyes into the Second Avice's cottage, he notices the absence of 'the "bo-fet", or double corner-cupboard, where the china was formerly kept'. Presumably the corrupted form of 'buffet' is to be thought of as the local usage of Pierston's childhood on the Isle of Slingers. Hardy himself may have called it a *bo-fet* until he started his French classes at King's College: his use of the same word, spelt 'beaufet', in quotation marks, with reference to a cottage in Mellstock parish in 'Enter a Dragoon' (*A Changed Man*) supports this view.

The preceding lists and examples will have conveyed something of the lexical dialect resources which Hardy employed to add local colour to his country scenes, of their distribution in his prose writings and, to a lesser extent, in his poems and *The Dynasts*, and of their often distant roots in earlier English. Although the dialect word or phrase is the principal means he uses to create the impression of rustic speech, it is not the only one: rather more sparingly, and rather less consistently from one book to the next, Hardy also indicates grammatical and phonetic divergences from standard English, as the following selective account will illustrate.

## II. GRAMMAR

Although pronouns and verbs are Hardy's main grammatical dialect indicators, they are not the only ones. Other categories are more sparingly involved.

In the case of nouns, a few points deserve notice. Thus we find the continuation, from Old English through southern Middle English into Hardy's Wessex, of the uninflected form of the plural of nouns after numerals in expressions of measure, as in 'forty couple', 'ten mile', 'thirty pound', 'twenty year'. We note an occasional use of plural forms in -*n*, which were common in southern and south-western Middle English, although for Hardy this was mainly a convenience of rhyme. The form *een* 'eyes' was common throughout England in the Middle Ages, and is used by Hardy in 'The King's Experiment' to rhyme with 'keen'. In the same poem, as well as in some others, he also uses *treen* 'trees'; in 'The Caged Thrush Freed and Home Again' it is one of six words all made to rhyme on the same sounds. It is worth recalling that Barnes uses similar forms, although, like *housen* in 'The Bachelor', not necessarily for rhyme. Maskell lists the form *vurzen*, 'furze' as current in Dorset in the mid-nineteenth century, and Udal, p. 256, records *vuz* and *vuzzen*.

Another dialectal feature involving nouns is the occasional ascription of the masculine gender to inanimate objects:

> 'And then they tried Samuel Shane's wagon, and found that the screws were gone from he, and at last they looked at the dairyman's cart, and he's got none neither!'
>
> (*Wessex Tales*: 'The Distracted Preacher', 7)

The comparison of adjectives retains not infrequently the older synthetic method which was gradually replaced in Middle English by the use of 'more' and 'most'. Hardy's predilection for older usages made him employ forms like *minuter*, *tearfuller*, *forwardest*, *raggedest*, even in straight narrative, although at times a 'period' effect is clearly intended, as when Tristram says to Iseult the White-handed in *The Famous Tragedy of the Queen of Cornwall*, xiv: 'Your father dealt me illest turn in this.' On the other hand, such forms are also marks of dialect: for example, the tranter's *civiller* in *Under the Greenwood Tree*; Grandfer Cantle's double superlative *most gallantest*, in *The Return of the Native*; or Tess's *properer* and the dairyman's *most rebellest* in *Tess of the d'Urbervilles*. The form *honestest* occurs in one of Hardy's literary notes.

In the formation of adverbs, Hardy's narrative and poetic usage is frequently as inventive as in other parts of speech: 'He closelier looked', 'written largelier', 'the road ascending whitely to the upland', 'more yellowly'; in dialect, on the other hand, adverbial endings are frequently omitted. For example: Suke Damson's 'Is he hurted very bad?' in *The Woodlanders*; Mr Penny's 'onmistakable well' in *Under the Greenwood Tree*; Robert Lickpan's 'My father used that joke regular at pig-killings' in *A Pair of Blue Eyes*; or Gabriel Oak's 'terrible trying' in *Far from the Madding Crowd*.

Hardy's use of pronouns displays considerable variety of forms. Those most characteristic of the south-west of England are the first person singular personal pronoun where it retains the Old English form *ic* /ɪtʃ/ in Grammer Oliver's usage ' 'ch woll', ' 'ch have' in *The Woodlanders*; the oblique forms of the third person singular masculine in-*n* derived from Old English *hine*; and the southern forms of the third person plural pronoun without initial *th-*. These are direct descendants of Old English *hī(e)*, *heom*, *heora*, which in standard English have been replaced by the forms of Norse origin, *they*, *them*, *their*. In Hardy's dialect, both types occur, not infrequently without regard to their traditional syntactic functions. Thus 'they' appears as *they* and *'em*: 'them' appears as *them*, *'em*, and *'em's*; and 'their' appears as *their* and *'em's*.

The singular forms show similar diversity and indifference to strict rules of grammar. They are, moreover, frequently reduced to a weakly stressed or unstressed shwa-sound /ə/, which Hardy represents by the letter *'a*: ' *'a* b'lieve' for 'I believe'; ' *'a* died' for 'she died'; 'that *'a* is' for 'that he is'.

The third person singular masculine 'he' shows some variation, appearing as *he*, *er*, *a*; in the oblique case the Old English *hine* generally survives in Hardy's forms *'n*, *'en*, *en*, *un* besides *him*, and even *he*, as in Marian's words to Tess: 'Then we could bring up Talbothays every day here afield, and talk of he.' The neuter pronoun, Old English *hit*, modern 'it', shares most of the masculine forms – *he*, *him*, *'n*, *'en*, *un*, as well as the modern standard *it*. The feminine 'she' is used for the oblique case as well: ' 'Tis hard for she', 'you can try your hand upon she'.

Nor do other pronouns escape this disregard of traditional case: ' 'Tis nothing to I', says Farmer Derriman in *The Trumpet-Major*; and 'us' frequently appears as *we* in the speech of Hardy's rustics; sometimes both figure incongruously side by side, as in John Durbeyfield's 'But she's nothing beside we – a junior branch of us, no doubt.'

The second person of the personal pronoun, both in the singular, *thou, ye, you*, and in the plural *ye, you* appears in Hardy's usage with little semblance of consistency. This probably represents the fluctuating usage among southern dialect speakers throughout the nineteenth century. Henchard, with fitting authorial irony, as Norman Page noted, slips from standard *you* to dialectal *ye* in a passage denouncing Elizabeth-Jane's use of dialect in Chapter 20 of *The Mayor of Casterbridge*. The older forms of the second person singular, personal and possessive, *thou, theee, thy, thine*, continued in dialect use, but were considered outmoded by the younger generation, of whom Fancy Day was clearly intended to be representative in mid-century:

The propriety of every one was intense, by reason of the influence of Fancy, who, as an additional precaution in this direction had strictly charged her father and the tranter to carefully avoid saying 'thee' and 'thou' in their conversation, on the plea that those ancient words sounded so very humiliating to persons of newer taste.

(*Under the Greenwood Tree*, V, Ch. 2)

Some of Hardy's speakers, however, not only the older ones as Martha Döll asserted, continued to use *thou*, except when addressing 'persons of quality'. John Loveday, for example, usually uses *you* to his brother, but slips into *thou* now and then:

'But it depends on how thou'st behave in future.'
(*The Trumpet-Major*, Ch. 39)

The hostler in the opening chapter of *The Hand of Ethelberta* addresses his interlocutor, the milkman, as *you*, but speaks to himself as *thou*: ' "Young man, young man", I think to myself, . . . "th' wouldstn't go doing hard work for play 'a b'lieve." ' And among the conversing rustics in *The Return of the Native* the older singular form, frequently implied and recognizable only by verbal inflection, occurs similarly alongside the ever more intrusive *you*:

' 'Tis a sad thing for ye, Christian. How'st know the women won't hae thee?'
'I've asked 'em.'
'Sure I should never have thought you had the face.'
(*The Return of the Native*, I, Ch. 3)

Again we can cite Joan Durbeyfield who, quite unwittingly, can be heard using both forms in the same breath, when addressing Tess: 'Y'll be fess enough, my poppet, when th'st know!' (Ch. 3).

The oblique forms of Hardy's *ye* and *you* are *ye*, *you*, and *'ee*, the latter also functioning occasionally as a nominative:

'Why – don't 'ee want to be happier than you be at present?' said Melbury.
(*The Woodlanders*, Ch. 30)

or in young Jude's outcry:

'Don't 'ee, sir – please don't 'ee!'
(*Jude the Obscure*, I, Ch. 2)

The interchangeability of *you* and *'ee* as oblique forms of the second person pronoun is as much part of the dialect of Hardy's rustics as the other variants we have noted. Hardy deliberately juxtaposes them, implying the speaker's indifference or unawareness. The Second Avice, for example, speaks to Pierston – a laundress addressing a 'person of quality' – in a manner wholly typical of Hardy's dialect use of *'ee* and *you*:

> 'O, sir, please go away! I can't bear the sight of *'ee* at this moment! Perhaps I shall get to – to like you as I did; but – '
> (*The Well-Beloved*, II, Ch. 12)

Alongside the pronoun *thou* survives the corresponding possessive form *thy*, as in the opening chapter of *Under the Greenwood Tree*: 'going to thy own father's house'. Some possessives are occasionally found in unstressed positions with reduced vowels, producing distinctive dialectal forms. For example, *yer*, as used by the malster and his friends in *Far from the Madding Crowd*, or in Fairway's 'Why did ye reveal yer misfortune, Christian?' in *The Return of the Native*, I, Ch. 3; or *ther*, as in the landlord's 'a Christian burial for ther children', in *A Laodicean*, I, Ch. 4.

In addition to such forms as *yer* and *ther* and *'a*, mentioned earlier, various pronouns are frequently shortened in unstressed positions, as in *y'll*, or *th'st*, or *'twould*, or occasionally dropped altogether, as in *dost*, *dostn't*, *canst*, or *how'st know*, *ask your pardon* (with omission of 'I'), *what art perusing?*, or *what the devil beest looking at?*

Some other pronominal forms which occur in Hardy's dialect merit brief mention.

The older forms of the reflexive pronoun survive in *hisself* and *theirselves*: for example, Creedle's 'he said to hisself' in *The Woodlanders*, Ch. 4; and the coachman's words to Cytherea Graye in *Desperate Remedies*, Ch. 5: 'Not at all – she never dismisses them – they go theirselves'; or Henery Fray's 'the sheep have blasted theirselves' in *Far from the Madding Crowd*, Ch. 21.

The demonstrative pronoun has several forms: alongside *this*, *that*, *these*, and *those*, occur *thik*, from Middle English *thilke*, which contains the Old English adjective *ilca*; *that there*; and some personal pronouns used demonstratively: 'Do you see they three elms?' asks the countryman in *The Hand of Ethelberta*, Ch. 12; 'I have been looking at they pigeons', says Marty South in *The Woodlanders*, Ch. 19. Hardy's construction 'Soon, soon that lover he came' may be regarded as 'a dialectal poeticism' in a poem, 'Julie-Jane', which contains some dialect forms, although it is not strictly a 'dialect poem' in the manner of 'Valenciennes' or 'The Bride-Night Fire'. It is worth recalling that all these demonstratives are found in Barnes's poems: 'they bells', 'they slopes' in 'A Pleace in Zight', or 'thik there wold yew' in 'Dobbin Dead', for example; but Hardy stopped short of imitating Barnes's retention of the Old English *thes*, *theos* in forms like 'theäse tower' ('Sheades'), except on very special occasions, as in 'The Ruined Maid', with its picturesque reminders of country speech:

> – 'At home in the barton you said "thee" and "thou",
> And "thik oon", and "theäs oon", and "t'other"; but now
> Your talking quite fits 'ee for high compa-ny!' –
> 'Some polish is gained with one's ruin', said she.

The frequent use of *who* for *whom* is also dialectal, as the latter is rarely used in any dialect. Not only rustic speakers, however, say *who*, for Hardy makes even Nelson ask 'Who have we lost on board here?' in *The Dynasts* I. v. 4.

Two points are noteworthy in Hardy's dialect treatment of the article. The first is the frequent use of *a'* instead of 'an' before a following vowel or diphthong, as in the speech of Mixen Lane in *The Mayor of Casterbridge*, where the landlady of Peter's Finger refers to 'a' old foolish thing' (Ch. 36); and the second is the frequent omission of the article altogether, which is common also in Barnes's poems. Hence the frequency in Hardy of such phrases as 'out o' window', 'up in chimley', 'coming in from station', 'down in barton', 'they got to church-door'.

In his treatment of verbs Hardy found ample scope for imparting dialectal colouring to his rustics' dialogue. Throughout the Middle English period, the inherited Old English system of conjugation underwent considerable changes, mainly in the direction of greater simplicity and uniformity. The old distinction between vocalic ('strong') and consonantal ('weak') verbs tended to break down, the former class decreasing, although modern English still retains a number of verbs which indicate preterite and past participle by a change of vowel or diphthong rather than by the addition of a dental suffix. In dialect, especially in southern dialects, the change to the latter mode is frequently carried further than in standard English, hence Hardy's forms *comed*, *gi'ed*, *growed*, *knowed*, *seed*, which are parallel to Barnes's *know'd*, *runned*, and the like.

Another indication of the same simplifying tendency is to blur the distinction between the preterite and past participle of vocalic verbs, which originally had different stem sounds: (I)*begun*; (he has)*bode*, *drove*, *forsook*; (we, you, they) *drunk*, *have took*, and so on. Similarly, past participles with loss of final -*n* occur, resulting in formal coalescence with the preterite, as in *have chose*, *have spoke*, *have stole*. Various irregular consonantal preterites and past participles are formed by adding -*ed* to infinitives, where standard English does not do so; thus: *builded*, *feeled*, *fleed*, *hurted*, *teached*, *weeped*. More 'irregular' variants still are *drownded* and *thoughted*. Similar usages occur in Barnes's poems, e.g. *runned*.

The Old English past participle prefix *ge*-, which remained in southern English throughout the Middle English period as *i*- or *y*-, figures occasionally in Hardy's dialect as *a*-, as in *a-builded*, *a-come*, *a-growed*, parallel to Barnes's retention of the same prefix in words like *a-vurrow'd*, *a-wheel'd*.

Occasionally, Hardy uses non-standard verbal forms in narrative and in his verse, where they impart an archaic flavour: 'As the wind sprung up stronger' (*The Hand of Ethelberta*, Ch. 43); 'the opportunity came which, while sought, had been entirely withholden' (*The Return of the Native* II, Ch. 3); *trode*, as a rhyming word, in 'Mute Opinion'; or *upclomb* in the first stanza of 'The Well-Beloved'. Such forms are found elsewhere in Victorian verse.

A characteristic feature of south-western dialects is the periphrastic use of 'do', which Barnes used frequently, and which occurs in such expressions as Jacob Smallbury's 'ye don't ought to count' in *Far from the Madding Crowd*, Ch. 8, or Tess's 'that's where my misery do lie' in *Tess of the d'Urbervilles*, Ch. 38.

Non-standard inflexional verbal endings are introduced more sparingly into Hardy's rustic dialogue than one might have expected. They reflect the tension in the south of England during the late Middle English and well into the early Modern English period between the older endings in -*th*, in the third person singular and plural of the present indicative, and the encroaching forms in -*s*. Standard English in due course restricted -*s* to the third person singular, and left the plural uninflected. In dialect, however, -*s* endings are used much more widely, and forms without endings also occur in the third person singular. Quite often, however, Hardy juxtaposes such forms with 'normal' ones, presumably not wishing to brand his rustic speakers as 'ignorant' in using forms so obviously regarded as solecisms in standard English. For example:

'What's that to a man in love? Pooh – I wish you would leave me, Picotee; I wants to be alone.'
(*The Hand of Ethelberta*, Ch. 28)

'I'm coming to that, if you'll leave me alone, Mister Oak!' remonstrated Cainy. 'If you excites me, perhaps you'll bring on my cough.'
(*Far from the Madding Crowd*, Ch. 33)

'What has happened to her, Mr Pierston? O what do it mean?'
(*The Well-Beloved*, III, Ch. 6)

'That's how we doos it – quite an obleeging young man!'
(*The Trumpet-Major*, Ch. 31)

'They downs their shutters at half-past six.'
(*A Changed Man*: 'The Romantic Adventures of a Milkmaid', I)

The older *-th* ending of the third person singular occurs infrequently in Hardy's dialect, although it figures of course in the scriptural passages which Hardy's rustics (and not only they) are prone to cite in conversation. Where it occurs otherwise it mostly represents the usage of the older generation. Squire Derriman, who is an old man in the first decade of the nineteenth century, can use *hath* with all propriety in a sentence like 'Ay; my nephew hath a scent of the place', in *The Trumpet-Major*, Ch. 40. Occasionally, the *-th* ending even slips into the first person, as in Jan Coggan's ' "Man", saith I in my hurry, but he were of a higher circle of life than that', in *Far from the Madding Crowd*, Ch. 8.

Hardy recognized the value of such features as the *-th* ending whenever he wished to archaize his diction, hence its occurrence outside dialect in such contexts as the scriptural 'the intuitive heart of woman knoweth not only its own bitterness, but its husband's' in *Tess of the d'Urbervilles*, Ch. 36; or in the speeches of the Spirits in *The Dynasts*; or in a sentence like 'Hath the old knave left?' in Scene xii of *The Famous Tragedy of the Queen of Cornwall*. But even in these works, Hardy's usage fluctuates greatly.

Such fluctuation is no less apparent in Hardy's handling of the verbs 'to be' and 'to do'.

In his war-time poem of 1915, 'The Pity of It', Hardy comments on the similarities between some Wessex expressions and their German equivalents – a thought somewhat less elegantly expressed in *The Dynasts*, II.i.7: 'The lingo of this place [Tilsit] has an accent akin to English' – and denounces those responsible for 'kin folk kin tongued' having to slaughter each other. The poem begins:

I walked in loamy Wessex lanes, afar
From rail-track and from highway, and I heard
In field and farmstead many an ancient word
Of local lineage like 'Thu bist', 'Er War',
'Ich woll', 'Er sholl', and by-talk similar,
Nigh as they speak who in this month's moon gird
At England's very loins, thereunto spurred
By gangs whose glory threats and slaughters are . . .

Barnes, who was also aware of such common Germanic roots, lists in the Grammar introducing his *Glossary* the following as being the Dorset forms of the verb 'to be': *I be*, *thou bist*, *he is*, *we be*, *you be*, *they be*; *I wer*, *thou werst*, *he wer*, *we wer*, *you wer*, *they wer*. Hardy uses all these forms in his rustic dialogue, as well as those derived from the Old English forms *eam*, *eom*, 'am'; *eart*, 'art'; *aron*, *earon*, 'are'; and the preterite singular *wæs* 'was'. Together with such negated forms as *ain't*, *bain't*, *idn'*, *idden*, *wadden*, Hardy's usage is much more diversified than Barnes's and much less consistent. The same speaker will use different forms without any sense of incongruity to denote identical grammatical functions; hence there are frequently juxtapositions of the kind *I am*, *I be*; *he be*, *he is*; *we are*, *we be*; *it wer*, *it was*, *it wez*; *we was*, *we were*; *you was*, *you wer*, *you were*; *they was*, *they were*. There is an instructive example in *Jude the Obscure*, V, Ch. 7: ' "You be the woman I thought wer my mother for a bit, till I found you wasn't", replied Father Time, who had learned to use the Wessex tongue quite naturally by now.'

Nancy Weedle, in 'The Superstitious Man's Story' (*Life's Little Ironies*), to give another example, says 'And we were frightened enough' at one point of this short tale, and 'it was darkish, and we was frightened' less than twenty lines further along. Or compare Miller Loveday's addressing his son with 'What art perusing, Bob?' in Ch. 22 of *The Trumpet-Major* with his saying to him 'th' beest hardly awake now', in Ch. 32.

Among auxiliary verbs, a few dialectal usages are worthy of note. Corresponding to Hardy's 'Ich wholl' in 'The Pity of It', quoted above, is Grammer Oliver's ' 'ch woll' in *The Woodlanders*, noted earlier in this chapter. She also uses the pronoun *er* 'he' ('er woll say', Ch. 17) which Hardy mentions in the poem as common to Wessex and Germany. Another uncommon form of the same verb is that used by Reuben Dewy in *Under the Greenwood Tree*, II, Ch. 8, when proposing marriage to his wife: 'Woot hae me?', that is, 'wilt thou have me?'. Even more elliptical is Farmer Baker's 'D'seem', that is, 'it would seem', in *Desperate Remedies*, Ch. 21.

Hardy appears to be making a subtle distinction with the help of apostrophes in Suke Damson's playful remark 'May'st kiss me if 'canst catch me, Tim!' in *The Woodlanders*, Ch. 20, where the first apostrophe seems superfluous and the second presumably indicates the omission of 'thou'. Once again, Hardy can be shown to be inconsistent, for in *The Trumpet-Major*, Ch. 15, the Miller says 'But how couldst forget so, Bob? – without apostrophe. Similarly, in one of the Wessex scenes of *The Dynasts*, I.ii.5, the First Old Man says: 'Canst be sharp enough in the wrong place as usual – I warrant canst!' If these are indeed Hardy's own punctuations and not the compositor's inconsistency, as Simon Gatrell has shown, is not unusual; but Suke's remark certainly illustrates Hardy's sensitive ear to the cadences of Wessex speech.

Hardy follows normal Dorset practice, as indicated by Barnes, in frequently using *have* for *has* as the third person singular: 'That there old familiar joke have been in our family for generations, I may say' (*A Pair of Blue Eyes*, Ch. 23). The deviation from standard English offends the 'impatient fastidiousness' of the boy in 'The Son's Veto' (*Life's Little Ironies*), as he corrects his mother's dialect usage:

'He have been so comfortable these last few hours that I am sure he cannot have missed us', she replied.

*Has*, dear mother – not *have*!' exclaimed the public-school boy, with an impatient fastidiousness that was almost harsh. 'Surely you know that by this time!'

Similarly, *do* frequently takes the place of *does* in Hardy's dialect, another usage given by Barnes; for example, in Mrs Leat's pious 'I trust the Lord will settle it all for the best, as He always do' (*Desperate Remedies*, Ch. 9). Once again, Hardy's usage is not consistent, but we should be on our guard against criticizing him too rashly. In the case of Tess there is often a lapsing into dialect in moments of stress, as when she cries out to her mother: 'Yes, yes; that's where my misery do lie!' (*Tess of the d'Urbervilles*, Ch. 38); and 'ordinary English' may give way to dialect in the same breath, as emotion swells:

'He does not leave me to work!' she cried, springing to the defence of the absent one with all her fervour. 'He don't know it! It is by my own arrangement.'
(*Ibid.*, Ch. 46)

'The auxiliary verb *may* and *might* is, in Dorset, *mid'*, (Barnes, *Glossary*). This is Hardy's usual form: ' "You mid last ten years; you mid go off in ten months, or ten days" '. (*Tess of the d'Urbervilles*, Ch. 3). He also spells it *med*; perhaps, in *Jude the Obscure*, to indicate the pronunciation of the northern part of Upper Wessex: 'Well ye med ask it, Mrs Williams', says Jude's great-aunt in I, Ch. 2; 'there med be in a week or two', says Arabella in I, Ch. 6, and similarly elsewhere. Sue, in IV, Ch. 5, gets *might* and *may* mixed up, a solecism encountered in present-day English even among educated speakers: 'If there had been a rope-ladder, and he had run after us with pistols, it would have seemed different, and I may have acted otherwise.'

It would needlessly extend this survey of Hardy's dialect grammar to list more instances of deviations from standard English. They readily declare themselves as such. This is also true of syntactic constructions which differ in some way from received usage, like ellipsis, double negatives, or unusual word-order. A few examples will suffice.

## Ellipsis

' 'Tis she that's come here schoolmistress.'
(*Under the Greenwood Tree*, I, Ch. 3)

'Ah! the business was done Sunday.'
(*Ibid.*, III, Ch. 2)

'A large farm?' she inquired . . . 'No; not large. About a hundred.' (In speaking of farms the word 'acres' is omitted by the natives, by analogy to such old expressions as 'a stag of ten'.)
(*Far from the Madding Crowd*, Ch. 3)

## Double negatives

'The young rascals got into my shirt and wouldn't be quiet nohow.'
(*Under the Greenwood Tree*, IV, Ch. 2)

'And at last they looked at the dairyman's cart, and he's got none neither!'
(*Wessex Tales*: 'The Distracted Preacher', 7)

*Word-order*

'Was ever heard such a thing as a young man leaving his work half done, and turning tail like this!'
(*Under the Greenwood Tree*, I, Ch. 5)

'You always will go poking into town in your working clothes. Beg you to change how I will, 'tis no use.'
(*A Pair of Blue Eyes*, Ch. 36)

### III. PRONUNCIATION

'An author may be said to fairly convey the spirit of intelligent peasant talk if he retains the idiom, compass, and characteristic expressions, although he may not encumber the page with obsolete pronunciations of the purely English words, and with mispronunciations of those derived from Latin and Greek. In the printing of standard speech hardly any phonetic principle at all is observed; and if a writer attempts to exhibit on paper the precise accents of a rustic speaker he disturbs the proper balance of a true representation by unduly insisting upon the grotesque element; thus directing attention to a point of inferior interest, and diverting it from the speaker's meaning, which is by far the chief concern where the aim is to depict the men and their natures rather than their dialect forms.'

Thus Hardy, in *The Athenaeum* of 30 November 1878, in one of his periodic comments on the use of dialect in fiction. Even a cursory glance at Hardy's representation of dialect pronunciation in his novels and short stories suffices to show that he made no attempt to 'exhibit on paper the precise accents of a rustic speaker'. To do so would have required in any case a more sensitive notation than occasional variant spellings or use of apostrophes and diaeresis. Nor would he have been much helped by Barnes's account of Dorset pronunciation, with its idiosyncratic terminology of breath-pennings and outekeing verbs, although Barnes's descriptions of sounds, once they are understood, are indeed an accurate representation of the more prominent features of central Dorsetshire speech in the age of Victoria.

Hardy, having grown up in their midst, did not need Barnes's help. He knew how people pronounced their versions of English in Dorset, and he was able to distinguish between the major divergences from standard English and those which affected individual words or limited combinations of sounds rather than whole classes of them. The former is clearly the more important group, as it characterizes

most of Dorset speech and is immediately recognized as such, especially, as Hardy hints in the Preface to his *Select Poems of William
Barnes*, 'by persons to whom the Wessex R and Z are uncouth
misfortunes'. In the following survey of Hardy's dialect
pronunciation, the major phonological features will be considered
first, to be followed by examples of such others as illustrate Hardy's
awareness of divergent pronunciations, also found in Wessex speech,
but used more sparingly in order to create some idiosyncrasy of
character or mood.

## Major phonological features

As the remark on 'Wessex R and Z' suggests, the most striking
characteristics of Dorset pronunciation are the voicing of /f/ to /v/
and of /s/ to /z/, and the strongly articulated /r/. The latter cannot be
indicated in ordinary spelling, except by such devices as the doubling
in *de-urr* for 'dear' in 'The Spring Call'; or the allusion to 'the
characteristic intonation of that dialect for this district being the
voicing approximately rendered by the syllable UR, probably as rich
an utterance as any to be found in human speech' (*Tess of the
d'Urbervilles*, Ch. 2). Hardy uses the doubled spelling to indicate the
Scottish /r/ in Farfrae's speech in *The Mayor of Casterbridge*, as in
*thirrough* and *jarreny*.

The voicing of /f/ and /s/ took place in southern England in the Old
English period, although the traditional spellings survived into
Middle English, except for some early Kentish documents which
have spellings like *zelf* 'self'. These voicings affected the whole of the
region that was to become Hardy's Wessex, and, although not confined to Dorset, they became a hallmark of his rustic speech. Hardy
does not use them consistently, but peppers his rustics' dialogue
sufficiently therewith to create a recurring impression of initial
voiced /v/ and /z/, and very occasionally also medially, as in *avore*.
Examples of initial voicing are plentiful: *vingers, vlee, vlock, voot*;
*zell, zid, zilver, zundays*, and so forth. It is worth noting that
Barnes's usage is much more regular than Hardy's. This also applies
to the recognition by Barnes of Dorset /dr/ for standard English /Θr/,
which Hardy notices in some cases, e.g. *dree* 'three'.

Another important consonantal feature, regularly found in
Barnes, is sufficiently distinctive for Hardy to use it as a Wessex
dialectal indicator: that is the modification of the final velar nasal

/ŋ/ to /n/ in the syllable -*ing*. This is spelt -*in* or -*en* by Hardy and
may be found from *Desperate Remedies* (*getten*, *overbearen*, and the
cumulative 'daddlen, and hawken, and spetten') to *The Well-Beloved*
(*wedden*, *mornen*), as well as in his verse. In a few cases, the disappearance of the final -*g* is indicated by an apostrophe, as in *lordlin's*;
or a grave accent is used to indicate that -*èn* stands for -*ing*, as in
*sweatèn*, *gapèn* ('Valenciennes'); or Hardy uses diaeresis where
ambiguity might otherwise exist: 'This upset of beën burnt out o'
home makes me very nervous' (*Desperate Remedies*, Ch. 11).

In many cases, consonantal sounds are lost altogether in initial,
medial, and final positions. This, too, is sufficiently indicative of
Wessex English to figure prominently in Hardy's dialect: for
example, *poun'*, *a'ter*, *on'y*, *culpet*, *pa'son*, *wi'*, *gie*, *hae*, *'ithout*,
*ath'art*, *ba'dy*.

The next major group of phonological variants from standard
English is a group of vowels and diphthongs which are characteristic
of Wessex. The most prominent are the diphthongal /ɪə/ for the
standard English vowel /iː/; the diphthongal /ɪə/ and /ɛə/ for
the standard English diphthong /eɪ/; and the several pronunciations, notably / ʊə / and / wʊə / for the standard English
diphthong / oʊ /. In all these cases Hardy's spellings range from the
received norm of contemporary usage to those favoured by Barnes,
as well as a few of his own. Thus he writes 'clean', *cleän* (in
'Valenciennes'), and *clane*; 'speak', *spaik*; 'tea', *tay*, for standard
English /iː/. The same sound is presumably intended in the spelling
*feymel* 'female'. He writes *speäker* (not in dialogue) for the stake used
by Grandfer Cantle in Ch. 3 of *The Return of the Native*. He
represents standard English / eɪ / by *aï eä*, in that *locus classicus* in
'The Waiting Supper' (*A Changed Man*), where 'the Squire's voice
was strongly toned with the local accent, so that he said "draïns" and
"geäts" like the rustics on his estate', and "maïd" later on as well.* In
'Valenciennes' Hardy writes *gapèn* 'gaping' for the same sound.
Standard English /oʊ/ from Middle English /ɔː/ had several pronunciations in Dorset, including some local variants, which Hardy's
various spellings – *o*, *oo*, *u*, *oa*, *aw*, *wu*, *wo*, *woa* – attempted to
indicate. The most common pronunciations were the diphthong
/ʊə/ and the triphthong / wʊə /, and the monophthong /uː/. For

---

* An example of deleted diaeresis occurs in 'The Bride-Night Fire' where the
manuscript reading *peäir*, retained in the 1898 edition of *Wessex Poems* for
the noun (but not for the verb), is finally replaced by *pair*.

example, 'home' is *home*, *hwome*; 'old' is *old*, *wold*, *awld*, and *wuld* /wʊəld/ (thus the old shepherd in *Tess of the d'Urbervilles*, Ch. 45); 'oak' is *oak* and *woak*; 'stone' is *stone* and *stwone*, and so on. The spelling *oo* appears to indicate /u:/ in several cases: 'Sir John's' *goo* in Ch. 1 of *Tess of the d'Urbervilles*, for example; and in *slooes* 'sloes' (*A Laodicean*, I, Ch. 5) and *tooes*, rhyming with 'loose' in 'The Bride-Night Fire'.

Another important difference in pronunciation is the lowering of /ɪ/ to /ɛ/ in Hardy's dialect, especially (but not solely) before a following dental consonant. Hardy uses the letter *e* when he wishes to indicate this pronunciation: *hent*, *het*, *med*, *peckle*, *prent*, *spet*. Here also belongs *sperrit* 'spirit' from Anglo-Norman *spirit*, older *espirit*, which Hardy frequently spells as shown. It is perhaps worthy of note, in passing, that this pronunciation, and the spelling *sperit*, is one of a number of south-western English dialect features transported by British colonists to the south-eastern United States. Cleanth Brooks, in an interesting study published in 1935, analysed these features for the Alabama-Georgia dialect, and my own experience confirms their persistence to this day in the pronunciation of certain sounds in North Carolina.

The opposite tendency is at work in a few instances where the proximity of a palatal consonant has caused /ɛ/ to become /ɪ/; thus Hardy writes *divel*, *git*, *jineral*.

Two other divergences from standard English pronunciation are sufficiently common to merit inclusion here. The first is the retention of the seventeenth-century pronunciation / aɪ / for the diphthong which became /ɔɪ/ in the course of the eighteenth century, possibly due to the influence of *oi*-spellings. Barnes's rhyme *smile*:*tweil* ('toil') in 'Good Measter Collins', for example, provides an instance of the pronunciation intended. Hardy usually replaces the standard spelling *oi* with *i* or *y*, as in *jine* 'join', *lynes* 'loins', but comes even closer to his intended pronunciation with *laitered* in 'The Bride-Night Fire'. To this group we might add the Squire's *gwine* 'going' in 'The Waiting Supper', where the same diphthong is being articulated, although its origin is different. This pronunciation, too, was transplanted to North America. Elsewhere, Hardy writes *goen*, besides normal *going*.

The other major remaining divergence from standard English is the monophthongization of /aɪ/ to /i:/, usually, although not invariably, spelt *ee* by Hardy, as in *flees*, *vlee*, *sheened*. Probably here also belong *oblege* and *obleeging*, as used by Cripplestraw and a member of the press-gang in Chapters 4 and 31 of *The Trumpet-Major* respectively; but it should be recalled that standard English pronounced 'oblige' with /iː/ until well into the nineteenth century, so that Hardy may here be indicating the normal usage of the first decades of that century rather than dialect. Finally, Hardy frequently writes *chiel*, as well as *chil'* and *chile*, for 'child', indicating the same Wessex pronunciation with /iː/.

## Minor phonological features

In many cases, we are here looking at isolated instances, occasional spellings used by Hardy to indicate some dialectal pronunciation without his making an attempt to extend these more systematically to a whole group. Perhaps the only incidence of cases large enough to warrant bundling together is the treatment of unstressed syllables in Hardy's dialect. It is a feature of stress-accented languages to weaken unstressed syllables, and sometimes to drop them altogether, and the colloquial nature of dialect speech presents fewer barriers to such development than a 'polite' language more scrupulously bounded by convention.

Hardy's examples of such 'weakened' pronunciation are many: for instance, *deppity*, *Goddy-mighty*, *hapeth* and *penneth*, *nater* and *picter*, *shadder* and *yaller*, *peanner* 'piano', *ruffens* 'ruffians', *varden* 'farthing', and the common reduction of *un-* to *on-* in such words as *onbearable*, *onfortunate*, *onpolite*. Personal and place-names tend to become weakened or distorted: thus *Marther Sarer* 'Martha Sarah' in 'The Distracted Preacher' (*Wessex Tales*) or *Crookhorn* 'Crewkerne' in the poem 'At Wynyard's Gap'.

Individual words tend to display Wessex dialect peculiarities, sometimes due to assimilation or dissimilation, as in *chimmer* 'chamber', *chimley* 'chimney', *hoss* 'horse', *sumple* 'supple'; or due to metathesis, as in *criddled* 'curdled'. An additional syllable develops in *linnit*, Grandfather William's way of saying 'lint' in *Under the Greenwood Tree*, I, Ch. 3. Occasionally, a final syllable, instead of being weakened in pronunciation, receives stronger articulation than in standard English: thus *chiney*, *chainey* 'china', with its weak final /ə/ raised to /ɪ/ or possibly diphthongized to /eɪ/.

Some consonantal variants are indicated by Hardy in spellings like *junks* 'chunks', with the sound /dʒ/, in *The Hand of Ethelberta*, Ch. 44, and *rubbidge*, with the same sound, in *Jude the Obscure*, IV, Ch. 3.

Similarly, Hardy makes use of variant spellings to indicate occasional vowels or diphthongs different from standard pronunciation in specific words. A small number of words, including *lags*, *stap*, *yaller*, show a lowering of /ɛ/ to /ʌ/ found in parts of Dorset and Somerset. The opposite tendency seems to be at work in *shet* 'shut' with /ʌ/ becoming /ɛ/, and in *inion* 'onion' and *sich* 'such', where /ʌ/ is raised to /ɪ/, all of them recorded in 'Lower Wessex'; but in Sunday Morning Tragedy' /ʌ/ becomes /ʊ/ in *strook*, rhyming with 'crook'. The spellings *drap* 'drop' and *gad* 'god' in several novels indicate a pronunciation /æ/ for standard English /ɒ/ in these words. There are a few indications of /ɔ:/ being pronounced /ɑ:/: *Jarge* 'George', the countryman's pronunciation in 'A Committee-Man of "The Terror" ' (*A Changed Man*); *Lard* 'Lord', the choir's intoning in *Two on a Tower*, Ch. 2, which, after the parson's correction, changes to *Lawd*; and Squire Everard's *taant* 'taunt' in 'The Waiting Supper' (*A Changed Man*). The same sound /ɑ:/ appears also, it seems, representing Dorset pronunciation, in *da'ter* 'daughter', and in *harnet* 'hornet', and *scarn* 'scorn', and more frequently in *martel* 'mortal', which occurs in a number of novels. The name *Draäts*, literally 'draughts', given to Egdon Heath in the poem 'The Sheep-Boy' presumably represents the Dorset pronunciation /dræ:ts/.

There are instances of long vowels being shortened in words like *kip* 'keep', *glum* 'gloom', or of a diphthong appearing as a short vowel as in *climmed* 'climbed'.

A few other uncommon spellings hinting at dialectal pronunciations deserve to be noted: *arrant* 'errand' is Dorset; *consarns* 'concerns' and *larning* 'learning', both showing Dorset dialect retention of the sixteenth-century standard English /ɑ:/ for later /ɜ:/; the variants *ees*, /i:/ Dorset, and *yaas*, / ɑ:/ 'Lower Wessex', for 'yes'; *tuens* 'tunes' represents one pronunciation / ʊə/ found in Dorset for standard English /ju:/, another is /u:/, which Hardy indicates by the spelling *Dook* 'duke' in the poem 'The Turnip-Hoer'; *wownd*, *wownded*, suggesting the Dorset diphthong / aʊ/ in 'wound'; and the rustic mouthful *wuzzes and flames* 'hoarses and phlegms' in 'The Three Strangers' (*Wessex Tales*). Sometimes Hardy also attempts to indicate peculiarities of pronunciation in 'polite' English: the choir's *towah* 'tower' in *Two on a Tower*, Ch. 2, for instance, and their *daown* 'down', corresponding to Miss Aldclyffe's *gaow* 'go', as reported by Robert, her coachman, in *Desperate Remedies*, Ch. 5. Finally, we need to recall Hardy's attempts to represent military utterances by appropriate spellings, like *Corpel*, *fawlocks*, *katridge*, *'tention*.

The preceding account does not claim to be any more exhaustive than Hardy's own treatment of Dorsetshire speech. What will have become apparent is Hardy's sensitive ear to nuances of regional pronunciation and his attempts to indicate these by appropriate spellings, both for whole groups of sounds and for individual words as used by a particular speaker or perhaps derived from some specific locale. The speech of Wessex in general and of Dorset in particular was distinctive enough, as Barnes's poems amply demonstrated, for Hardy to have here a linguistic reservoir hitherto untapped for the purposes of fictional narrative. Despite Hardy's own cavalier dismissal of George Eliot – 'she had never touched the life of the fields' (*Life*, p. 98) – the latter's example as well as Sir Walter Scott's as purveyors of fictional dialects, inevitably springs to mind. Hardy was still a pupil in Hicks's office, and next door to Barnes's school, when *Adam Bede* appeared in 1859, rich in the north-west-midland dialect of the Poysers. Hardy paid more attention to phonological characteristics than George Eliot, but both writers used dialect for similar ends, although George Eliot's use is more tinged with irony. It was thus not so much a breaking of new ground for Hardy as a look in another direction, naturally enough to that southern region whose sounds and grammar, words and phrases had been intimately familiar to him since childhood and were to remain so throughout his long life. Dorsetshire English and that of the wider Wessex regions adjacent proved an immensely fertile, time-honoured resource in the moulding of Hardy's English.

# CHAPTER IV

# A Dictionary Word

𝕾𝕾𝕾𝕾𝕾𝕾

> 'Don't think of me like that!' she begged. 'A
> mere chattel.'
> 'A what? Oh, a dictionary word. Well, as
> that's in your line I don't forbid it, even if it
> tells against me', he said good-humouredly.
> And he looked her proudly up and down.

HERE, in this little exchange between Melbury and Grace in Chapter 12 of *The Woodlanders*, we have a metaphor of Hardy's English: its mobility from one level or register or stylistic mode to another – a 'chattel', after all, is primarily 'a movable possession'; its eclectic, learned, ponderous character – 'a dictionary word' implies collection, reference, consultation; Grace's 'line' *versus* Melbury's – educated speech juxtaposed with the local dialect; and the feeling of social superiority which attaches to those whose command of the Queen's English places them above the rest. The basic contrast is between the dictionary word and the language of ordinary discourse, between the opaque and the transparent. Hardy, as we know, cultivated both.

The backbone of Hardy's language is of course the modern English of the second half of the nineteenth century. This differs in some, albeit relatively minor, ways from the English of, say, Jane Austen, and rather more markedly from the English of the nineteen-eighties, subjected to pressures of technological demands, commercialism, changes of emphasis in education, and various forms of manipulation. Hardy's wide popularity as a writer of fiction owes much to the single fact that most of his writing is easily understood: the 'asymptote' may be conspicuous in his sentence, but it does not rule it. For many readers of his own time Hardy presented fewer difficulties still. They may have carped, as the reviewers often did, at the unevennesses of style, the quirks of diction, the occasional involutions of syntax, but they did not require the copious notes of The

New Wessex Edition to elucidate biblical or classical quotations, to explain references in *The Woodlanders* to, say, Spinoza, Sterne, and St. Stephen. They knew their Bible, their Shakespeare, their Homer and Virgil, which is certainly not the case among many of Hardy's readers today.

But even to Hardy's contemporaries certain features of his diction were unfamiliar: those who knew their way around the works of Greuze and Nollekens may have floundered among Early Flourballs and Thompson's 'Wonderfuls', or been confounded by the megatherium and the myledon and the other elephantine forms conjured up before the eyes of the helpless Knight clinging to his cliff in *A Pair of Blue Eyes*. Hardy's 'technical' vocabulary, to use a convenient shorthand, ranges widely across the arts and sciences and many of its 'dictionary words' call for explanation now as they did then. But there is yet a further element to be considered here: Hardy's propensity to drop words or phrases from other languages into his English sentences, from the Virgilian *nullo cultu* in the first chapter of *Desperate Remedies* to 'the *passée* wife' in the last chapter of *The Well-Beloved*. In what follows, we shall glance at both the more familiar sources of Hardy's 'dictionary words' – taking this term to denote almost everything a modern editor feels inclined to annotate – and the less familiar ones. Such a survey will complement the preceding chapter on dialect by focussing on another important source of Hardy's English.

The literary influences which helped to shape Hardy's thought and work have by now been so plentifully scrutinized as to make further toil in this particular vineyard largely supererogatory. But no account of his language can afford to ignore the role they played in the enrichment of his diction and the modulations of his prose sentences as well as the cadences of his verse. Of all these influences the most pervasive and persistent is that of the English Bible and of the liturgy of the Church of England with which Hardy was familiar from boyhood. His personal absorption of biblical and liturgical words and phrases, as well as his knowledge of hymns, is reflected in the speech of those characters in his fiction to whom these elements are not so much a second language as an integral part of their mother tongue. Joseph Poorgrass, for example, in *Far from the Madding Crowd*, Ch. 8, instinctively recites the Lord's Prayer, the Creed, the Ten Commandments, and other familiar lines, when 'lost by Lambing-Down Gate' one dark night:

'My heart died within me, that time; but I kneeled down and said the Lord's Prayer, and then the Belief right through, and then the Ten Commandments, in earnest prayer. But no, the gate wouldn't open; and then I went on with Dearly Beloved Brethren, and, thinks I, this makes four, and 'tis all I know out of book, and if this don't do it nothing will, and I'm a lost man. Well, when I got to saying After Me, I rose from my knees and found the gate would open – yes, neighbours, the gate opened the same as ever.'

These prayers, as indispensable as 'charms' in a moment of peril as Christian Cantle's 'Matthew, Mark, Luke, and John, bless the bed that I lie on . . .' (*The Return of the Native*, I, Ch. 3), may be all that Joseph knew 'out of book', as far as the order of service was concerned, but he knew his Bible thoroughly. Hardy sums up not only Joseph's 'scripture manner' but his own in the final paragraph of the novel:

'Yes; I suppose that's the size o't', said Joseph Poorgrass with a cheerful sigh as they moved away; 'and I wish him joy o' her; though I were once or twice upon saying to-day with holy Hosea, in my scripture manner, which is my second nature, "Ephraim is joined to idols: let him alone." But since 'tis as 'tis, why, it might have been worse, and I feel my thanks accordingly.'
(*Far from the Madding Crowd*, Ch. 57)

Although Joseph cites St. Matthew as readily as the Second Book of Samuel in the same breadth, or at least on the same page, Hardy's preferences, temperamentally and theologically at least, lay in the Old Testament. Here narrative and poetry, rather than doctrine and exegesis, furnish matter for exemplifying story and elucidating character, and, no less important, provide the ready-made phrase or image in narrative, description, or authorial commentary. Hardy, throughout his long life, in his work, in his letters, and in his conversation, drew upon the language of Scripture, the liturgy, and hymns, for this was as integral and fully assimilated a part of his own vocabulary as was Dorsetshire speech. Both were embedded in his mother tongue.

Thus it came naturally to him, when describing Aunt Charlotte in *The Hand of Ethelberta*, Ch. 33, to note 'no point in her causing the slightest suggestion of drops taken for the stomach's sake'; or to say of the enamoured Swithin in *Two on a Tower*, Ch. 15, that 'the lover had come into him like an armed man, and cast out the student'. The modern editor who asterisks these passages in order to show their biblical sources in I Timothy and Proverbs respectively, may be rendering a service to the student unfamiliar with the Bible, but he is rendering a disservice to Hardy by pointing an annotating finger at something that is so thoroughly and characteristically a part of Hardy's mode of saying things.

Although Hardy, as is well known, suffered in early manhood what Robert Gittings in *Young Thomas Hardy* describes as 'the dramatic loss of faith which was such a feature of the lives of well-educated people in the mid-Victorian era,' he retained a sentimental attachment to the Church, its buildings, its traditions, its music, and its language. And despite the Bishop of Wakefield's ferocious re-action to *Jude the Obscure* and the unkind cut administered to the Bishop of Melchester in *Two on a Tower*, Hardy retained life-long respect for upright Christians among his acquaintance, among whom members of the Moule family figured prominently. It is typical of such attachment that Hardy should have remembered in 1919 the text used by the Vicar of Fordington 'one Sunday evening about 1860' (*Life*, p. 390); or that he was speaking, a few weeks before his death, of that fellow-pupil in Hicks's office nearly seventy years earlier, with whom he had, among other matters, discussed questions of baptism. Henry Robert Bastow, long since lost sight of in Australia, 'was a Baptist and evidently a very religious youth, and T.H. was devoted to him', as Florence Hardy records (*Life*, p. 443), adding, 'I felt, as he talked, that he would like to meet this man again more than anyone in the world.'

Such reminiscences may be dismissed as the not uncommon phenomena of old age, but they point to the depths of impression made upon Hardy by his intellectual and emotional involvement with Christianity in his formative years. It is not surprising then to find its language so deeply embedded in Hardy's writings. It is there, as we have seen, unobtrusively in the narrative; it is on the lips of most of his characters; it provides images and functions as symbol; it can, as in *Jude the Obscure*, become the dominating idiom of an entire novel.

In *Far from the Madding Crowd*, to return to Joseph Poorgrass, Hardy's 'scripture manner' is firmly and lastingly established. Nearly everyone here quotes or talks Scripture. Carl J. Weber has counted 'no less than thirty-eight Biblical quotations or allusions, the Old Testament appearing more than twice as often as the New': Maryann quotes a psalm; Billy Smallbury *Thessalonians*; Oak, Boldwood, Troy – they all think at crucial moments instinctively in biblical phrases. Gabriel, we are deliberately told, 'at this time of his life had outgrown the instinctive dislike which every Christian boy has for reading the Bible, perusing it now quite frequently, and he inwardly said, " 'I find more bitter than death the woman whose heart is snares and nets!' " This was mere exclamation – the froth of the storm. He adored Bathsheba just the same' (Ch. 22).

No such *apologia* is deemed necessary in most instances, however, as when Boldwood voices Jonah: 'I had some faint belief in the mercy of God till I lost that woman. Yes, He prepared a gourd to shade me, and like the prophet I thanked Him and was glad. But the next day He prepared a worm to smite the gourd and wither it; and I feel it is better to die than to live!' (Ch. 38).

But *Far from the Madding Crowd* had predecessors, and already in 'How I Built Myself a House' there is an echo of *Exodus* in the wife's 'turning to me with a glance in which a broken tenth commandment might have been seen'. *Desperate Remedies* provides the first of Hardy's Scripture-citing devils, of whom more in a moment, as well as rustics quoting Genesis or Deuteronomy as readily as *Robinson Crusoe*. *Under the Greenwood Tree* adds the scriptural grandfathers, more echoes of Genesis from Enoch, as well as such utterances befitting the clerical Mr. Maybold as the prophetic 'A Laodicean lukewarmness is worse than wrongheadedness itself' (II, Ch. 4). Elfride and Knight cite Scripture in *A Pair of Blue Eyes*; and the roll-call continues all the way to Jude's *Jobiad* as he lies dying in Christminster, and indeed beyond into the diction of *The Dynasts*, as Louis Morcos has shown, and into that of much of Hardy's verse.

There are many facets to this use of scriptural and liturgical language. A simple image, for example:

> The lower half of the garden, furthest from the road, was the most snug and sheltered part of this snug and sheltered enclosure, and it was well watered as the land of Lot.
> (*The Trumpet-Major*, Ch. 10)

Or an image endowed with added force by a touch of irreverence:

> 'Your face is like the face of Moses when he came down from the Mount.'
> She reddened a little and said, 'How can you be so profane, Giles Winterborne!'
> (*The Woodlanders*, Ch. 9)

Or the juxtaposition of two images, one commonplace, the other biblically exotic:

> The furze-cutter was so absorbed in the business of his journey that he never turned his head; and his leather-legged and gauntleted form at length became to her as nothing more than a moving handpost to show her the way. Suddenly she was attracted to his individuality by observing peculiarities in his walk. It was a gait she had seen somewhere before; and the gait revealed the man to her, as the gait of Ahimaaz in the distant plain made him known to the watchman of the king. 'His walk is exactly as my husband's used to be', she said; and then the thought burst upon her that the furze-cutter was her son.
>
> (*The Return of the Native*, IV, Ch. 5)

For Hardy, the simile of the moving handpost, itself reflecting the instability in its beholder's mind, and that of the gait of Ahimaaz, with its ironic reversal of the messenger's 'All is well' – for all is *not* well on Egdon – represent the same use of language, however different their sources. Any nagging doubt as to the decorum of putting such seemingly esoteric culling from the Old Testament into the consciousness of Mrs. Yeobright is allayed by our knowledge that to a woman of Egdon the Bible was what it was to Hardy himself, a natural way of thinking and speaking. Not surprisingly, the same chapter from II Samuel furnishes Hardy with another apt image elsewhere, that of the oak branches recalling Absalom's death in Chapter 14 of *Two on a Tower*.

The use of a biblical name can thus denote a simple likeness as well as evoke richly symbolic connotations, and Hardy is well aware of the fecundity of this linguistic resource. He can, in the same way, play – in no pejorative sense – with the words and concepts of sacred Christian mysteries. There is a dexterous perversion of St. Paul's reference to Christ ('I protest by your rejoicing which I have in Christ Jesus Our Lord, I die daily', I Corinthians XV, 31) in Pierston's allusion to his female goddesses:

> 'You may be right; but I think you are wrong', said Pierston. 'As flesh she dies daily, like the Apostle's corporeal self; because when I grapple with the reality she's no longer in it, so that I cannot stick to one incarnation if I would.'
>
> (*The Well-Beloved*, I, Ch. 9)

More complex, and more accomplished in its linguistic fusion of natural setting, erotic symbolism, and irony is a passage like the following, with its central symbol of Resurrection, its foreboding mention of Mary Magdalen, and its suggestion of transfigured beings:

> The mixed, singular, luminous gloom in which they walked along together to the spot where the cows lay, often made him think of the Resurrection hour. He little thought that the Magdalen might be at his side. Whilst all the landscape was in neutral shade his companion's face, which was the focus of his eyes, rising above the mist stratum, seemed to have a sort of phosphorescence upon it. She looked ghostly, as if she were merely a soul at large. In reality her face, without appearing to do so, had caught the cold gleam of day from the north-east; his own face, though he did not think of it, wore the same aspect to her.
>
> (*Tess of the d'Urbervilles*, Ch. 20)

As an even more complex example of Hardy's scriptural indebtedness, we may glance at a passage from Chapter 27 of *The Woodlanders*. Trees, in this novel, rule the universe of the Hintocks as the stars rule that of Welland. Fitzpiers was approaching Felice Charmond's house through one of those finely observed woodland scenes in which this novel is particularly rich:

> The morning had been windy, and little showers had scattered themselves like grain against the walls and window-panes of the Hintock Cottages. He went on foot across the wilder recesses of the park, where slimy streams of fresh moisture, exuding from decayed holes caused by old amputations, ran down the bark of the oaks and elms, the rind below being coated with a lichenous wash as green as emerald. They were stout-trunked trees, that never rocked their stems in the fiercest gale, responding to it only by crooking their limbs. Wrinkled like an old crone's face, and antlered with dead branches that rose above the foliage of their summits, they were nevertheless still green – though yellow had invaded the leaves of other trees.
>
> (*The Woodlanders*, Ch. 27)

As Fitzpiers enters the darkened chamber, fire-lit 'though it was not cold', Felice hurls passionately uttered questions at him, questions which the trees outside had long since answered for themselves, for they had learnt to crook their limbs 'in a world like this'. Fitzpiers responds with 'You must eat of a second tree of knowledge before *you* can do it, Felice Charmond' – a response that immediately re-opens the vista of the park outside and we realize that a 'slimy' moment in another garden is being re-lived, for Fitzpiers is intruder and tempter in the world of *The Woodlanders*, and the imagery of wrinkles and fading colours bodes travail yet to be endured by the woman seeking to have *her* eyes opened. Fitzpiers's biblical response is absorbed into the rich symbolic texture of the passage, itself emblematic of the whole novel. For Hardy, the satanic presence in Eden was anathema; its remembrance, as the final page of the *Life* tells us, was Hardy's dying thought, as he listened to his wife reading to him the stanza from the *Rubáiyát of Omar Khayyám* beginning

> Oh, Thou, who Man of baser Earth didst make,
> And ev'n with Paradise devise the Snake . . .

Even the gleam of emerald, looking ahead to the rainbow in *Revelations*, is insufficient to inspire comfort, let alone hope, in the gloomy scene here being enacted.

Hardy's use of biblical language and allusion thus becomes frequently a complex interplay of narrative relevance and ironic innuendo. It is thus with the Eden images in *Tess of the d'Urbervilles* and it is apparent also in the case of his 'Mephistophelian visitants' – Hardy's own term in *The Return of the Native* – of whom, as J.O. Bailey has shown, there is a considerable number. They readily protest the Scriptures, all the more effectively as Hardy remembered Antonio's words – with their rustic image – in *The Merchant of Venice*, I, iii:

> The devil can cite Scripture for his purpose.
> An evil soul, producing holy witness,
> Is like a villain with a smiling cheek,
> A goodly apple rotten at the heart.

The citations vary of course, for not all Hardy's visitants are fiends. Diggory Venn, for example, the strangest of all Hardy's visitants, has Mephistophelian characteristics; is, like Egdon itself, 'Ishmaelitish'; and appears to Timothy Fairway as a 'fiery mommet', with all the infidel connotations of that rustic word – yet his is no destructive intrusion; unlike Dare's in *A Laodicean*, who is twice referred to as 'Mephistophelian' and indeed proudly identifies himself with the Devil in answer to de Stancy's 'Where do you come from?'

> 'From going to and fro in the earth, and walking up and down in it, as Satan said to his Maker. – Southampton last, in common speech.'
> (*A Laodicean*, II, Ch. 5)

Such bluntness is not typical of Hardy's visitants, however. Like Troy, that 'juggler of Satan' as Bathsheba soon realized, they could talk 'winningly',* producing holy witness even in an engaging image of pastoral hedonism, as when he rebukes her, in an apt Old Testament echo, for taking from him 'the one little ewe-lamb of pleasure that I have in this dull life of mine' (*Far from the Madding Crowd*, Ch. 26). This is neatly said, a considerable advance on the biblical mouthings of Hardy's founding fiend, Aeneas Manston in *Desperate Remedies*, who at a moment of shocked discovery can quote aloud to himself 'a line from the book of Jeremiah – A woman shall compass a man' (Ch. 9), or find cool comfort amid the entanglements of his matrimonial affairs in the thought 'But anything for a change – Abigail is lost, but Michal is recovered' (Ch. 14). Hardy was to travel a long way from such unpromising beginnings to the moment when Alec d'Urberville, still mouthing Scripture, shoots 'hot archness' from his eyes and says 'You temptress, Tess; you dear damned witch of Babylon – I could not resist you as soon as I met you again!' (*Tess of the d'Urbervilles*, Ch. 46). It is the indispensable 'damned', the cadence of 'dear damned witch', and the pretiguring of the woman drunken with blood, that makes all the difference.

Not every reader of Hardy, certainly not every critic, has been willing to accept wholeheartedly the intimate knowledge of the Bible which he ascribes even to, and especially to the more unsophisticated of his rustic people. R.H. Hutton, reviewing *Far from the Madding Crowd* in the *Spectator* of 19 December 1874, voiced this disquiet, asking 'whether all the vivacious description we have here is quite trustworthy . . . And here the reader who has any general acquaintance with the civilization of the Wiltshire or Dorsetshire labourer . . . will be disposed to say . . . that if any one society of agricultural labourers were at all like that which we find here, that class, as a whole, must be a treasure-house of such eccentric shrewdness and profane-minded familiarity with the Bible, as would cancel at once the reputation rural England has got for a heavy, bovine character, and would justify us in believing it to be a rich mine of quaintness and oddities, all dashed with a curious flavour of mystical and Biblical transcendentalism.'

The answer to such charges is twofold. In the first place, Hardy's own background exemplifies the closeness of the village people, be

---

* One recalls that the original title of *A Pair of Blue Eyes* was *A Winning Tongue Had He*.

they stone-masons or 'workfolk', to their church and their constant exposure to its words. From boyhood onwards Hardy was one of them. He was still 'an exceptional attender at church all through the 1860s', as Gittings records, and remained 'churchy' all his life. It was an era when the spoken word, the reiterated spoken word, came not through disembodied electronic media but from the pulpit, so that its impact was personal, repetitious, and powerful. My suggestion that Mrs. Yeobright might not have been unfamiliar with the affecting episode involving David and the messengers is based upon such recognition, and on the fact that II Samuel XVIII provided the first lesson at Morning Prayer on St. George's Day. That this chapter was a favourite of Hardy's – 'the finest example of its kind that I know', he wrote in *The Fortnightly Review* in August 1887 – does not disprove the point that others will also have been familiar with it.

The Bible, moreover, continued not only to be heard, but read. There is no reason to doubt the wider applicability of Hardy's allusion to Oak's frequent perusal of the Bible, in Chapter 22 of *Far from the Madding Crowd*. In the preceding chapter Joseph Poorgrass 'was sitting at home looking for Ephesians' when the news of the sheep getting blasted is brought to him. Negative evidence, as it were, is adduced by the reference in the same novel to Cain Ball's mother as 'not being a Scripture-read woman', whence her 'mistake at his christening, thinking 'twas Abel killed Cain, and called en Cain, meaning Abel all the time' (Ch. 10). Similarly, we are told that Giles Winterborne possessed a Psalter, even if it was used 'mainly for the convenience of whetting his penknife upon its leather covers' (*The Woodlanders*, Ch. 43). Here is truly 'profane-minded familiarity with the Bible', yet familiarity it is.

These things were no doubt changing in the second half of the nineteenth century amid changes in the rural economy of southern England and in the modes of living among the workfolk, but, as Michael Millgate has repeatedly emphasized, Hardy was writing not about 'the immediate present but about periods somewhat vaguely located in the recent past', evoking 'a remote and almost timeless rural world', whose 'pastness' includes habits of thought and speech, beliefs, superstitions, and other 'folkways', which were far from bovine.

What is relevant here, then, is Hardy's awareness of the role the Bible played in the regular worship, and frequently the reading habits, of the villagers whom he chose to depict in his fiction. But there is a second answer to Hutton's criticism and that is, precisely, that Hardy's fiction *is* fiction. For Hardy, the kind of realism aimed at, in this as in other aspects, is, as he writes in 'The Science of Fiction', 'an artificiality distilled from the fruits of closest observation'. 'The best fiction', he says in another essay, 'The Profitable Reading of Fiction', 'like the highest artistic expression in other modes, is more true, so to put it, than history or nature can be'. But close observation, the noticing of such things, is always at the heart of what Hardy writes: the material circumstance is both acknowledged and transfigured.

We may thus conclude that the villagers at times turned to the Scriptures for ready-made speech material, much as their modern descendants have recourse to the commercial and political slogans, vogue words and clichés to which they are exposed. We may also affirm that Hardy recognized their doing so under stress of emotion as being an instinctive turning towards religious support. Finally, we may explain Hardy's own frequent use of biblical language and imagery, in both his prose and his verse, as the result of a sometimes deliberate, often probably quite unconscious, recourse to a source of English expression that had inspired English writers for generations. Even today the language of the Authorized Version of the Bible and the lovely cadences of the Prayer Book, what Matthew Arnold called the Church's 'unconscious poetry' remain, despite all recent modernizations and innovations, deeply embedded in the language of English speakers throughout the world.

So does the language of Shakespeare.

'Young Thomas', so Hardy informs us, was twelve years old when he read Shakespeare's tragedies 'for the plots only, not thinking much of *Hamlet* because the ghost did not play his part up to the end as he ought to have done' (*Life*, p. 24). A few years later he saw Phelps's performances at Drury Lane, following the text from 'a good edition' of each play in the front row of the pit, meanwhile continuing his reading of 'various plays of Shakespeare' along with many other books. Fifty years later he was still jotting down thoughts on Shakespeare: 'The people in Shakespeare act as if they were not quite closely thinking of what they are doing, but were great philosophers giving the main of their mind to the general human situation' (*Life*, p. 386). And, according to a note in Carl J. Weber's *Hardy of Wessex*, Hardy is reported by his wife to have spoken of Shakespeare a few hours before his death. Weber has traced Hardy's involvement with Shakespeare in two papers published in 1934, and, in the book just cited, sums up Hardy's indebtedness in these words:

'The most easily recognised part of Hardy's debt to Shakespeare is, of course, the direct borrowings from the plays. *Hamlet* is the one most frequently quoted, but Hardy knew them all, from the earliest to the latest. He quotes from twenty-six of the plays. He knew the lines that everyone knows, but he quotes unusual and little-known lines as well. He began to quote Shakespeare when he was twenty-five and he was still at it sixty years later. It is safe to say that the list of his direct quotations from Shakespeare cannot be paralleled in the work of any other novelist. The Shakespearean trail runs through all fourteen of the Wessex novels, through three of the four books of short stories, and is seen in at least two of the books of Hardy's poetry.'

Weber quotes some fifty examples of quotations and paraphrases in his articles, to which E.P. Vandiver, Jr., has added some thirty more. Pinion's thorough search has increased the total yet further. But more illuminating than bland statistics are, as is the case with Hardy's scriptural language, the range and the use of this Shakespearean inheritance as part of his own language, and its distribution throughout his work.

Direct quotations occur variously: in the title of *Under the Greenwood Tree*\*; in a chapter heading, like 'Too like the Lightning' in *The Well-Beloved*; or as epigraph, as in the question from Sonnet 73 introducing Part Third of the same novel. They may be spoken by a character and acknowledged as such:

> 'Now!' she said, shaking her head with symptoms of tenderness and looking into his eyes. 'What have you just promised? Perhaps I like you a little more than a little, which is much too much! Yes, – Shakespeare says so, and he is always right.'
> (*A Laodicean*, III, Ch. 9)

A quotation may be acknowledged in order to evoke connotations attaching to a particular play, as David Lodge justly surmises in his note to this passage in The New Wessex Edition, where 'Grace may be "slily" reminding Fitzpiers that the play turns upon various kinds of sexual misdemeanour':

> 'It is a different kind of love altogether', said he. 'Less passionate; more profound. It has nothing to do with the material conditions of the object at

---

\* Geoffrey Grigson prefers to derive this title from the ballad of that name (New Wessex Edition, p. 19). But cp. Millgate on Hardy and *As You Like It*, *Thomas Hardy: His Career as a Novelist*, pp. 44 ff.

all; much to do with her character and goodness, as revealed by closer observation. "Love talks with better knowledge, and knowledge with dearer love." '

'That's out of *Measure for Measure*', said she slily.
(*The Woodlanders*, Ch. 45)

Or a quotation may be acknowledged obliquely, as in Chickerel's letter to Ethelberta in *The Hand of Ethelberta*, Ch. 7, where a line from *Twelfth Night* is accompanied by an explanatory 'as it says in that book of select pieces that you gave me'. A butler's familiarity with Shakespeare required more explaining than his daughter's facility for citing Scripture.

The roll-call of characters quoting Shakespeare is of course shorter and much more selective than that of those whom Hardy portrays as well versed in biblical phrase and story: The Bishop of Melchester, the Rector of Endelstow, Dr. Fitzpiers, Lady Constantine, the actress Matilda Johnson, Richard Phillotson, and Jocelyn Pierston are obviously well qualified by education or profession to be acquainted with the Bard. Springrove, we are told by Owen Graye in *Desperate Remedies*, Ch. 2, 'knows Shakespeare to the very dregs of the foot-notes', although the novel offers no evidence for this. In *A Laodicean*, which is especially rich in Shakespearean quotations, one might almost say dependent upon them, both Paula and Dare are prone to them, matched only by the narrator himself. Into this novel, so Hardy told William Lyon Phelps, he put more of the facts of his own life than he had done elsewhere; and these 'facts' certainly included those features of his English – Scriptural passages, quotations from Shakespeare, a wide range of technical vocabulary, considerable use of foreign words, and catalogues of the names of architects, painters, and others – which are particularly in evidence in *A Laodicean*.

Angel Clare quotes Shakespeare almost as often as he is described by Hardy in Shakespearean terms. Alec d'Urberville also has his Shakespearean moments: Tess may not recognize them for what they are ('the allusion was lost upon Tess', Ch. 9), but she has her own kind of Shakespearean awareness:

She was conscious of the notion expressed by Friar Laurence: 'These violent delights have violent ends.'
(*Tess of the d'Urbervilles*, Ch. 33)

The entire novel is dominated by Shakespearean thought and

imagery, from the title-page – 'Poor wounded name! My bosom as a bed/ Shall lodge thee' – to the description of Angel's love for Tess, in its past phase, as 'a love "which alters when it alteration finds" ' (Ch. 53), echoing from Sonnet 116 Shakespeare's most succinct statement of the nature of true love, which had clearly haunted Hardy ever since he first quoted it in *Desperate Remedies* (Ch. 11) twenty years earlier.

We are not here directly concerned with the wider and deeper influences exerted upon Hardy's thought and art by his intimate knowledge of and response to Shakespeare; only with their more audible verbal manifestations. No alert reader of Hardy's fiction can help being aware of the pervasiveness of this influence: it can be heard in the often comic dialogue of the country folk and in the 'grave-diggers' scene' in the Luxellian vault in Chapter 26 of *A Pair of Blue Eyes*; it is there in the passionate scene between Clym and Eustacia in *The Return of the Native*, V, Ch. 3, which carries along with its verbal echoes of Webster's *The White Devil* reminiscences of *Othello*; it leads Henchard inexorably to the hovel on 'the heath to the north of Anglebury'; it furnishes variations on the themes of rival families and the destructive power of Time to the peculiar orchestration of *The Well-Beloved*.

Some of the novels, like *A Laodicean*, *Two on a Tower*, and *Tess of the d'Urbervilles*, are more overtly Shakespearean in diction than others, but in most cases it is Hardy himself rather than his characters who slips into a Shakespearean image or phrase. Their range parallels that of scriptural usage. A simple image may be called up, sometimes with comic intent: 'There was a regular collapse of the tea-party, like that of the Hamlet play scene' (*The Trumpet-Major*, Ch. 17); or:

> A more attractive feature in the case was that the same youth, so capable of being ruined by flattery, blandishment, pleasure, even gross prosperity, should be at present living on in a primitive Eden of unconsciousness, with aims towards whose accomplishment a Caliban shape would have been as effective as his own.
> (*Two on a Tower*, Ch. 1)

Although not by any means one of Hardy's more successful sentences either in syntactic structure or in its imagery, it illustrates aptly his habitual recourse to the ready-made diction with which his mind was so well stocked.

Much more effective, in being less contrived, is the seemingly artless incorporation of a Shakespearean phrase, sometimes hauntingly reminiscent, sometimes openly familiar, into the narrative texture:

> The wire sang on overhead with dying falls and melodious rises that invited him to follow.
> (*A Laodicean*, I, Ch. 2)

'That strain again! It had a dying fall', says Duke Orsino in the opening speech of *Twelfth Night*. And in this instance Hardy immediately follows this echo with another musical borrowing, quoting – still in the same sentence – Lorenzo's 'Still quiring to the young-eyed cherubim' from *The Merchant of Venice*. One clearly suggested the other.

Among other narrative examples are: 'The captain, wisely taking the current when it served, already had it in the gallery' (*A Laodicean*, III, Ch. 3) echoing Brutus's 'And we must take the current when it serves' from *Julius Caesar*, and recalling Hardy's earlier use of the same phrase, applied to Matilda Johnson in *The Trumpet-Major*, Ch. 36; 'O the pity of it, if such should be the case!' (*Two on a Tower*, Ch. 5), echoing Othello's familiar words; 'a soul's specific gravity constantly re-asserts itself as less than that of the sea of troubles into which it is thrown' (*The Woodlanders*, Ch. 4), echoing Hamlet's soliloquy in III, i; 'Angel, in fact, rightly or wrongly (to adopt the safe phrase of evasive controversialists), preferred sermons in stones to sermons in churches and chapels on fine summer days' (*Tess of the d'Urbervilles*, Ch. 23), echoing the exiled Duke's lines from *As You Like It*:

Finds tongues in trees, books in the running brooks,
Sermons in stones, and good in everything.

Some Shakespearean borrowings declare themselves by direct quotation: 'circles where men pile up "the cankered heaps of strange-achieved gold" ' (*A Changed Man*: 'The Romantic Adventures of a Milkmaid', X); or by forms of language, as in 'that worm i' the bud – Henchard' (*The Mayor of Casterbridge*, Ch. 34); or by an archaism, like Angel's self-addressed 'Thou art in a parlous state, Angel Clare' (*Tess of the d'Urbervilles*, Ch. 40); or by the mention of the name of a character or a play: 'Many bathers had there prayed for a dry death from time to time, and, like Gonzalo also, had been unanswered'

(*Far from the Madding Crowd*, Ch. 47), recalling Gonzalo's 'but I would fain die a dry death' in the opening scene of *The Tempest*; or: 'Twice a week the pair went in the dusk to Hintock Churchyard, and like the two mourners in *Cymbeline*, sweetened his sad grave with their flowers and their tears' (*The Woodlanders*, Ch. 45), recalling Arviragus's lines:

> With fairest flowers
> While summer lasts and I live here, Fidele,
> I'll sweeten thy sad grave.

Although somewhat less frequently, Shakespearean diction directly enters Hardy's poetry also. The verb 'betumble' in 'Weathers', for example, is Shakespearean; the 'Rosalind' poems have their obvious echoes, and there is another, rather more facile, 'making do' with a phrase from *As You Like It* – 'mankind in its ages seven' – in 'The House of Silence'. The title of 'The Pity of It' declares its ancestry, as does the line

> She owned that she had loved too well

in 'A Sunday Morning Tragedy'. So, for that matter, also from *Othello*, is the grandiloquent invocation of the Spirit Sinister by the Spirit of the Years in *The Dynasts* I.i.6:

> Thou Iago of the Incorporeal World.

If the early sonnets in *Wessex Poems* are rather obviously modelled on Shakespeare, and the Shakespearean phrases in other poems are no less obviously derivative, there are occasional transmutations of a Shakespearean inspiration into authentic Hardy, like the 'Iago of the Incorporeal World' just cited. Also from *The Dynasts*, I.iv.3, is this passage – the words are those of the Archduke Ferdinand at Ulm:

> But it seems clear to me that loitering here
> Is full as like to compass our surrender
> As moving hence. And ill it therefore suits
> The mood of one of my high temperature
> To pause inactive while await me means
> Of desperate cure for these so desperate ills!

This is a metamorphosed Macbeth deliberating, much as there is a shadowy Ulysses delivering himself of weighty oratory behind Napoléon's soliloquy in II, v. 1.

In its Shakespearean quality, particularly in its often inconspicuous absorption of Shakespearean phrases, Hardy's English is representative of the English language since the seventeenth century. Shakespeare, like the Bible, we know, is 'full of quotations', most of them no longer recognized as such by speakers of English of whose vocabulary they form an inherited portion. That Hardy's English should be especially 'full of quotations' is thus doubly to be expected: he inherited a language already impregnated with the cadences of the age of Elizabeth and James, and he brought to it his own harvest of a life-time's reading and response. When we read Hardy, we are, willy-nilly, in Shakespeare's company. As Hardy said in his anniversary tribute 'To Shakespeare' in 1916:

> Through human orbits thy discourse to-day,
> Despite thy formal pilgrimage, throbs on
> In harmonies that cow Oblivion,
> And, like the wind, with all-uncared effect
>     Maintain a sway
> Not fore-desired, in tracks unchosen and unchecked.

Hardy's deliberately cultivated 'pastness' found in Shakespeare both the direct verbal inspiration illustrated above, and models for imitation which he followed with a strong feeling for the particular 'harmonies' as well as the lexical potential of Renaissance English.

When William R. Rutland wrote his pioneering study of Hardy's writings and their background, he chose not to include a chapter on Shakespeare. But he did devote one to 'Hardy and the Classics', a theme ever since then the object of critical attention, both in general terms affecting Hardy's art and his outlook on life, and with specific reference to those especially of Hardy's works which make direct allusion to classical models or invite comparison with them.

*The Return of the Native*, for instance, has frequent references to Homer, Virgil, Aeschylus, and Sophocles, and even if, as John Paterson has argued, 'Hardy failed to produce a formal and structural parallel with Greek tragedy, he managed to achieve, consciously or unconsciously, a reasonable artistic equivalent'. Some readers have responded less guardedly to Hardy's attempt in this novel to approximate to the classical unities of place and time and action, and to the invitation, in its opening paragraphs, to respond to the connotations of such allusions as 'Titanic form' and 'the new Vale of Tempe may be a gaunt waste of Thule'. Hardy is more explicit in the opening chapter of *The Woodlanders*:

> It was one of those sequestered spots outside the gates of the world where may usually be found more meditation than action, and more listlessness than meditation; where reasoning proceeds on narrow premisses, and results in inferences wildly imaginative; yet where, from time to time, dramas of a grandeur and unity truly Sophoclean are enacted in the real, by virtue of the concentrated passions and closely-knit interdependence of the lives therein.

Like Egdon, Little Hintock is a closely defined, circumscribed locale whose literary ancestry is here more openly hinted at.

No classical allusion in all Hardy's work has received more attention, and indeed notoriety, than the opening sentence of the final paragraph of *Tess of the d'Urbervilles*: ' "Justice" was done, and the President of the Immortals, in Æschylean phrase, had ended his sport with Tess.' As John Laird has demonstrated, this was an afterthought on Hardy's part, as the insertion to the manuscript shows; and Hardy might have saved himself much misunderstanding and bitterness had he employed in the editions of the novel either the variant used in the *Graphic* serial version – 'Time, the Arch-satirist, had had his joke out with Tess' – or the even more 'primitive' version printed, in Laird's words, in the *Sydney Mail* from a 'set of proofs which was apparently sent off virtually untouched'. And this simply read: ' "Justice" was done. The two speechless gazers bent themselves down to the earth, as if in prayer . . .'

The point here is not that Hardy thought of *The Return of the Native* as a direct novelistic evocation of the ancient world, nor that he was writing Greek drama in *The Woodlanders*, nor again that he was providing an Aeschylean world-picture for *Tess of the d'Urbervilles*. It is rather that in his maturest work the classics had changed for him from being accident to being more in the nature of substance; from being incidental and adumbrative to providing him with a literary frame of reference which the reader could recognize as appropriate for the histories being unfolded. His earliest uses of classical allusions and quotations, in *Desperate Remedies*, are all of the incidental kind. By the time Hardy was adding his 1912 Post-script to *Jude the Obscure*, however, he expressed the 'hope that certain cathartic, Aristotelian qualities might be found therein'. The progress of his indebtedness to the thought and language of classical literature is from its surface to its heart.

The early displays of classical learning may be dismissed as a pardonable exhibitionism, that same linguistic self-consciousness previously noted. It is often heavy-handed and protrudes like the 'asymptote' on which I have harped before. Virgil is prominent:

> And this flexibility and elasticity had never been taught her by rule, nor even been acquired by observation, but, *nullo cultu*, had naturally developed itself with her years.
> (*Desperate Remedies*, Ch. 1)

> Indeed, the *Quos ego* of the whole lecture had been less the genuine menace of the imperious ruler of Knapwater than an artificial utterance to hide a failing heart.
> (*Ibid.*, Ch. 9)

> *Talibus incusat.* Manston then left the house, and again went towards the blackened ruins, where men were still raking and probing.
> (*Ibid.*, Ch. 11)

Yet more obtrusively so in:

> Against the wall a Dutch clock was fixed out of level, and ticked wildly in longs and shorts, its entrails hanging down beneath its white face and wiry hands, like the fæces of a Harpy ('fœdissima ventris proluvies, uncæque manus, et pallida semper ora').
> (*Ibid.*, Ch. 16)

Or in that other verse from the *Æneid*, quoted at the end of Section 1 in Chapter 19:

> Non illa colo calathisve Minervæ
> Fœmineas assueta manus.

The display continues generously in *A Pair of Blue Eyes*, with a number of Latin tags, including some medieval legalese, and with Virgil now only just ahead of Catullus, Horace, Juvenal, and Livy. In *Desperate Remedies* Virgil had but Terence to compete with in the original. Thereafter, however, the direct quotation becomes rarer: a chapter heading in *Far from the Madding Crowd*; another Horatian echo in *The Hand of Ethelberta*; an adaptation of a verse from the *Æneid* in *Two on a Tower*; a piece of Ovid, whom she had 'just been construing', from Elizabeth-Jane in *The Mayor of Casterbridge*; a conspicuous 'Socratic $\epsilon$' . . . λρωνεία' in *The Woodlanders*; an echo from the *Georgics* applied to Angel Clare; and a verse of Horace in English introduced by its familiar opening '*Integer vitae*', quoted by him in *Tess of the d'Urbervilles*; and the title of the New Testament in Greek capitals, a portion of I Corinthians in transliterated Greek, and an Ovidian part-title in *Jude the Obscure*. Sheridan quotes '*Nec Deus intersit*' in the first act of *The Dynasts*, and the Spirit of the Years quotes '*Si diis immortalibus placet*' in the last act. There is the learned 'spell' '*Hi, hae, haec, horum, harum, horum*' in *Our Exploits at West Poley*, Ch. 2, suggesting memories of Latin grammar learnt more than thirty years earlier, and the name of the Master of Biblioll College in *Jude the Obscure*, II, Ch. 6, which suggests memories of Greek verbs. Finally, there are a few more Latin and Greek phrases, poetic and scriptural, scattered here and there through the novels and stories, the poems and *The Dynasts*, along with some French and German ones and proverbs from Italy and Spain, and the unforgettable biblical 'It was the Τετέλεσται of her union with Troy' in Chapter 43 of *Far from the Madding Crowd*.

Hardy outgrew the temptation thus openly to parade his self-taught classical learning. Already in *Under the Greenwood Tree* he recognized that, for all its georgic affinities, the setting was inappropriate for the classical dressing so generously bestowed upon the other early novels. Its absence in *A Laodicean* with its 'Neo-Greek' heroine is perhaps surprising, but is amply compensated for in this novel by its heavy reliance upon other sources of linguistic prolixity. Instead, he henceforth turned to more subtle modes: the evocation of a name, an incident, an emblematic episode, or a phrase or quotation rendered into English and thus more easily assimilated into the flow of a sentence, perhaps with a mere hint of its origin: ' "A perplexing and ticklish possession is a daughter", according to the Greek poet, and to nobody was one ever more so than to Melbury' (*The Woodlanders*, Ch. 12); or 'Henchard was stung into bitterness; like Bellerophon, he wandered away from the crowd, cankered in soul' (*The Mayor of Casterbridge*, Ch. 17); or 'As Antigone said, I am neither a dweller among men nor ghosts' (*Jude the Obscure*, VI, Ch. 9).

The technique thus becomes similar to that which Hardy employed in his use of the Bible and of Shakespeare, but classical literature never achieved for him the same degree of absorption into the language of narrative or into that of his characters. It remains extrinsic, proclaiming a different genesis. One could with some justice over-simplify these sources of Hardy's diction by saying that the Scriptures were inborn, Shakespeare inbred, the Greek and Latin classics inherited. His earliest instinct as a writer was to treat them all alike, but then he learnt to distinguish, not least among those of his characters to whom knowledge of such registers of language could be properly ascribed. Hence the relative few who quote Shakespeare, contrasted with the ubiquitousness of the Scriptures; hence the similar handful who know the classics among the rural retreats of Wessex, among them Mr Swancourt especially, who spouts Catullus and Juvenal and Horace, the latter putting Stephen Smith on his mettle in that brief Horatian antiphonal in Chapter 7 of *A Pair of Blue Eyes*. Father and son de Stancy, Swithin and Lady Constantine, Elizabeth-Jane, Angel Clare, and Jude – it is a list which suggests care in the compiling. Should doubts linger about Sir William de Stancy's qualifications, Hardy tries to allay them: 'The world has not yet learned the riches of frugality, says, I think, Cicero, somewhere,' – thus Sir William in a manner that could hardly be more tentative. On the other hand, Jude broods on the *Agamemnon* as Hardy undoubtedly did himself (*Jude the Obscure*, VI, Ch. 2). There are other parallels: Young Hardy 'soliloquizing in Latin' at sixteen, as the autobiography tells us (*Life*, p. 28), is surely present in this memorable scene:

> On a day when Fawley was getting quite advanced, being now about sixteen, and had been stumbling through the 'Carmen Sæculare', on his way home, he found himself to be passing over the high edge of the plateau by the Brown House. The light had changed, and it was the sense of this which had caused him to look up. The sun was going down, and the full moon was rising simultaneously behind the woods in the opposite quarter. His mind had become so impregnated with the poem that, in a moment of the same impulsive emotion which years before had caused him to kneel on the ladder, he stopped the horse, alighted, and glancing round to see that nobody was in sight, knelt down on the roadside bank with open book. He turned first to the shiny goddess, who seemed to look so softly and critically at his doings, then to the disappearing luminary on the other hand, as he began:
> 'Phoebe silvarumque potens Diana!'
> (*Jude the Obscure*, I, Ch. 5)

Over half a century after soliloquizing on the road to and from Dorchester, Hardy still heard Horace ringing in his memory, and incorporated his *'concordia discors'* into the final verses of the Years in the After Scene of *The Dynasts*:

> Why the All-mover,
> Why the All-prover

Ever urges on and measures out the chordless chime of Things.

Nor is this the last echo, for in the poem 'Genitrix Laesa' in *Human Shows, Far Phantasies, Songs, and Trifles*, published in 1925, occurs the parenthetical

> (Yes; so deem it you, Ladye –
> This *'concordia discors'*!)

From his youth to his old age the world was bathed for Hardy in ancient hues, right down to a passing face seen on an omnibus, 'perfect in its softened classicality – a Greek face translated into English' (*Life*, p. 220). At its subtlest and most integrated, Hardy's own 'classicality' is just that: 'a Greek face translated into English'.

Sometime in 1886 Hardy listened to 'some music of Wagner's', and in the following February he finished *The Woodlanders*. Perhaps the reference to Tannhäuser in Chapter 28 of this novel was inspired by the concert, to which Hardy refers in the *Life* (p. 181). Whatever interpretation we may choose to place on this metaphor, by itself it does not signify more than Hardy's propensity to incorporate recent experience as well as bygone jottings into current writing; but there may be more to it in this instance. *The Woodlanders* is unusual in containing a number of references to northern mythology which constitute an interesting departure from Hardy's more accustomed classical linguistic resource.

Perhaps we should speak of a blending rather than a departure, for Tannhäuser as well as Faustus, mentioned in Chapter 2, combine a German origin with legendary classical associations: Tannhäuser spent years of revelry with Venus, Faustus was associated with Helen of Troy. In the novel the allusion to Tannhäuser plays upon Fitzpiers's infatuation for Felice Charmond; that to Faust upon his temptation by the Devil being re-enacted between Marty and Percomb. Both these themes are reinforced in *The Woodlanders* by several other images of which those derived from Scandinavian mythology are the most unusual.

In Chapter 3 occur two of these: 'The night in all its fulness met her flatly on the threshold, like the very brink of an absolute void, or the ante-mundane Ginnung-Gap believed in by her Teuton forefathers'; and, towards the end of the chapter:

> She would not turn again to the little looking-glass out of humanity to herself, knowing what a deflowered visage would look back at her and almost break her heart; she dreaded it as much as did her own ancestral goddess the reflection in the pool after the rape of her locks by Loke the Malicious.

In Chapter 7, the ugliness and deformities of the woodland traversed by Melbury and his daughter, followed at some distance by Winterborne, recall 'the fabled Jarnvid wood'; and in Chapter 13, Giles, rejected by Grace, 'continued motionless and silent in that gloomy Niflheim or fogland which involved him'.

There is in all these allusions an interest in the mythology of a people more primitive than those of classical antiquity* which is strikingly in keeping with the ethos of the novel as David Lodge has described it: 'As readers of the novel we are situated in the semi-wild heart of the woods, where human life corresponds more closely to the primitive, in the anthropological sense of the word, than perhaps anything else in Hardy ('primitive' is, indeed, a word used in the novel on certain important occasions).' The primeval northern lands denoted by these Norse images are specifically contained in 'the great web of human doings then weaving in both hemispheres from the White Sea to Cape Horn' to which Hardy refers, also in Chapter 3.

These allusions are, moreover, reinforced by others in which Hardy draws upon his knowledge of ancient rites and superstitions deeply embedded in Germanic folklore. Prominent among these is the divination rite practised by the Hintock maidens on Midsummer Eve, in Chapter 20. Fifteen years earlier Hardy had recorded one such 'old Midsummer custom' in his *Memoranda I Notebook*, and in the year following the completion of *The Woodlanders* he noted another game that used to be played at Bockhampton to determine the vocation of a girl's future husband.

The 'weird shadows and ghostly nooks of indistinctness' of the Midsummer woodland scene, where the 'nocturnal experiment' is undertaken, emphasize its superstitious basis and evoke echoes of

---

* The contrast is pointed sharply in Hardy's description of Eustacia Vye in *The Return of the Native*, I, Ch. 7. Her 'classical' mouth, he writes, 'did not come over from Sleswig with a band of Saxon pirates'.

ancient beliefs in *wyrd* and spectres, and visions of places enveloped in mist and darkness, such as Niflheim was, the misty region to the north of the Ginnung-Gap, itself a huge emptiness. The connotations of the Norse creation myth, on which Hardy was drawing, embraced giants as well as the old gods, among whom Loki was an enigmatic figure, and it is not overstating the case to suggest that there is a symbolic affinity also between the world-ash Yggdrasil and the tall elm that haunts and finally kills John South.

The northern echoes are still audible as the story draws to its close, particularly in the vivid imagery of the stormy night in Chapter 41, with its spectral manifestations, its devilry, and its 'gigantic hand'. These are elemental forces, belonging to the same world of 'witches and demons' that caused the horse Darling to be *hag-rid*, as the groom insisted (Ch. 28); a world partly conjured up for Hardy by the very same Wagnerian music which he had been listening to while writing *The Woodlanders*:

> It was *weather* and *ghost* music – whistling of wind and storm, the strumming of a gale on iron railings, the creaking of doors; low screams of entreaty and agony through key-holes, amid which trumpet-voices are heard.
> (*Life*, p. 181)

The essence is here, to be expanded thus in the novel:

> The wind grew more violent, and as the storm went on it was difficult to believe that no opaque body, but only an invisible colourless thing, was trampling and climbing over the roof, making branches creak, springing out of the trees upon the chimney, popping its head into the flue, and shrieking and blaspheming at every corner of the walls. As in the grisly story, the assailant was a spectre which could be felt but not seen . . . Sometimes a bough from an adjoining tree was swayed so low as to smite the roof in the manner of a gigantic hand smiting the mouth of an adversary, to be followed by a trickle of rain, as blood from the wound.
> (*The Woodlanders*, Ch. 41)

It was of course not only Wagner who was at work on Hardy's mind while he was writing such passages in *The Woodlanders*. He was acquainted with some of the Norse sagas translated by Eiríkr Magnússon and William Morris*, and he had presumably stored in

---

* See *Literary Notes*, 1110–1112, and the note to 1110.

his memory, although not in his notes, the northern myths mentioned by Carlyle in *On Heroes and Hero-Worship* and by Arnold in 'Balder Dead'.* Such recollections served to furnish an occasional image, like the playful 'spittoon of the Jötuns' applied to Casterbridge Ring in *The Mayor of Casterbridge*, Ch. 11, or the reference to 'old Skrymer', the giant, snoring, in 'The Wind's Prophecy'. It also helped to add the name of Freya to the list of those who might have been the love-queen of Pierston's isle in *The Well-Beloved*, II, Ch. 12. There may even be a Norse echo in the image of the awakening hills in 'Life and Death at Sunrise', as Pinion has suggested in *A Commentary on the Poems of Thomas Hardy*, p. 210.

Moreover, Hardy's antiquarian interest in local traditions is evident throughout his writings. There are allusions to the Germanic past, for instance, in several episodes in *The Return of the Native*, of which the first is the lighting of fires on Egdon Heath to commemorate the Gunpowder Plot, the most recent in a long line of folk customs, which included 'jumbled Druidical rites' and such 'Saxon ceremonies' as the 'Festival fires to Thor and Woden'. The chapter (I, 3) is appropriately entitled 'The Custom of the Country'. Later in the novel, in describing the orgiastic gipsying attended by Eustacia and Wildeve, Hardy remarks that 'for the time Paganism was revived' in the hearts of the dancers (IV, Ch. 3); – patently, it was always slumbering just beneath the surface among the people of Egdon:

> The instincts of merry England lingered on here with exceptional vitality, and the symbolic customs which tradition has attached to each season of the year were yet a reality on Egdon. Indeed, the impulses of all such outlandish hamlets are pagan still: in these spots homage to nature, self-adoration, frantic gaieties, fragments of Teutonic rites to divinities whose names are forgotten, seem in some way or other to have survived mediaeval doctrine.
>
> (*The Return of the Native*, VI, Ch. 1)

These northern echoes are deeply rooted in Hardy's linguistic consciousness, for not only do they provide allusions and images, but Norse words embedded in English dialects find their way into his language to reinforce the sense of the past which was so much part of his vision.

---

* See Mary Jacobus, 'Tree and Machine: The Woodlanders', in *Critical Approaches to the Fiction of Thomas Hardy*, ed. Kramer, pp. 116–34.

The first chapter of Hardy's autobiography traces both his genealogical and his literary ancestry, and we recall his maternal grandmother's familiarity with the writings of Addison and Steele, of Richardson and Fielding, 'and, of course, with such standard works as *Paradise Lost* and *The Pilgrim's Progress*'. The 'of course' is significant: it was inevitable that from his grandmother and his mother, who also 'read omnivorously', Thomas should have, in his turn, acquired his familiarity with the standard works of English literature, a heritage to which he added his own life-long reading of English and foreign writers, past and contemporary. There is no need to attempt here a rehearsal of who they all were, for almost every study of Hardy, in books and numerous essays, has drawn attention to Hardy's indebtedness to other writers. Nor is there need here to prove the point by many examples. Let one or two suffice: the sudden echo of *The Rape of the Lock* – 'With powder, puff, or patch' – in Hardy's poem 'An Expostulation'; or the reminiscence of Keats's well-known sonnet in the closing line of Hardy's 'To a Tree in London': 'Smelt the landscape's sweet serene'; or the title 'So Various', straight from Dryden. Apart from Shakespeare and in his own way Barnes, some writers stand out above the rest: Milton and Dryden, Shelley, Keats, and Wordsworth, Tennyson, Browning, and Swinburne, among the poets; Fielding, Scott, Ainsworth, Hawthorne among the novelists. The literary notebooks contain entries from scientific and philosophical writings, many of which furnished Hardy with ideas, occasional verbal expressions, and direct quotations. Comte's *System of Positive Polity* provides more entries than any other single work. Other writers much in evidence are Arnold, Carlyle, Herbert Spencer, and Leslie Stephen, as well as Darwin, Huxley, and J.S. Mill. For Hardy's English it was a process of continuing enrichment.

As with the Scriptures, with Shakespeare and the classical poets and dramatists, other writers are ubiquitous in Hardy's work: they furnish titles, epigraphs, chapter headings; they are quoted by Hardy's characters; they are, above all, absorbed into Hardy's own diction, consciously or unconsciously, set in quotation marks or simply incorporated. There are not many pages in Hardy's fiction where his own omnivorous reading has not borne fruit in a word or phrase or sentence, sometimes awkwardly intrusive, often easily assimilated. That highly popular novel *John Inglesant : A Romance* by J.H. Shorthouse, to give one example, was probably in Hardy's mind when he wrote parts of *The Mayor of Casterbridge*, especially its well-known ending. Into his *Literary Notes* Hardy had copied the following passage from this novel which, it is worth noting, went through ten editions within the first two years after its publication in 1881:

> From those high windows behind the flower-pots young girls have looked out upon life, which their instincts told them was made for pleasure, but which year after year convinced them was, somehow or other, given over to pain.

There is a notable parallelism between this passage and that describing Lucetta and Elizabeth-Jane looking out of the windows of High-Place Hall in *The Mayor of Casterbridge*, Ch. 22:

> They sat in adjoining windows of the same room in Lucetta's great stone mansion, netting, and looking out upon the market, which formed an animated scene.

And there are further reverberations of *John Inglesant* in the final paragraph of *The Mayor of Casterbridge*, with its reference to Elizabeth-Jane,

> whose youth had seemed to teach that happiness was but the occasional episode in a general drama of pain.

While such absorption into his own language is not uncommon, Hardy frequently acknowledges a particular indebtedness:

> His was the passion of Congreve's Millamant, whose delight lay in seeing 'the heart which others bled for, bleed for me'.
> (*The Woodlanders*, Ch. 29)

> But so far was she from being, in the words of Robert South, 'in love with her own ruin', that the illusion was transient as lightning.
> (*Tess of the d'Urbervilles*, Ch. 13)

The acknowledgement may even be accompanied, fittingly so from the Rural Dean, by a little advertising: '. . . in the words of good Robert South (whose sermons might be read much more than they are) . . .' (*A Group of Noble Dames*: 'The Marchioness of Stonehenge').

The acknowledgement is sometimes more oblique:

> 'Your trenches, zigzags, counterscarps, and ravelins may be all very well,

and a very sure system of attack in the long run; but upon my soul they are almost as slow in maturing as those of Uncle Toby himself.'
(*A Laodicean*, III, Ch. 4)

'And be a perfect representative of "the modern spirit"?' she inquired, 'representing neither the senses and understanding, nor the heart and imagination; but what a finished writer calls "the imaginative reason"?'
(*A Laodicean*, VI, Ch. 5)

Uncle Toby is Sterne's creation in *Tristram Shandy*; the 'finished writer' is Matthew Arnold. At its most clandestine, the quotation simply disappears into Hardy's sentence, absorbed with other eclectic elements into his diction:

We have been told what happens when a woman deliberates; and the epigram is not always terminable with woman, provided that one be in the case, and that a fair one.
(*The Return of the Native*, I, Ch. 5)

Her cheeks had lost for ever that firm contour which had been drawn by the vigorous hand of youth, and the masses of hair that were once darkness visible had become touched here and there by a faint grey haze, like the Via Lactea in a midnight sky.
(*Two on a Tower*, Ch. 41)

To be sure, with such pleasing anxious beings as they were, the boy's coming also brought with it much thought for the future, particularly as he seemed at present to be singularly deficient in all the usual hopes of childhood.
(*Jude the Obscure*, V, Ch. 5)

Gray, Addison, Milton, not in that order – the reader is invited to isolate the quotations and assign each to its author – for that is precisely what Hardy is asking us to do; not, of course, as a form of parlour game, but in that implicit manner in which cognoscenti discourse among themselves. Or is this to assume too much, especially when Hardy's fiction was serialized in family magazines whose readership included not only the educated but those anxious to educate themselves? We remember young Hardy himself perusing, and learning from, Victorian periodicals, among them *The Saturday Review*, *The Cornhill Magazine*, and *The Graphic*. One way to encourage the reading of good literature is to whet the appetite by judicious quotation; a frequent practice with Hardy, who will quote anything from a line of verse to a stanza, from a phrase or sentence of prose to a paragraph, both with authorial voice, at times straining credulity, from the lips of such as Miss Aldclyffe, Christopher Julian, Fitzpiers, Sue and Jude, all quoting lines from Shelley. Alec d'Urberville quotes extracts from *Paradise Lost* because, he says, 'I used to be quite up in that scene of Milton's when I was theological' (*Tess of the d'Urbervilles*, Ch. 50); Angel, by contrast, has a thought of Pascal's 'brought home to him' – in French (Ch. 18); whereas Giles Winterborne 'could have declared with a contemporary poet' – two whole stanzas of a poem by Edmund Gosse. The hinted possibility, however, remains wisely unrealized.

Such ascription to a character's utterances or musings of passages dear to Hardy himself is a favourite mode of his, but he will as readily do so in his own voice, and here it is the context which determines decorum, whether the chosen lines are apt or not. There is something rather overwhelming in the spectral anthology which comes to Jude at Christminster (*Jude the Obscure*, II, Ch. 1) in the manner of Macbeth's ghostly procession. On the other hand, it seems wholly right that Phillotson should walk out of Shaston (*ibid.*, IV, Ch. 4) to the ironic accompaniment of a few lines of Barnes's poem 'Shaftesbury Feair' (slightly misquoted). While there is fitting irony of a different kind in making Oak and Bathsheba at long last sit together in Oak's house, in the penultimate chapter of *Far from the Madding Crowd*, where, also in Barnes's words, the old furniture was

all a-sheenen
Wi' long years o' handlen.

In both instances, Hardy acknowledges Barnes in a footnote, but he does not say that the latter lines come from what is perhaps his finest poem, 'Woak Hill', whose singular appropriateness to the scene in Oak's cottage the reader is left to discover for his or her self.

Hardy's direct indebtedness to the philosophical writings of his time may be illustrated by examples of the use he makes in his fiction of the works of J.S. Mill and Auguste Comte. Mill made a strong impression on Hardy, personally as well as intellectually, for he recalled, in a letter to *The Times* of 21 May 1906, hearing Mill addressing a public meeting in London forty-one years earlier. There is an unforgettable image in his description of Mill: 'He stood bareheaded, and his vast pale brow, so thin-skinned as to show the blue veins, sloped back like a stretching upland, and conveyed to the observer a curious sense of perilous exposure' (*Life*, p. 330). Hardy's involvement with Mill's writings is visibly reflected in the markings in his copy of Mill's *On Liberty* and in the 'modern' attitudes adopted by some of his more progressive and unorthodox characters. Sue Bridehead quotes from *On Liberty* (*Jude the Obscure*, IV, Ch. 3), for example; and that devoted disciple of its philosophy, Ethelberta, reads several extracts from *Utilitarianism* before our eyes in Chapter 36 of *The Hand of Ethelberta*.

Hardy was also strongly impressed by the ideas of Auguste Comte, notably the latter's treatment of man's psychological development through a series of stages from a primitive, *fetichistic* one to a modern religion of humanity, in a form of social progress which Hardy called 'a looped orbit', a concept elucidated in his notes by an accompanying diagram. This notion of progress 'in the lapse of ages' is ascribed to Angel in *Tess of the d'Urbervilles*, Ch. 26, as he ponders on Tess's 'unsophisticated open-air existence'. The fetichistic phase interested Hardy particularly as being close to primitive beliefs and superstitions of the kind that play their part in the traditions of his Wessex countryside. The word itself found its way into his writings, for Hardy was speaking the literal truth when he asserted (*Life*, p. 98) that some of the expressions of 'Comte's Positive Philosophy, and writings of that school' had passed into his own vocabulary, as they had into that of George Eliot. The copious notes jotted down from Comte bore such fruit as Sue Bridehead's description of Christminster as 'a place full of fetichists and ghost-seers' or her reference to Jude's now being 'in the Tractarian stage' (*Jude the Obscure*, III, Ch. 4), or Joan Durbeyfield's 'curious fetichistic fear' of her fortune-telling book (*Tess of the d'Urbervilles*, Ch. 3). Tess herself links the first and third of Comte's phases of man's theological stage by giving voice to a rhapsody on her descent into the Valley of the Great Dairies that was 'a Fetichistic utterance in a Monotheistic setting' (Ch. 16).

'Monotheism . . . always in collision with Intellect', Hardy had jotted in his *Literary Notes*, a notion that re-echoes through much of his writing, as does that of the biological interdependence of man and organic nature, similarly noted: 'Biological Dependence' – 'The nobler phenomena are everywhere subordinate to those which are grosser, but also simpler and more regular . . . Man is entirely subordinate to the World – each living being to its own environment.' Perhaps the most memorable expression of this notion is in *The Woodlanders*, where Giles 'looked and smelt like Autumn's very brother', causing Grace's senses to revel 'in the sudden lapse back to Nature unadorned' and her 'veneer of artificiality' to be discarded, so

that she 'became the crude country girl of her latent early instincts'
(Ch. 28). In Chapter 38 the same idea is further elaborated:

> He rose upon her memory as the fruit-god and the wood-god in altern-
> ation: sometimes leafy and smeared with green lichen, as she had seen him
> amongst the sappy boughs of the plantations: sometimes cider-stained and
> starred with apple-pips, as she had met him on his return from cider-
> making in Blackmoor Vale, with his vats and presses beside him.

The polytheistic allusion to Comte's second phase is as unmistakable
as the powerful image of man's interdependence with the natural
world.

Comte left his verbal imprint on Hardy's diction, even though
later in his life Hardy considered the positivist notion of evolutionary
progress towards an alliance of religion and rationality 'a forlorn
hope, a mere dream'. Writing, a few years after the First World War,
in the 'Apology' prefaced to *Late Lyrics and Earlier*, he harks back
once more to Comte's notion of looped-orbit advance as holding out
what slender hope there is of such an alliance. From our present
vantage point, sixty years later, Hardy's scepticism certainly appears
justified.

The 'dictionary words' absorbed into Hardy's English have many
other sources in human thought and endeavour besides those considered thus far. The second half of the nineteenth century was a
period of lively activity in several fields of science in which Hardy
took an interest, which, in turn, is reflected in his work. His
'Drinking Song' in *Winter Words* is a rollicking parade of well-
known names – a kind of anticipatory limerick on a large scale – in
which figure Thales, Copernicus, Hume, Darwin, the biblical
scholar T.K. Cheyne, and Einstein. They all interested him, and so
did early psychologists like Henry Maudsley, whose *Natural Causes
and Supernatural Seemings* influenced *Jude the Obscure*, as Patricia
Gallivan has demonstrated. Biology and geology, and what they
revealed about evolution, furnished Hardy with words and images
and reinforced his vision of age-old places like Egdon Heath or that
'enormous many-limbed organism of an antediluvian time' which
provides the setting for 'A Tryst at an Ancient Earthwork' in *A
Changed Man*. The most celebrated geological excursus in Hardy's
fiction is the description of Knight's rapid survey of 'the varied scenes
that had had their day between this creature's epoch and his own' as
he contemplates 'an imbedded fossil' in the cliff face upon which he is

suspended in *A Pair of Blue Eyes*, Ch. 22, but there are other examples of Hardy's use of geological and biological data. In *Tess of the d'Urbervilles*, Ch. 26, for example, Hardy speaks of a 'mental epiderm'; in the opening chapter of *The Well-Beloved*, the Isle of Slingers is described in a manner half poetical – Shelley, in this instance – half-scientific, so characteristic of Hardy, which M.A. Goldberg has described as 'this constant pull between two worlds':

All now stood dazzlingly unique and white against the tinted sea, and the sun flashed on infinitely stratifed walls of oolite,

> The melancholy ruins
> Of cancelled cycles, . . .

The 'pull' may be between rather different worlds, of course, as between the esoterica of science and the utterly homely:

> A crooked file of men was approaching the back door. The whole string of trailing individuals advanced in the completest balance of intention, like the remarkable creatures known as Chain Salpæ, which, distinctly organised in other respects, have one will common to a whole family. Some were, as usual, in snow-white smock-frocks of Russia duck, and some in whitey-brown ones of drabbet – marked on the wrists, breasts, backs, and sleeves with honeycomb-work. Two or three women in pattens brought up the rear.
> (*Far from the Madding Crowd*, Ch. 9)

In *The Trumpet-Major*, Ch. 39, a jagged streak on Bob's cheek is 'like the geological remains of a lobster'; in *The Woodlanders*, Ch. 40, 'the inertion of Grace's pool-like existence was disturbed as by a geyser'; in *Tess of the d'Urbervilles*, Ch. 36, within Angel's constitution 'lay hidden a hard logical deposit, like a vein of metal in a soft loam'; in *Jude the Obscure*, II, Ch. 2, Jude has yet to learn that 'mediævalism was as dead as a fern-leaf in a lump of coal'; and in *The Well-Beloved*, III, Ch. 4, occurs the third Avice's irresistibly funny reaction to Pierston's revelation of his earlier infatuation for her mother and her grandmother:

> 'My mother's, and my grandmother's', said she, looking at him no longer as at a possible husband, but as a strange fossilized relic in human form.

The technical diction of geology, biology, and astronomy, the latter particularly plentiful in *Two on a Tower*, added a not inconsiderable element to Hardy's linguistic resources. He took some trouble, as he relates in the *Life* (p. 151), to acquaint himself with matters astronomical in order to lend authenticity to *Two on a Tower*. He visited Greenwich Observatory, had probably read R.A. Proctor's *Other Worlds Than Ours* (1870) and owned a copy of his *Essays on Astronomy* (1872), and sought technical information on lens-grinding from Professor W.C. Unwin, author of *The Elements of Machine Design*, to which Hardy refers in his letter to Unwin of 13 December 1881. The hero of the novel, Swithin St Cleeve, hoping to be 'the new Copernicus' (Ch. 4), is thus well equipped for his role and peppers his discourse with appropriate technicalities about 'streams of satellites or meteors', 'primary and secondary planets', 'fixed stars', 'yawning spaces', 'immensities', 'an equatorial', 'ascensions and declinations', 'scintillation . . . merely a matter of atmosphere', 'the occasional green tint of Castor', 'the Transit of Venus', and the like. And Hardy himself, wishing, as he says in the Preface to *Two on a Tower*, 'to set the emotional history of two infinitesimal lives against the stupendous background of the stellar universe', does the same in his narrative and dialogue, comparing a bed of snowdrops to 'a nether Milky Way' and a whiplash cut on a cheek to a meridian. Dialogue is couched in technical figures:

'But you will never realise that an incident which filled but a degree in the circle of your thoughts covered the whole circumference of mine. No person can see exactly what and where another's horizon is.'

(*Two on a Tower*, Ch. 6)

Or: 'I have never ordinated two such dissimilar ideas' (Ch. 12), with its verbal derivative of a technical term in geometry. Even the course of Swithin's and Viviette's emotional history is charted with something approaching mathematical exactitude: 'To such had the study of celestial physics brought them in the space of eight months, one week, and a few odd days' (Ch. 15).

The attention devoted to the stellar universe, to telescopes and lenses, paid off in other novels and stories too, although Hardy was of course familiar with magnifying glasses long before he consulted Professor Unwin. To this early familiarity we owe the splendid image in *Far from the Madding Crowd*, Ch. 35:

The creeping plants about the old manor-house were bowed with rows of heavy water drops, which had upon objects behind them the effect of minute lenses of high magnifying power.

The unbridgeable distances of the skies are appropriately evoked as Jude watches the academic procession in Christminster on 'Remembrance Day' from which he was separated by similar immensities:

> The procession of Heads of Houses and new Doctors emerged, their red and black gowned forms passing across the field of Jude's vision like inaccessible planets across an object glass.
> (*Jude the Obscure*, VI, Ch. 1)

Two final examples, to illustrate the linguistic convergence of Hardy's fondness for country dancing with his mental sweeping across the galaxies in unusual imagery:

> And so the dance whizzed on with cumulative fury, the performers moving in their planet-like courses, direct and retrograde, from apogee to perigee, till the hand of the well-kicked clock at the bottom of the room had travelled over the circumference of an hour.
> (*Wessex Tales*: 'The Three Strangers')

In *The Return of the Native* Eustacia is dancing with Wildeve at the gipsying, and here Hardy draws both his image and his verbal inspiration straight from Proctor, the prolific astronomer, as this entry in his *Literary Notes* suggests:

> The planet Mercury is always seen on the bright background of a full twilight sky & does not make a striking appearance even if the most brilliant of the planets.
> Proctor.

And thus Eustacia:

> Like the planet Mercury surrounded by the lustre of sunset, her permanent brilliancy passed without much notice in the temporary glory of the situation.
> (*The Return of the Native*, IV, Ch. 3)

That Hardy derived some of his astronomical imagery and diction from Tennyson's 'The Palace of Art', including the deleted stanzas used by Proctor as an epigraph to his *Essays on Astronomy*, has been convincingly argued by Michael Millgate.

It required patient application to familiarize himself with the scientific technicalities which Hardy absorbed into his language, but the case is different with architecture. Hardy's training equipped him professionally with expert knowledge in architectural history, theory, and practice, compared with which his acquaintance with the sciences, even with the botany of Dorset, was but that of an interested amateur. During the ten years between 1862 and 1872, while Hardy was working in architectural offices in Dorchester, London and Weymouth, he filled most of the pages of his surviving *Architectural Notebook*. This is rich in sketches and diagrams and notes, as well as in details of building crafts like masonry, carpentry and joinery, and plumbing, with which Hardy was clearly familiarizing himself, as Somerset must have done in *A Laodicean* III, Ch. 11, as C.J.P. Beatty has noted.

Translated into his writing, architecture provided Hardy with concepts of form and structure, of architectonic relationships, as well as with the ability to describe buildings with an expert's eye and the vocabulary to do so. But he saw more than the mere buildings themselves: he saw their histories, their changing functions, their human connections; he saw into their souls as well as seeing their external features. At its most basic level, architectural diction figures in the description of buildings which Hardy copied from real places. Knapwater House in *Desperate Remedies* was suggested by Kingston Maurward House in the parish of Stinsford, and the resemblance is strengthened by revisions Hardy introduced into the description in the edition of 1912. He changed 'Greek classicism' to plain 'classicism' early in the novel (Ch. 5), and 'columns' to 'pilasters' in the final chapter. The earlier description is severely factual with its omniscient awareness of the ground plan, the court, the ice-houses, laundries, and stables, such as an architect might have drawn up; and Hardy did indeed draw up a groundplan on p. 45 of his *Architectural Notebook*, which bears closer resemblance to his description in the novel than to the actual building, as Beatty has noted. The later description is of the house as seen by Clerk Crickett and the reporter by moonlight; the architect is still present, but so now is the poet:

> It was a magnificent picture of the English country-house. The whole of the severe regular front, with its pilasters and cornices, was built of a white smoothly-faced freestone, which appeared in the rays of the moon as pure as Pentelic marble. The sole objects in the scene rivalling the fairness of the façade were a dozen swans floating upon the lake.
>
> (*Desperate Remedies*, Sequel)

A particularly elaborate account is that of Enckworth Court in *The Hand of Ethelberta*, Ch. 38. It relies heavily on technical details – as Philippa Tristram has said: 'The architect's vocabulary is at times obtrusive in his prose' – but while observing and describing the building, Hardy allows himself a number of critical observations on the modern portion which had risen alongside the original medieval structure, the latter now 'a mere cup-bearer and culinary menial beside it', and the only thing, Hardy maintains, that was 'honest' in the entire complex. His most succinct comment is that 'it was a house in which Pugin would have torn his hair' – but characteristically, Ethelberta's tastes are more pragmatic:

> 'How lovely!' said Ethelberta, as she looked at the fairy ascent. 'His staircase alone is worth my hand!'

Pugin, whom Hardy admired, reappears elsewhere: for example, in Sue's 'Gothic is barbaric art, after all. Pugin was wrong, and Wren was right' (*Jude the Obscure*, V, Ch. 6), and in the disquisition on contemporary trends of which Hardy delivers himself in the opening chapter of his most architectural novel, *A Laodicean*. There is a lavish display of names here that recalls Hardy's own apprenticeship, a display that is paralleled elsewhere where names or technical terms are paraded in the manner of medieval 'enumeratio':

> He asked for the foreman, and looked round among the new traceries, mullions, transoms, shafts, pinnacles, and battlements standing on the bankers half worked, or waiting to be removed. They were marked by precision, mathematical straightness, smoothness, exactitude: there in the old walls were the broken lines of the original idea; jagged curves, disdain of precision, irregularity, disarray.
> (*Jude the Obscure*, II, Ch. 2)

Hardy's eye roves, approvingly or critical, over all sorts and conditions of buildings while his pen notes the technical details: the Tranter's 'long low cottage with a *hipped roof* of thatch' in *Under the Greenwood Tree*, I, Ch. 2; the shearing-barn in Chapter 22 of *Far from the Madding Crowd*; the mill in *The Trumpet-Major*, Ch. 2, which had '*hips instead of gables*, giving it a round-shouldered look'; the long gallery with its '*coved ceiling* of *arabesques*' at Stancy Castle in *A Laodicean*, I, Ch. 3; High-Place Hall in Casterbridge, which, Hardy says, 'was *Palladian*, and like most architecture erected since the Gothic age was a compilation rather than a design' (*The Mayor of*

*Casterbridge*, Ch. 21). In *The Well-Beloved*, Pierston's renunciation of his quest and his break with the past are symbolized in the final chapter by his scheme to provide reticulated water, and by his 'acquiring some old moss-grown, mullioned Elizabethan cottages, for the purpose of pulling them down because they were damp; which he afterwards did, and built new ones with hollow walls, and full of ventilators.'

The philanthropy here displayed was at loggerheads, within Hardy himself, with an antiquarian delight in old buildings. He realized both the need to modernize uncomfortable and inconvenient domestic dwellings and the urgency to restore crumbling medieval edifices if they were to remain in use as churches or as memorials of past workmanship. On p. 49 of the *Architectural Notebook*, for example, in Beatty's words, 'a handsome Ruskinian knocker shares the top of the page with details of stables and the floor of a church or chapel, while the rest of the page is taken up with "Cesspool to school W.C.'s"', a simple plan for a double architrave, ground floor windows, rafters and other details.' At the same time, Hardy recognized the revolution brought about by the use of modern materials like cast and rolled iron in building, and the birth of new architectural temples to take the place of the old:

> 'Shall we go and sit in the Cathedral?' he asked, when their meal was finished.
> 'Cathedral? Yes. Though I think I'd rather sit in the railway station', she answered, a remnant of vexation still in her voice. 'That's the centre of the town life now. The Cathedral has had its day!'
> (*Jude the Obscure*, III, Ch. 1)

'The ministration of the temporary outlasting the ministration of the eternal' is the lesson here, as Hardy had previously worded it in *Tess of the d'Urbervilles*, Ch. 35, where 'the mill still worked on, food being a perennial necessity; the abbey had perished, creeds being transient'. The description of the great barn in *Far from the Madding Crowd* had prompted similar thoughts, for to Hardy no building could be divorced from what in 'Memories of Church Restoration' he called the 'personal relation'; its intimate connection with the people who dwelt there, worked there, or worshipped there. Hence the integration of his architectural vocabulary, when not purely descriptive or merely enumerative, into his narrative diction and imagery: Dare 'standing as still as a *caryatid*' (*A Laodicean*, III, Ch.

4); Eustacia's lips forming 'the curve so well known in the arts of design as the *cima-recta, or ogee*' (*The Return of the Native*, I, Ch. 7), an image to which Hardy returns in *The Mayor of Casterbridge*, Ch. 22; or the noses of listeners 'ranged as regularly as *bow-windows* at a watering-place' (*The Hand of Ethelberta*, Ch. 16). If buildings prompted thoughts of people, people suggested architectural comparisons, albeit not always wholly feliciticiously.

One attempt to trace the 'personal relation' is Hardy's poem 'The Abbey Mason', in which he presents his version of the origin of the English Perpendicular style in Gloucester Cathedral. Like 'The Church Builder' in *Poems of the Past and Present*, it makes use of architectural diction:

> The *ogee arches transom-topped*,
> The *tracery-stalks* by *spandrels* stopped,
>
> Petrified lacework – lightly lined
> On ancient massiveness behind . . .

The poem was written when Hardy was seventy-one, published in *Harper's Monthly Magazine* in 1912, and reprinted two years later in *Satires of Circumstance*. Hardy himself gives an account of its genesis in his autobiography (*Life*, p. 357). This and the poem itself acknowledge his continuing interest in architecture and the deep embedment of its technical terminology in his vocabulary, from his first novel to his last, from the

> high halls with *tracery*
> And open *ogive-work*,

of one of his earliest poems, 'Heiress and Architect', dedicated to Arthur Blomfield, to images of '*architraves* of sunbeam-smitten

cloud' and 'the last *entablature* of Time' in *The Dynasts*, Fore Scene, and I. v. 4, and to his last poems, as in

> The *aisles*, the *roof's new frame*,
> And the *arches*, and *ashlar* with coloured bands.
> (*Winter Words*: 'Whispered at the Church-Opening')

In his late poem 'Concerning Agnes', several of Hardy's interests – dancing, music, monumental sculpture, classical literature –

find brief expression. Although not a great poem, its diction is a characteristic reflection of these varied influences: the poem recalls his dancing with 'that fair woman', Agnes Grove, echoes 'the booms / Of contrabassos', and pictures her now lying 'white, straight, features marble-keen', like some figure out of Greek mythology – Aphrodite or Kalupso or Amphitrite or one of the Muses, 'grown stiff from thought'. Many of Hardy's poems are similarly eclectic in their diction.

Contrabassos boom elsewhere, as in 'At the Entering of the New Year', where the language of dancing is more explicit:

> Our *allemands*, our *heys*, *poussettings*,
> Our *hands-across* and back again,
> Sent rhythmic throbbings through the casements.

The names of popular dances crop up here and there: for example in the poem 'One We Knew', at the tranter's party in *Under the Greenwood Tree*, I, Ch. 7, or in the stage directions in *The Dynasts*: ' "Speed the Plough" is danced to its conclusion, and the band strikes up "The Copenhagen Waltz" ' (II. vi. 7). Not only the names of dances, but of other pieces of music – songs, hymns, psalms – are witnesses to Hardy's love of 'Story, and Dance, and Hymn', as he writes in 'The Vatican: Sala delle Muse', but the love of country dancing was unquestionably deep-rooted. Asked whether she could dance, Hardy's romantic milkmaid recites this inventory:

> 'Reels, and jigs, and country-dances like the New-Rigged-Ship, and Follow-my-Lover, and Haste-to-the Wedding, and the College Horn-pipe, and the Favourite Quickstep, and Captain White's dance.'
> (*A Changed Man*: 'The Romantic Adventures of a Milkmaid', III)

– not quite what the Baron expected. In 'The Fiddler of the Reels' (*Life's Little Ironies*) Hardy brings out the primitive appeal and hypnotic force of the persistent rhythms that emanate from the instrument, 'crowds of little chromatic subtleties, capable of drawing tears from a statue'. In *A Pair of Blue Eyes* music is an important ingredient in a romantic scene that impresses ineradicably upon Stephen Smith Elfride's 'form in which she was beheld during these minutes of singing' (Ch. 3). She has 'a pretty contralto voice'; we are given names of songs and song-writers; two lines of French verse from de Leyre; and four lines from Shelley's 'The Flight of Love'.

Elfride is pictured 'trilling forth, in a tender *diminuendo*, the closing words' of Shelley's poem, and later discovers that 'her harmonies had fired a small Troy, in the shape of Stephen's heart'. Here the diction naturally draws upon musical technicalities; but there are instances where it is not immediately drawn out of the context, but derives from Hardy's life-long response to music, dating back to his boyhood fiddling and piano-tuning (see *Life*, pp. 22–3).

Musical metaphors are embedded in Hardy's diction as firmly as those drawn from other arts, especially painting and architecture. Some draw on musical instruments: Sue Bridehead's tense personality suggests several times the taut strings of a harp 'which the least wind of emotion from another's heart could make to vibrate as readily as a radical stir in her own' (*Jude the Obscure*, V, Ch. 3), so were 'the fibres of her nature . . . strained like harp-strings (IV, Ch. 3). The image recurs elsewhere:

> We sent the covered carriage to meet the train indicated, and waited like two newly strung harps for the first sound of the returning wheels.
> (*A Changed Man*: 'Alicia's Diary', IV)

Some musical metaphors draw on notation: two of Hardy's heroines have arched brows resembling 'nothing so much as two slurs in music' (*Under the Greenwood Tree*, I, Ch. 7); and like Fancy's brows so are Ethelberta's (*The Hand of Ethelberta*, Ch. 33). Colonel Heymès's ill-omened expression elicits from a sullen Napoléon the apt comment 'And his face shows what clef his music's in!' (*The Dynasts*, III. vii. 6). Other metaphors draw on other musical concepts:

> But to attempt to gain a view of her – or indeed of any fascinating woman – from a measured category, is as difficult as to appreciate the effect of a landscape by exploring it at night with a lantern – or of a full chord of music by piping the notes in succession.
> (*Desperate Remedies*, Ch. 1)

In the same novel appears the first of Hardy's poems to see the light of day, 'Eunice', in Ch. 16, which contains the unusual image 'A pinkly pictured melody', although originally Hardy had written, rather less daringly, 'A kind of pictured melody', which he then changed in the edition of 1912. The cliché of a musical voice is turned into 'that lingual music' as one of the attractions of Pierston's ideal woman in *The Well-Beloved*, II, Ch. 1. In 'The Sleep-Worker' we read of

> Fair growths, foul cankers, right enmeshed
>      with wrong,
> Strange orchestras of victim-shriek and song,
> And curious blends of ache and ecstasy.

And in 'A Young Man's Exhortation':

> Send up such touching strains
> That limitless recruits from Fancy's pack
> Shall rush upon your tongue, and tender back
>      All that your soul contains.

'A full chord of music', 'a melody', 'strange orchestras', 'touching strains' – the diction is not particularly distinctive, yet at times the context makes it memorable. As Hardy invariably tried to get his colours just right, a theme to which we shall return, so he tried to indicate sounds, either onomatopoeically or by selecting what he deemed appropriate words. Hence the nightingale's final comment 'Tippiwit! swe-e-et! ki-ki-ki! Come hither, come hither, come hither' at the end of *Under the Greenwood Tree*; and the 'coo' of the ancient fossil bird of 'In a Museum', and the 'carolings' of the bird which 'Had chosen thus to fling his soul / Upon the growing gloom' in 'The Darkling Thrush'. Hardy's trees are all symphonic, especially so in *The Woodlanders*, nestling, sighing, moaning, even chanting 'melancholy Gregorian melodies' (Ch. 13). 'Sights and Sounds draw the Wanderers together' is the title of Chapter 9 in Book Fifth of *The Return of the Native*, in which the little pools of light illuminate the deadly pool of Shadwater Weir with its 'vortex formed at the curl of the returning current', and the 'roaring of a ten-hatch weir' rising above the 'din of weather' in which 'the loosened gravel and small stones scudded and clicked together before the wind'.

Similar sound-effects are aimed at elsewhere. The other notorious weir in Hardy's fiction is the Ten Hatches in *The Mayor of Casterbridge*, Ch. 41, whose moorland water-music is strikingly orchestrated:

To the east of Casterbridge lay moors and meadows through which much
water flowed. The wanderer in this direction who should stand still for a

few moments on a quiet night, might hear *singular symphonies* from these waters, as from a lampless orchestra, all playing in their *sundry tones* from near and far parts of the moor. At a hole in a rotten weir they executed *a recitative*; where a tributary brook fell over a stone breastwork they *trilled cheerily*; under an arch they performed *a metallic cymballing*; and at Durnover Hole they *hissed*. The spot at which their *instrumentation* rose loudest was a place called Ten Hatches, whence during high springs there proceeded *a very fugue of sounds*.

It is instructive to note how the humble seed of the 'lantern' and the 'full chord of music' in *Desperate Remedies*, quoted above, has brought forth this rich verbal harvest of 'a lampless orchestra' playing 'a very fugue of sounds', and all the modulations in between. The language of music continues to sound throughout *Tess of the d'Urbervilles*, from the opening dancing at the club-walking to the humming of Stonehenge, on which 'the wind, playing upon the edifice, produced a booming tune, like the note of some gigantic one-stringed harp' (Ch. 58). Even the cows at Talbothays are drawn in, as the dairyfolk sing ballads to induce them to let down their milk.

We are not here directly concerned with Hardy's own verbal music, but with the linguistic resources which his love and knowledge of music had placed at his disposal. It is obvious from the story of his life, from his attendance at concerts and operas, and from his continuing interest in church music, that this was a life-long passion.* In his later years, his involvement with the Hardy Players revived an active interest in the incidental dances and music accompanying their performances. In his verbal art, music and dance were not only another fertile source of figurative language but added their own rhythms, sounds, and cadences both to his verse and to his prose:

'You be bound to dance at Christmas because 'tis the time o' year; you must dance at weddings because 'tis the time o' life . . .'
     (*The Return of the Native*, I, Ch. 3)

Perhaps it is, more than any other word, the recurring verb *throb* that reflects Hardy's verbal indebtedness to the 'language' of music, linking as it does the rhythm of music and dance to the beating of the

---

* Cp. Elna Sherman, 'Music in Thomas Hardy's Life and Work', *The Musical Quarterly* XXVI (1940), 419–45.

human heart, perhaps nowhere more succinctly expressed than in this allusion to Bathsheba:

> The swift music of her heart became hubbub now, and she throbbed to extremity.
> (*Far from the Madding Crowd*, Ch. 31)

The influence of painters and paintings on Hardy's language is inevitably less direct than that of music and dance, for the latter arts involve sounds and rhythmic patterns as words do, whereas painting is wholly visual, even where it leads on to 'abstract imaginings'. All arts, of course, have their proper names and their jargon, although the technical vocabulary of painting is the critic's rather than the artist's. Critics talk of pictorial 'composition', of 'movement' in pictures, of 'form' and 'plane' and 'line' and 'chromatic effect', sometimes relying for their vocabulary on other arts, sometimes letting the picture suggest its own. The painter may give to his picture a title but offers no helpful 'andante' or 'presto' to its interpreter. The closest Hardy comes to doing so is the subtitling of *Under the Greenwood Tree* as 'A Rural Painting of the Dutch School'.

Hardy trained himself to understand the great paintings of the past and to learn about schools and styles of painting by spending hours in the National Gallery during his early London years and by 'confining his attention to a single master on each visit, and forbidding his eyes to stray to any other' (*Life*, p. 52). The fruits of this early training were a facility for seeing landscapes and people and incidents with a painter's eye, often framed like a picture in isolation from their surroundings. Marty South is first seen thus, by Mr Percomb, as he looks out of the darkness at the girl through the uncurtained window of her cottage (*The Woodlanders*, Ch. 1), and the language deliberately focuses: 'The interior, as seen through the window, caused him to draw up with a terminative air and watch.' There is deliberate ambiguity in Hardy's use of *terminative*, which refers not solely to Percomb's having reached his destination and being about to conclude his errand, which is the sense the *Oxford English Dictionary* ascribes to this passage and which is similar to Hardy's usage elsewhere, for example in Chapter 10 of *A Pair of Blue Eyes*, but also to the boundary of the scene, the physical framing of the lighted window, which both attracts and restricts the spectator. Norman Page in his *Thomas Hardy* has drawn attention to this 'framing' device in Hardy's fiction as well as to Hardy's frequent reduction of human figures to tiny specks in a landscape, another of the more obviously 'pictorial' of his narrative devices. Other readers have noted these also.*

The language Hardy uses in such cases is often that of the art historian or critic:

> The picture thus presented to a spectator in the Town Hall was curious and striking. It was an illuminated miniature, framed in by the dark margin of the window, the keen-edged shadiness of which emphasised by contrast the softness of the objects enclosed.
> (*Desperate Remedies*, Ch. 1)

> This picture of to-day in its frame of four hundred years ago did not produce that marked contrast between ancient and modern which is implied by the contrast of date.
> (*Far from the Madding Crowd*, Ch. 22)

or in this 'optical poem':

> And as if to complete the picture of Grace personified and add the one thing wanting to the charm which bound him, the clouds, till that time thick in the sky, broke away from the upper heaven, and allowed the noonday sun to pour down through the lantern upon her, irradiating her with a warm light that was incarnadined by her pink doublet and hose, and reflected in upon her face.
> (*A Laodicean*, II, Ch. 7)

Miller Loveday in Chapter 17 of *The Trumpet-Major* sees 'two specks the size of caraway seeds on the far line of ridge where the sunlit white of the road met the blue of the sky'. In the story of 'The Honourable Laura', the last in *A Group of Noble Dames*, the narrator twice refers to the distant human figure in the landscape – 'a black spot on the distant white' – the second time on the road 'that margined the coast'. The pictorial diction is manifest. The same is true of descriptions in which reference is made to an actual picture, or detail of a picture, which Hardy recalls and expresses in quite specific terms. In many cases he uses this technique to portray a woman's face:

---

* For example, C.J.P. Beatty, 'Desperate Remedies 1871', *The Thomas Hardy Year Book* 2, 1971, pp. 29–38.

Those who remember Greuze's 'Head of a Girl', have an idea of Cytherea's look askance at the turning.
(*Desperate Remedies*, Ch. 4)

The picture in the National Gallery which Hardy has in mind here may not in fact have been by Greuze, as Alastair Smart has noted, but 'the sweet and somewhat arch expression' Hardy is trying to convey will be immediately suggested by the reference to Greuze to any reader who knows anything of the latter's work.

There are many similar examples, more insistently so in the earlier novels, and they range from a single incisive evocation, of, say, 'the angry crimson of a Danby sunset' (*Far from the Madding Crowd*, Ch. 20), to a composite portrait drawn from several sources, literary and pictorial:

Elfride had as her own the thoughtfulness which appears in the face of the Madonna della Sedia, without its rapture: the warmth and spirit of the type of woman's feature most common to the beauties – mortal and immortal – of Rubens, without their insistent fleshiness. The characteristic expression of the female faces of Correggio – that of the yearning human thoughts that lie too deep for tears – was hers sometimes, but seldom under ordinary conditions.
(*A Pair of Blue Eyes*, Ch. 1)

Landscapes are similarly visualized and described in terms of styles or specific paintings: leaves are 'varnished' by rain-drops as brightly as 'in the landscapes of Ruysdael and Hobbema' (*Far from the Madding Crowd*, Ch. 46) – landscapes, as Hardy says elsewhere of Hobbema and his school, 'which have been imprinted on the world's eye' (*A Changed Man*: 'The Romantic Adventures of a Milkmaid', IX). A single landscape picture of Hardy's may draw upon imagery from many sources, like the description of the Valley of the Great Dairies in Chapter 16 of *Tess of the d'Urbervilles*. In its interweaving of landscape and the mood of the beholder, and by its eclectic diction with its reminiscences of the 'three strands' of Hardy's life, this chapter illustrates well how the diction of painting is fused with that of music and architecture, of the Bible and Comtean philosophy, of modern science and the ancient world, of rustic life and 'military display'. Even the typical Hardy speck is there in the figure of Tess 'like a fly on a billiard-table of indefinite length, and of no more consequence to the surroundings than that fly'. The diction, as in many other landscape descriptions, evokes the 'feel' as well as the looks of pictures: '*a glossy smoothness*', 'a *carpeted* level', 'slopes *encrusted* with vivid green moss'. There is technical jargon: *distance*, *pattern*, *perspective*, *elevation*, *horizontal*, *flatness*, *outline*; and there is the recollection of painterly styles: 'The green lea was speckled as thickly with them as a canvas by Van Alsloot or Sallaert with burghers.' It is an instructive chapter for the reader seeking to explore the 'technical' resources of Hardy's English.

Norman Page explains many of Hardy's allusions to painters and paintings as springing 'from the attempt to compensate for the inadequacy of our language to describe colour'. This may be the case as far as it applies to all languages, but Hardy had an unusual gift for expressing in words shades of colour so subtle and so variegated that the frequent reference to painters, especially in the earlier novels, is more likely due to that urge to display his self-acquired knowledge which we have noted previously. Tony Tanner's remark that 'More than make us judge, Hardy makes us see', may be interpreted at its literal level to point to Hardy's talent for verbal pictorialism, of which colours are an essential ingredient. Paintings may have been an important source of his appreciation of colour, but it is Hardy the artist who makes them vivid in words. We shall return to this theme in the next chapter.

The autodidacticism underlying Hardy's many references to painters is visibly exemplified in the methodical listing and annotations in his *Schools of Painting Notebook*, the earliest of his extant notebooks, dated 12 May 1863, the period of Hardy's first sojourn in London which led in due course to his systematic study of the Old Masters in the National Gallery. Of especial interest in our present enquiry are some of Hardy's annotations, verbal anticipations of phrases and images in his subsequent writings: Correggio has the note 'great knowlge. of lights & shades', which prompts 'the greenish shades of Correggio's nudes' in *Desperate Remedies*, Ch. 12. The 'insistent fleshiness' of Rubens in *A Pair of Blue Eyes*, Ch. 1, is anticipated in the note 'Living life. voluptousness'; 'the landscapes of Ruysdael' in *Far from the Madding Crowd*, Ch. 46, by the stark entry in the notebook: 'Jacob Ruysdael – 1636. landscape'; and the reference to Ethelberta's dress which 'would have drawn approval from Reynolds' in *The Hand of Ethelberta*, Ch. 38, by the note 'correct taste' applied to Reynolds in the notebook. The 'uncommon light' noted against Rembrandt's name re-appears as 'a highlight portrait' in *A Laodicean*, I. Ch. 15. In *The Woodlanders*, Ch. 28, the association of the horse Darling with the Dutch painter Wouwerman recalls the note 'P. Wouwerman – horses introduced'.

The *Life* contains several references to Turner, the last of which, written in 1906, links him with Wagner: 'I prefer late Wagner, as I prefer late Turner' (*Life*, p. 329). This was relatively late Hardy, in 1906; a good deal later still, in 1921, Hardy pasted into his *Memoranda II Notebook* these words by Ernest Newman from *The Sunday Times* of 31 July 1921, underlined by himself: 'Wagner has survived *not because he theorised well, but because he wrote first-rate music*' – a comment applicable *mutatis mutandis* to Turner's painting and Hardy's own writing. Turner was recorded as 'much decried, mad, late-Turner' in a note in early 1887, the period of the final instalments of *The Woodlanders*, when, as the note also says, 'the "simple natural" is interesting no longer' (*Life*, p. 185). Landscapes are no longer simply descriptive – if indeed they ever were wholly such, even in *Desperate Remedies* – so that the metaphorical diction becomes more insistent. The other reference to Turner, made two years later, in January 1889, explains Hardy's reaction to him more fully: 'At the Old Masters, Royal Academy. Turner's water-colours: each is a landscape *plus* a man's soul . . . What he paints chiefly is *light as modified by objects*' (*Life*, p. 216). Samuel Hynes has discussed the implications of Turner's approach to landscape painting for Hardy's own art (*The Pattern of Hardy's Poetry*, pp. 109 ff.), in which the problem of translating such objective-subjective pictures into language remained paramount. Hardy's italics stress the significance he saw at the heart of Turner's technique which compelled him to experiement ceaselessly with light and shade and darkness and to seek constantly for appropriate words of tints and hues and colours, of which he 'invented' – in every sense – a considerable number. One such successful 'translation' in the manner suggested by Turner is Jude's vision of Christminster with its 'points of light' and its Turneresque ingredients of alternating 'transparency' and 'shining spots', its 'varied outlines that were faintly revealed' and then 'became veiled in mist'. The light and the objects interplay: 'The foreground of the scene had grown funereally dark, and near objects put on the hues and shapes of chimæras' (*Jude the Obscure*, I, Ch. 3). This is Turner verbalized, landscape *plus* a human soul, emblematic of the grotesque imaginings which lead ultimately to the funereal darkness of Jude's encounter with the real Christminster.

Some of this quality of Turner is already appreciated in Hardy's earlier fiction. In *A Pair of Blue Eyes*, Ch. 14, he describes the effect of gaslight on butchers' stalls, again linking the pictorial with a musical image and using appropriate technical diction like *glared*, *splotches*, *purl*, *pitch*, and other words:

> Gaslights glared from butchers' stalls, illuminating the lumps of flesh to splotches of orange and vermilion, like the wild colouring of Turner's later pictures, whilst the purl and babble of tongues of every pitch and mood was to this human wild-wood what the ripple of a brook is to the natural forest.

The 'human wild-wood' is again landscape *plus* a soul, while the 'splotches' of Turneresque colour recur in Hardy's next novel, *Far from the Madding Crowd*, Ch. 5, in a passage whose chromatic exuberance bids fair to equal Turner's. The impressionistic quality of Turner's 'Snowstorm and a Steamboat' which Hardy mentions in the reference to the Old Masters at the Royal Academy, is probably responsible, as Evelyn Hardy has suggested, for the 'strange birds from behind the North Pole' in a landscape of 'a disordered medley of grays', which likens the dreary exposed downs of Flintcomb-Ash to 'an achromatic chaos of things' (*Tess of the d'Urbervilles*, Ch. 43). Turner's influence on Hardy's art is thus clearly reflected in language which sought to express similar spiritual as well as objective realities.

Theatre and drama provided another source of inspiration for Hardy. He wrote some of his works in dramatic form, notably *The Dynasts*. He dramatized *Far from the Madding Crowd* into *The Mistress of the Farm*, as well as *Tess of the d'Urbervilles*, and *The Three Wayfarers*, based on 'The Three Strangers', one of the stories collected in *Wessex Tales*.* He acted as a young man, and, as an old man, assisted The Hardy Players, as the Dorchester Debating and Dramatic Society eventually came to be called, in various ways. Joan Grundy, in the chapter on 'Theatrical Arts' in *Hardy and the Sister Arts*, has suggested some of the ways in which Hardy's interest in drama and the theatre has found its way into his prose and verse. Inevitably, Hardy's English reveals elements deriving from the same source.

There are technical words suggesting theatrical arrangements, spectators' viewpoints, and dramatic method. The 'watchers' are carefully positioned in that nocturnal episode of multiple concealment in Ch. 19 of *Desperate Remedies*, for example; and there is a

---

* For details of these dramatizations, see Purdy, pp. 28–30, 77–80, and, more recently, D. Hawkins, *Hardy: Novelist and Poet*, Appendix 2.

careful grouping of *dramatis personae* at Troy's highly theatrical entrance, where he is described as 'wrapped up to his eyes' in the manner of a stage direction, before the fatal shooting in Chapter 53 of *Far from the Madding Crowd*. To look *into* a window tends to suggest pictorial diction to Hardy; to look *out of* a window tends to be expressed in theatrical terms: 'the scene from the Town Hall windows', for example, in *Desperate Remedies*, Ch. 1, or 'and then she regarded the scene outside the uncurtained window', in *Jude the Obscure*, VI, Ch. 2. Such 'scenes' are common; in the poems, too, Hardy uses the word with theatrical connotations:

> On this scene enter – winged, horned, and spined –
> A longlegs, a moth, and a dumbledore.
> ('An August Midnight')

Such words as *scene, stage,* even *stagery* (in the Preface to *The Dynasts*), *performance, spectator, actor, comedy, tragedy*, are integral to dramatic incidents in which Hardy's fiction and much of his verse abound. They are of course not unique to Hardy and represent probably the least original of his 'technical' words.

Hardy was no scientist, and his use of scientific and technological language is incidental rather than, like so many of his other resources, integral to his diction. He evinces some familiarity with chemical processes of a simple kind, as in this simile, still playing on 'scenes':

> Emotions will attach themselves to scenes that are simultaneous – however foreign in essence these scenes may be – as chemical waters will crystallize on twigs and wires.
> (*Desperate Remedies*, Ch. 1)

or this:

> The speakers, sundry phantoms of the gone,
> Had risen like filmy flames of phosphor dye.
> ('Spectres that Grieve')

He knows enough about telegraphy to use its technology in *A Laodicean*, to talk of "telegraphic signs of affection" in 'The Romantic Adventures of a Milkmaid', XVI, and to employ a term from it in this figure:

And the corners of his mouth twitched as the telegraph-needles of a
hundred little erotic messages from his heart to his brain.
(*The Hand of Ethelberta*, Ch. 40)

He refers to 'that breathing refrigerator, her uncle' in *A Laodicean*,
III, Ch. 11, very much in the manner of Dickens's 'He moves among
the company, a magnificent refrigerator' in *Bleak House*. And he is
fond of images involving clocks and similar mechanisms:

> These flesh-hinged mannikins Its hand upwinds
> To click-clack off Its preadjusted laws.
> (*The Dynasts*, Fore Scene)

> . . . a creature in airy clothing, translucent, like a balsam or sea-
> anemone, without shadows, and in movement as responsive as some
> highly lubricated, many-wired machine, which, if one presses a particular
> spring, flies open and reveals its works.
> (*The Well-Beloved*, II, Ch. 2)

There is Knight's critical reference to 'compensation pendulums' as a
motif for ear-rings in *A Pair of Blue Eyes*, Ch. 19, along with
'the governor of a steam-engine', part of the mechanism of such a
machine. There is the incongruous simile of the 'Nasmyth hammer'
coming down on Fancy Day's shoulder in *Under the Greenwood
Tree*, I, Ch. 8. And there are such passing allusions as to what 'the
scientific might say', to 'statisticians', to 'a neurologist' in 'The
Fiddler of the Reels', and to 'a figure on a lantern-slide' in what the
Spirit Ironic calls 'your phantasmagoric show' (*The Dynasts*, I. iv. 5).
There are references to machinery of various sorts, both direct and
figurative, as to the 'agricultural piano' that has arrived in Casterbridge and to the 'portable repository of force' at Flintcomb-Ash
Farm, or to the ancient maltster's movement 'being as the turning of a
rusty crane' in *Far from the Madding Crowd*, Ch. 8. The arrival of a
fashionable new dance is hailed thus:

> A new motive power had been introduced into the world of poesy – the
> polka, as a counter-poise to the new motive power that had been intro-
> duced into the world of prose – steam.
> (*A Changed Man*: 'The Romantic Adventures of a Milkmaid', V)

There are jottings in Hardy's notebooks revealing brief encounters
with the natural and physical sciences which reverberate in his

works. His tendency to see living things as through a microscope, for example, is well known and has produced some memorable instances, of which probably the best-known is the view of the peoples of Europe, in the Fore Scene of *The Dynasts*, as 'writhing, crawling, heaving, and vibrating' creatures which

gyrate like *animalcula*
In tepid pools.

The same process finds 'independent worlds of *ephemerons*' in a muddy spot on Egdon Heath (*The Return of the Native*, IV, Ch. 5), and one may well wonder whether this typical Hardyan point of view received at least some of its impetus from encounters like this, recorded in his *Literary Notes*:

> *Alive* According to Professor Ehrenberg, one of the highest authorities on microscopic science. Berlin stands upon a stratum composed entirely of living infusoria.
> Echo.

'The Deaf Dr. Kitto', mentioned in Herbert Spencer's *Principles of Biology* as having developed an unusual sensitiveness to vibrations 'as by ears', appears in another note in Hardy's *Literary Notes*, and duly re-appears in *The Return of the Native* II, Ch. 3. What Robert Gittings, referring to Hardy's notes, has called his 'raw material', proved unceasingly useful in the verbal manufactory of his writings.

Not all his technical knowledge, however, came to Hardy from the books or from the journals so carefully condensed, like an early *Reader's Digest*, in his notebooks. He observed the natural world around him from his childhood on and noticed such things as birds and moths and hedgehogs, and the leaves in May 'delicate-filmed as new-spun silk', as he says in 'Afterwards'. He knew how animals anticipated a thunderstorm, and observed how toads moved 'humbly', and he recognized the ticking sound of the love-making of the grasshopper. His knowledge was neither methodically acquired nor scientific, and he was more at home with the popular names of plants than with their botanical ones. It is part of that informal, yet informed, mastery of the rustic life and its pursuits which is at the heart of most of his novels, and which brought with it a plentiful vocabulary of agricultural and horticultural terms, 'dictionary words' of a more homely sort than those looked at so far.

There are plants like *horehound* and *sengreen* and *boy's-love* and *withwind*, and entire catalogues – in the manner so dear to Hardy – of flowers, both familiar, such as those Troy planted on Fanny's grave:

> There were bundles of snowdrop, hyacinth and crocus bulbs, violets and double daisies, which were to bloom in early spring, and of carnations, pinks, picotees, lilies of the valley, forget-me-not, summer's farewell, meadow-saffron and others, for the later seasons of the year.
> (*Far from the Madding Crowd*, Ch. 45)

– and less familiar, like those of the Weatherbury pastures in early June:

> Flossy catkins of the later kinds, fern-sprouts like bishops' croziers, the square-headed moschatel, the odd cuckoo-pint, – like an apoplectic saint in a niche of malachite, – snow-white ladies'-smocks, the toothwort, approximating to human flesh, the enchanter's night-shade, and the black-petaled doleful-bells.
> (*Ibid.*, Ch. 22)

This description of 'the vegetable world in and about Weatherbury at this teeming time' anticipates that of the garden at Talbothays 'damp and rank with juicy grass' in *Tess of the d'Urbervilles*, Ch. 19; but in the latter Hardy creates a superbly sensuous scene emblematic of the burgeoning love between Tess and Clare without mentioning a single plant by name: the evocation of 'blooth' and colour and tactile sensations is achieved by subtler means.

There are other flowers: convolvulus flowers looping the heroine's dress in *The Hand of Ethelberta*, Ch. 4; roses 'from the Maiden's Blush, through all varieties of the Provence down to the Crimson Tuscany' to do justice to Bathsheba's blush in Chapter 3 of *Far from the Madding Crowd*. Roses, perennial as poetic symbols, also appear along with other flowers in Hardy's verse. 'The Spell of the Rose', for example, is not the finest, yet it is a moving poem in *Poems of 1912–13*, where the plant is, traditionally, 'queen of trees'. More imaginative than this or the 'pink primrose' which fails to flourish alongside 'of pansies, pinks, and hollyhocks' in 'The Unplanted Primrose', is the blackbird's 'crocus-coloured bill' in 'I Watched a Blackbird', and the re-appearance of the *picotee* as a term of endearment in 'A Sunday Morning Tragedy' twenty years after the heroine's 'pink-cheeked' sister had been thus called in *The Hand of Ethelberta*.

Hardy clearly knew the names of many flowers, their colours, their aroma, and their values as symbols. He knew his way around the woodlands, too, and it requires no pedantic listing here to remind ourselves of Hardy's lifelong response to his arboreal environment, of his anthropomorphic response to the growth and decay of trees, their ceaseless motion, and their varied harmonies. As early as *Desperate Remedies* the link is established, as Cytherea 'looked at all the people as they stood and sang, waving backwards and forwards like a forest of pines swayed by a gentle breeze' (Ch. 12). Thenceforth trees furnish Hardy with inexhaustible imagery, its diction drawing on their every aspect: 'like a bowed sapling'; 'unyielding twigs'; 'a steady stertorous breathing from the fir-trees'; 'crash like trees at felling-time'; 'beech leaves, that yellow the noon-time'; 'the yew-tree arms, glued hard to the stiff stark air'; 'pollard willows, their twigs just bared'. *The Woodlanders* in particular accords to trees a life of their own, from its opening paragraph's mention of 'their lower limbs stretching in level repose over the road, as though reclining on the insubstantial air' to Marty South's concluding solemn affirmation, 'Whenever I plant the young larches I'll think that none can plant as you planted'. We shall return to this arboreal language in Chapter Six.

Trees are part of the economy of Hardy's Wessex, forest trees as well as fruit trees, and among the latter apple-trees in particular. Some of the names of apples Hardy mentions are undoubtedly 'dictionary words' to urban readers, although some of them, like Farmer Springrove's *griffins*, fail to qualify for such status in even major dictionaries. There are varieties like *quarrenden* and *ribstones*; there are those specially selected to produce certain qualities in cider:

> *Horner* and *Cleeves* apple for the body, a few *Tom-Putts* for colour, and just a dash of *Old Five-corners* for sparkle.
> (*The Trumpet-Major*, Ch. 16)

Grace Melbury's educated loss of touch with country ways is succinctly illustrated by the inability she has developed to distinguish between *bitter-sweets* and *John-apple trees* (*The Woodlanders*, Ch. 6). Knowledge of such things is inbred in his rural characters, as it was in Hardy himself: to lose it is to abandon one's birthright. Not so, of course, the rustics in *Far from the Madding Crowd*, who not only knew their apples – *costard*, *biffin*, and the rest – but invented new ones:

'Cainy's grandfather was a very clever man', said Matthew Moon. 'Invented a' apple-tree out of his own head, which is called by his name to this day – *the Early Ball*. You know 'em, Jan? A *Quarrenden* grafted on a *Tom Putt*, and a *Rathe-ripe* upon top o' that again.'
　(*Far from the Madding Crowd*, Ch. 33)

But Grace's knowledge returns, we are led to believe, by Chapter 25 of *The Woodlanders* when, looking out upon the Chattertonian 'scene' at large and Giles's mobile cider-press in the yard below her, 'she saw specimens of mixed dates, including the mellow countenances of *streaked-jacks*, *codlins*, *costards*, *stubbards*, *ratheripes*, and other well-known friends of her ravenous youth'. The diction of the opening paragraphs of this chapter combines the technical language of cider-making, including this list of apple varieties and such phrases as 'wringing down the pomace', with echoes of Keatsian sensuousness to evoke the autumn season of a part of Wessex which 'was a debatable land neither orchard nor sylvan exclusively'. Hardy effectively uses words and phrases suggestive of mellow fruitfulness: there are 'gardens and orchards now bossed, nay encrusted, with scarlet and gold fruit'; 'sweet juice gushed forth into tubs and pails'; 'the blue stagnant air of autumn which hung over everything was heavy with a sweet cidery smell'. There are verbs like *bursting*, *sticking*, and *quivering*; adjectives like *prolific* and *abundant*; and substantives like *superfluity* and *windfalls* and *harvest*. The scene not only draws forth a sigh from Grace, it acts as symbol of her relationship with Giles: on the one hand, the wall and window, like her recent marriage to Fitzpiers, divide them; on the other hand, the rural scene with its activities and its reminders of 'her ravenous youth' links them as indissolubly as her nuptial vow ties her to Fitzpiers. In this scene we are not far from the garden at Talbothays where 'sticky blights which, though snow-white on the apple-tree trunks, made madder stains' on Tess's skin. It is in such passages that Hardy's language, drawing upon his countryside, comes most fully into its own.

　Nor are its resources yet exhausted. There are images of apples, both comic in import and tragic: to speak of Maryann Money, the charwoman in *Far from the Madding Crowd*, Ch. 9, 'was to raise the image of *a dried Normandy pippin*', suggesting rotundity as readily as faded yellow colouring; and for Tess the metaphor of stars as worlds seen 'like the *apples on our stubbard tree*' was as natural as the elaboration – 'most of them splendid and sound – a few blighted' –

was fraught with sadness, for our star, as she tells Abraham, is 'a blighted one' (*Tess of the d'Urbervilles*, I, Ch. 4).

It is in such diverse ways that Hardy uses the language of the land, of its trees and flowers, plants and fruits, implements and labour, so succintly summed up by two of her women in answer to Bathsheba's question 'What have you been doing?':

'Tending thrashing-machine, and wimbling haybonds, and saying "Hoosh!" to the cocks and hens when they go upon your seeds, and planting Early Flourballs and Thompson's Wonderfuls with a dibble.' (*Far from the Madding Crowd*, Ch. 10)

While these wield their *dibble* to plant potatoes, Gabriel wields his *trochar*, Bob Loveday opens the *bolter*, and Marty South makes *spars* with her *bill-hook*. Not content with introducing Tess to Mrs d'Urberville's 'community of fowls' in Chapter 9 of *Tess of the d'Urbervilles*, Hardy reverts to his old habit of 'enumeratio': 'Hamburghs, Bantams, Cochins, Brahmas, Dorkings', just as he had done with breeds of sheep at Greenhill Fair in Chapter 50 of *Far from the Madding Crowd*. This is a lengthy catalogue, admittedly enlivened by descriptive and appraisive comments indicative of Hardy's familiarity with the breeds of sheep mentioned, but its insertion into a vivid account of these 'bleating, panting, and weary thousands' being guided into their pens is yet another instance of Hardy's dropping his morsels of learning and technical knowledge, howsoever acquired, into his narrative, in Richard H. Taylor's apt phrase 'like raisins into a bun'. Let the reader judge for himself or herself:

Men were shouting, dogs were barking, with greatest animation, but the thronging travellers in so long a journey had grown nearly indifferent to such terrors, though they still bleated piteously at the unwontedness of their experiences, a tall shepherd rising here and there in the midst of them, like a gigantic idol amid a crowd of prostrate devotees.

The great mass of sheep in the fair consisted of South Downs and the old Wessex horned breeds; to the latter class Bathsheba's and Farmer Boldwood's mainly belonged. These filed in about nine o'clock, their vermiculated horns lopping gracefully on each side of their cheeks in geometrically perfect spirals, a small pink and white ear nestling under each horn. Before and behind came other varieties, perfect leopards as to the full rich substance of their coats, and only lacking the spots. There were also a few of the Oxfordshire breed, whose wool was beginning to curl like a child's flaxen hair, though surpassed in this respect by the effeminate Leicesters, which were in turn less curly than the Cotswolds. But the most picturesque by far was a small flock of Exmoors which chanced to be there this year. Their pied faces and legs, dark and heavy horns, tresses of wool hanging round their swarthy foreheads, quite relieved the monotony of the flocks in that quarter.

All these bleating, panting, and weary thousands had entered and were penned before the morning had far advanced, the dog belonging to each flock being tied to the corner of the pen containing it. Alleys for pedestrians intersected the pens, which soon became crowded with buyers and sellers from far and near.

There is, throughout Hardy's writings, a tension between this enumerative display of technicalities and the imaginative transformation of some technical detail into the stuff of poetry, not only in verse. The latter does not necessarily exclude the former. The following description of Thomasin, now married to Wildeve, on a visit to Mrs Yeobright, breathes the girl's soul into what might else have been merely an ornithological catalogue:

The oblique band of sunlight which followed her through the door became the young wife well. It illuminated her as her presence illuminated the heath. In her movements, in her gaze, she reminded the beholder of the feathered creatures who lived around her home. All similes and allegories concerning her began and ended with birds. There was as much variety in her motions as in their flight. When she was musing she was a kestrel, which hangs in the air by an invisible motion of its wings. When she was in a high wind her light body was blown against trees and banks like a heron's. When she was frightened she darted noiselessly like a kingfisher. When she was serene she skimmed like a swallow, and that is how she was moving now.

(*The Return of the Native*, III, Ch. 6)

Plant and bird are combined later in the same novel, VI, Ch. 1, in the image of a kind of love that 'would be a plant of slow and laboured growth, and in the end only small and sickly, like an autumn-hatched bird'. These are not 'dictionary words', of course, but they imply insight of a kindred sort, as does the description of Uncle Benjy's corpse, 'dry and fleshless as that of a dead heron found on a moor in January' (*The Trumpet-Major*, Ch. 40).

The 'dictionary words', properly so called, involve yet other branches of knowledge and pursuits. *The Trumpet-Major Notebook*, for example, contains numerous technicalities, painstakingly garnered, which Hardy used in the novel as well as, much later, in *The Dynasts*. Even an occasional early nineteenth-century idiom finds its way into these pages, as the editor of the *Notebook*, Richard H. Taylor, has observed; like this entry from the *Morning Chronicle of* 11 October 1805: 'Oath of the period "Damn my wig" ', which duly appears as 'Dash my wig' in the mouth of Festus Derriman half a dozen times in *The Trumpet-Major*. There are details of dress too in this novel accordant with the fashions of the Napoléonic age, both military and civilian, including ladies' costumes such as that described in Chapter 25: 'She was fashionably dressed in a green spencer, with "Mameluke" sleeves, and wore a velvet Spanish hat and feather.' There is reference to pheasant's and ostrich feathers on page 165 of the *Notebook*, and there are sketches accompanying some of the notes, all testifying to Hardy's methodical homework.

Military language, words of command, the names of weapons, of military installations, and of battles, find their way into direct narrative or imagery, culminating in the vast panorama of *The Dynasts*. A dinner at the King's Arms is 'Henchard's Austerlitz', Dare's forehead is 'vertical as the face of a bastion' while Ethelberta's neck is 'firm as a fort'. Sergeant Troy's sword-play in *Far from the Madding Crowd*, Ch. 28, displays close acquaintance with this particular sport, with its 'cuts' and 'guards' and 'thrusts', and the use of the technical fencing term *passados*, apropos of Troy in Chapter 25, suggests the same. And there are other sports and games and rural pastimes with their appropriate diction in Hardy's writings, like the game of 'cross-dadder' or the reference to the 'Muzio gambit' in chess, although none can equal the 'fascination' of Chapter 8 of the book of that name (III) in *The Return of the Native*, where Venn and Wildeve play at dice by the light of glow-worms on Egdon, watched by staring heath-croppers. Their gambling table was a 'little flat stone, which to them was an arena vast and important as a battle-field', and upon this they cast their dice, scoring now 'a raffle of aces', now 'a triplet of sixes', and clinching Venn's success with a 'blank is less than one' of the split die.

It would be tedious to prolong this catalogue of the sources upon which Hardy drew for what I have loosely called 'dictionary words'. All 'three strands' are here represented, and both Hardy's habit of conscientious note-taking and his practice of referring to his notes throughout his writing career help to account for the important 'technical' element in his diction. There remains, however, one category of 'genuine' dictionary words yet to be considered: words and idioms culled from foreign languages, other than the direct quotations from the classical tongues noted earlier.

Principal among Hardy's foreign words and phrases are those which he remembered from his early training in Latin and from his French classes in London while he was working for Blomfield. I have counted over a hundred from French and over fifty from Latin, and to these may be added at least another twenty from Italian, German, and Spanish. Altogether, Hardy introduced around two hundred non-English words and phrases into his writing, and for the most part these are made prominent in the text by being italicized. The greatest numbers occur in *The Mayor of Casterbridge*, *A Laodicean*, *A Pair of Blue Eyes*, and *The Woodlanders*; the smallest numbers in *Under the Greenwood Tree*, *The Return of the Native*, and *The Trumpet-Major*. Foreign words and phrases are uncommon in the poems and, surprisingly so, in *The Dynasts*. In these Hardy tended to create his own diction into which non-English words or such originally foreign archaisms as the poetic *sans* 'without' (as in 'sans a single shot' in *The Dynasts*) are easily absorbed. Foreign words may creep into a poem unannounced, as it were, perhaps for rhyme:

> The formal faced *cohue*
> Will then no more upbraid
> With smiting smiles and whisperings two . . .
>     ('The Conformers')

where the italics are not Hardy's; or to evoke deliberately foreign associations:

> By many a *Fiord*, and *Strom*, and *Fleuve*
> Have I since wandered . . .
>     ('The Tree')

where again Hardy does not italicize. Equally inconspicuous is the unitalicized use of the French form *aurore* in 'A Woman's Trust'.

There is an inevitable air of self-consciousness about many of Hardy's italicized foreign words and phrases, similar to those other displays of erudition which we have noted – the classical allusions, the painterly metaphors, all the 'raisins in the bun'. Hardy's characters rarely make use of them, but when they do there is often an impression of affectation. Cytherea Graye is talking informally to her brother about Springrove, so that the phrase 'His *tout ensemble* is striking?' sounds artificial (*Desperate Remedies*, Ch. 2). So does de Stancy's 'You carry on your work at the castle *con amore*, no doubt?' to Somerset in *A Laodicean*, V, 6, although this is spoken in a scene stiff with formality and therefore carries perhaps a little more conviction. Lucetta writing to Henchard (*The Mayor of Casterbridge*, Ch. 22) casually drops a couple of French expressions into her letter: *mon ami*, she calls him, and then talks of her *étourderie*, presumably expecting Henchard to understand her meaning. Fitzpiers is more likely to be understood by Mrs Charmond when he talks of his *trouvaille* (*The Woodlanders*, Ch. 26), but again the use of the foreign word suggests artifice.

Hardy's sparing use of this form of linguistic side-stepping in dialogue suggests that he did not intend to use it as a means of characterization. He was less circumspect, however, in narrative, where foreign expressions extrude self-consciously, in many cases at the expense of perfectly good English alternatives. A few examples should suffice to illustrate the point. All of them are italicized by Hardy:

'Dear me – very awkward!' said Stephen, rather *en l'air*.
(*A Pair of Blue Eyes*, Ch. 5)

Even her ambiguities and *espièglerie* were but media of the same manifestation.
(*Ibid.*, Ch. 30)

She was thus convinced that the reddleman was a mere *pis aller* in Mrs Yeobright's mind.
(*The Return of the Native*, II, Ch. 7)

Hardy uses the same phrase when he refers rather ponderously to Mixen Lane as 'the *pis aller* of Casterbridge domiciliation' in *The Mayor of Casterbridge*, Ch. 26.

Whatever mysterious merit might attach to family antiquity, it was one which her adaptable, wandering, *weltbürgerliche* nature had grown tired of caring about.
(*The Woodlanders*, Ch. 8)

Another characteristic nineteenth-century German word is used of Alec d'Urberville when his evangelical phase had passed and his 'original *Weltlust* had come back' (*Tess of the d'Urbervilles*, Ch. 47).

Latin words are scattered as widely, albeit not as numerously, as French ones. Nor do they protrude quite so patently. Whereas most French words embedded in the English language were adopted in the Middle Ages, so that modern French words like *espièglerie* have a distinctly foreign appearance, both Renaissance and modern scientific Latin adoptions fit less awkwardly into English sentences. Thus Phillotson can mount 'beside his box of books and other *impedimenta*' (*Jude the Obscure*, I, Ch. 1, Hardy's italics) and cause little semantic difficulty even for a reader not trained in Latin. Indeed, but for the italics the word would hardly be recognized as foreign. This is true of many of Hardy's Latinisms, like *genius loci*, *primum mobile*, 'an *ex-cathedrâ* air', even the *aurora militaris* created by Troy's sword-play in *Far from the Madding Crowd*, Ch. 28.

Certain foreign words recur in a number of places in Hardy's work, suggesting a predilection for them: *fiasco*, for example, and *coup d'oeil*, *sang-froid*, *tête-à-tête*, *pari passu*; others recall his reading: '*non lucendo* principles', or *coup-de-Jarnac*, or the Italian and Spanish proverbs paraded by Dare in *A Laodicean*. Yet other words of foreign origin, like *hauteur*, were sufficiently part of English speech in the nineteenth century not to be italicized by Hardy. In some cases, however, he seemed unsure. Thus he usually italicizes *tête-à-tête*: for example in *The Trumpet-Major*, Ch. 5; in *The Woodlanders*, Ch. 5; in *The Well-Beloved*, III, Ch. 4; but not in *The Well-Beloved*, II, Ch. 1. There does not seem to be any obvious reason for such discrepancies; they are probably fortuitous.

Finally, it is worth noting that a number of words which are fully assimilated into contemporary twentieth-century English, were still felt by Hardy to be sufficiently exotic to require italicizing. Such words include *annexe*, *aplomb*, *début*, *naïveté*, *nonchalance*, *penchant*, *rôle*, and *vivâ voce*. The accents have mostly disappeared in contemporary English along with the italics. But even in the nineteenth century, attitudes to such words varied considerably. Thus, for example, *annexe*, *naïveté*, and *nonchalance* were not usually italicized, and *début* and *rôle* sometimes were, sometimes not. On the other hand, *vivâ voce*, with or without accent, was usually italicized. Hardy's usage throughout means either that he was playing safe in according to such words their foreign status, or that he was deliberately displaying them as exotica in his vocabulary. Either is possible, the latter is the more likely.

This conclusion is in keeping with the tenor of the present chapter. In the use of what I have called his 'dictionary words', Hardy the autodidact is constantly looking over the shoulder of Hardy the artist. The results are by no means uniformly or even generally displeasing. We can sympathize all the more readily with some of Paula Power's idiosyncrasies, if we recall her *'prédilection d'artiste* for ancestors . . . like the de Stancys' (*A Laodicean*, I, Ch. 14). We relish the biblical mouthfuls uttered by rustic characters like Joseph Poorgrass, just as we rejoice in numerous apt echoes of Shakespeare or Virgil or Shelley. On the other hand, we may find some of Hardy's displays tiresome, whether of painters or of potatoes, and worse still, there are what look like lapses of tact where a 'borrowed' word, as it were, seems out of place. Would such a word as *niaiseries* really occur to Tess in a moment of irritability, or is Hardy here simply playing about with language, unwilling to heed a dissonance which his ear was generally so sensitively attuned to detect? Consider the passage:

> She went on peeling the lords and ladies till Clare, regarding for a moment the wave-like curl of her lashes as they drooped with her bent gaze on her soft cheek, lingeringly went away. When he was gone she stood awhile, thoughtfully peeling the last bud; and then, awakening from her reverie, flung it and all the crowd of floral nobility impatiently on the ground, in an ebullition of displeasure with herself for her *niaiseries*, and with a quickening warmth in her heart of hearts.
> (*Tess of the d'Urbervilles*, Ch. 19)

In such a passage Hardy's English is reaching for the heights. The balance of short emotive phrases – 'her bent gaze', 'her soft cheek' – with the Romance sonority of 'an ebullition of displeasure' provides a satisfying equilibrium, as does the contrast between the pensive adverbs 'lingeringly' and 'thoughtfully' and the explosive 'impatiently'. There is the poeticism of the 'floral nobility' reminiscent of Augustan periphrasis, balanced by the Wordsworthian 'quickening warmth in her heart of hearts'. And there is the inconspicuous homely botany of 'lords and ladies'. The only word which seems oddly out of place is *niaiseries*. None of the others is so incongruously intrusive, for *reverie* has been familiar since Chaucer used it, and *ebullition* is a good Renaissance word. Admittedly, *niaiseries* is found in the seventeenth century according to the *Oxford English Dictionary*, but it remains alien. Hardy may have picked it up with a few other exotic words in *Fraser's Magazine*, but the reader may well wonder whether the discord in such a passage as the above escaped Hardy's usually sensitive ear, or whether he courted it deliberately.

# CHAPTER V

# Acres of Words

𝕞𝕞𝕞𝕞𝕞𝕞

THE phrase is Henchard's; but it may be applied to Hardy's own verbal fecundity even more aptly than to Lucetta's epistolary effusions in *The Mayor of Casterbridge*. In this chapter I shall consider Hardy's lexical inventiveness, both in its current sense of creating new words and in its older sense of finding earlier words and usages and endowing them with new life. Hardy's linguistic resourcefulness, like Shakespeare's, knew no bounds, but he was clearly disturbed by critical condemnation of neologisms and archaic or dialectal usages. Robert Graves's anecdote in Chapter 28 of *Goodbye to All That* is worth recalling, although Robert Gittings in *The Older Hardy* casts doubt upon the reliability of the 'record' which Graves claims to have kept of his talk with Hardy at Max Gate a few years before the latter's death:

> He regarded professional critics as parasites, no less noxious than autograph-hunters, wished the world rid of them, and also regretted having listened to them as a young man; on their advice he had cut out from his early poems dialect-words which possessed no ordinary English equivalents. And still the critics were plaguing him. One of them complained of a line: 'his shape smalled in the distance'. Now, what in the world else could he have written? Hardy then laughed a little. Once or twice recently he had looked up a word in the dictionary for fear of being again accused of coining, and found it there right enough – only to read on and discover that the sole authority quoted was himself in a half-forgotten novel!

The story may be apocryphal, but its substance is true enough. There are, according to Yoshinoshin Goto, more than a thousand citations from Hardy in the *Oxford English Dictionary*, and probably more still in its supplements, of which a considerable proportion are his own coinages.

Some of these may appear exotic, but it needs to be stressed that

Hardy followed traditional patterns of English word-formation, active in the language since Anglo-Saxon times. These include the transference of words from one grammatical category to another, as in the example 'smalled' in Graves's story, although in this instance the critic should have known better: 'small' as a verb, both transitive and intransitive, is recorded in the language well before Hardy used it. There are frequent examples in Hardy's work of coinages using prefixes and suffixes, some of them, like *un-*, extremely common, others, like *en-*, rather less so. And above all, because they are distinctive especially as metaphors and as descriptive epithets, there are Hardy's many compound words, composed of what in technical language are called free forms: elements which function in the language as separate words, to distinguish them from bound forms which, like affixes, do not function independently.

Hardy's compounds share with those of Gerard Manley Hopkins a strong affinity with those of Old English poetry in their metaphorical substance and their not uncommon internal alliteration. In Old English the poetic compound was the mainstay of figurative diction, and in Hardy's verse and occasionally in prose it often serves a similar function, also at times an ironic one, as when Picotee sees her sister 'as the chief figure of a glorious *pleasure-parliament* of both sexes' in *The Hand of Ethelberta*, Ch. 29. In using such compounds as *heart-heaves* or *soul-swoon*, *world-weaver* or *foam-fingered*, Hardy is drawing upon a tradition harking back to such Old English words as *heort-hogu* 'heart-care', or *woruld-wuldor* 'world-glory', or *fāmig-heals* 'foamy-necked'. The particular merit of such words is their ability to compress an often complex concept or image into a single word, dispensing with the need of syntactic expansion into phrases or even sentences. The economy of diction thus attained is particularly noticeable in Hardy's verse:

> And my remedy – what kind?
> *Wealth-wove* or *earth-hewn*?
> '*Earth-hewn*'.
> ('The Echo-Elf Answers')

But into his prose, too, Hardy introduces such compounds, and here they go some way towards counteracting his more expansive style with its occasional tendency towards complex sentences. In *Jude the Obscure* II, Ch. 2, Sue Bridehead 'looked right into his face with liquid, untranslatable eyes'; in the following chapter she becomes *liquid-eyed*. In Chapter 4 of Part III the 'contralto note of tragedy coming suddenly into her silvery voice' becomes an 'emotional *throat-note*' a couple of pages later. In *The Well-Beloved*, Pierston's restless emotional and social condition is succinctly summed up by the phrase 'without any *soul-anchorage*' (I, Ch. 9), an effective poetic image in the midst of Hardy's circumstantial prose. By letting Paula Power accede 'to the unstable throne of *queen-beauty*' (*A Laodicean*, VI, Ch. 3), Hardy was anticipating by forty years the American invention of the 'beauty-queen'. And, to give one more example, there is the graphic distinction drawn by Angel Clare, eulogizing Tess to his parents, between life lived as a poem and the dead words on the page:

> 'She's brim full of poetry – actualized poetry, if I may use the expression. She *lives* what *paper-poets* only write.'
> (*Tess of the d'Urbervilles*, Ch. 26)

*Paper-poets* is but one of many such telling coinages to be found in his prose.

But whether in verse or prose, the Hardy compound comes in various shapes. The second element can be noun, adjective, adverb, preposition, or verb, and the first, or modifying, element is similarly diversified, although verbal forms are not common and, where they do occur, as in *reporting-book*, they are generally verbal nouns. One use to which Hardy puts his lexical fecundity is to employ compounds in prosodic or syntactic functions. In his poem 'To Outer Nature', for example, he uses a five-line stanza of short lines in which compounds are conveniently accommodated, in some cases filling half the line, in two cases the entire line: '*Omen-scouting*' and '*Darkness-overtaken*'. The differing grammatical functions of the modifying elements become clear if we paraphrase the first by 'I was scouting for omens' and the second by 'You were overtaken by darkness'. B. Groom calls these, respectively, 'objective' and 'instrumental' compounds. There are also instances of compounds being suggested by rhyme. In his triolet 'Birds at Winter Nightfall' Hardy uses as rhymes for the thrice-recurring 'faster' both an original coinage *crumb-outcaster* and the etymologically restored compound *cotonea-aster*. Another poem, 'The Respectable Burgher', employs a single rhyme for its thirty-six lines beginning with 'declare' and ending with 'Voltaire'. Hardy uses four compounds to supplement the supply of rhymes available in the language, two of which bear his personal stamp, as it were: *furnace-flare* and *God-obeyer*.

Syntactically, a compound can be substituted for a longer phrase, thereby achieving that economy of diction already mentioned. In the following examples, not all the compounds are original coinages, but their adverbial functions are similar:

> In her days of prosperity Lady Constantine had often gone to the city of Bath, either frivolously, for shopping purposes, or *musico-religiously*, to attend choir festivals in the Abbey.
> (*Two on a Tower*, Ch. 17)

> The result of the rain had been to flood the lane *over-shoe* to a distance of some fifty yards.
> (*Tess of the d'Urbervilles*, Ch. 23)

In the same novel, Ch. 43, the snow lies *sole-deep* upon the floor; in *The Mayor of Casterbridge*, Ch. 26, Jopp is 'standing *hands-pocketed* at the street corner'; in *The Return of the Native*, I, Ch. 1, Hardy speaks of 'surroundings *oversadly* tinged'. The words *over-sad* and *over-shoe* are recorded in English in the seventeenth and sixteenth century respectively, but the latter, used as 'over-shoes' by Shakespeare and found in America, may have helped to inspire Hardy's coinage *sole-deep* in *Tess of the d'Urbervilles*.

Prosodic and syntactic considerations account, however, for only a small proportion of Hardy's numerous original or resuscitated compounds. Mostly, they are an indispensable linguistic tool for expressing his personal vision in appropriate diction. In the preface to his edition of Barnes's poems, published in 1908, Hardy refers to Barnes's compounds 'the *blue-hill'd* worold', 'the *wide-horn'd* cow', 'the *grey-topp'd* heights of Paladore', as a wholly warranted and congenial mode of achieving the older poet's 'closeness of phrase to his vision'. It was probably Barnes's example, familiar to Hardy from his early Dorchester days, that inspired his own frequent recourse to this traditional English mode of word-invention – again in both senses of this word. Hardy wrote to Coventry Patmore on 11 November 1886: 'I have lived too much within his [Barnes's] atmosphere to see his productions in their due perspective'; and in his poem about Barnes, 'The Collector Cleans His Picture', by the use of such Barnesian compounds as *easel-lumber, soon-reached* city, *artfeat, brushcraft,* and *grimefilms* – whether deliberately imitative or not – Hardy is exemplifying the older poet's influence. Throughout his verse Hardy persisted in the use of compounds from the earliest of *Wessex Poems* ('for a *breath-while*', 'my *life-deed*') to *The Dynasts* (*carcase-care*, *tedious-timed*, *roughish-mouthed*) and to his final collection, *Winter Words* (*self-glamourer*, *laugh-loud*). In his prose fiction, too, he frequently makes use of compounds, from *Desperate Remedies* (*brass-faced*, *many-membered*, *crazy-religious*) to *The Well-Beloved* ('a *ready-money* man', 'that *science-man*') and *Jude the Obscure* (*heart-hurt*, *strong-lunged*). In 'The Melancholy Hussar of the German Legion' (*Wessex Tales*), *home-woe* literally renders German *Heimweh*, a concept rendered by *home sorrow* in the poem 'Before Marching and After'.

By far the majority of Hardy's compounds are attributive, describing personal features, emotions, or states of mind; places, trees, and various objects; while his absorbing pre-occupation with Time engendered such words as 'our *breathing-time*', or 'a *breath-while*' or *tedious-timed*. Either or both components may be time words in such instances: 'a breath-while' occurs in several of Hardy's poems and may have suggested itself to him by the act of 'breathing' a horse, that is allowing a horse time to recover from exertion. In the story 'The Withered Arm' (*Wessex Tales*), Gertrude Lodge, traversing Egdon Heath, 'drew rein to breathe her bearer'. In the poems, the connotations range more widely: in the first of *Wessex Poems*, 'The Temporary the All' – a poem distinguished by much unconventional diction – 'a breath-while' means 'a short time', emphasizing the link between breathing and living. A similar effect is attained in 'The Graveyard of Dead Creeds' where the poet points an ironic contrast between the sepulchred dead and their sudden arousal 'like wakened winds that autumn summons up'. There is irony also in the use of 'for a breath-while' to suggest a breathing-space amid 'high carouse' in 'The Dead Quire'. A 'breath' for Hardy was more than a merely physiological phenomenon; it was a symbol of life, a measure of time, a mode of utterance as in Tess's exhausted *underbreath* (*Tess of the d'Urbervilles*, Ch. 48), a nineteenth-century usage Hardy may have remembered from Meredith or Swinburne.

Analogous to 'breath-while' are such words as *blight-time*, *bright-time*, *mirth-time*, *claytime*, *gnat and cobweb-time*, *song-time*, *pray-time*, *month-night*, *sun-sweep* and *time-rail*, all signifying time-spans endowed with more meaning that the mere clocking of passing minutes. Words like *yestereve*, *yestertide*, *yester-summer* were popular among Victorian poets, as in Swinburne's *yesterage*, but not so the substantive *yester*, as in Hardy's 'Yester's quick greenage' in

'At the Royal Academy'. As a prefix *yester-* had long been familiar in English. In the poem 'In a Eweleaze near Weatherbury', Hardy writes of *'never-napping* Time', contributing his own word to a long line of similar participial compounds in English letters. In 'A Broken Appointment', there is poignant emphasis on 'marching Time' drawing on until 'the *hope-hour* stroked its sum', leaving the *time-torn* man disappointed by the woman's non-appearance. With the 'time-torn' man of this moving poem we may compare the picture of the *rose-necked* maiden in 'The Maid of Keinton Mandeville' who is now an old woman *'Time-trenched* on cheek and brow'. The action of Time, or of 'Time-wraiths', as they are in 'To an Unborn Pauper Child', is mostly seen to be destructive, of life, of youth, of hopes, of buildings, eventually covering all 'with *years-deep* dust' ('Shut Out That Moon'). But the picture is not wholly gloomy: The 'family face' lives on, in 'Heredity', as

> The *years-heired* feature that can
> In curve and voice and eye
> Despise the human span
> Of durance – that is I;
> The eternal thing in man
> That heeds no call to die.

The polysyllabic 'years-heired feature' gains prosodic as well as semantic prominence in a stanza composed largely of monosyllables.

But there is usually some irony in Hardy's brighter reactions to Time: The *'long-sunned* day' in 'The Peasant's Confession' is no summer idyll as it might be in Tennyson, but the incongruous backdrop to continuous gunfire; and 'the *years'-long-binned* Madeira', evoking perhaps a more acceptable picture of *'years-deep* dust', turns out to be a ghostly vision in that 'filmy phantasy' of a poem, 'The Re-Enactment'.

The triple compound just cited recalls some of Browning's and Hopkins's longer coinages, like 'foolish-face-foremost' or 'a nine-hundred-years-old name', 'no-man-fathomed' or 'brown-as-dawning-skinned', but Hardy does not have many of these. One such is *new-brought-forth* in 'The Two Houses', another 'The *All-Earth-gladdening* Law / Of Peace' in 'A Christmas Ghost-Story', which could be Hopkins's but for the bitter irony with which it is imbued. In his prose we find such longer compounds occasionally in Hardy's more informal narrative manner, as in the reference to

Stephen Smith in Chapter 6 of *A Pair of Blue Eyes*, as 'not the man to care about *passages-at-love* with women beneath him', or in the description in *Far from the Madding Crowd*, Ch. 4, of Gabriel Oak's 'nicely adjusted' dress as 'between *fine-market-day and wet-Sunday* selection', which reproduces the tone of colloquial grammar, as does the phrase '*Sunday-clothes* folk' in *Desperate Remedies* (Sequel). The same novel uses the phrase 'a nice ghastly *hair-on-end* story' in dialogue (Ch. 5), the coachman speaking to Cytherea in a manner that combines informality and some dialect with somewhat un-expected displays of literary learning as well as familiarity with the Bible. These modes of speech are better suited to Joseph Poorgrass in *Far from the Madding Crowd*, who utters the happy phrase: to 'stand godfather to poor little *come-by-chance* children' (Ch. 8).

Hardy's real strength, however, lies in loading the rift of every descriptive compound with ore, embellishing, explanatory, defining, figurative, ironic. To this end he employs a variety of morphological means, combining different parts of speech with one another in order to exploit a wide range of semantic possibilities. It was probably Hardy's vision of the world as constantly 'unfolding', as the Spirit of the Years says in *The Dynasts*, III. vii. 9, which made him express himself so often in verbs, even to the point of coining or reviving verbs derived from nouns or adjectives, like 'turmoiled' or 'colding'. In the case of compounds this element of mutability is present in the many words constructed on a participial base, present or past. He speaks, for example, in *In Tenebris III*, of furbishing the soil into 'a *summer-seeming* order', a word suggesting both unreality and transience, appearance and seasonal change. There is implicit development, hence change, in music that is *battle-breathing* and *forward-footing* ('The Bridge of Lodi'); in 'eyewounds' that are *dream-endangering* ('Genoa and the Mediterranean'); in circumstances that are '*love-kindling, passion-begetting*' (*A Laodicean*, II, Ch. 6); in fancies that are *thick-coming* (*ibid.*, V, Ch. 13); in air that is *just-awakening* (*A Pair of Blue Eyes*, Ch. 7).

Where the base is a past participle, either historical or created by parasynthesis – Hardy's most common type of attributive compound – the connotations are of passivity, of change accomplished, of a fate determined. The sun is *God-curst* in 'Neutral Tones'; mankind is *ail-stricken* in 'Copying Architecture in an Old Minster'; Henchard has become a '*self-alienated* man' (*The Mayor of Casterbridge*, Ch. 45); the lovers in 'A Spot' are *transport-tossed*; feet in 'The Supplanter' are *travel-tarnished*. In 'Music in a Snowy Street' Hardy writes of '*love-satiate* things' and 'the *flake-laden* noon'.

Many such compounds describe emotions, states of mind, psychological upheavals, as Hardy probes his own soul in his poems or the souls of his characters in his fiction. The second stanza of 'In a Wood' begins with the lines:

> *Heart-halt* and *spirit-lame*,
> *City-opprest*,
> Unto this wood I came
> As to a nest . . .

where the three compound epithets illustrate both the cause of distress (the city), and the effect of oppression (the heart and the spirit are both halt, lame). These compounds are often memorably expressive: *passion-goaded*, *pleasure-caught*, *thought-worn*, or *life-shotten* in 'A Philosophical Fantasy', which has as its epigraph Walter Bagehot's words 'Milton . . . made God argue' and which makes Hardy's 'Causer' say:

> 'A universe to marshal,
> What god can give but partial
> eye to frail Earth – *life-shotten*
> Ere long, extinct, forgotten . . .'

where 'life-shotten' has not only the obvious connotations of being wounded and exhausted, but the dialectal ones of milk turning sour. Certain elements tend to recur in this group of epithets: *heart*, *life*, *mind*, *thought*, *nature*, *nerve*, *passion*, *soul*, *spirit*, sometimes as the bases of the compound, sometimes as modifiers: *small-hearted*, *heart-swollen*; *life-brief*; *absent-thoughted*; *middle-natured*; *elastic-nerved*; *passion-tossed*; *soul-subliming*, *whole-souled*, *fervent-souled*, *sanguine-souled*, *subtle-souled*; *spirit-torn*.

Other morphological variations occur: the first element may be an adverb, as in *drily-kind* or *subtly-jovial* or *soberly-sweet*; or a proper name, as in *Miranda-like*; or even an infinitive, as when Eustacia is berated by Wildeve with these words: 'One moment you are too tall, another moment you are too *do-nothing*' (*The Return of the Native*, I, Ch. 9). The second element is occasionally a noun, not used participially but attributively in the manner very familiar from contemporary English usage: 'A *one-part* man'; '*slow-coach* men'; 'in the *jolly-companion* way children want to like folks'. Or a compound may expand into a phrase: 'such *double and treble-barrelled* hearts'.

Hardy was less prolific in his attributive compounds relating to personal appearance or features. These formed part, often a minor part, of a much wider descriptive repertoire which exploited other linguistic resources, several of which we have glanced at in the two preceding chapters. It is worthy of note that in the 'Queen of Night' chapter (Ch. 7) of the first book of *The Return of the Native*, which is wholly devoted to a portrait of the heroine, Hardy uses hardly any descriptive compounds. We learn that Eustacia Vye is *full-limbed* and that one could fancy 'the colour of Eustacia's soul to be *flame-like*'. For the rest, Hardy's method is to expatiate upon Eustacia's attributes in his most eclectic manner, drawing upon history and literature, music and mythology for exemplars, as in his final sentence: 'In heaven she will probably sit between the Héloïses and the Cleopatras.' The portrait Hardy here paints of Eustacia is indeed, as Pinion writes in *A Hardy Companion*, 'out of all proportion to the young woman of the novel'.

He can be more incisive with personal appearance, as he is in descriptions of places, of animals, of objects, when concentrating his vision upon a single feature and matching this with an appropriate compound: the glazier in Chapter 8 of *The Mayor of Casterbridge* is a '*bucket-headed* man'; the constables in Chapter 39 of the same novel are *rusty-jointed*; Sue Bridehead is not only *liquid-eyed*, but, characteristically, *light-footed* (*Jude the Obscure*, II, Ch. 3), which is more subtly allusive than the overt mention of Artemis, Athena, and Hera in the portrayal of Eustacia. Some memorable epithets of this kind occur in the poems and *The Dynasts*: *languid-lipped*, *scoop-eyed*, *rotten-fleshed*. Occasionally, the economy and concentration achieved by an image-compound could hardly go further: 'Thence to us came she, *bosom-burning*' ('By Henstridge Cross at the Year's End').

Hardy's often magnificent evocation of place owes part of its success to the same ability to concentrate a pictorial impression into a poetic compound, whether in verse or prose. 'The *foam-fingered* sea' in 'The Old Gown', with its echoes reverberating through Swinburne back to Old English elegiac poetry, contrasts with the *rain-reek* of woodlands in the same poem. The Isle of Portland is *many-caverned* ('The Souls of the Slain') just as the lowland in the story 'The Withered Arm' (*Wessex Tales*) is *many-dairied*, and a galaxy is *many-mortaled* (*The Dynasts*, I. i. 6). A slope is *bent-bearded*, a valley is *copse-clothed*, a street is *history-haunted*, a sea-side town is *wave-washed*, a lawn is *dew-dashed*. Cornfields are *mire-bestrowed* in *The Dynasts*, III. vi. 8, whereas in the poem 'A Wet Night' 'my clothing clams me, *mire-bestarred*', a subtly ironic play on specks of mud replacing stars made invisible by *'rain-shafts* riddling me'. A *low-chimneyed* house or a *high-shouldered* arch are not particularly original descriptions, but they focus on essentials in appearance, just as Barnes does in his *'twelve-tunn'd* house' or his *'grey-wall'd* height o' the tow'r'.

And as Hardy would distinguish between *mire-bestrowed* and *mire-bestarred*, because the first directs one's vision downward and the other up, so he does by calling mosses *quaint-natured* halfway down a well (*The Return of the Native*, III, Ch. 3), and *delicate-patterned* in the open woodlands (*The Woodlanders*, Ch. 19). In 'To Outer Nature' two successive compounds similarly imply contrasting attitudes: Hardy is describing fading light, so that *glow-forsaken* implies disappearance, evanescence, and loss; to be immediately followed by a word that is both synonym and antonym, *Darkness-overtaken*, with its dual connotations of conquest and defeat, victor and victim.

Such tension may occur in the same word, as when Hardy uses the old compound *dead-alive*, which has been recorded in English since the Renaissance; or the compound *sorry-smiling* in 'The History of the Hardcomes' (*Life's Little Ironies*) which succinctly sums up the ambivalent circumstances into which their impulsive bride-swapping had precipitated the two Hardcome cousins.

An important link with the tradition of poetic compounds harking back to Old English is the tendency to compose them of words that are bound by alliteration, of which *sorry-smiling* is an instance, although the two parts here pull in different semantic directions.* More commonly, alliteration is an effective means of underwriting sense by sound:

It was snowing with a *fine-flaked* desultoriness.
   (*The Woodlanders*, Ch. 17)

'She won't open the door, sir, not to nobody at all!' said the chambermaid with *wonder-waiting* eyes.
   (*Desperate Remedies*, Ch. 13)

---

* For a list of Hardy's alliterating compounds in his poems, see E.C. Hickson's list G.

A *soberly-sweet* expression sat on her face.
   (*Two on a Tower*, Ch. 12)

When the *love-led* man had ceased from his labours Bathsheba came and looked him in the face.
   (*Far from the Madding Crowd*, Ch. 21)

> Against the horizon's *dim-discernèd* wheel
>    A form rose.
> ('A Meeting with Despair')

> And corpses wore his *glory-gleam*.
> ('The Sick Battle-God')

Sometimes Hardy fits an alliterating compound into a larger alliterative pattern, even more strongly reminiscent, as Hopkins so often is, of early English alliterative poetry:

> *S*o, *s*canning my *s*ire-*s*own tree.
>    ('The Pedigree')

> *C*ruelly *c*rossed by *m*alversations,
>       *M*arring *m*other-*m*inistry
> To your *m*ultitudes.
>    ('Genitrix Laesa')

> These *w*elfare-*w*asting *w*ars.
>    (*The Dynasts*, II. i. 1)

   In order to appreciate the full force and particular flavour of Hardy's compounds, one needs of course to see, and even more to hear them, as it were, in action. The first of Hardy's 'Poems of Pilgrimage' in *Poems of the Past and the Present* is not one of his best or best-known poems, but its diction is 'classic Hardy' and it will be for most readers devoid of the associations that cling to better-known poems like 'The Oxen', 'The Darkling Thrush', or those in *Poems of 1912–13*. I shall here quote it in full.

   'Genoa and the Mediterranean' describes a visit to Italy in March 1887, but, as Hardy informs us in the *Life* (p. 187), it was written 'a long time after'. Apart from its compound nouns and participial compounds there are other characteristic Hardy usages, some of which have yet to be discussed: compounds using prefixes as in *up-browed*; the adverbial compound *thereacross*; the use of a rare noun, *Dowd*, compared with the more familiar adjective *dowdy*, and the Miltonic *marrings*, a word of venerable Old English ancestry; the use of an 'unpoetical' technical word in *ochreous*, and the Latinism *Superba* derived from Baedeker's *Italy*.

O epic-famed, god-haunted Central Sea,
Heave careless of the deep wrong done to thee
When from Torino's track I saw thy face first flash on me.

And multimarbled Genova the Proud,
Gleam all unconscious how, wide-lipped, up-browed,
I first beheld thee clad – not as the Beauty but the Dowd.

Out from a deep-delved way my vision lit
On housebacks pink, green, ochreous – where a slit
Shoreward 'twixt row and row revealed the classic blue through it.

And thereacross waved fishwives' high-hung smocks,
Chrome kerchiefs, scarlet hose, darned underfrocks:
Often since when my dreams of thee, O Queen, that frippery mocks:

Whereat I grieve, Superba! . . . Afterhours
Within Palazzo Doria's orange bowers
Went far to mend these marrings of thy soul-subliming powers.

But, Queen, such squalid undress none should see,
Those dream-endangering eyewounds no more be
Where lovers first behold thy form in pilgrimage to thee.


Many of the compounds here are Hardy's own, for the greater part participial or parasynthetic. The opening line uses its two compounds to establish and re-inforce the city's link with the past, by playing on the literal meaning of Mediterranean as the 'Central Sea' and directing the reader's mind to classical epic. Deliberate contrasts are set up between this *'epic-famed, god-haunted'* past, the sordid present of *housebacks* and 'darned *underfrocks*', and the City's continuing *'soul-subliming* powers', the latter an enduring antidote to the temporary *'dream-endangering eyewounds'* which mar the poet's first impressions. It is not claiming too much to say that the poem is carefully poised between its classical image and its present blemishes by means of strategically placed, highly charged compounds.

Another moment of balance is achieved by the *'deep-delved* way' of the traveller's approach to Genoa, through a series of railway tunnels, opening upon '*high-hung* smocks' blurring the poet's vision of the sea's 'classic blue'. The promised ascent from depth to height is made ironically disenchanting.

The word *multimarbled*, comparable to the reference to Plymouth as 'The Marble-Streeted Town' in the poem of that title, is Hardy's coinage, a deliberate shorthand for what is more expansively described in the *Life*, on the opening page (187) of Chapter XV, 'Italian Journey', as 'that city – so pre-eminently the city of marble – "everything marble", he writes, "even little doorways in slums" '. And there is another short prose equivalent in *Jude the Obscure*, III, Ch. 9, where Hardy says that one of the most splendid views in Christminster – based on the prospect of the High from Carfax, in Oxford – is 'in picturesqueness unrivalled except by such Continental vistas as the Street of Palaces in Genoa'. As so often in his figurative language Hardy is drawing on personal knowledge or experience, which in the poem centres on the recovery from disillusioning first impressions to the recognition of 'Afterhours Within Palazzo Doria's orange bowers' which 'Went far to mend these marrings'. It is both the vista of Genoa's architectural splendours and the contrast between the refreshing 'orange bowers' and the hideous 'pink, green, ochreous' colours of the backs of houses with their chrome and scarlet laundry, that mark the turning point of the poem.

Even a brief analysis of such a poem as 'Genoa and the Mediterranean' can indicate some of the important functions performed by Hardy's compounds. In 'A Broken Appointment' the two crucial compounds *hope-hour* and *time-torn* occupy identical stressed positions in the penultimate lines of the two stanzas which make up the poem. In 'The Going' there is a steady building up of emotional tension to the moment of retrospection in stanza 4 – so characteristic of the mood of *Poems of 1912–13* – with an emphatic 'You' introducing a twofold vision, one of place, one of the person addressed, in which poetic compounds are given prosodic and semantic prominence:

> You were she who abode
> By those *red-veined* rocks far West,
> You were the *swan-necked* one who rode
> Along the beetling Beeny Crest . . .

These are the only compounds of their kind in the poem. Another poem of this group, 'A Dream or No', similarly expresses the poet's vision of the departed, this time using four compounds in one drawn-out line to create a visual impression of Emma Lavinia Hardy which anticipates the delineation of Iseult in *The Famous Tragedy of the Queen of Cornwall* ten years later:

> *Fair-eyed* and *white-shouldered*, *broad-browed*
> and *brown-tressed*.

In several other poems of *Poems of 1912–13* Hardy envisions his lost wife in appearance, or in places embedded in his memory, with the aid of evocative poetic compounds: in 'I Found Her Out There' the poet recalls the cliff where he found her, with its '*salt-edged* air', her face *fire-red* in the sunset, her '*wind-tugged* tress' flapping her cheek, while she listened to the sound of the sea 'With a *thought-bound* brow'. In 'Lament' there is poignant contrast between the opening evocation of a merry party, Emma '*bright-hatted* and gloved' and the sombre ending recognizing that she is now shut 'In her *yew-arched* bed'. In 'After a Journey' he remembers her

> With your *nut-coloured* hair,
> And gray eyes, and *rose-flush* coming and going,

and in the most haunting of all these poems, 'The Voice', 'Even to the original *air-blue* gown!' In 'The Phantom Horsewoman', she is 'A *ghost-girl-rider*', now unchanging and unchangeable, while the poet '*toil-tried* . . . withers daily'.

It is plain from these examples and the many others that could be adduced how readily Hardy's poetic imagination found voice in a group of related linguistic forms that enabled him to express and to compress in one word his private vision of persons, places, moods, and experiences. That he must have been aware of the tradition upon which he was drawing, in the first place through Barnes, is made evident by the reliance placed upon such compounds in *The Famous Tragedy of the Queen of Cornwall*, one of his last works, published in 1923, although its composition was begun several years previously, as Purdy makes clear. The diction of this play is deliberately archaized; the archaisms for which Hardy has been so frequently criticized are here at least thoroughly at home. There are over thirty such compounds in this short work, some of them variations on the same theme: Iseult, the second, is *finger-white*,

*white-handed*, *white-palmed*, and *pale-palmed*. What is a *banquet-ing-hall* in a stage direction becomes in the text the more direct *feasting-hall* which is, despite its originally French element, closer to the several Old English variations on this word, like the 'mead-hall' of *Beowulf*. The fateful love potion is both a *love-drink* and a '*love-compelling* vial', and its tasting makes Iseult '*heart-aflame* / For Tristram'. The tragic tenor of the play is underscored by telling compounds: Tristram is '*gloom-born* / In his mother's death'; both he and Iseult are *Fate-haunted*. Iseult, unsuspecting of her name-sake's deceit, exclaims that '*Sudden-shaken* souls guess not at guile', and later comments with cruel unconcern on her rival's '*self-sown* pangs'.

Although the play is far removed in legend, its protagonists are enacting 'in their *long-faded* sphere' what is a timeless drama. In *The Dynasts*, on the other hand, Hardy was not out 'to raise / An antique spell', but to make more recent history come alive to a generation poised uneasily between two wars, both of which he viewed with gloom and protest. Most readers of Hardy will be familiar with such Boer War poems as 'Drummer Hodge' or 'The Souls of the Slain', and with his 'Poems of War and Patriotism' in *Moments of Vision* of which the best-known is the splendid lyric 'In Time of "The Breaking of Nations" ', dated 1915, in which the theme of *The Dynasts* is echoed in the poet's contemplation of life going on 'though Dynasties pass'. The very much larger scope of *The Dynasts* inevitably prompted a more diffuse style and diversified language than these poems, and a more typical stylistic *mélange* than Hardy permitted himself in *The Famous Tragedy of the Queen of Cornwall*. All the familiar ingredients are present: dialect, colloquial diction, literary echoes and foreign quotations, archaisms and neologisms, and numerous compounds of both the latter sorts. These contribute in their particular manner of figurative compression to the major themes of *The Dynasts*. They sum up aspects of the Immanent Will and its nescient workings in such words as 'the *All-mover*' and 'the *All-prover*', and 'the *all-urging* Will'; while its abiding-place is allusively questioned by the Chorus Ironic in these lines:

> Is it where *sky-fires* flame and flit,
> Or solar craters spew and spit,
> Or *ultra-stellar night-webs* knit?
> (II. vi. 5)

The mechanical activities of 'the Great *Foresightless*' are succinctly expressed in words like *random-fashioned* and *mechanic-drawn*, and are made the spectacle of *puppet-watchers*. The human condition viewed disinterestedly or ironically or compassionately by the Spirits is similarly commented on. What men do is *foretimed*; they themselves are '*flesh-hinged* mannikins' of '*flesh-built* frame'; their dreams are *high-doctrined*; their world is *ill-contrived*.

War, with its suffering and futility, is another major theme of *The Dynasts*, to which Hardy's compounds contribute some characteristic expressions. The movement of entire armies, crawling across the map of Europe, is regularly narrowed down to detailed glimpses of particular battles, in order to focus on '*Steel-cased* squadrons swathed in *cloud-drift*, plunging to doom' at Eylau, or on French reinforcements at Talavera '*new-primed* in their plump battalions', or on '*Hot-hasting* succours of light cannonry' at Quatre Bras. Individuals are spotted as they 'Beheld the grazing *death-bolt* with a smile' on their *death-spot*; the normal traffic of a beleaguered city is reduced to a 'mad current of *close-filed* confusion'; even butterflies are doomed 'to die of a worse than the *weather-foe*', as the Chorus of the Years anticipates the slaughter of Waterloo.

The passage of time, the absorption of the past in the present, the possibility of change even within the Unconscious Will are familiar themes in *The Dynasts*, and as in his poems and his fiction Hardy makes use of compounds to crystallize aspects of Time in one word: *foretimed, tedious-timed*, '*deedless* years', Napoléon's 'last *empery-hour*', '*far-ranged* aions past all fathoming'.

Kenneth Marsden in his valuable chapter on Hardy's poetic vocabulary (*The Poems of Thomas Hardy: A Critical Introduction*, Ch. VII) asserts that Hardy 'was a frequent user of compounds, without being able to achieve striking effects from them', a comment repeated later in a somewhat modified form. It is certainly not difficult to find among Hardy's compounds, of the type so far discussed, examples of clichés, of commonplace, even empty, words which add nothing to the reader's pleasure or profit. Some are singularly inept, at best just uninformative, and one suspects that metrical reasons in a poem, or the persistent urge in Hardy to alliterate, in prose as in verse, may have determined their use. But that is only part of the picture, and the lesser part at that. I have used the word 'poetic' to describe certain of Hardy's compounds, not so much to emphasize their traditional associations, as in *foam-fingered*, or their more exotic powers of evoking unfamiliar responses, as in *rain-reek*, but to stress their importance in the texture of Hardy's work, as important bearers of his meaning, as vital links in his poetic matching of vision and phrase. To say, as Groom does, that 'of the delicate touch which transforms the ordinary into the poetic, they show not a trace', is plain nonsense, for in not a few of them is to be found that quintessence of poetry which 'it is the capacity of the form to contain'.

It would be no great step, nor a very original one, to move from Shakespeare's 'sable-coloured' or Milton's 'sable-vested' to 'sable-clad', but Hardy goes one step further yet to point an ironic contrast between the genuine mourner in 'She at His Funeral' who watches from nearby, 'Unchanged my gown of garish dye', and the 'griefless' mourners who are standing round and whose attire is *sable-sad*. This is an early poem (1873), yet the skill to manipulate language towards a complex poetic response is already present. And this ability to vary a conventional word, or to coin one to function with ironic import or allusive play or descriptive force is one of the continuing strengths of Hardy's English. Some of his poems are rescued from indifference by a well-chosen compound: the final mournful *sorrow-wrung* of 'The Faded Face', for example, is its only redeeming feature. On the other hand, in some of his finest poems, a well-chosen compound adds its own vibrations to the poetic melody, like the figure of *'hill-hid* tides' throbbing, 'throe on throe', in 'Weathers'; or the *spectre-gray* frost and the *'blast-beruffled* plume' in 'The Darkling Thrush', setting the desolate, wintry, ghostly scene and stressing the paradox between the aged, frail, vulnerable bird, symbol of mortality, and its

> *full-hearted* evensong
> Of joy illimited,

symbol of faith, of 'some blessed Hope' unknown to the poet. To deny that such words produce 'striking effects' or possess that delicate transforming touch into the poetic is to be deaf to their subtleties and imaginative force.

In his novels and stories compounds can be just as dull, and just as effective, as in Hardy's poems. Such words as *ever-regardful* applied to Melbury in *The Woodlanders*, or *horizontal-headed* applied to trees in *The Hand of Ethelberta*, or the prosaic *noon-clear* in the phrase 'In her *noon-clear* sense that she had never loved him' in *Far from the Madding Crowd*, Ch. 31, Hardy is substituting mechanical language for the imaginative diction of which he was capable. Yet a compound, like any other well-chosen word, need not be elaborately contrived. In the description of Tess as *'naked-armed* and *jacketless'* at a turning point in her life (*Tess of the d'Urbervilles*, Ch. 29), Hardy is not merely describing the informality of Tess's attire, but emphasizing yet again both the sensuousness and the vulnerability of his heroine, yet the words he uses so effectively could hardly be plainer. Equally simple means are employed in Jude's plaintive words to Sue: 'We've both re-married out of our senses. I was made drunk to it. You were the same. I was *gin-drunk*; you were *creed-drunk*' (*Jude the Obscure*, VI, Ch. 8). 'Of course the book is all contrasts', Hardy wrote to Gosse on 20 November 1895, and here, *in parvo*, Jude's disastrous weakness of the flesh and Sue's moral obduracy are once again contrasted in stark simplicity with the aid of just two compound words.

In his description of the cliffs in Ch. 7 of *A Pair of Blue Eyes*, where Elfride and Stephen find themselves on a brink that is, so to speak, both topographical and emotional, Hardy sums up the external panorama of the 'toothed and zigzag line' of the cliffs as well as the amorous agitation of the lovers in the phrase *'storm-torn* heights'. This is an effective as well as an original variant of the more common-place *storm-tossed* or the Tennysonian *storm-worn*, and the insight of this moment of poetic vision is made all the more apparent when contrasted with Hardy's ponderous pontification some lines further on, after Elfride has received her first kiss: 'In fact, the art of tender-ing feminine lips for these amatory salutes follows the principles laid down in treatises on legerdemain for performing the trick called Forcing a Card.' Here, indeed, is a cliff-fall into bathos.

A second major group of compounds consists of words formed with the help of affixes, which may be free morphemes, like *after*, *in*, *out*, *up*, *like*, *wise*, or bound morphemes not found as separate words, like *be-, en-, -ish, -ness*. Hardy has a considerable number of compounds of this type, the largest single group being words begin-ning with *un-*, a phenomenon sometimes explained as the product of his negative, pessimistic view of things. But in the history of English word-formation *un-* is not only a negative or pejorative prefix, but may express the reversal of a previous action, as in *unjailed*:

> 'Yet I saw that a joy, as of one *unjailed*,
> Now shone in his gaze.'
> ('A Conversation at Dawn')

Here the emphasis is on a positive state, a previous infliction reversed, so that it is somewhat facile to draw general philosophical conclusions from Hardy's usage. It is more relevant to point in this context, as in others, to Hardy's response to traditional modes of English expression. He retains in a number of instances the original semantic force of affixes like *un-* or *be-*, or *-some* or *-wise* which is as a rule no longer felt in modern English. Or it may have been replaced by more recent semantic development, as in the case of *-wise*, which originally indicated the manner of something or its direction, as in Hardy's '*Bedwise* he fares' in 'The Bird-Catcher's Boy', but which in current English usage is often affixed to a noun to indicate reference to something, taking the place of a phrase, as in 'the trip was successful *weatherwise*'.

There can be no doubt that Hardy's insistent reliance on compounds formed with affixes is one of the principal reasons for the seemingly exotic character of much of his diction, not least where he runs counter to usual modern English practice of tmesis by preferring the compound to the separation of its parts:

> *Uprises* there
> A mother's form upon my ken,
> ('The Roman Road')

compared with such normal usage as 'She *fired up* at once' (*Far from the Madding Crowd*, Ch. 31). This is so common a feature of Hardy's English that one instinctively seeks an explanation. One of several suggestions made by C.H. Salter* is that Hardy may have cultivated a form of compound that brought English closer to other languages, both classical and modern, in order to emphasize both his recognition of man's smallness in the universe, and his frequent assertions 'of how little Wessex has changed since the Heptarchy'. Salter draws attention to the fact that at least one example in *The Dynasts* – 'The bridge of Lindenau has been *upblown*' (III. iii. 5) – is spoken by a German. Another suggestion Salter makes is that as compounds with *out-*, *up-*, and *on-* are inversions Hardy used them because he thought inversions poetical, and sometimes used them simply for that reason. He also, according to Salter, used this type of Thomas Hardy's Verse', *Victorian Poetry* XI (1973), 261.

---

* C.H. Salter, 'Unusual Words Beginning with *un*, *en*, *out*, *up* and *on* in Thomas Hardy's Verse', *Victorian Poetry* XI (1973), 261.

compound occasionally 'for good reasons and with a good effect', for example, *unbe*, *enghosted*, *outshape*, *upblown*.

But the most basic explanation is that at the root of Hardy's practice is the metrical model he found in Barnes's verse. Barnes has examples of compounds containing bound morphemes, although compounds made up of free morphemes far outnumber them. 'With feet *unsandall'd*, and *disorder'd* dress', for example, is from one of his early non-dialectal poems, 'The Death of Adonis'; while in his first collection of dialect poems occurs this example:

> We left the beds our mossy thatch
> Wer never mwore to *overstratch*.
> ('Leady-Day, an' Ridden House')

But the real trademark, as it were, of Barnes's diction is the use of the dialectal prefix *a-*, which derives from Old English *an-*, *on-*, *ge-*, *a-*, and the preposition *on*, representing for the poet both a conspicuous dialectal feature and an extremely useful metrical device. Barnes attaches this prefix to present and past participles where it helps the metre, and omits it where it does not:

> An' there the unlatch'd doors did creak,
> *A-swung* by winds, *a-streamen* weak
> Drough empty rooms, an' *meäken* sad
> My heart . . .
> (*Ibid.*)

How important the prefix is to Barnes's prosody may be gleaned from these lines:

> There's a cloud over Blackmwore, about ov our height,
> Wi' his sheädow *a-zweepen* the ground in his flight,
> An' *a-climen* the tow'r, an' *a-sheäden* the boughs,
> An' *a-leäpen* the stream, an' *a-dark'nen* the cows . . .
> ('On the Hill')

These are the rhythms that nurtured young Thomas Hardy's early poetic stirrings, but for him the prefix *a-* obviously had much more limited usefulness than it had for the richly dialectal muse of Barnes. He uses it, on occasions, in both verse and prose: in 'A Sound in the Night', for example, which re-tells an old local story, Hardy's 'a-blowing' and 'a-thumping' are archaisms, just as Henchard's 'a little small new cottage just a-builded' (*The Mayor of Casterbridge*, Ch. 1) is dialectal. Other examples, in most cases deriving the prefix from an original preposition, are *abrim*, *a-coast*, *achime*, *aflush*, *agroan*, *ahorse*, *a-perch*, and *aswing*. In *a-groaning* Hardy uses the prefix before the present participle in the dialectal manner favoured by Barnes.

Clearly, the metrical model of Barnes could not be satisfied by a prefix which Hardy felt disinclined to attach to any but a very limited number of standard English words. He therefore turned to others, of which *un-* became by far the most prominent. Maybe his tendency to take 'a full look at the Worst' had something to do with this, but not by any means all his *un-*compounds express negation, deprivation, or a pessimistic view of things. The point was made earlier that Hardy is quite capable of making a positive statement by means of an *un-*word: 'And my trustful daring *undoubt*' in 'A Self-Glamourer' is an obvious example. 'The square *unembattled* tower of Knollsea Church' in *The Hand of Ethelberta*, Ch. 44, is not so much a hankering for something missing as a straightforward architectural impression. The reduction of the frightening mass of mankind to its '*unformidable*, even pitiable' units (*Tess of the d'Urbervilles*, Ch. 13) expresses, as the collocation of the two adjectives makes clear, a positive sense of something manageable. The argument is strengthened by such instances as '*No unwarped* mind can doubt' in the political jargon of Ponsonby (*The Dynasts*, III. v. 5), where the double negative enforces some such positive sense as 'fair-minded'; or the description of Laura's mansion as '*no unhandsome* one' in 'The Honourable Laura' (*A Group of Noble Dames*). Such instances of understatement are by no means uncommon in English usage from as far back as *Beowulf*.

Some of Hardy's *un-* compounds, whether revivals like *unreasons* or coinages like *uneagerness* and *unsuccesses*, are patently used in deliberate contrasts with their antonyms:

> Mr Melbury overlooked the infinite throng of other possible *reasons and unreasons* for a woman changing her mind.
> (*The Woodlanders*, Ch. 11)

> 'We have triumphed: this achievement turns the bane to antidote,
> *Unsuccesses to success*'.
> ('Friends Beyond')

Or, more subtly, by accentuating the antithesis by means of contrasting tenses:

> Nor God nor Demon can *undo the done*,
> *Unsight the seen*.
> Make muted music *be as unbegun*.
> ('To Meet, or Otherwise')

The majority of Hardy's more unusual *un-* compounds occurs in *The Dynasts* and in his poems, those in his prose writings being for the most part less exotic. Their frequent use in verse raises prosodic questions, although there are of course other reasons to be considered. In one of his earliest poems, 'Hap', Hardy writes:

> And why *unblooms* the best hope ever sown?

As a participial adjective *unbloomed* is recorded in the sixteenth century, but as an active verb Hardy's usage appears to be original. He could have written 'And why blooms not the best hope ever sown?', thereby achieving similar, albeit not quite the same, sense, but lessening the impact of the double alliteration in the line. The compound carries evenly divided stress over its two parts, thus ensuring vocalic alliteration on *un-* and *ever*, and consonantal alliteration on *-blooms* and *best*. The other version would tend to place too much stress on *not*. But *unblooms* connotes more than 'does not bloom', as Pinion glosses in *A Commentary on the Poems of Thomas Hardy*. It suggests growth following upon the sowing, but thwarted before the flower opens; the previous line similarly acknowledges the fact of joy while lamenting its termination.

If this is considered over-subtle, it may be of value to consider Hardy's word *unbe*. This is not his coinage, as some critics have thought, but Hardy's connotations are more complex than is the case in earlier recorded occurrences. Hardy's best-known example is in the poem 'Tess's Lament':

> It wears me out to think of it,
> To think of it;
> I cannot bear my fate as writ,
> I'd have my life *unbe*.

The word also occurs in the original manuscript version of 'The Impercipient':

> Yet would I bear my shortcomings
>     With equanimity,
> But for the charge that blessed things
>     I'd rather to *unbe*.

Hardy made several changes here: 'equanimity' finally becomes 'meet tranquillity', and the last line quoted eventually appears as 'I'd liefer not have be', the last three words restoring his first, but deleted, manuscript version. These revisions do not suggest second thoughts about the archaic nature of *unbe*, for *liefer* is a much older English word and felt to be more archaic, but rather hesitation on Hardy's part how his meaning could best be expressed. Traditionally, the word *unbe* can mean either 'to be non-existent' or 'to make non-existent', and Hardy's use, certainly his later use in 'Tess's Lament', represents a conflation or co-existence of these two meanings: Tess would rather not have lived at all, not solely to be now annihilated, but to have her whole life's story unwritten. This is a phenomenon not unknown in totalitarian countries, defined by a writer in *The Times* (19 June 1981) as '[disappearance] into the political void of unpersons'. In the antiphonal songs of the two semi-choruses in *The Dynasts*, I. vi. 3, the word *unbe* has one of its primary meanings of 'to be non-existent' and was probably chosen for metre and rhyme, while in the original version of 'The Impercipient' *unbe* may have been felt by the poet to be too forceful, even violent, whereas he was aiming here to express the calmer notion of wishing to dispense with 'blessed things'. Admittedly, there is, as L.E.W. Smith has recently noted, 'a cutting edge of bitterness' in the poet's 'answering back' at this point in the poem: he certainly wishes to refute the charge that he considers 'blessed things' redundant, but there is to be no suggestion of violent termination. Hence the more moderate tone of the final version.

Other *un-* compounds pose similar problems. The notion of 'impercipience', for example, recurs in several forms, stressing, with the help of the prefix, lack of awareness, of understanding, of knowledge, as in *unware*, *unawareness unmindfulness*, *unknow*, *unknowingness*, *unweeting*; or lack of vision, inability to see, spiritual blindness, as in *unrecognize*, *unsee*, *unsight*, and *unvision*. Several titles of poems express similar notions: 'Unknowing', 'Unrealized', 'The Self-Unseeing', 'Self-Unconscious'. Napoléon's charisma on the eve of Austerlitz, voiced by the Chorus of the Pities in the words 'Strange suasive pull of personality!' evokes the ironic retort:

His projects they *unknow*, his grin *unsee*!
(*The Dynasts*, I. vi. 1)

Human ignorance and blindness are simply facts of existence, easily manipulated, but such clouds of unknowing arouse compassion for the sufferings they engender, so that the Pities, here at least, have the last word:

Their loyal luckless hearts say blindly – He!

These are perennial themes with Hardy, and in one poem, 'The Aerolite', he traces the appearance of 'sentience' in our world, which came on a meteorite

And operated to *unblind*
Earth's old-established ignorance . . .

where *unblind* combines the senses of giving sight, bestowing consciousness, and, like *unscreens* in *The Dynasts*, III. i. 9, opening shutters on the world. Characteristically, the poem ends with the ironic observation:

Maybe now
Normal *unwareness* waits rebirth.

Hardy himself was probably quite unaware much of the time whether he was reviving an obsolete word, or using a current one, or coining a new one on a familiar morphological pattern. He juxtaposes them without feeling any of the incongruity that may strike the reader, as in the last line of the third stanza of 'At Mayfair Lodgings': 'Unpardoned, unadieu'd', or by using in the same poem ('A Watering-Place Lady Inventoried') the nonce word *unnarratable* alongside familiar words like *unsurpassed* and *unforgettable*. He gave a new lease of life to a number of English words of respectable antiquity, directly as in *unhope*, or indirectly by prefixing them with *un-* as in Caxton's and Gray's *storied*, which appears in the line 'By cromlechs *unstoried*' in 'My Cicely'. This happens, albeit more rarely, also in Hardy's prose. Thoughts are described as '*unowned*, *unsolicited*' in *The Mayor of Casterbridge*, Ch. 42; here the first word of the pair, with its meaning of 'unacknowledged' is possibly an echo of Samuel Richardson's similar usage ('latent or unowned inclination') in *Clarissa Harlowe*, a work singled out for special commendation in Hardy's essay 'The Profitable Reading of Fiction'. Sir Thomas Browne's *uncarnate* reappears as a proper epithet for the spiritual, almost disembodied Sue in *Jude the Obscure*, III, Ch. 9. Browne, among others, also uses *unteach*, which finds its way into Hardy's observation 'Experience *un*teaches – (what one at first thinks to be the rule in events)' (Hardy's italics. *Life*, p. 176).

A characteristic revival is the Renaissance word *unwombs*, whose choice is partly semantic and partly metrical. The positive connotation of escaping from the confinement of the womb into individual freedom is immediately contradicted by the threat implied in the balancing rhyme word *foredooms*, while the metre of the poem ('In Childbed') requires the stress patterns which the two compounds are constructed to provide.

There are of course many *un-* compounds whose meanings are quite straightforward. This is particularly so in Hardy's prose. The word *unmarry*, for instance, is simply a synonym for 'divorce' in 'Nothing could *unmarry* them' (*An Indiscretion in the Life of an Heiress*, II, Ch. 7), the *un-* prefix here connoting reversal to an earlier condition rather than asserting negation. A more light-hearted occurrence, tinged with irony, in *The Dynasts*, III. ii. 3, describes the end of a casual liaison rather than of a marriage. *Unstrategic*, possibly borrowed from Carlyle, is clarified by the accompanying *unambitious* to describe Charles Darton's nature in 'Interlopers at the Knap' (*Wessex Tales*). Carlyle's Professor in *Sartor Resartus* similarly glosses the word by adding 'undiplomatic'. Both writers are perhaps unconsciously following the practice of earlier centuries in such juxtaposing of a less familiar with a more familiar word. Chaucer, who anticipated Hardy's propensity for *un-* words to a marked degree, offers some instructive examples.

Even in Hardy's prose, however, an *un-* compound may retain or assume a distinctly poetic flavour. The 'creeping chilliness' felt by Yeobright as he emerges into 'the *unsunned* morning air' to question young Johnny about Mrs. Yeobright's death (*The Return of the Native*, V, Ch. 2) recalls Shakespeare's 'unsunn'd snow' in *Cymbeline*, II, v, as well as more recent instances in Coleridge or Tennyson. Another possible Shakespearean echo is the rare word *unsexed*:

> Though she was unknown to fame, this was a great gift in Faith, since to have an *unsexed* judgment is as precious as to be an *unsexed* being is deplorable.
> (*The Hand of Ethelberta*, Ch. 8)

The poetic flavour of such words, by their association with well-known earlier instances, is probably more a part of the reader's response than the author's intention. Hardy's readiness to pick his words indiscriminately, although by no means undiscriminatingly, from any source needs no further emphasis here. William Archer made the now familiar comment, in his review of *Wessex Poems* in 1898, that 'there are times when Mr Hardy seems to lose all sense of local and historical perspective in language, seeing all the words in the dictionary on one plane, so to speak, and regarding them all as equally available and appropriate for any and every literary purpose.' Hardy thought that 'seeing all the words of (*sic*) the dictionary on one plane' was a 'happy phrase' (Letter to Archer of 21 December 1898).

Archer's comment derives particular support from the random distribution of rare or nonce compound words among Hardy's characters. A Cabinet Minister at a party in the house of a Lady of Quality (*The Dynasts* I. i. 5) prophesies that the troops of the Alliance will '*un-French* Italy / From shore to shore'; at the other end of the social scale, also in a Napoléonic context, a peasant says:

'Safe was my stock; my capple cow *unslain*';
('The Peasant's Confession')

Bob Loveday, in *The Trumpet-Major*, Ch. 19, uses figuratively a dialect word that was once in literary use: 'Any little vulgar action *unreaves* their nerves like a marline-spike.' The maltster in *Far from the Madding Crowd*, Ch. 8, calls Oak's grandfather 'a nice *unparticular* man'. Lady Hester (*The Dynasts*, I. vi. 8) refers to the dying Pitt's 'unmuscled hand', another possible Richardsonian echo, which occurs again in III. vii. 7, in the words of an Aide:

And those who are left alive of it
Are so *unmuscled* by fatigue and thirst
That some relief, however temporary,
Becomes sore need.

For the most part, however, except in the dramatic dialogue of *The Dynasts*, Hardy's *un-* compounds are uttered by his own voice, in poems and in prose narrative, and this is true also of many other compounds formed in the same manner. Many of these also are verbs, Hardy's most characteristic grammatical element; some are verbal nouns. His favourite prefixes, after *un-*, are *up-* and *out-*; others, in approximate order of frequency, include: *en-* and *em-*, *fore-*, *over-*, *in-*, and *on-*; *in-* representing not only the preposition, as in *inbe* 'to dwell within', but also a variant of *un-*, as in *inexist*, which is the semantic counterpart to *unbe*.

The list of prefixes occurring in Hardy's more unusual words is of course much longer, as these examples will illustrate: *a-coast*, *after-haps*, *bedrench*, *byspeak*, *deparked*, *disillude*, *miscompose*, *remutinied*, *subtrude*, *underwhistle*. In its few occurrences, as in 'Reminiscences of a Dancing Man' and in *The Dynasts*, the archaic *yclept* retains the Middle English form of the Old English prefix *ge-*.

Apart from neologisms, like most of the above, the primary interest attaching to Hardy's compounds of this type lies in his preference for unseparated forms in verbs normally subject to tmesis. This is a common feature in his verse, but Hardy thought it inappropriate in prose, except in a few isolated instances where some semantic subtlety is intended, as in these cases:

> Warren's Malthouse was enclosed by an old wall *inwrapped* with ivy.
> (*Far from the Madding Crowd*, Ch. 8)

Here the parallelism between *enclosed* and *inwrapped* deliberately stresses the doubly snug seclusion of the house, introduced in this opening sentence of the cosiest chapter in the novel.

> The superstratum of timidity which often *overlies* those who are daring and defiant at heart had been passed through.
> (*The Return of the Native*, V, Ch. 3)

The retention of an older word here, in a figurative manner, strengthens the geological image, with its connotations of pressure from above.

> Every conceivable aid, method, stratagem, mechanism, by which these last desperate eight hundred yards could be *overpassed* by a human being unperceived, was revolved in her busy brain, and dismissed as impracticable.
> (*Far from the Madding Crowd*, Ch. 40)

The dual connotations of 'to traverse' and 'to overcome, to conquer' lend particular poignancy to the use of the word *overpassed* in the agonizing scene of Fanny's travail on Casterbridge Highway. One wonders whether Hardy ever came across the haunting refrain in the Old English poem 'Deor's Lament', '*þæs ofereode, |þisses swa mæg*', which could be translated 'that was overpassed, so may this'.

C.H. Salter in the article previously cited has claimed that Hardy's '*out*- words mean the same as they would mean if the *out* followed the verb instead of preceding: they do not have the meaning "exceed someone in doing something" '. This needs modification. In a case like 'Who had no arts, but what *out-arted* all' ('Panthera'), the meaning is clearly 'to exceed', but this is not a tmetic verb, that is a compound verb which permits separation of its parts by the inter-polation of one or more words. The same is not true, however, of 'whose years *out-count* your own' ('The Revisitation'), for this is a tmetic verb and there are doubtful cases of tmetic verbs where Hardy's meaning is ambiguous. Even in so prosaic a context as the topographical stage direction at the beginning of Part First, Act Sixth, Scene I, of *The Dynasts* there is ambiguity: 'In the front mid-distance the plateau of Pratzen *outstands*, declining suddenly on the right to a low flat country.' This may be merely idiosyncratic Hardy, but it is more probably a deliberate playing on a figurative as well as a straightforward topographical meaning. The plateau is not only prominent; it dominates, as the subsequent battle makes clear. A similar duality of meaning is present in the description of 'the land's sharp features' in 'The Darkling Thrush', which

> seemed to be
> The Century's corpse *outleant*.

The word suits metre and rhyme, but clearly has a different meaning from 'to lean out'. Indeed, its connotations go further than merely 'stretched out' (Pinion), even allowing for the sense of the dead century reaching out into the future, for the archaic verb *lean* adds its meaning of 'to become or make lean' to that of the verb meaning 'to incline'. Hardy's wintry, 'hard and dry' landscape is not merely spread out, corpse-like, before the speaker's eyes, but is made lean, fleshless, and withered.

An obvious case of the compounded form having a different meaning from the tmetic form occurs in Hardy's poem 'Memory and I'. Each stanza asserts the continuing presence of 'him' or 'her' as spectre or phantom, lingering, wandering, haunting. In the fourth stanza this theme is expressed thus:

'I saw her in a ravaged aisle,
    Bowed down on bended knee;
That her poor ghost *outflickers* there
    Is known to none but me.'

By *outflickers* Hardy means a fitful but continuing flickering:
the parallels with the other verbs in the poem require this;
whereas 'flickers out' would have denoted a flash or two followed by
extinction.

Such cases should warn us against assuming too readily that
Hardy's compounds of this type are merely idiosyncratic reversals
of normal usage. That in many cases his choice was dictated by metre
or rhyme cannot be doubted. The example of Barnes remained
insistent. But there is a further reason. Many of Hardy's prefixes,
and suffixes, for that matter, were not free forms and could not
therefore be detached from the base, and of such words Hardy
availed himself as readily as he did of other kinds. It was therefore
natural to treat tmetic compounds whenever it suited his prosody or
his meaning as if they were non-tmetic. Of the latter kind some are
revivals of obsolete words, like *disillude* or *enarch*, some
are Hardy's own coinages, like *re-ponder* or *re-wive*. For the
most part, such words have the same 'poetic' aura about them as
words of the *outleant*-type, which inevitably tends to 'poeticize'
Hardy's diction, more obviously so in his poems, in *The Dynasts*,
and in *The Famous Tragedy of the Queen of Cornwall*. That Hardy
himself thought such words to be somehow different from others of
more common registers is unlikely; they are all part of the same
verbal acreage. For the reader, however, they generate a heightened
response because they do not belong to his or her 'normal' language:

'I am a sculptor,
    A worker who
Preserves dear features
    The tombs *enmew*.'
    ('A Jingle on the Times')

or:

. . . our momentary bereavement
*Outshapes* but small.
    ('After the last Breath')

or:

> Right! Lady many-spoused, more charity
> *Upbrims* in thee than in some loftier ones.
> (*The Dynasts*, I. vi. 7)

or:

> Fluttering with fear,
> *Out-tasked* her strength has she!
> (*The Famous Tragedy of the Queen of Cornwall*, scene xiv)

The reader's feeling that this is 'poetic' language is of course reinforced by such other linguistic signs as the compound *many-spoused*; alliteration as in 'Fluttering with fear'; inverted syntax as in the line 'Out-tasked her strength has she!'; or words traditionally regarded as poetic like 'aureate nimb':

> Did her gifts and compassions *enray* and *enarch* her sweet ways
> With an aureate nimb?
> ('Thoughts of Phena')

There is yet a further reason for Hardy's predilection for compound verbs of this type. The accentual pattern of such words in English is to put the stress either on the verb-base, as in *outflickers*, or to divide it about evenly between prefix and base, as in *re-wive*; whereas in a separated compound, the main stress tends to fall on the preposition, as in 'rolled up', which clearly has a different stress pattern from

> That the Thames-side lanes have *uprolled*,

with its rhyming 'fold' and 'cold' in the same stanza of 'A Wife in London'. Hardy's practice of leaving the prefix attached to the verb, even when separable, and his preference for verbs with non-separable prefixes, are indications of the emphasis he places on the verb. This is particularly apparent where the verb-base carries rhyme, as in the example just quoted. We are therefore looking at linguistic choices influenced by a complexity of semantic and prosodic factors, and the reader's response depends very much on arriving at a satisfactory balance of these. Sometimes Hardy helps. In the line

> When he would have *unslung* the Vessels *uphung*
>      To his arm . . .
>      ('The Lost Pyx')

the internal rhyme indicates that the two prefixes play a relatively minor role. On the other hand, in the line

> *Undeeming* great scope could *outshape* in
>      A globe of such grain,
>      ('The Mother Mourns')

the opening prefix by its position and negative import requires even stress with *deeming*, whereas in the second compound the prefix is semantically unimportant, as the contrast in magnitude which it indicates is already implied in Hardy's juxtaposition of 'great scope' and 'such grain'. The prefix appropriately carries weaker stress than the verb it modifies.

Hardy was aware of the different etymological functions of some of the prefixes he so readily employed, as has been noted in the case of *un-*. He distinguishes, for example, between the several possible senses of *en-*, *em-*. This can mean 'to put into or upon', as in Hardy's *enearth*, *enjailed*, *ensepulchred*, *ensphered*, or *embay*, and it can also mean 'to put into a certain state or condition', as in the word *enghost*, which Hardy uses several times with striking effect to mean both 'to make a ghost of' and 'to become a ghost'. The dead soldiers in Napoléon's Russian campaign 'are enghosted by the caressing snow' (*The Dynasts*, III. i. 9), where the sense is not only that they are now dead, but that the snow which *enmews* them (another Hardy word, used of tombs) gives them a spectral appearance. A similar concentration of meaning is achieved in 'The Re-Enactment':

> That here some mighty passion
>      Once had burned,
> Which still the walls *enghosted*,
>      I discerned,
> And that by its strong spell mine might be overturned.

The passion survives as a ghostly remembrance, the actors themselves having previously in the poem briefly enacted a phantasmal scene; but *enghosted* by the walls also implies the confinement of this particular drama within this particular chamber. Hardy manages to squeeze a lot of meaning out of this one word, and he plays yet another variation in describing the ancestral drama in 'Family Portraits' as 'Their restless *enghostings*'. It was not simply that the word fitted neatly into these various contexts; it expresses a visionary experience characteristic of Hardy's retrospective, somewhat morbid, temperament.

The prefix *en-* also has traditionally an occasional intensive function, as in the verb *enkindle*, which is more emphatic than *kindle*. In 'The Distracted Preacher' (*Wessex Tales*) Stockdale's attractive young landlady is aptly described as *enkindling*, a word dating from the sixteenth century.

Another prefix which has several meanings is *over-*. Its most literal meaning is that of the preposition *over*, meaning above something, as in '*over-topping* the wall in general level was the graveyard' (*A Pair of Blue Eyes*, Ch. 4). At a figurative level this becomes descriptive of a dominating influence, as in 'Slowly a drowse *overgat* me' ('In Tenebris III'), or the description of the disappointed bride as *overborne* in 'The Satin Shoes'. The two senses are combined in such cases as 'the sudden resolution . . . which sometimes impels a plump heart to rise up against a brain that *overweights* it' (*The Hand of Ethelberta*, Ch. 2). A distinctive word, widely distributed in English dialects is *overlook* 'to look on with the evil eye, to bewitch' as used by Christian Cantle in *The Return of the Native*, IV, Ch. 7. Another sense denotes excess; in a verb:

> But I am so *overgloomed*
> By its persistence . . .
> ('Bereft, She Thinks She Dreams')

or in a substantive:

> . . . judgment of that hue
> Which *over-hope*
> Breeds from a theoretic view
> Of regal scope.
> ('A King's Soliloquy')

None of these *over-* compounds was invented by Hardy. Although Elizabeth Hickson* claimed that *overborne* was Hardy's

---

* Hickson, p. 125, where the wrong page reference is given.

coinage, it is in fact found in the sense 'oppressed' in Renaissance English. The word *over-hope*, which occurs in Middle English, is the antonym of Hardy's *unhope*. Coleridge uses *overgloomed*; and *overweight*, in the sense in which Hardy uses the verb, is recorded in several nineteenth-century contexts, but not apparently before. Hardy's painstaking revisions, as we saw in the case of *unbe*, can mean the occasional discarding of a compound; but they can also lead to the substitution of a compound for a phrase. In 'The Satin Shoes', for example, the line 'All day the bride, as overborne' first appeared, in *Harper's Monthly Magazine*, as 'All day the bride, as one down borne', which is both more ambiguous and less striking than the resurrected Renaissance word which Hardy introduced into the version printed four years later, in 1914, in *Satires of Circumstance*.

One other comment may be made on these compounds. Quite apart from the impression of poetic diction created by words like *enarch* or *upbrims* or *overborne*, many of them contribute in considerable measure to the Latin sonority of much of Hardy's diction. In other words, they act as reminders of Renaissance English. Such words as *disillude*, already mentioned, or *retrocede*, or *superinduced*, are of this kind, and some of Hardy's own inventions match them almost imperceptibly:

> And, grieved that lives so matched should *miscompose*,
> Each mourn the double waste.
> ('At a Bridal')

> For those happy suns are past,
> *Fore-discerned* in winter last.
> ('Before and after Summer')

*Superinduced* appears in *Desperate Remedies*, Ch. 18, and there are many other instances of such compounds in Hardy's prose, like *dis-esteem* in *Tess of the d'Urbervilles*, Ch. 49, *insuavity* in *The Return of the Natives*, V, Ch. 2, and so forth.

These comments about the poetic and Latinate character of this aspect of Hardy's diction apply with equal force to compounds employing suffixes. A word such as *presciencelessness*, in 'Thoughts at Midnight', is a characteristic Hardy creation; one feels tempted to say doubly so, with its dual suffixes *-less* and *-ness*. The word fills practically the whole line, and is made to measure for the dactylic metre:

Led by sheer senselessness
And presciencelessness
Into unreason.

A similar example occurs in one of Hardy's finest poems, 'The Voice', where the final version of the line 'You being ever dissolved to wan *wistlessness*' is a substitution for his earlier 'You being ever consigned to *existlessness*'. Both these exotic compounds are neologisms, and both are characteristic of numerous words in *-less* or *-ness* or *-lessness*, found alike in his prose and verse. The suffix *-less* can denote either a state of deprivation or inability to do something, of which the former is more common with Hardy. Many of these words, out of context, are quite mundane, like *breakfastless*, *supperless*, *jacketless*, which simply carry on the late nineteenth-century, and subsequent, vogue for compounds, many of them nonce-words, of this kind. Some are more typical of Hardy's diction, like the Spenserian *weetless*, the Byronic *stirless*, or the word *stayless*, meaning 'unable to stop, ceaseless', also first recorded in the sixteenth century, which occurs in the sibilant phrase 'in Time's stayless stealthy swing' in 'God's Funeral'.

When Hardy felt the need to employ these traditional lexical tools to construct a new word, he did so, in this way as in others, without compunction:

Retty used to draw me down
  To the turfy heaps,
Where, with yeoman, squire, and clown
  *Noticeless* she sleeps.
    ('Retty's Phases')

The word *noticeless* implies both 'un-noticed' and 'un-noticing', a happy conflation of the two senses of the suffix. It shows Hardy's sensitive revision, by means of such a compound, of a more prosaic earlier version. The poem exists in an early draft, dated 'June 22, 1868' (reproduced from the Dorset County Museum manuscript in Purdy, facing page 242, and more recently on page 700 of Gibson's Variorum Edition) and in fact represents the earliest surviving manuscript of a poem by Hardy. The above lines originally read:

# Acres of Words

Retty used to draw me down
To the green church-hay
Where with yeoman squire and clown
Her little body lay.

The loss of the archaic *church-hay*, a good Dorsetshire word, recorded in Haynes's *Vocabulary* and preserved in Hardy's poem 'My Cicely', is to be regretted; but the later version, as printed in *Human Shows* gains immeasurably by the invention and inclusion of *noticeless* in the calm flow of the line.

There are other coinages in *-less*: *breachless, brookless, fore-thoughtless, logicless, vexless, wealth-wantless*, all in Hardy's verse; and there are some of contrary import using the suffix *-ful*, like *acheful, exploitful, pleadful, shudderful*, and *whimful*, while both suffixes figure in words describing a condition or state by means of the additional suffix *-ness*: *bloomfulness, chancefulness, featfulness, musefulness, tristfulness, famelessness*, of which the latter occurs in Hardy's Revised Preface to *The Woodlanders*.

It is worthy of note that Hardy uses a number of archaic or poetic words with the suffix *-ness* in prose as well as in verse in preference to more usual alternatives: *oddness* rather than *oddity*: 'This impression of indescribable *oddness* in Stephen's touch' (*A Pair of Blue Eyes*, Ch. 7); *silentness* rather than *silence*: 'They . . . made their tiny movements with a soft, spirit-like *silentness*' (*Desperate Remedies*, Ch. 1); *inevitableness* rather than *inevitability*: 'The waterfall hissed sarcastically of the *inevitableness* of the unpleasant' (*A Changed Man*: 'The Waiting Supper'); *nescientness* rather than *nescience*: 'Dungeoned in an eternal *nescientness*' ('Aristodemus the Messenian'); and *absentness*, which occurs in 'On a Discovered Curl of Hair' is glossed 'absentmindedness' by the *OED* rather than *absence*, which is Hardy's meaning. Not all such pairs are exactly synonymous, however: *antiqueness* in 'The Pedigree' is different from *antiquity*, for example; similarly, when in 'God's Funeral' Hardy speaks of the 'phantasmal *variousness*' of the strange form being carried, he is using the word not merely for rhyme but in order to convey the sense of 'changeableness', which was no longer current for the word *variety*.

Of the many other suffixes present in the words that make up Hardy's more unusual diction, some have become largely unproductive in English, like *-ance* or *-hood* or *-some*, while others, like *-ish, ism, -like, -wise* continue to be active elements in the creation of new words. This distinction creates differences in response for the modern reader, to whom words like *frustrance*, *mongrelhood*, and *eyesome* will appear archaic, whereas *townish*, *indifferentism*, *careless-like*, and *music-wise*, have a modern ring, although such words, too, may be of venerable antiquity: *townish*, for example, occurs in Lydgate's *Troy Book*.

Hardy's prose offers examples of his fondness for words containing these and other suffixes which would not perhaps always have fitted easily into his poetry:

'Through the whole past evening *touchable*, *squeezable* – even *kissable*!'
(*Under the Greenwood Tree*, I, Ch. 8)

He could on occasion close the mouths of his dependents by a good *bomb-like* oath.
(*A Group of Noble Dames*: 'The Duchess of Hamptonshire')

'Their dislike of other people's [children] is, like class-feeling, patriotism, *save-your-own-soul-ism*, and other virtues, a mean exclusiveness at bottom.'
(*Jude the Obscure*, V, Ch. 3)

He was a *wickedish* man, the squire was, though now for once he happened to be on the Lord's side.
(*Life's Little Ironies*: 'Absent-Mindedness in a Parish Choir')

The opposite is no less true; namely, that there are other such compounds more appropriate for poetry than for prose fiction:

Your nuptial *plightage* and your rightful glory.
(*The Dynasts*, III. v. 4)

The courts of their *encompassment*.
(*The Famous Tragedy of the Queen of Cornwall*, Scene vi)

But such distinctions are rather hazardous to make in Hardy's case, for, as we see again and again and as William Archer noted, Hardy himself paid little attention to them. Thus we find the neologism *mollyish*, which Pinion in his Glossary in *A Hardy Companion* defines as 'soft, yielding, weak', in a poem ('In the Room of the Bride-Elect'), and the poetic Renaissance word *faultful* in *Jude the Obscure*: 'the purest moment of his *faultful* life' (IV, Ch. 3). An interesting neologism, not recorded in the dictionaries, is Hardy's *necrophobist*, which occurs in 'The Doctor's Legend', I, a story first published in America in 1891 and not re-printed until Pinion included it in *Old Mrs Chundle and Other Stories* in The New Wessex Edition, 1977. The words *No-God-ist* and *God-ist* appear in Hardy's autobiography *sub anno* 1883 (*Life*, p. 161), perhaps modelled on the seventeenth-century word *religionist*, still current in the nineteenth century, or an anglicization of *deist*. That Hardy rather fancied words in -*ism* and -*ist*, reflecting his interest in various schools of thought and belief, is suggested by his use of words such as *indifferentism* and *indifferentist*, *personalism*, *theologism*, and the rare *subtlist* in *The Woodlanders*, Ch. 45: 'A subtlist in emotions'. In the same novel, Ch. 14, this passage refers to Fitzpiers:

> Strict people of the highly respectable class, knowing a little about him by report, said that he seemed likely to err rather in the possession of too many ideas than too few; to be a dreamy 'ist of some sort, or too deeply steeped in some false kind of 'ism.

Two particularly common groups of words in Hardy's vocabulary are those ending in -*er* and -*(e)ry*, for the most part words revived from earlier usage, in some cases coined by him analogically. It may be of interest here to list some of the more unusual ones as a further illustration of the element of verbal exoticism attaching to Hardy's diction: *awaiters, bread-bringer, Causer, courter, darers, diers, dismantlers, doers, elbowers, farer, flingers, forecaster, God-obeyer, hard-hitter, horner, improver, in-dwellers, laugher, livers, liviers, marrer, misadventurer, misrepresenter, money-taker, muser, onbearers, oneyer, outcaster, outsetter, passager, passer, reasoners, responders, ruers, rumourers, scorner, self-glamourer, soul-lifters, spouter, surrounders, tightener, upstanders, Urger, well-meaner, Wellwiller, Willer, World-weaver.* The following words ending in -*(e)ry* all occur in *The Dynasts*, a few of them also in other works: *bombastry, bridalry, cannonry, charactery, cheatery, demonry, empery, enginry, footmanry, hazardry, slaughtery, stagery, wardenry, weedery.* There are also the proper nouns *Bourbonry, Britishry, Englishry, Saxonry.* Elsewhere, Hardy also has *coxcombry, dreamery, householdry, leafery* (corresponding to the more prosaic *leafage* in *Life* p. 235), *phantastry, servantry; Churchwardenry* in the essay 'Memories of Church Restoration'; *Dogedomry* in the *Life*; *villagery* in one of his letters. These do not exhaust the list, but they make their point.

The -*er* suffix, of Germanic origin, is a regular formative for agent-nouns and emphasizes the close link between doer and doing, noun and verb, which clearly appealed to Hardy. The *-ry* suffix is a reduced form of *-ery*, of French origin, which denotes a quality, state, or condition, lending a dimension of universality to the actors and events in *The Dynasts* which formed part of Hardy's intention in presenting the Napoléonic drama largely as seen from above, *sub specie aeternitatis*. In one or two cases Hardy's usage differs from that of earlier writers: *footmanry* in *The Dynasts* means 'infantry', not the occupation of a footman; *wardenry* means 'guardianship', not the office or jurisdiction of a warden; and *weedery* refers to garments, not as in usual nineteenth-century usage to weeds.

My main reason for harrowing this large acreage of Hardy's words is less to demonstrate yet again the exotic quality of much of his diction and its eclecticism, than to illustrate how deeply rooted are the formative influences which have continued to fashion the English language, upon which Hardy drew with an instinctive sense of propriety. Many of the words containing such affixes as we have examined are Hardy's coinages, and they conform to traditional modes of English word formation. But many more of his less familiar words are in fact revivals of archaic, obsolete, or dialectal words endowed with new life in his verse and prose. Those critics who cavil at 'a lone cave's *stillicide*' may need to be reminded of the venerable Renaissance ancestry of the word. Those who may find something a trifle odd in 'A *haggish* creature of about fifty presided' (*The Mayor of Casterbridge*, Ch. 1), will find a precedent in *All's Well That End's Well*. The choice of *surplusage* instead of the more usual *surplus* in *The Dynasts*, III. v. 2, probably made for metrical reasons, may easily be justified by an even more venerable ancestry. The word *whorage*, also found as *horridge*, is a Dorsetshire word defined by Barnes (*Glossary*) as 'a house or nest of bad characters'; more literally it means 'a collection of whores', and thus Hardy uses it in *Tess of the d'Urbervilles*, Ch. 10, while in this poem 'The Fight on Durnover Moor', *whorage*, rich in innuendo, refers not only to the 'biggening' wenches, but also to the scrimmage beyond the bridge. Critics may wonder why Hardy felt it necessary to coin the word *dolorifuge* in *Tess of the d'Urbervilles*, Ch. 6:

> The children, who had made use of this idea of Tess being taken up by their wealthy kinsfolk (which they imagined the other family to be) as a species of *dolorifuge* after the death of the horse, began to cry at Tess's reluctance.

The answer is probably the one Hardy gave Robert Graves: 'Now, what in the world else could he have written?' He would have found no other quotation in the *Oxford English Dictionary*. And yet the word conforms to the pattern of such as *febrifuge*, a seventeenth-century coinage, favoured by Scott and De Quincey and Ruskin and Charles Reade, whose popular novel *The Cloister and the Hearth* Hardy probably read in his early twenties. The suffix *-fuge*, based on Latin *fugāre* 'to drive away', may not be common in modern English, but its existence was sufficient warrant for the neologism in *Tess of the d'Urbervilles*. The resultant phrase 'a species of *dolorifuge*' is a characteristic Hardyan enrichment of our language.

This is not always the case, however, and one may wonder at Hardy's modernity in coining such a word as *flattites* to describe dwellers in flats, in a letter to his sister Katharine of 11 June 1899, while at the same time one deplores the unhappy neologism itself. Yet here, too, Hardy was but using an active suffix, *-ite*, to form a new word.

The resurrection of obsolete words was not merely a linguistic necessity in Hardy's constant quest for the right word, but a means of conveying the sense of timelessness, of past merging into present, which is an important dimension of the Wessex novels and of many of Hardy's poems. The juxtaposition of an antique word and one wholly familiar in contemporary usage helps to strengthen the impression of continuity of rustic life in which a phrase remained as unchanged for generations as the beliefs and superstitions of the people, or for that matter the heath and the seasons. Since Hardy hailed from a corner of England where traces of West-Saxon speech were still audible, it is hardly surprising that such an Old English word as *ceorl* should suddenly surface in *The Trumpet-Major*, Ch. 2, or *The Woodlanders*, Ch. 38, or that Hardy should have recourse to the Old English *hrædnes*, in its later form *ratheness* to complete the line

Yea, to such rashness, ratheness, rareness, ripeness, richness,
  Love lures life on.
  ('Lines To a Movement in Mozart's E-Flat Symphony')

There are such verbal forms as *chaunted*, *littled*, *meseemed*, *pomped*, *strown*, *worsed*, *yclept*, with their inescapable overtones of archaic diction. There are numerous antique words like *accompt*, *forsooth*, *hinds*, *intermell*, *olden*, *somewhiles*, *tass*, *unruth*, *whoso*, and obsolete meanings as in 'impending over him'. To these and other good English words fallen into desuetude, like Coverdale's *daysman*, Hardy granted temporary reprieve, words which, as he said in a letter to Gosse of 14 February 1899, 'every true friend of the language is anxious to restore', although we should remember that some of them could still be heard in Dorset speech. A few examples must suffice:

> The *daysman* of my thought.
> ('He Abjures Love')

'I can call to mind that we've lost three chickens, a tom-pigeon, and a weakly sucking-pig, one of a *fare* of ten.'
(*The Trumpet-Major*, Ch. 6)

There was a naïveté in her *cheapening* which saved it from meanness.
(*Far from the Madding Crowd*, Ch. 12)

> From these *inimic* hosts defiling down
> In homely need towards the little stream.
> (*The Dynasts*, II. iv. 5)

> Stone-deaf *therence* went many a man
> Who served at Valencieën.
> ('Valenciennes')

He *fain* could hope, in the secret nether chamber of his mind that something would happen . . .
(*The Woodlanders*, Ch. 11)

The two last examples illustrate Hardy's fondness for adverbs either obsolete or at least so rarely used as to be felt by most readers to be archaic. These include several formed with the suffix *-wise*, like *elsewise*, *suchwise*, *thencewise*, *thuswise*, which is then extended to adverbial compounds like *chancewise*, *furtive-wise*, or *wooingwise*, or

> The sour spring wind is blurting *boisterous-wise*,
> ('An Unkindly May'),

and occasionally Hardy forms adverbial phrases, making up compound nouns with the substantive *wise* in a manner which the *OED* describes as 'illogical', like 'in nursing-wise', 'in jealous-wise', 'in idle-wise', 'in selfish-wise'. Furthermore, there are unusual adverbs in *-ly*: *forwardly*, *inventorially*, *leftwardly*, *liegely*, *momently*, *nextly*, *samely*, *troublously*, or

> And my dream was scared, and expired on a moan,
>     And I *whitely* hastened away.
> ('The Dream-Follower')

The transference of a word from one grammatical category to another is frequently achieved without such lexical formatives as *-ly* in the creation of adverbs. The loss of inflectional endings in Middle English facilitated the exuberant disregard of inherited grammatical distinctions between nouns and verbs and adjectives which is such a marked feature of Renaissance English. 'Wouldst thou be *window'd* in great Rome?' asks Mark Antony, a question that has – grammatically speaking – echoed through the language ever since. Those modern purists who take exception to similar latitude in contemporary English, like the critic objecting to Hardy's 'his shape *smalled* in the distance', should pause for a moment to contemplate the rich harvest our language has reaped from this device and the great advantage it enjoys over less pliant, inflected languages like French or German.

In this respect as in so many others Hardy's English is rooted in tradition, and his ingenuous retort to Graves needs to be accepted at face value.

It is of course possible to write modern English prose or verse without having recourse to archaisms, neologisms, poetic diction, dialect, technical jargon, private allusions, foreign languages, literary echoes, and other devices used by writers to achieve certain effects, but at what cost to the integrity of their vision? As well might a painter forgo certain colours because they possess connotations irritating to some viewers. Hardy had no such compunctions. He knew that the word *god* had been used as a verb by such poets as Spenser, Shakespeare, and Tennyson; hence he did likewise. But he also went further and made a verb of *goddess*, which no one else had yet done:

> So dowered, with letters of credit
>     He wayfared to England,
> And spied out the manor she *goddessed* . . .
>     ('The Flirt's Tragedy')

The bold coinage is happily in keeping with the ironic note implied in the general theme of 'Time's Laughingstocks' to which 'The Flirt's Tragedy' belongs. Another such shifting of categories occurs in the phrase 'He *downed* to breakfast' in 'Squire Hooper', a deliberately prosaic expression to describe a prosaic action, yet one imbued with the pathos of the dying man's last hours. The verb was known in English before Hardy, but in the sense of 'to descend' he appears to have been among the first to use it. It occurs again, paired with the verb *up*, in 'The Wind's Prophecy'.

Both these examples are verbs, and it is especially to furnish verbs, participial adjectives like 'these *turmoiled* years', and verbal nouns like the Miltonic *oraclings*, that Hardy turns to such instances as he could find in earlier English of words derived from others by grammatical transference. Another such example is the verb *whim*, derived, as Dr Johnson noted, from the noun, in the line 'But she's *whimmed* her once too often, she'll see!' in 'One Who Married Above Him'. When there were no earlier instances, Hardy did his own transferring, although such examples are relatively few especially when compared with his many innovative compounds.

Among a handful of verbs derived from adjectives by means of the suffix *-en* Hardy had a distinct liking for *largen*, which occurs in several poems and in *The Dynasts*, and is representative of several such words popular among nineteenth-century writers. These include the verbs *closen*, *golden*, *louden*, *olden*, *richen*, and *stouten*, whereas *biggen* and *greaten* are found two centuries earlier. Some of Hardy's verbs, derived unchanged from adjectives, are of even greater antiquity: *greened* occurs in Old English; *darks*, *darked* in Middle English, *gayed* in the Renaissance. A few verbs derive from other parts of speech: for example, *forth'd* from the adverb *forth* dates back to Old English, *upped* from the preposition *up* to the seventeenth century in the sense in which Hardy uses it in the line 'And she *upped* like a bird' in 'The Catching Ballet of the Wedding Clothes'.

The majority, however, of verbs and verbal nouns and participial adjectives in *-ing* and *-ed* belonging to this group of words involving shifted grammatical categories, derive from substantives. Many of these were coined in Hardy's own century which was second only to the Renaissance in its fecundity of such transferences. To the nineteenth century we owe such Hardy usages as these:

His clothes were of fustian, and his boots hobnailed, yet in his progress he

showed not the mud-accustomed bearing of hobnailed and *fustianed* peasantry.
(*Wessex Tales*: 'The Three Strangers')

Her lips were red, *without* the polish that cherries have, and their redness *margined* with the white skin in a clearly defined line.
(*A Pair of Blue Eyes*, Ch. 18. The first italics are Hardy's).

'And saves much sad *good-nighting*.'
('A Jog-Trot Pair')

In this fair niche above the unslumbering sea,
That *sentrys* up and down all night, all day.
('A Singer Asleep')

To the same period belong such forms as *diamonded* and *paean'd*, in *The Dynasts*, and *treed* ('the tumulus *treed* with pine' in 'The Moth-Signal') which Hardy was to take a step further in 'the *apple-tree'd* old house' in 'The Second Visit'. Cleanth Brooks, in the passage quoted in Chapter 1 of this book, pounces on the oddity of the verb *lip*, which Hardy may have derived from Keats's 'I heard my name / Most fondly lipp'd' in *Endymion*. Hardy uses it with some discernment, for alliteration in 'A Musical Incident': ' "Liar!" / I lipped'; to describe silent movement of the lips, as in *The Woodlanders*, Ch. 46: ' "Ah, I thought my memory didn't deceive me!" he lipped silently'; and, in the sense of 'to raise to the lips' in the compound 'a trumpet *uplipped*' in 'A Two-Years' Idyll'. Although very sympathetic to Hardy's linguistic resourcefulness, I did however find myself balking at 'White *lippings* above the Delphic tripod / Mangle never their message! And they *lip* such', in 'Aristodemus the Messenian'.

Many of these words had been used by other poets besides Keats and they may have been reverberating in Hardy's memory before re-appearing in his prose and poems. Shakespeare had used *bellied*, *exampled*, *kinged* and *palating*; and the verb *sheet* occurs in a passage in *Antony and Cleopatra* (I, iv):

Yea, like the stag, when snow the pasture *sheets*,
The barks of trees thou browsed'st –

which may well have inspired Hardy's line

213

When the moon *sheets* wall and tree,
('The House of Hospitalities')

with its similarly blanching connotation. As Hardy recalls in the epigraph to Chapter 5 of *A Pair of Blue Eyes*, Milton had used *bosomed* in 'L'Allegro', '*Boosom'd high* in tufted Trees', and thus Hardy uses it in 'Fellow-townsmen' (*Wessex Tales*): 'It was so *highly bosomed* in trees and shrubs . . .'. Similarly, Milton's verb *pillows* in 'On The Morning of *CHRISTS* Nativity' finds its way into *The Woodlanders*, Ch. 13. Hardy's verb *west* in 'Drummer Hodge' is used several times by Chaucer as well as by Spenser; and there are other examples of such precedence, including Byron's '*Carnation'd* like a sleeping infant's cheek' in *Manfred*, which appears in *The Hand of Ethelberta*, Ch. 33, applied to the heroine, 'her cheeks *carnationed* by the wind'.

With such antecedents to guide him, Hardy coined more words by the same means. For example:

From the *battered* hornwork the cannoneers
Hove crashing balls of iron fire.
('San Sebastian')

Thuswise a harpsichord, as 'twere from
*dampered* lips.
('Haunting Fingers')

Let your chambers show no sorrow,
Blanching day, or *stuporing* morrow.
('To a Well-Named Dwelling')

Ay, all well-nigh, ere Time have *houred* three-score.
(*The Dynasts*, III. vi. 2)

Yet *haggarded*, in the morning light,
By too *late-houring* overnight.
('A Victorian Rehearsal')

In 'the fiddlers *six-eighted*' in 'At a Pause in a Country Dance' a numeral becomes a verb, and in 'The Mongrel' Hardy follows recent nineteenth-century usage of *out* as an intransitive verb in the line 'And, the tide still *outing* with brookless power'. Even the facetious verb *autumn* in a letter (13 August 1900) – 'Cannot you winter, or at least *autumn*, in London . . .' – was probably a spontaneous neologism for Hardy, although an obscure citation in the *Oxford English Dictionary* predates it by over a century.

To verbal nouns like the Miltonic *oraclings* in *The Dynasts* may be added a good many others. Shakespeare has 'a kind of *gain-giving* as would perhaps trouble a woman' (*Hamlet*, V, ii); Hardy writes:

> Scared momently
> By *gaingivings*.
> ('A Spot')

Tennyson's *sing-songing* appears in the Hussar's song 'Budmouth Dears' in *The Dynasts*, III. ii. 1, while in 'To an Unborn Pauper Child' Hardy writes of 'our *songsingings*'. Shelley's *undervoice* becomes Hardy's *undervoicings* in 'A Commonplace Day'. Dryden's '*Southing* Sun' becomes Hardy's 'The moon in its *southing*' in 'Plena Timoris'. Other substantives derive from other parts of speech without altering their form:

> To bring about the highest possible average of *takes* within the year.
> (*Desperate Remedies*, Ch. 4)

> A *flit* is made upstairs.
> (*Under the Greenwood Tree*, I, Ch. 8)

> 'See if you can borrow some larger candles than these *fourteens*'
> (*Ibid.*, I, Ch. 2)

– an instance of this usage, referring to fourteen candles to one pound, which antedates the first citation in the *Oxford English Dictionary* by several years.

> 'Papa won't have *Fourthlys* – says they are all my eye.'
> (*A Pair of Blue Eyes*, Ch. 4)

Few such words are Hardy's coinages, however, although the jocular *Fourthlys* is. Such nouns as *attain*, *auditory*, *dismals*, *owings*, *says*, *shines*, *steep*, *tentative*, can all be traced at least to the eighteenth century and in most cases to the late Middle Ages or the sixteenth century. In the eclectic environment of Hardy's verse such words are less conspicuous than in his prose, where a usage like 'the whole collection of *shines* nearly annihilating the weak daylight from outside' (*Desperate Remedies*, Ch. 13), suggests some linguistic eccentricity which was probably less unintentional in Hardy's first, rather mannered, novel than in his later fiction. He did, after all, develop some views about what was and what was not admissible, to the point of branding, in one of his letters to Florence Henniker (11 February 1896), the word *cablegram* an 'illegitimate word!', although it had by then been in use for a generation. Also in *Desperate Remedies* occur the substantives *auditory*, *seeming*, *smooth*, *takes*, and *yesses*, of which the first occurs also in *Under the Greenwood Tree*, but thereafter such words are more likely to be used in verse. Even the phrase *by littles*, which Dickens had used in prose and Hardy likewise in *Tess of the d'Urbervilles*, finds its way into a Hardy poem:

> We see *by littles* now the deft achievement
> Whereby she has escaped the Wrongers all.
> ('After the Last Breath')

Hardy rather liked to use *peradventure* as a noun, a usage frowned upon by Dr Johnson and never widespread. For example:

> 'Awake! I'm off to cities far away',
> I said; and rose, on peradventures bent.
> ('The Chimes Play "Life's a Bumper!" ')

Another verbal link with the past is Hardy's deliberate retention or revival of obsolescent or obsolete meanings as in the case of *impending*, meaning 'hanging' or 'leaning', a sense which in the nineteenth century had become much less common than that of 'being imminent'. Similarly, Hardy writes 'The mother thus *invoked* ran upstairs' (*The Trumpet-Major*, Ch. 1), using the word in the general sense of 'to call out to someone', although the several specific meanings of the word, like 'to appeal to', 'to summon as aid or witness', were then, as they are now, the usual ones. The original meaning of *concur* is retained, in the sense of 'to come together, coincide', in the clause

> When the periodic cessations between the creaks of the engine *concurred* with a lull in the breeze.
> (*Desperate Remedies*, Ch. 19)

The obsolete meaning of *distract*, 'to draw asunder, divide', is revived in 'Barnet had a wife whose presence *distracted* his home'

(*Wessex Tales*: 'Fellow-townsmen'); and in *The Return of the Native*, IV, Ch. 7, the traditional popular meaning 'to look upon with the evil eye' is retained in Christian Cantle's 'There's folks in heath who've been *overlooked* already.' Originally to be found in literary usage, as in Shakespeare, the word survived in this sense in various dialects, including Dorset where Barnes listed it in his *Glossary*. It is one of a number of such words whose semantic history diverges in standard English and in dialect.

Although the examples of such semantic revivals quoted so far all occur in Hardy's prose, he employed the same device in his verse. A characteristic example occurs in 'The Inscription':

> And showed him the words, ever gleaming
> > upon her pew,
> *Memorizing* her there as the knight's eternal wife.

By the time this poem was written (1907), the meaning 'to perpetuate the memory of someone, to record' had become obsolete and the word *memorize* had become restricted to its current meaning.

There is, in all these modes of compounding, and coining, and shifting, and reviving, an insistent urge to defeat Time, to restore to life and to keep alive treasures which the language had relegated or discarded altogether. Hardy had no illusions about the changes to which English, like any living tongue, was subject. He tells us in his autobiography (*Life*, p. 318) that he drew up the memorial to his progenitors' musical services in Stinsford church in Latin because he 'was guided by his belief that the English language was liable to undergo great alterations in the future, whereas Latin would remain unchanged'. He acknowledges the fact of linguistic change by pointing a comical finger at one of the effects of the Great Exhibition of 1851 in the opening paragraph of 'The Fiddler of the Reels' in *Life's Little Ironies*:

> None of the younger generation can realize the sense of novelty it produced in us who were then in our prime. A noun substantive went so far as to become an adjective in honour of the occasion. It was "exhibition" hat, "exhibition" razor-strop, "exhibition" watch; nay, even "exhibition" weather, "exhibition" spirits, sweethearts, babies, wives – for the time.

More seriously, he realized that, whatever the loss incurred, each generation had to clarify and re-define its concepts in the light of changing circumstances. Speaking of Tess's 'ache of modernism', Hardy reflects – in the mind of Angel – 'that what are called advanced ideas are really in great part but the latest fashion in definition – a more accurate expression, by words in *logy* and *ism*, of sensations which men and women have vaguely grasped for centuries' (*Tess of the d'Urbervilles*, Ch. 19). That the gain may be specious the twentieth century with its surfeit of -*logies* and -*isms* has amply demonstrated. But for Hardy the loss was even greater when it meant the disappearance of ancient and legitimate words whose usefulness he did not deem to have come to an end.

In his sober moments he acknowledged the inevitability of such change; but as an artist he ignored it, allowing the turn of a single phrase to remain unaltered for ten generations and more. We can thus see the hauntings and seemings, the preoccupation with the past, with memories and re-appearances, so frequently remarked upon by his critics, made linguistically manifest by Hardy's treatment of his English as if it were all of a piece, as if the passage of centuries of linguistic change were irrelevant. This attitude provides a key, perhaps the master key, to Hardy's linguistic eclecticism, to the co-existence in his English of so many diverse elements, many of them long since assigned to oblivion by other writers. It was one of the principal weapons he chose to 'make war upon this bloody tyrant Time'.

Shakespeare had done so before him, and if other authority were needed, there was Horace's warrant in *Ars Poetica*, encouraging the poet not only to make 'a familiar word new', but to invent words not heard before, and moreover reminding him of the ebb and flow of language:

> Multa renascentur quae iam cecidere, cadentque
> quae nunc sunt in honore vocabula.
>  (70–1)*

Hardy knew his Horace: 'Read some Horace', he notes in the *Life*, p. 48, and a few pages later: 'Through this winter the following note continually occurs: "Read some more Horace".' The latter's words

---

* I am grateful to Professor Gordon Williams for drawing my attention to his discussion of this passage in his book *Figures of Thought in Roman Poetry*, (New Haven and London, 1980), pp. 278 ff.

fell on receptive ears, and kept reverberating, as in the essay 'The Profitable Reading of Fiction'.

But these same ears were also attuned to the speech of his own day. Perhaps 'day' is an inadequate description of a life that began less than a decade after the death of Crabbe and ended more than half a decade after the publication of *The Waste Land*. Hardy has been well described as a nineteenth-century novelist and a twentieth-century poet, and there is a good deal in his English which the twentieth-century reader will recognize as closely akin to modern colloquial English, including clichés, jargon, and slang.

It is important, however, to distinguish here between Hardy's own voice and those of his characters. Some of the latter employ colloquial turns of phrase, just as others lapse into dialect. The use of slang, however, is more restricted. Jargon and clichés, on the other hand, are mostly the narrator's. As Robert B. Heilman noted in his article on the style of *The Mayor of Casterbridge*, Hardy's 'verbal woolliness' is frequently a form of jargon, akin to such familiar contemporary phenomena as business English, 'legalese' and 'officialese'. He cites examples like these from the novel: 'two persons not unconnected with that family' (Ch. 3); 'guarantees for the same' (Ch. 14); 'the by-road aforesaid' (Ch. 40); 'the day which closed as in the last chapter' (Ch. 45).

Hardy's jargon, as these examples suggest, takes several forms. At its simplest, he prefers a periphrastic to a direct expression:

> But the next morning Manston found that *he had been forgetful of* another matter . . .
> (*Desperate Remedies*, Ch. 9)

Talking about the weather can lead to such circumlocution as this piece of 'officialese':

> Mr Japheth Johns now opportunely arrived, and broke up the restraint of the company, after *a few orthodox meteorological commentaries had passed* between him and Mrs Hall by way of introduction.
> (*Wessex Tales*: 'Interlopers at the Knap', III)

Cytherea's feminine attractions are couched in the jargon of an economic survey:

> To look in the glass for an instant at the reflection of *her own magnificent resources in face and bosom*, and to mark their attractiveness unadorned,

was perhaps but the natural action of a young woman who had so lately been chidden . . .
(*Desperate Remedies*, Ch. 6)

A sentence may begin quite innocuously, only to conclude upon a stretch of ponderous verbiage reminiscent of the worst kind of bureaucratic English:

> She seemed to feel, after a bare look at Diggory Venn, that the man had come on a strange errand, and that he was not so mean as she had thought him; for her close approach did not cause him to writhe uneasily, or shift his feet, or show any of those little signs *which escape an ingenuous rustic at the advent of the uncommon in womankind*.
> (*The Return of the Native*, I, Ch. 10)

Hardy was particularly prone to generic observations of the type illustrated by 'the uncommon in womankind'. One recalls Bathsheba observing herself 'as a fair product of Nature in the feminine kind' (*Far from the Madding Crowd*, Ch. 1); or the phrase 'young women of fragile and responsive organisation' in 'The Fiddler of the Reels' (*Life's Little Ironies*). It is because Hardy saw in his rustic dramas epitomes of wider humanity that he found himself drawn to thinking of 'kinds' and 'classes' and 'sorts': 'His mouth was a triumph *of its class*' (*A Pair of Blue Eyes*, Ch. 4); and:

> Though Wildeve's fevered feeling had not been elaborated to real poetical compass, it was *of the standard sort*.
> (*The Return of the Native*, III, Ch. 6)

> From an upper window Festus Derriman was leaning with two or three kindred spirits *of his cut and kind*.
> (*The Trumpet-Major*, Ch. 13)

The danger of lapsing into jargon is unfortunately ever present when employing stereotyped diction, and Hardy is liable to succumb to it. He uses such phrases as 'the present writer', 'the subjoined facts', 'the taller division of middle height', 'an additional precaution in this direction', 'anxious regard for Number One', 'critical situations of the passive form', 'initiated into the proportions of social things', and speaks of Tess's emotional potential as 'what she herself was capable of *in that kind*'; an unhappy stylistic anticlimax to a sentence promising better (*Tess of the d'Urbervilles*, Ch. 3). That Hardy was liable to write like this outside his fiction may be illustrated from this sentence in a letter to Sir George Douglas (3 March 1898): 'When I do start I am going to do wonders *in the visiting line.*'

Perfectly capable of calling a spade by its usual name, Hardy often seems at pains to avoid doing so, even as I have just done. He talks ponderously of '*the hard-handed order* in general' when he means the working classes or, better still in his own familiar Dorset phrase, the 'workfolk' (*The Hand of Ethelberta*, Ch. 28). He makes do at times with vague words strung together in a manner dear to modern politicians, as when he speaks of Swithin St Cleeve as

> A student of *the greatest forces in nature*, he had, like *many others of his sort, no personal force to speak of in a social point of view*, mainly because he took no interest in *human ranks and formulas*; and hence he was as docile as a child in her hands *wherever matters of that kind were concerned*.
>
> (*Two on a Tower*, Ch. 23)

Hardy's characters now and then lapse into similar utterances: '*What meaning have you*, Harry?' asks Elfride, *A Pair of Blue Eyes*, Ch. 34; 'and, though I may say *no great things as to happiness* came of it . . .', says the second Avice, *The Well-Beloved*, III, Ch. 3; and even in his poems there are such awkward moments of jargon as the lines in 'In a Waiting-Room' which made Edmund Blunden point a finger at Hardy's 'stuffed-owl simplicities':

> The table bore a Testament
> For travellers' reading, *if suchwise bent.*

This is uncomfortably closely akin to business English such as Hardy used when writing to tradesmen:

> Gentlemen:
>     Please to warehouse the cases and boxes sent herewith, and numbered as follows . . . A receipt for same will oblige.
>     (Letter of 19 March 1875)

One of Hardy's favourite clichés is 'at this point of time', which in our own day is being used, as Eric Partridge noted in *A Dictionary of Catch Phrases*, 'to a nauseating extent'. Used in several novels and stories, the expression re-appears in a poem of 1899, 'An August Midnight', in a manner that redeems it from outright condemnation as an empty, outworn phrase:

Thus meet we five, in this still place,
At this point of time, at this point in space . . .

The colloquial tone implicit in such phrases as 'at this point of time'
or 'There's no accounting for taste' or in proverbial expressions
scattered here and there in his prose (' "But I thought honesty
was the best policy?" said Picotee', in *The Hand of Ethelberta*,
Ch. 20) can be detected easily enough in a good deal of Hardy's
dialogue. Indeed, it is when he succeeds in catching a colloquial
cadence that Hardy comes closest to reporting authentic English
speech, apart from his representation of dialect. In narrative he
employs colloquialisms sparingly:

> Meanwhile Louis Glanville had returned to the House and told his sister in
> the most innocent manner that he had been in the company of St Cleeve
> that afternoon, *getting a few wrinkles on astronomy*.
> (*Two on a Tower*, Ch. 30)

The phrase may well be Glanville's although Hardy is narrating;
in either case, it represents a late nineteenth-century colloquial
development of the meaning 'to get a piece of useful information, a
tip', from the earlier sense of *wrinkle* 'a fib, a trick'. The use of *what
not* in narrative is a form of colloquial shortcut which Hardy may
have acquired from Richardson's *Pamela*, along with other verbal and
stylistic traits. Speaking of Henchard, Hardy writes that 'he had
become Mayor and churchwarden *and what not*' (*The Mayor of
Casterbridge*, Ch. 17); and later: 'And thus the once flourishing
merchant and Mayor *and what not* stood as a day-labourer in the
barns and granaries he formerly had owned' (Ch. 32). The ironic
disparagement of Henchard's worldly achievements is succinctly
conveyed by the colloquial *what not*. There is irony of a kindred
sort in the depiction of the cathedral's statues '*pondering whatnot*,
giddy or grave' beneath the appropriately 'yawning' dome and nave
('In St Paul's a While Ago'). Other colloquialisms find their way into
Hardy's verse occasionally, to the disquiet of some critics:

> . . . And for earthing *a corpse or two*,
> And for *several other such odd jobs round here* . . .
> ('The New Dawn's Business')

> But how could that be? *They anyway buried her*
> *By her mother's side*.
> ('The Whaler's Wife')

or 'So it mayn't have bent it' and 'Anyhow' in 'A Gentleman's Second-Hand Suit'. There is an authentic note of uninhibited relief in the colloquial exchange between Liddell and Scott in the poem of that name, beginning with 'Well . . .' and ending with the exhausted couplet:

> 'I feel as hollow as a fiddle,
> Working so many hours', said Liddell.

No less colloquial is the fruity phrase 'She's a plum' in 'Bags of Meat' or the expression 'I was a peach for any man's possession' in 'A Beauty's Soliloquy during Her Honeymoon'.

It would be supererogatory to quote extensively from Hardy's many instances of colloquial dialogue. No matter how extensive, such an exercise could not exonerate him from the charge that his dialogue can be very wooden and unnatural especially where, as frequently in *Jude the Obscure*, it serves but as a vehicle for the author's own ideas. Yet, he often catches just the right note:

The maid Unity: '. . . for the full blow would have knocked his hand abroad, and in reality *it is only made black-and-blue like.*'
(*A Pair of Blue Eyes*, Ch. 9)

Mr John Smith: '*That's about the size o't.*'
(*Ibid.*, Ch. 10)

Sol Chickerel: 'My mate bears the title of Honourable, whether or no; *so let's have none of your slack.*'
(*The Hand of Ethelberta*, Ch. 44)

Thomasin: 'He takes no notice of what I say, *and puts me off with the story of his going on a journey, and will be home to-morrow, and all that*; but I don't believe it.'
(*The Return of the Native*, V, Ch. 8)

Bob Loveday: '*About that harp thing, I mean. I did make it.*'
(*The Trumpet-Major*, Ch. 22)

'Haymoss' Fry: 'Now sound A, neighbour Sammy, and *let's have a slap at* Heav'n's high tower again.'
(*Two on a Tower*, Ch. 2)

Giles Winterborne: '*Pooh – we can polish off the mileage as well as they, come to that.*'
(*The Woodlanders*, Ch. 6)

A student: '*She'll have it hot* when she does come.'
(*Jude the Obscure*, III, Ch. 3)

Arabella: '*O I beg your pardon, I'm sure.*'
(*Ibid.*, VI, Ch. 3)

Selina Paddock: 'It is really too old-fashioned, and so folded and fretted out, *you can't think*.'
(*A Changed Man*: 'Enter a Dragoon', III)

And an example from Hardy's poems:

> *And when you'd a mind to career*
> *Off anywhere – say to town –*
> You were all on a sudden gone
> Before I had thought thereon,
> Or noticed your trunks were down.
> ('Without Ceremony')

The boundary between colloquial English and slang is notoriously hard to draw, nor can it be drawn once and for all. One generation's slang may become accepted, 'received' usage for the next. Eric Partridge, very sensibly, talks of 'unconventional English' and in many cases expresses his own uncertainty, as does the *Oxford English Dictionary*, by the dual label 'slang or colloquial'. Against one of the entries, on 'Spiritual belief' (No. 1297), in his *Literary Notes*, Hardy wrote *bosh*, which according to Björk is 'the strongest comment of disapproval on any entry' (*The Literary Notes of Thomas Hardy*, II, p. 375), and to which the *Oxford English Dictionary* applies its dual label.

I do not propose to be dogmatic about these distinctions, but assume that Hardy knew what he was doing when he ascribed utterances of 'unconventional English' to such of his characters as Alec d'Urberville, Elfride Swancourt, Alfred Neigh, and Louis Glanville. Both the latter use the term *a flat* for a 'fool, simpleton', a word recorded as slang by Partridge from the middle of the eighteenth century. It is listed in Francis Grose's *A Classical Dictionary of the Vulgar Tongue*. Elfride Swancourt uses the phrase 'They are *all my eye*' (*A Pair of Blue Eyes*, Ch. 4) which also dates from the eighteenth century, and later in the novel, Ch. 29, repeats the phrase 'She's the *nobbiest* girl on the boat', picked up from a couple of cricketers. Alec d'Urberville says to Tess 'Come here, and I'll see what *grub* I can find' (*Tess of the d'Urbervilles*, Ch. 5), a word still regarded as slang by modern English dictionaries. Both Humphrey ('some *rum* job', III, Ch. 2) and Venn ('a *rum* course', VI, Ch. 2) use the slang word *rum* 'odd, peculiar' in *The Return of the Native*.

References to getting married are liable to be couched in 'unconventional' language by diverse kinds of people. There is, for example, an informal conversation 'below stairs' in Ch. 13 of *Desperate Remedies*, in which one of the speakers refers to 'lady Hinton's reason for choosing yesterday *to sickness-or-health-it*'. In *Two on a Tower*, Ch. 31, Louis Glanville refers to the Bishop's proposal of marriage to his sister with suitably colloquial irreverence as 'now that *the question has actually been popped*', a phrase probably still considered slang in the eighteen-eighties; and in 'Interlopers at the Knap' in *Wessex Tales*, Japheth Johns refers to his imminent proposal as 'to speak practical', while in the poem 'The Brother' Hardy uses the phrase 'we *churched it*', a colloquial development of the sixteenth-century 'to go to church', meaning to get married.

Along with unconventional language of the kinds illustrated we find exclamations and expletives in Hardy's dialogue, varying from an innocuous *why*! or *O, my*! to rather more forceful expressions of emotion like *O damn*! or *what the hell*! Hardy's major characters are not much given to swearing, with the notable exception of Henchard, whose tempestuous personality occasionally explodes into outbursts like *curse me*, *be hanged*, *'Od damn it*, *by heavens*, *dammy*, *Good God*. A few characters have their idiosyncratic oaths: Mr Penny in *Under the Greenwood Tree* favours *'Od rabbit it all'*, an eighteenth-century imprecation, possibly a perversion of *drat*, found amid a plethora of colourful oaths in Smollett and Fielding; the milkman in *The Hand of Ethelberta* favours *dang*, a euphemism for *damn*, which Hardy also associated with such other 'hard-handed' workers as the glazier in *The Mayor of Casterbridge*; Festus Derriman's boastful and cantankerous disposition several times expresses itself in the early nineteenth-century military imprecation *Dash my wig* and its variants, as well as in such mouth-filling oaths as 'O, my heart and limbs!' and 'hang me if I don't!'. Pennyways in *Far from the Madding Crowd* swears by 'My eyes and limbs', Coggan by 'Heaven's high tower', and Wildeve in *The Return of the Native* 'by my crown'. Giles Winterborne, in *The Woodlanders*, on the other hand, is content with an occasional pensive or questioning 'h'm'.

The majority of profane imprecations are euphemistic, like some of those already mentioned: *nation* for *damnation* is used by several characters, so is *daze* for *damn*, besides *dang* and *dash*. *Begad*, *what the dickens*, *zounds*, *chock' it all*, *be jiggered*, *what the deuce*, and *'Od* for 'God' are distributed with some semblance of verisimilitude among such characters as de Stancy, Mr Swancourt, Bob Loveday, Widow Edlin, the Hangman in 'The Three Strangers', and lawyer Downe in 'Fellow-townsmen'. Edward Springrove just stops short of taking the name of the Lord in vain with a 'Good –!' in *Desperate Remedies*, Ch. 11; George Somerset is content with a mild 'Dear me'; Angel Clare exclaims 'My heavens' in adoration of Tess (*Tess of the d'Urbervilles*, Ch. 34); while in Chapter 46 Alec d'Urberville exclaims 'Angels of heaven!' in ironic unconsciousness of the play on the name which he is trying to ascertain. The irony is underscored by Alec's pious 'God forgive me for such an expression' immediately following.

But there are plenty of full-blooded oaths in Hardy's fiction invoking the deity: 'Good heart of God!' says Clym Yeobright in a moment of acute anguish (*The Return of the Native*, V, Ch. 2); 'O, my great God!' exclaims Grace, as the truth of her husband's involvement with Mrs Charmond strikes her (*The Woodlanders*, Ch. 33); and 'My good God!' and 'The Lord-a-Lord!' utters Mrs Durbeyfield in consternation at Tess's confession to her husband (*Tess of the d'Urbervilles*, Ch. 38), the latter expression echoed in *The Well-Beloved* by Ruth Stockwool (III, Ch. 6). Arabella invokes the Lord readily enough, as one would expect, but her genteel aspirations are nicely pointed as she corrects herself, when speaking to Sue: 'Lord – I mean goodness gracious – what is there to cry about?' (*Jude the Obscure*, V, Ch. 7).

Others, including reverend gentlemen, are less fastidious. Parson Toogood is made to exclaim 'Good God, clerk, don't drive me wild! . . . Why the hell didn't I marry 'em, drunk or sober!', to which the storyteller of 'Andrey Satchel and the Parson' adds the exonerating comment 'Pa'sons used to cuss in them days like plain honest men' (*Life's Little Ironies*). The Vicar of Durnover is another of them pa'sons (in *The Dynasts*, III. v. 6) with his pipe and perpendicular spitting, and his 'Well, I'm d– Dear me – dear me! The Lord's will be done', as characteristic a clerical cadence as is to be found anywhere in Hardy. Also in *The Dynasts* are English echoes of good French profanities as in Napoléon's furious outburst in III. vii. 6:

Infantry! Where the sacred God thinks he
I can find infantry for him!

Others swear in *The Dynasts* as the spirit of battle moves them, if
anything less violently and less frequently than men really do in war:
'By God' and 'Oh! Hell!' exclaim the deserters in Spain; 'Blast-me-
blue!' says a postilion; 'What the hell!' says Hill; 'By God', exclaims
Wellington as his *aide-de-camp* falls mortally wounded; 'Ah,
Heaven!' mutters an officer at Wagram.

George Gillingham's 'By the Lord Harry!' in *Jude the Obscure*,
IV, Ch. 4, sounds affectedly archaic even for such a traditionalist,
whereas Sir Andret's 'God's 'ounds' and ' 'Od's blood' in *The
Famous Tragedy of the Queen of Cornwall* are wholly in keeping
with the profane medieval habit of tearing 'Christ's blessed body' all
to pieces, denounced by Chaucer. In Hardy's poems, on the other
hand, oaths are rare, even in the colloquial context of his balladry
where he permits himself at best an occasional *Gad*, or *O damn*, or
*Damn me*, or *My God*, among a handful of even less nocuous
exclamations. 'An East-End Curate' finishes with an emphatic *God
wot*! a suitably ironic finale to a depressing poem.

A considerable portion of Hardy's verbal acreage consists of
idiomatic expressions which suggest to the twentieth-century reader
a quaintness which they did not possess for Hardy or his contemporaries a century ago. The sympathetic reader will recognize 'a *pile*
of flats' or 'they had moved house *in mass*' as equivalent to our 'block
of flats' and *en masse*. He or she will be aware that Fitzpiers's
protestation 'honour bright' in *The Woodlanders*, Ch. 20, has its
parallels in Dickens and George Eliot and other writers of that
period. We accept that 'his unconscious wife' in *Far from the
Madding Crowd*, Ch. 50, or 'the unconscious horseman' in 'Master
John Horseleigh, Knight' (*A Changed Man*), meaning 'unaware,
unheeding', preserve one of the senses of *unconscious* which we
would no longer employ in this fashion. Such changes are inevitable,
but they may mislead 'the unconscious reader' into believing Hardy's
language to be more singular than it really is.

The meaning of such earlier usages, now for the most part
obsolete, is rarely in doubt. When Miss Aldclyffe says to Cytherea 'if
you must have loved him *off-hand*' (*Desperate Remedies*, Ch. 6), the
sense is plainly that of the modern idiom 'at first sight', although
elsewhere Hardy uses *off-hand* also in the senses still current today.
Similar idioms readily spring to mind: 'please to leave me'; 'a press of

matters to attend to'; 'thank you much' and 'much thanks'; 'in a pet'; 'she has been hardly used'; 'on the stretch with curiosity'; 'but a minute bygone'; 'for the inside of a fortnight'; 'such an one' and 'out upon such'; 'to painfulness' in the sense in which we might say 'until it hurt' or even *ad nauseam*; 'I'm all abroad' meaning 'confused'; and 'at any count'.

The nineteenth century of course contributed its own share to semantic change. The phrase 'for the nonce', for instance, which used to mean 'on purpose, for the occasion', as in *Hamlet* – 'I'll have prepared him / A chalice for the nonce' (IV, vii) – came to acquire the meaning 'for the time being, temporarily', which is how Hardy uses it, for example, in this passage:

> As he watched, the dead flat of the scenery overpowered him, though he was fully alive to the beauty of that untarnished early summer green which was worn *for the nonce* by the poorest blade.
> (*The Return of the Native*, III, Ch. 5)

It required the invention of the railway to extend the use of the verb *save* to catching a train:

> There was a train at six o'clock . . . which by great exertion he might *save* even now.
> (*A Laodicean*, III, Ch. 6)

Another nineteenth-century usage, still occasionally heard today, is the phrase *shake down*, used several times by Hardy, meaning 'to settle', usually temporarily, a rather more polite cousin to the modern slang expression 'to shack up with'. Mrs Melbury uses it thus in *The Woodlanders*, Ch. 11, and Angel Clare in *Tess of the d'Urbervilles*, Ch. 36, but when Arabella says of Jude, 'He'll shake down, bless 'ee – men always do', in *Jude the Obscure*, I, Ch. 9, she is using the phrase in the extended sense of 'to get used to something', which is also a nineteenth-century development.

Obsolescence is a relative term. When Hardy used such phrases as 'passing well' or 'passing mean' he may or may not have been aware that they were beginning to sound a little quaint, not to say *passé*; just as he may or may not have been aware that to put the phrase 'passably well put' into a rustic mouth would have seemed odd to such of his contemporaries as the anonymous reviewer of *Far from the Madding Crowd* who objected to it in the *Athenaeum* in December 1874.

When Hardy introduced genuine archaisms he often did so for a specific purpose. In *The Famous Tragedy of the Queen of Cornwall*, such obsolete expressions as 'for a leastness' or 'with deathy mien' are obviously intended to contribute audibly to the sense of a bygone age. Similarly, in *The Trumpet-Major*, as we have noted previously, Hardy endeavoured to re-create the age of Napoléon by narrative and descriptive means including the use of obsolete words and expressions. Such is, for instance, Bob Loveday's 'Who can have blown upon me?' (Ch. 31), here used in its earlier sense of 'to tell tales of someone', or the same speaker's 'I made myself her beau' (Ch. 29), which would have sounded distinctly old-fashioned when the novel was written in the last quarter of the nineteenth century. The intention behind the use of an archaism may be ironic: in *Two on a Tower*, Ch. 21, for instance, Hardy uses the obsolete 'in good sooth' at a moment in the narrative when the familiar motif of the poor man in love with the lady of ancient lineage is aired yet again. The timelessness implied by the survival of old modes of speech is, as much as their sense of period, an important linguistic ingredient of Hardy's Wessex.

Many of Hardy's idioms are country sayings, some of them long embedded in folk speech, some of them reminiscent of proverbs. Mrs Smith, in *A Pair of Blue Eyes*, utters whole strings of them:

'I'm sure . . . if there'd been so much trouble to get a husband in my time as there is in these days – when you must make a god-almighty of a man to get him to hae ye – I'd have trod clay for bricks before I'd ever have lowered my dignity to marry, or there's no bread in nine loaves.'
(Ch. 10)

Also in this novel occurs the expression 'in a turk of a mess' (Ch. 23) which has its parallel in the phrase 'a turk of a while' in *A Laodicean*, VI, Ch. 4, and a more distant analogue in the expression 'the Turk can't open [the door]' in *A Pair of Blue Eyes*, Ch. 2. Turks were considered to be cruel and savage, a hangover from the Middle Ages, so that the word came to denote anyone or anything big and formidable. Hardy's characterization of Troy as one who 'was moderately truthful towards men, but to women lied like a Cretan' (*Far from the Madding Crowd*, Ch. 25), illustrates another traditional proverbial denigration of foreigners.

More obviously rustic are such colloquial idioms as these: Joseph Poorgrass's 'I've had the news-bell ringing in my left ear quite bad enough for a murder, and I've seen a magpie all alone!' (*Far from the Madding Crowd*, Ch. 8) – both of them indicative of ill luck; and in the same novel Jan Coggan's picturesque asseveration 'Straight on, as sure as God made little apples' (Ch. 32), akin to Humphrey's 'They say he can talk French as fast as a maid can eat blackberries' in *The Return of the Native*, II, Ch. 1. In *The Woodlanders*, Ch. 9, Hardy uses the phrase 'from cellar to apple-loft'; in 'The Withered Arm' (*Wessex Tales*) cows are described as being 'in full pail'; in *Tess of the d'Urbervilles*, dairyman Crick describes the ill-used young woman from Mellstock 'ballyragging Jack by side and by seam' (Ch. 21); in *Jude the Obscure*, Arabella spouts such sententious saws as 'A contented mind is a continual feast' (V, Ch. 8), and Tinker Taylor 'To be sure, halfpence that have been in circulation can't be expected to look like new ones from the Mint' (VI, Ch. 7). In the same breath this worthy connoisseur refers to Arabella in country fashion as 'a little bit thick in the flitch perhaps', as rounded a description of her as Hardy manages anywhere in the novel. In 'The Waiting Supper' (*A Changed Man*) occurs the expression 'she's left in very lean pasturage' to describe Christine Bellston's straitened circum-stances and in 'The Romantic Adventures of a Milkmaid' in the same collection, Vine describes the horses pulling the grand coach with Margery in it as rattling on 'like hell-and-skimmer', a phrase that preserves the dialect meaning of *skimmer* denoting rapid movement.

Pairs of words are frequently conjoined in such colloquial idioms: 'neck and crop', 'use nor principal', 'by inching and pinching', 'beyond sniff and snaff', 'by long and by late', 'front and foremost'. Idiomatic expressions may be used to add colour to a particular character's speech, like the tranter's in *Under the Greenwood Tree*: 'He's all in a mope, as might be said' (IV, Ch. 4) or 'Chanticleer's comb is a-cut then' (V, Ch. 2); or Mr Penny's 'That'll put the stuns upon a man' (*ibid.*) where the substantive *stun* is a derivative of the verb *stun*, cognate with *astound*, which means 'to startle, surprise'. In *Far from the Madding Crowd*, Jacob and Mark Clark ask, in unison, 'What's a-brewing, Henery?' (Ch. 8), as apposite a question as any in this bibulous story. In *The Trumpet-Major*, the Lovedays' social standing, a matter of great import to Mrs Garland, is con-stantly signalled by appropriate diction that would some years ago have been categorized as non-U. The miller is not above admitting to such popular superstitions as 'there *was* a letter in the candle' (Ch. 12) while Bob goes in for idiomatic turns of phrase like 'That's just the shape of it' (Ch. 33), which resembles Sailor Cornick's colloquial

'You all seem struck of a heap wi' that' (Ch. 36).

Nat Chapman, in *Two on a Tower*, Ch. 13, responds to the question 'How are you?' with as good an idiomatic résumé of conventional church-going Christianity as Hardy achieved any-where: 'One hour a week wi' God A'mighty and the rest with the devil, as a chap may say.' Other facets of rustic devotional life are expressed no less colourfully: 'Ye might have tried till the end of Revelations' in *A Pair of Blue Eyes*, Ch. 23, suggests quite literally the long road through all the books of Scripture, as well as the distant prospect of Doomsday. Old Timothy Tangs in *The Woodlanders*, Ch. 22, utters an idiom – 'that will take the squeak out of your Sunday shoes, John!' – which incidentally conveys something of the importance of the Sabbath in village social life. No less idiomatic is the reckoning of time by the Church calendar, as in 'by Lady Day', as well as by seasonal manifestations and more mundane signposts like 'in the dog days' or 'last tatie-digging'. Early rising has its colloquial idiom in the phrase 'to go cock-watching', an innocent enough expression on the face of it, but the cock's crowing has Christian associations which hint at duplicity in even the most innocuous context. Mr Swancourt may have noticed that Stephen Smith 'seemed averse to explanation' when he referred to the latter's going 'cock-watching the morning after a journey of fourteen or sixteen hours' (*A Pair of Blue Eyes*, Ch. 4). And there is even more explicit suspicion in the waggoner's remark to Winterborne:

'That was she – Mrs Charmond! Who'd ha' thought it? What in the world can a woman that does nothing be cock-watching out here at this time o' day for?'
(*The Woodlanders*, Ch. 13)

There are idiomatic expressions to indicate a person's age, like the Second Avice's 'Going in nineteen' (*The Well-Beloved*, II, Ch. 4), or Hardy's description of Corporal Tullidge as on 'the shady side of fifty' (*The Trumpet-Major*, Ch. 4), or Mrs Cuxsome's reminiscence: 'I was getting up husband-high at that time – one-half girl, and t'other half woman, as one may say' (*The Mayor of Casterbridge*, Ch. 13).

'As one may say', indeed. Hardy's use of this and similar phrases in a tone half explanatory and half apologetic hints at his awareness that some of the expressions he employs may be unfamiliar to his readers or deemed unconventional. Not every reader could be expected to

possess the same familiarity as the author with dialect, colloquialisms, idiolects, archaic English, and such occasional literary quibbles
as 'one who out-Farfraed Farfrae' or 'I have out-Sued Sue' or 'the
mean bread-and-cheese question', and biblical ones like Ethelberta's
'A coronet covers a multitude of sins' or Eustacia's 'I have certainly
got thistles for figs in a worldly sense.'

In his constant search for the right verb, Hardy employed many
verb phrases current at the time but since then either modified or
discarded altogether from the language. The verb *to do*, for instance,
could be attached as readily to tea as to a door or a person:

'Now, are you sure you have quite done tea?'
(*Desperate Remedies*, Ch. 5)

'Well – don't do the door. That's all I say.'
(*Jude the Obscure*, VI, Ch. 6)

'You've done for yourself by this, young man', said she. 'I don't know
whether you know it.' 'Of course I do. I meant to do for myself.'
(*Ibid.*, VI, Ch. 9)

In *Desperate Remedies*, Ch. 6, Miss Aldclyffe says to Cytherea:
'Think over the whole matter, and *get cooled*', and in *A Pair of Blue
Eyes*, Ch. 9, Mr Swancourt refers to the possibility of getting rid of
Stephen as '*get shot of* him again'. In the same novel, Ch. 7, Stephen
uses the phrase '*hob and nob* with him', which acquired its modern
form without the connective in the second half of the nineteenth
century. The taciturn reporter in *Desperate Remedies* (Sequel), who
will not divulge his 'line o' life', as Crickett calls it, says 'I am no
trade', which has a precursor in Dryden's 'A Captain is a very gainful
Trade', noted in Johnson's Dictionary, but it was not a common
expression.

The following examples, scattered throughout Hardy's fiction, are
more obviously idiomatic phrasal verbs: 'To *help away* the tedious
hours', 'who *own to* no moral code' (*Desperate Remedies*); 'Knight
again found himself *thrown with* Elfride' (*A Pair of Blue Eyes*); 'I do
hope Daisy will *fetch round* again' (*Far from the Madding Crowd*);
'Do you brave me? do you *stand me out*?' (*The Return of the Native*);
'We must needs *be put-to* for want of a wholesome crust'; 'Maybe I'll
walk on till the coach *makes up on* me'; 'when he had tried to *hang
near* her' (*The Mayor of Casterbridge*); 'Look here, *cut off home* at
once' (*The Woodlanders*); 'She had *loved herself out*'; 'When his

step-children had grown up and were *placed out* in life' (*Wessex Tales*: 'Interlopers at the Knap'); '*bending himself to* a rapid walk' and 'she . . . *bent her steps*'; 'it was the season for "*taking up*" the meadows' (*Tess of the d'Urbervilles*); 'It *had place in* one of the minor parks' (*Life's Little Ironies*: 'The Son's Veto'); 'they would *make out* a holiday' (*ibid.*: 'Andrey Satchel and the Parson and Clerk').

Sometimes Hardy's phrases have a very modern ring: 'You can hardly find a girl whose heart has not been *had*', says Miss Aldclyffe in *Desperate Remedies*, Ch. 6, the emphasis here being Hardy's; yet at other times he is either deliberately old-fashioned (as in 'forgetting of 'ee', in *The Trumpet-Major*) or just appears to be so to the modern reader: 'I make no doubt', (*The Hand of Ethelberta*); 'Bethinking himself of a wiser plan'; 'where he had used to sit' (*The Return of the Native*); 'He might have searched Europe over' (*Life's Little Ironies*; 'On the Western Circuit'); 'our calling cousins when really strangers' (*Jude the Obscure*).

The difference between Hardy's nineteenth-century English and the language of a century later is quite often confined to a single grammatical element, as some of the above examples make clear. Hardy repeatedly writes 'on a sudden', or 'on sight of', for instance, or 'there's an end on't', displaying a tendency towards adverbial phrases which leads to occasional ponderousness of expression. Thus he writes *in reality* for 'really', *to a certainty* for 'certainly', *in ordinary* for 'ordinarily', *to the full* for 'fully'. He retains the old-fashioned 'for a wonder', 'without the door', and 'by your help', and he uses expressions like 'collected together' and 'vanished away' where the adverbs are plainly tautological.

Hardy's idiomatic range is impressive. At its least successful it displays a leaning towards cliché or verbosity; at its best it draws upon colloquial idiom or rustic speech or deliberately revivifies older usages to enliven narrative and dialogue, to add individuality to character, or to shed an ironic light upon person or incident. The modern reader needs to be circumspect in not confusing normal nineteenth-century usage with genuine archaism, and in being aware of changes in the language occurring during Hardy's long lifetime.

The example, quoted earlier, of Hardy's preferring 'in mass' to *en masse*, both of which were current in nineteenth-century English, illustrates the occasional incursion into his language of phrases modelled on French idioms. The influence was probably quite unconscious in most cases: 'She became teacher in a school' (*Elle est devenue institutrice*); 'How sorry I am' (*Comme je suis triste*); 'they are all known to me very well' (*je les connais tous très bien*). In Hardy's Preface to *Wessex Tales* we find a sentence beginning 'In those days, too, there was still living an old woman', which reads much like French *de ce temps, aussi, il vivait encore une vieille*. And in his paper 'Memories of Church Restoration' occurs the phrase 'architects the most experienced' which is idiomatic French rather than English and has its parallels in similar post-nominal placing of adjectives not only in some of Hardy's poems, but also in his fiction from *Desperate Remedies* to *Jude the Obscure*: 'during the spring succeeding' (*durant le printemps suivant*); 'book-shelves ordinary and extraordinary'; 'a consumption too great'; and with adjectives in the superlative in cases like these: 'rooms the best'; 'breezes the freshest'; 'women the most delicate'; 'events the most impressive'; 'men the most honourable'; 'mischief the most dire'. When Henchard overhears Farfrae speaking to Lucetta in Chapter 27 of *The Mayor of Casterbridge*, the Scotsman is speaking 'with the unmistakable inflection of the lover pure' which, as Hardy no doubt knew, is the exact equivalent of French *de l'amant pur*, which means 'pure' in the sense of unblemished, chaste, whereas the pre-nominal alternative *du pur amant* means 'pure' in the sense of single-minded. The element of ambiguity in Hardy's phrase is no doubt intentional.

'Hardy's concern for accuracy of communication of idea', in the words of J.G. Southworth (*The Poetry of Thomas Hardy*, p. 131), is evident in his ceaseless search for the right word or phrase to express his vision, a search that led him, as we are constantly made aware, along a variety of rarely trodden linguistic byways branching off the main road of nineteenth- and early twentieth-century English. Hardy's vision was a strongly pictorial one, and it is in concrete description rather than abstract discussion that he achieved his greatest successes as a stylist. We may remember the gist of some of Ethelberta's arguments or of the often stilted dialogue between Sue and Jude, but the unforgettable moments in Hardy's fiction are those in which – whatever their symbolism – the pictorial details of a scene, a landscape, or a person's appearance are imprinted on the reader's mind and memory: Knight poised on the cliff-face; Troy's sword-play; Rainbarrow; Casterbridge, 'clean-cut and distinct, like a chess-board on a green table-cloth'; Marty South framed in her cottage window; Tess's eyes; Talbothays and Flintcomb-Ash; Jude's vision of Christminster. Hardy's observant eye and his architectural training prompted his modes of composition: the arrangement of figures in a landscape; the balance between foreground and distance;

the framing or delimiting of the given scene; but it is his feeling for movement and his strong sense of colour that breathe life into these pictures. In terms of language, verbs supply the movement while the remarkable richness of Hardy's lexical paintbox supplies the colour.

Hardy's sense of colour was nurtured from childhood. He used to sit on the staircase at Bockhampton, as he recalls in the *Life*, p. 15, and wait for the evening sun to enhance the 'Venetian red' of the walls while reciting Isaac Watts's 'And now another day is gone'. The memory of these colourful moments persists in those numerous sunsets that punctuate the lives of his characters. His later visits to galleries and exhibitions brought detailed awareness of the problems of translating a mental picture on to canvas: the importance of 'harmony and softness', 'light and shade', 'shadow and contrast', 'charm of colour', 'darkness and clouds', 'design', 'dignity', 'drollery', 'power in portraits', 'truth', 'colour and accuracy', and all the other elements of pictorial composition he jotted in his *Schools of Painting Notebook*. His growing familiarity with individual painters and paintings further deepened his discrimination between colours and made him grope for words accurate enough to convey tints and shades to match those in pictures or, increasingly, in nature herself. His first attempt at verbal pictorialism in verse, the early poem 'Domicilium', has a solitary 'red roses' to indicate colour; but by the time he wrote 'Neutral Tones' in 1867, some eight or ten years later, he was able to use two simple words of colour to evoke scene and mood with astonishing deftness:

> We stood by a pond that winter day,
> And the sun was white, as though chidden of God,
> And a few leaves lay on the starving sod;
>     – They had fallen from an ash, and were gray.

From these beginnings sprang quickly and with growing assurance Hardy's ability to express in words the colours, the light and shade, contrasts and harmonies, that characterize his numerous descriptions and images. The first of his many memorable 'framed' pictures is Cytherea's glimpse of the figures on the scaffolding surrounding the spire in the opening chapter of *Desperate Remedies*, a picture suggesting 'an illuminated miniature, framed in by the dark margin of the window, the keen-edged shadiness of which emphasized by contrast the softness of the objects enclosed'. Cytherea herself had already been introduced into the story, with a single brush stroke that anticipated the numerous images of the later novels, as 'an exceptional young maiden who glowed amid the dulness like a single bright-red poppy in a field of brown stubble.' The heroines of Hardy's next two novels are similarly set off against their surroundings: Fancy 'like a flower among vegetables', with her dark eyes, her dark-brown hair, and her 'gauzy dress of white with blue facings' (*Under the Greenwood Tree*, I, Ch. 7), and Elfride 'appearing amid the dingy scene like a rainbow in a murky sky' (*A Pair of Blue Eyes*, Ch. 29).

Images like these rely on sharply contrasting colours, lines, and concepts. The effect is sometimes one of shock and not always felicitous: 'The sun was resting on the hill like a drop of blood on an eyelid' (*The Mayor of Casterbridge*, Ch. 35) is a notorious example. More successful are the various nocturnal images involving Hardy's sensitiveness to shades of black, and contrasting these with red where appropriate, the two dominant colours in *The Return of the Native*. The nocturnal bonfires on Egdon, for example, with their connotations of ancient pagan ceremonies, are aptly described as 'glowing scarlet-red from the shades, like wounds in a black hide' (I. Ch. 3). Eustacia and Wildeve, traversing the dark undergrowth of the heath are glimpsed as by 'an eye above', their faces illumined by moonlight, 'amid the expanse like two pearls on a table of ebony' (IV, Ch. 3). No less startling are images involving degrees of blackness: young Charley appearing 'on the dark ridge of heathland, like a fly on a negro' (II, Ch. 4); or the 'knot of stunted hollies, which in the general darkness of the scene stood as the pupil in a black eye' (IV, Ch. 4). There is a 'keen-edged', deliberately unpleasant, quality in the reference to one of the de Stancy ancestors painted with 'a mole on his cheek, black and distinct as a fly in cream' (*A Laodicean*, III, Ch. 1). Less stark is the bird's-eye view of the sheep-washing pool in *Far from the Madding Crowd*, Ch. 19, reflecting the light sky, 'as a glistening Cyclops' eye in a green face'; or the wood-smoke above Geoffrey Day's cottage drooping 'over the roof like a blue feather in a lady's hat' (*Under the Greenwood Tree*, II, Ch. 6). Green and blue are softer colours and their impact is correspondingly less forceful. So are pink and grey, hence the gentler image of a youthful face, 'fresh in colour . . . like the light under a heap of rose-petals' (*Wessex Tales*: 'The Withered Arm', 2.); or of the 'pervasive grayness [which] overspread her once dark brown hair, like morning rime on heather' (*ibid*.: 'Fellow-townsmen', IX). Angel Clare is persistently reminded of 'the old Elizabethan simile of roses filled with snow', as he contemplates Tess's profile 'keen as a cameo cut from the dun background of the cow' in a scene richly painted in pinks and whites, at whose centre is 'that little upward lift in the middle of her red top lip . . . distracting, infatuating, maddening' (*Tess of the d'Urbervilles*, Ch. 24), later in the novel referred to as those 'deep red lips like Cupid's bow' (Ch. 39). Red and white, as Tony Tanner has well demonstrated, are the focal colours of this novel and their symbolic impact is inescapable from the first mention of Tess's ironically medicinal 'peony mouth' to the 'scarlet blot' on the white ceiling which 'had the appearance of a gigantic ace of hearts', signalling the murder of Alec d'Urberville, who had been, from the moment of their first meeting, 'the blood-red ray in the spectrum of her young life' (Ch. 5).

The 'peony mouth', the 'scarlet blot', and the 'blood-red ray' give some indication of Hardy's endeavour to indicate different tints of red in a novel which also tells of 'the crimson brick lodge' leading to The Slopes, Mrs. d'Urberville's house, of 'the same rich red colour . . . which rose like a geranium bloom against the subdued colours around' (Ch. 5); of 'stripes like red-hot pokers'; of 'liquid fire'; of 'madder stains on her skin', of the evening sun 'like a great inflamed wound in the sky'; of 'a Last Day luridness in this red-coaled glow'; and so on to yet another 'large red-brick building' on the final page. Red is but one of a dozen colours on which Hardy plays ingenious verbal variations throughout the entire range of his work. Faces, places, gowns, sunrises and sunsets, are painted in varying shades of red: a girl 'redly weeps' in 'The Christening'; a face is 'reddish-fleshed' or 'ruddy' or 'the colour of light porphyry' or with 'rose-flush coming and going' or even, in Arabella's case, 'spirituous crimson'; cheeks are of 'peony hues' or 'crimsoned' or 'cherry' or were 'once rosy-red'; the old maltster's eyes were 'vermilion-red' like the sunsets over Deadman's Bay; Lizbie Browne's hair was 'bay-red'; and one of the three strangers in the story of that name sported a few 'grog-blossoms' in 'the neighbourhood of his nose'. Other hues are indicated by 'carmine', 'redbreast red', 'rust-red', 'russet-red', 'winy red', 'golden red', and 'crimson bright'. The rising sun is 'red upedging' or 'ruby-red'; the setting sun is 'like a crimson wound'; and the colour of war is 'red' or 'crimson' in *The Dynasts* and in the poem 'Channel Firing' with its unforgettable

> All nations striving strong to make
> Red war yet redder.

There is an ironic *double entendre* in the reference to Henchard at a fateful moment of recognition, with the aid of a French gambling term: 'the rich *rouge-et-noir* of his countenance underwent a slight change' (*The Mayor of Casterbridge*, Ch. 10); while in *The Woodlanders*, Ch. 42, 'evening came at last' with a change of colour rather more forcefully painted:

> The evening came at last; the sun, when its chin was on the earth, found an opening through which to pierce the shade, and stretched irradiated gauzes across the damp atmosphere, making the wet trunks shine, and throwing splotches of such ruddiness on the leaves beneath the beech that they were turned to gory hues.

The colour blue enters Hardy's fiction with Elfride Swancourt's eyes:

> These eyes were blue; blue as autumn distance – blue as the blue we see between the retreating mouldings of hills and woody slopes on a sunny September morning. A misty and shady blue, that had no beginning or surface, and was looked *into* rather than *at*.
> (*A Pair of Blue Eyes*, Ch. 1)

Such misty blue eyes are rare; Stephen Smith's, by contrast, are 'bright sparkling blue-gray', in the same novel; Gertrude Lodge's in 'The Withered Arm' (*Wessex Tales*) are, more vaguely, 'of a bluish turn'. The colour can denote a 'cold blue quality' as readily as a 'soft azure landscape' and ranges from vague 'misty blues' to 'deep blue':

> The atmosphere beneath is languorous, and is so tinged with azure that what artists call the middle distance partakes also of that hue, while the horizon beyond is of the deepest ultramarine.
> (*Tess of the d'Urbervilles*, Ch. 2)

Shades of blue include the 'sapphirine hue' of the sky in spring; a 'greenish-blue sky'; 'dark blue fragments of cloud'; the 'bright blue hue of new paint' on the turnip-slicing machine at Flintcomb-Ash; the 'bluish pallor' of a white dress; a 'sky-blue dress'; the 'air-blue gown' of 'The Voice'; 'greenish-blue satin' and a 'greenish-blue sky', both in *The Well-Beloved*, and 'the blue narcotic haze' of Alec d'Urberville's cigar. In 'A Spellbound Palace'

> The stirless depths of the yews
> Are vague with misty blues,

and in the same collection of poems, *Human Shows, Far Phantasies, Songs, and Trifles*, another poem begins with the lines

> At four this day of June I rise:
> The dawn-light strengthens steadily;
> Earth is a cerule mystery,
> As if not far from Paradise
> > At four o'clock.
> > ('Four in the Morning')

Eyes fascinated Hardy. This is obvious from the pains he took to describe their colours. Elfride's misty September eyes were only the beginning. Various shades of grey were attributed to others, like Elizabeth-Jane's 'aerial-grey eyes', or the 'green-gray' eyes in 'The Chosen', or the memory of Emma Lavinia's 'gray eyes' in 'After a Journey'. Matilda Johnson's eyes 'would have been called brown, but they were really eel-colour, like many other nice brown eyes', exactly the same shade of brown, be it noted, as the tree pictures on the drinking cups served on Sundays at the Three Mariners in Caster-bridge. The first Avice has 'bright hazel' eyes to match her 'brown tresses of hair'; the romantic Margery's eyes 'were of a liquid brown'. But the most lustrous of all were Tess's eyes, so much more poly-chromatic to their creator than the green eyes of Nastassia Kinski in Roman Polanski's film. Hardy's first grandiloquent description of Tess's eyes is in fact an admission of defeat; her eyes are indescribable:

> Large tender eyes, neither black nor blue nor gray nor violet; rather all those shades together, and a hundred others, which could be seen if one looked into their irises – shade behind shade – tint beyond tint – around pupils that had no bottom.
> (*Tess of the d'Urbervilles*, Ch. 14)

Angel, looking into Tess's eyes later in the story,

> plumbed the deepness of the ever-varying pupils, with their radiating fibrils of blue, and black, and gray, and violet, while she regarded him as Eve at her second waking might have regarded Adam.
> (*ibid*., Ch. 27)

This is a more typically Hardyan picture than the preceding one, with its deliberate rare *deepness* in preference to 'depth'; its use of an uncommon technical word, *fibrils*, which George Eliot ascribed to Mirah's dark curly hair in *Daniel Deronda*, and which Hardy here uses to evoke numerous minute strands of strong positive colours; and its persistent biblical symbolism. To his mother, Angel later described these unfathomable eyes rather lamely as 'violety-bluey-blackish' (Ch. 39), but what in the world else could he have said?

Sue Bridehead presents Hardy with an ocular problem of a different kind: her eyes are not so much indescribable in terms of colour, as 'untranslatable' in terms of character. They are 'liquid' eyes in several places, and they are both 'bright' (in III, 1) and 'dark' (in II, 4 and III, 6), all three of them words that denote qualities of temperament and mood rather than actual colours, which is in keeping with the neutral tones and paucity of strong colours in *Jude the Obscure*.

'Gray', writes Samuel Hynes in *The Pattern of Hardy's Poetry*, p. 113, echoing J.G. Southworth, 'is by far Hardy's favorite color – it is, in fact, about as colorful as his dark world ever gets.' This is a comment which, however appropriate to some of Hardy's poetry, is not true of his fiction. Here Hardy's characteristic colour is brown, or rather a whole spectrum of browns. There are 'whitish-brown' tints produced by the friction of lime and stone upon grandfather James's garments in *Under the Greenwood Tree*, I, Ch. 3; there is the action of dust upon gaiters and shoes, turning them 'whitey-brown' in *The Trumpet-Major*, Ch. 1 (the spelling is 'whity-brown' in the 1897 edition); in *The Hand of Ethelberta*, Ch. 2, Faith's little green-leather sheath is 'worn at the edges to whity-brown' (*sic*); and in *The Woodlanders*, Ch. 4, Melbury says 'how the whitey-brown (*sic*) creeps out of the earth over us', referring to the wintry mud on his horse's hoofs. Later in the same novel, Melbury's companions appear in the doorway, their clothes 'whity-brown' (*sic*). This somewhat soiled colour recurs several times in *Tess of the d'Urbervilles*, where Hardy applies it to Tess's rough wrapper in Ch. 42, to the landscape of the uplands in Ch. 44, to the women-workers' pinners in Ch. 47. The occasional orthographic variants do not signify any subtle distinctions, but the colour itself connotes wear and toil even when applied to landscapes.

Then there is 'grayish-brown', which, despite its form, denotes a shade of grey in a piece of landscape painting in which Hardy is visibly mixing his colours to achieve the right tints:

The long-armed trees and shrubs of juniper, cedar, and pine varieties, were

grayish-black; those of the broad-leaved sort, together with the herbage, were grayish-green; the eternal hills and tower behind them were grayish-brown; the sky, dropping behind all, gray of the purest melancholy.
(*A Pair of Blue Eyes*, Ch. 5)


Brown tints are frequently indicated by suggestive nouns: 'a brick-brown street', 'chocolate-toned rocks', 'mud-coloured clouds', 'snuff-coloured stone', 'nut-brown soil', 'dove-coloured silk' with its suggestion of a greyish sheen. Brown hair is common among Hardy's heroines: Ethelberta's is 'squirrel-coloured', which might puzzle the modern reader accustomed to grey squirrels rather than their red precursors; Tess's, early in the novel, Ch. 5, is described as 'then earth-coloured', an epithet as full of symbolic import as it is characteristic of Hardy's vision of the soil as embracing various shades of brown from nut-colour through mud-colour to the dreary 'blank agricultural brownness' of a field stripped of its crop. Some-where in the middle range of brown is Paula Power's hair 'of good English brown, neither light nor dark'. Marty South's hair is of a shade of brown, 'a rare and beautiful approximation to chestnut', that allows a strong reddish tint to stand out such as 'you can't match by dyeing', as barber Percomb professionally remarks (*The Woodlanders*, Ch. 2). In the same novel, Grace Melbury's eyebrows call up memories of days spent in galleries: 'She had well-formed eyebrows which, had her portrait been painted, would probably have been done in Prouts's or Vandyke brown' (Ch. 5). The latter colour, a fine deep brown, is that of Hardy's father's 'dark Vandyke-brown hair' as he remembers it in his autobiography (*Life*, p. 13). Emma's hair is remembered as 'nut-coloured' in 'After a Journey', and Hardy's description of her as the 'young lady in brown' (*Life*, p. 78), clearly derived from the 'soft deep dark coloured brown habit' (p. 69) which she wore at their first meeting, as much as from her brown tresses, which re-appear in the first Avice in *The Well-Beloved*. Arabella's first impression upon Jude is that of a 'brown girl' with 'the rich complexion of a Cochin hen's egg' (*Jude the Obscure*, I, Ch. 6), dark-eyed, and well-built, whose later physical decline is succinctly indicated by the alcoholic reddening of her countenance. Another form of change is that of the poem 'Every Artemisia':

> '. . . My hair, then auburn-brown,
> Pangs have wanned white.'

A characteristic Hardy word is the verb *embrown*, used both transitively and intransitively, a poetic word he had found in *Paradise Lost*, and which he tended to associate with night-fall: 'embrowning twilight', 'Egdon Heath embrowned itself moment by moment', 'the wood was embrowned with the coming night'. The meaning is not so much a literal becoming brown as to grow dusky, a Turneresque fusing of earth and its objects with the darkening sky creating shades of darkness in contrast with each other: 'The shadowy black figures of pedestrians moved up, down, and across the embrowned roadway' (*The Well-Beloved*, II, Ch. 11). Occasionally the word is, however, to be taken more literally, as in this picture of Tess's face, in which Hardy's sensitive response to hues and texture finds subtle expression:

> Her countenance, a natural carnation slightly embrowned by the season, had deepened its tinge with the beating of the rain-drops; and her hair, which the pressure of the cows' flanks had, as usual, caused to tumble down from its fastenings and stray beyond the curtain of her calico bonnet, was made clammy by the moisture, till it hardly was better than seaweed.
>
> (*Tess of the d'Urbervilles*, Ch. 30)

In the same novel, Ch. 24, Hardy effects a more violent change to brown by describing how 'Ethiopic scorchings browned the upper slopes of the pastures', an emotive description of a kind not unfamiliar in Hardy's use of colour.

When Hardy uses the word *drab*, he is primarily thinking of the dull light-brown or yellowish-brown colour denoted by the word in normal nineteenth-century usage; but by the end of the century the common modern connotation of dullness and shabbiness had become accepted, so that an element of ambiguity sometimes enters into Hardy's usage. His meaning can be quite unequivocal: Alec d'Urberville is wearing 'a dandy cap, drab jacket, breeches *of the same hue*' (*Tess of the d'Urbervilles*, Ch. 7); on the other hand, the word is used with emotive overtones in the picture of the swede-field at Flintcomb-Ash as 'in colour a *desolate drab*' (Ch. 43), and something of the same force attaches to the dawn breaking on a cool, rainy morning 'in hues of drab and ash' (*Far from the Madding Crowd*, Ch. 38).

The connotations of Hardy's browns are for the most part those of the natural world, of living creatures and hard, honest toil, of squirrels and chestnuts, of ploughed fields and stones and rocks, of muddy lanes, and of the interaction of country folk with their surroundings:

> 'You looked so weather-browned,
>   And brown in clothes, you seemed to be
>   Made of the dusty ground!'
>   ('A Thought in Two Moods')

By contrast, words such as *ash* or *ashy* and others depicting shades of grey are frequently as much expressions of states of mind and moods as of colours. Hynes's implication that Hardy's world is predominantly a grey one is true of that side of his nature which brooded on morbid themes, which dwelt on 'rose-coloured' dreams toned down 'to a greyish tinge', on a pretty, sensitive mouth turning to 'ashy lips', on things spectral and mournful and gloomy. And so grey becomes the colour 'of the purest melancholy' as early as *A Pair of Blue Eyes*. The connotations persist:

A zinc sky met a leaden sea on this hand, the low wind groaned and whined, and not a bird sang.
   (*The Hand of Ethelberta*, Ch. 31)

Clare arose in the light of a dawn that was ashy and furtive, as though associated with crime.
   (*Tess of the d'Urbervilles*, Ch. 36)

. . . the whole bush or tree forming a staring sketch in white lines on the mournful gray of the sky and horizon.
   (*Ibid.*, Ch. 43)

With the shifting of the clouds the faces of the steeps vary in colour and in shade, broad lights appearing where mist and vagueness had prevailed, dissolving in their turn into melancholy gray, which spreads over and eclipses the luminous bluffs.
   (*A Changed Man*: 'A Tryst at an Ancient Earthwork')

In 'The Darkling Thrush' frost was 'spectre-gray', in 'The Tree and the Lady' the tree speaks of 'Icicles grieving me gray', while 'In a Waiting-Room' the melancholy mood of the scene is aggressively painted in the opening lines:

> On a morning sick as the day of doom
>   With the drizzling gray
>   Of an English May
> There were few in the railway waiting-room.

The cycle of the seasons reverts to greyness:

> And month after month lapsed, graytime to
> green and to sere,
> ('One Who Married Above Him')

which has its prose counterpart in this:

> The gold of the summer picture was now gray, the colours mean, the rich
> soil mud, and the river cold.
> (*Tess of the d'Urbervilles*, Ch. 37)

Rarely has the dreariness of winter been more bleakly sketched in so few words.

The melancholy connotations of the colour predominate, but Hardy was by no means blind to its various shades. He distinguishes, for example, 'blue-gray', 'purplish-grey', 'green-gray', 'greenish-grey', 'reddish-gray', as well as 'pearly grey' and 'sky-gray', and hints at more specific colours still with such phrases as 'a chinchilla shade' of whiskers, or the 'mouse-coloured trunks' of beeches, or Jim Hayward turning 'as pale as rendlewood', the latter a dialect word denoting bark ripped off an oak-tree which Hardy had replaced elsewhere by the less unfamiliar 'barked-oak twigs', but retained in 'The Romantic Adventures of a Milkmaid'.

In October 1896 (according to *Life*, p. 284) Hardy noted 'a novel, good, microscopic touch in Crabbe': 'He gives surface without outline, describing his church by telling the colour of the lichens.' The reference is to the opening of Letter II of Crabbe's *The Borough* and to Nature's 'living Stains' compared with the artist's perishable 'Greens and Greys'. It is in the use of his own greens that Hardy comes closest to Crabbe's 'microscopic touch': his careful tinting of moss, for example, in the case of old tiles on a steep, sloping roof 'being overgrown with rich olive-hued moss' (*Desperate Remedies*, Ch. 15), an early reaction to Crabbe, possibly, whom he seems to have first read in his twenties (cp. Pinion, *Companion*, p. 202). Perhaps closer still, with its mention of 'lichened', is the face of the railway tunnel in *A Laodicean*, I, Ch. 12:

> The vertical front of the tunnel, faced with brick that had once been red, was now weather-stained, lichened, and mossed over in harmonious rusty-browns, pearly greys, and neutral greens, at the very base appearing a little blue-black spot like a mouse-hole – the tunnel's mouth.

Here, too, is 'surface without outline' and Hardy sees his colours much as Crabbe saw them, which,

> while they meet, their due distinctions keep;
> Mix'd but not blended.

There is similar emphasis on surface colour in 'the green-faced time-keepers' in *Far from the Madding Crowd*, Ch. 1, and the striking image in 'Last Look round St Martin's Fair':

> The moon presents the lustre-lacking face
> Of a brass dial gone green
> Whose hours no eye can trace.

Another image in which shape is subordinated to colour occurs in 'A Countenance':

> And her lips were too full, some might say:
> I did not think so. Anyway,
> The shadow her lower one would cast
> Was green in hue whenever she passed
> Bright sun on midsummer leaves.

As with other colours, Hardy took pains to suggest the shades of green he wished to depict: 'neutral, green hills'; 'monotonous gray-green grass'; the contrasting greens of the Vale of Blackmoor – where 'hedgerows appear a network of dark green threads overspreading the paler green of the grass'; the 'dingy green' of the trees along the dusty road to Weydon-Priors; the 'scarecrow green' of Joshua Jopp's coat, faded by sunlight; the 'chalky-green' of the sea along the shore at Sandbourne; the 'neutral green-and-blue tongues of water' at Barwith Strand. There are 'green-rheumed clouds' in 'The Pedigree'; 'warm yellowy-green' birch-leaves in 'The Upper Birch-Leaves'; plants of 'blueish green' in 'The Turnip-Hoer'; and the moon, by and by, turning 'a yellow-green, / Like a large glow-worm in the sky' in 'At Moonrise and Onwards'.

In many instances Hardy's greens lack the vibrant freshness usually associated with that colour. He seems always to be seeing the sere beyond, so that to don green at all is but an act of temporary assertion, 'bravery of greenth', in a characteristic phrase. 'The so-called spring was but winter overlaid with a thin coat of greenness', is

Hardy's vision applied to Clare seeking his deserted wife. Beneath the transient green of the Hardy country lies the ever persistent agricultural brownness of centuries of ploughed soil, and of fields of brown stubble doomed to wintry decay.

There are various hues of yellow in Hardy's chromatic vocabulary, although it is not one of his characteristic colours. He paints the sky as 'a lemon-hued expanse' in chapter 8 of *A Pair of Blue Eyes*, and in 'orange-yellow' as 'a familiar September sunset' in Chapter 11. By contrast, the awakening sky is 'primrose-hued' in *Far from the Madding Crowd*, Ch. 46. Topaz hues, ranging from yellow to pink, are introduced to add their own variety to a scene:

> The weather changed; the sunlight, which had been like tin for weeks, assumed the hues of topaz.
> (*The Mayor of Casterbridge*, Ch. 26)

> Behind the perpendicular, oblique, zigzagged, and curved zinc 'tall-boys', that formed a grey pattern not unlike early Gothic numerals against the sky, the men and women on the tops of the omnibuses saw an irradiation of topaz hues, darkened here and there into richest russet.
> (*The Well-Beloved*, III, Ch. 5)

Yellow can be the colour of a blackbird's 'crocus-coloured bill' on Easter Day ('I Watched a Blackbird'), and of a 'kindly yellow day of mild low-travelling winter sun' ('A Spellbound Palace'), but it is more typical of autumn, where Hardy finds 'green and yellowish leaves' in one scene, and, in another, more vividly:

> The various species of trees had begun to assume the more distinctive colours of their decline, and where there had been one pervasive green were now twenty greenish yellows, the air in the vistas between them being half opaque with blue exhalation.
> (*The Hand of Ethelberta*, Ch. 12)

'Blue and yellow autumn-time' he calls it in *Life's Little Ironies*, not very original perhaps, but significant in Hardy's personal kaleidoscope: blue is his calmest, most serene colour, while yellow, with its prospect of autumnal decline, is melancholy. He speaks of 'the yellow melancholy of this one-candled spectacle' in one place in *Tess of the d'Urbervilles*, Ch. 3, and of 'the sad yellow rays which the morning candles emitted' in another, Ch. 29. Even the perpendicular stalks of oats are 'amber-yellow' only as they fall to the scythe.

Orange and blond, gold and silver are rare colours in Hardy's vocabulary, although here also he distinguishes different hues: 'ochreous' and 'ensaffroned'; 'corn-coloured' and 'aureate'; 'silver-wiry' and 'steely'. Sue's voice is 'silvery'; a 'tarnished moon' has a face 'resembling the outworn gold-leaf halo of some worm-eaten Tuscan saint'; mists and twilight hazes are 'aureate' and 'ochreous'.

Purple, on the other hand, is closer to home with its reminders of plum and mulberry and heather and hillocks. Donald Davie has commented in *Agenda* on Hardy's 'purple' in those passages where the sense is that of the Virgilian *purpureus*, which Lewis and Short in *A Latin Dictionary* define as 'brilliant, shining, bright, beautiful' – vivid colours, not confined to the colour purple alone. Such, as Davie points out, are the 'purples' in 'Beeny Cliff' and 'the bloom of dark purple cast, that seems to exhale from the shoreward precipes' in the 1895 Preface to *A Pair of Blue Eyes*. Such perhaps also are 'the magnificent purples . . . / Of those near mountains' in 'Alike and Unlike', although hills and heath are literally purple when heather blooms, as in 'A yawning, sunned concave / Of purple' in 'The Sheep-Boy', unless 'embrowned' by the sun:

> The sun had branded the whole heath with his mark, even the purple heath-flowers having put on a brownness under the dry blazes of the few preceding days.
> (*The Return of the Native*, IV, Ch. 5)

A dark reddish-purple colour adds a distinctive tint by means of 'amaranthine glosses' to 'a green and pellucid expanse in the western sky' at a melancholy moment in Bathsheba's tempestuous emotional life (*Far from the Madding Crowd*, Ch. 31). Mrs. Yeobright's laborious journey across the Heath takes place under an August sky whose 'sapphirine hue' had been replaced by a 'metallic violet', a description that conveys heat as forcibly as colour. And when, in *Jude the Obscure*, II, Ch. 4, Hardy speaks of 'the purple or lurid light' of dramatic developments consequent upon innocent beginnings, we are made aware yet again of a colour symbolism that marks such phrases as 'amaranthine glosses' and 'metallic violet' as more than merely decorative tints.

Rose and pink are similar colours, and they too play symbolic roles in Hardy's diction. Pink is the colour of flesh among Europeans, a connotation that is made explicit by Mrs. Swancourt's remark to Henry Knight:

'That is a flesh-coloured variety', said Mrs Swancourt. 'But oleanders, though they are such bulky shrubs, are so very easily wounded as to be unprunable – giants with the sensitiveness of young ladies.'
(*A Pair of Blue Eyes*, Ch. 17)

Hardy's young ladies, his 'muslined pink young things', are frequently shown to possess pink faces or pink arms, to be 'rosy-mouthed' or 'rose-necked' or 'pink-faced'; a more realistic colouring – in some cases tending to brown or crimson, as we have seen – than the traditional poetic 'You were the swan-necked one' of 'The Going' or the several white epithets applied to white-handed, finger-white Iseult in *The Famous Tragedy of the Queen of Cornwall*. Tess's sensual appeal is strongly emphasized by reference to her pink arms and hands, which are 'of the pinkness of the rose', while her face is described as 'a natural carnation', a more attractive colouring than Marian's more stolid 'chronic pinkness'. Even Tess's figure is sensuously sketched by the phrase 'her pink-gowned form' – into which it had ripened from the earlier 'pink print pinafore' – in the milking scene in Chapter 24 previously referred to. Hardy's lifelong sympathy with the animal world expressed itself in various ways, of which the imagery of the trapped animal in *Tess of the d'Urbervilles* is one instance; in this context it is noteworthy that the pinkness of human beings is shared by some of his farm animals, the 'pink-white nostrils' of Bathsheba's Devon cows come to mind or the 'salmon-tinted' sheep among those countless weary flocks at Greenhill Fair.

Not many mornings are pink in Hardy, although the phrase 'as soon as daylight begins to pink in' is used by one of his rustics, Jim Owlett, in 'The Distracted Preacher' (*Wessex Tales*), and there is 'a hint of pink nebulosity' in another reference to daybreak, in *Tess of the d'Urbervilles*, Ch. 50. In both these instances it is the thought of dawn in the mind of the character that matters, not the spectacle as painted by the author. So it is with the 'rose-coloured dream' which acquires a greyish tinge in 'The Waiting Supper' (*A Changed Man*), and with the figure attributed to Manston in the poem 'Eunice' which appears in Chapter 16 of *Desperate Remedies*:

> Lit by the light of azure eyes
> Like summer days by summer skies:
> Her sweet transitions seem to be
> A pinkly pictured melody,
>     And not a set contour.

'A pinkly pictured melody' was a late substitution for the line 'A kind of pictured melody' found in the novel until Hardy discarded it in the edition of 1912; the use of *pinkly* here is in keeping with the sensuous connotations this colour had for him.

Hardy's artistic feeling for colour, naturalistic, figurative and symbolic, expresses itself both in contrast and in harmony. He clearly gave much thought to the many and often subtly different-iated hues introduced into his writing and had undoubtedly learnt much from the paintings so assiduously studied in his early man-hood. There is something painterly, perhaps in rather primitive style, about the pairing of 'pink and white' and 'white and green' in the opening stanza of 'A Thought in Two Moods', and the contrast with 'weather-browned' in the final stanza, to give one obvious example. On page 100 of his *Architectural Notebook* he jotted down 'Harmonious Contrasts in Col.^d Decoration', listing a dozen pairs of colours which he deemed harmonious, among them violet and pale green, chocolate and bright blue, maroon and warm green, claret and buff. When he included in this list 'Deep blue and pink', had he forgotten, one wonders, the Dorset form of the old colour proverb:

> Green and white,
> Forsaken quite;
> Pink and blue,
> Will never do . . .

Some of this painstaking schoolwork was to prove useful, in the decorations of Ethelberta's house, for example, with its 'general flat tint of duck's-egg green', patterned with designs 'done in bright auburn, several shades nearer to redbreast-red than was Ethelberta's hair, which was thus thrust further towards brown by such juxta-position' (*The Hand of Ethelberta*, Ch. 17). But Hardy saw more meaning in such juxtapositioning than merely colours that harmonized or clashed. The many hues and tints that make up his chromatic vocabulary – more than two hundred words – are rich in emotive connotations, reflecting in their variety and patterning not merely the changing landscapes and seasons of his dramas but the characters themselves, their personalities, their moods, and their fortunes. That Hardy recognized this symbolism is plain from our preceding discussion and from such overt comments as this: 'Contrasting colours heighten each other by being juxtaposed; it is the same with contrasting lives' (*A Changed Man*: 'The

Romantic Adventures of a Milkmaid', II). That Hardy employed such symbolism of colour is widely appreciated, more especially in such novels as *The Return of the Native* and *Tess of the d'Urbervilles*. What needs to be stressed here is the richness of his colour vocabulary; his verbal skill in indicating shades and tints and hues comparable to the almost endless resources of a painter's palette; and finally, and of equal importance, his dexterous use of contrasting light and shade and of nuances of white and black to express in words a vision that embraced many facets of human experience, from the brightest of full-starred heavens to 'the blackness of unutterable night'.

Light tends to be more figurative than actual in Hardy's work; and many important episodes take place at night, or at least in subdued, colourless, neutral, or lurid light – all of them words used by him to indicate a sobriety of setting that tends to match the mood of the characters enacting their dramas against it. He recognized the dramatic importance of the absence or monotony of colours as much as their presence and variety, and his vocabulary was equal to the task. The poem 'Neutral Tones', written when he was twenty-seven, is an early indication of this, to be followed by others in which such phrases as 'colourless thoughts' and 'muddy monochrome', 'neutral-tinted haps' and 'the fields are a water-colour washed out' are not uncommon. Here, too, belong those 'sober' or 'nameless' or 'non-descript' secondary and tertiary hues occasionally introduced into his fiction; and the bitter connotations of such a phrase as 'an achromatic chaos of things' describing the wild, wintry scene at Flintcomb-Ash, of which Evelyn Hardy wrote: 'Here, surely, is Turner's "Snowstorm" remembered, and transmuted into words.'

Dawn often breaks on mornings equally lurid and depressing. We have already noted daybreak, in *Far from the Madding Crowd*, Ch. 38, 'in hues of drab and ash'; and the light of a dawn, in *Tess of the d'Urbervilles*, Ch. 36, 'that was ashy and furtive, as though associated with crime'. Later in the same novel, darkness 'began to turn to a disordered medley of grays' (Ch. 43), and in *The Wood-landers*, Ch. 4, 'the bleared white visage of a sunless winter day emerged like a dead-born child', an image that recurs in 'the pale corpse-like birth / Of this diurnal unit' in 'A Commonplace Day'. The word 'disordered', the metaphorical language of crime and still-birth, are deliberate, perhaps over-rhetorical adjuncts to the wan colours, or the lack of colours, in such scenes.

Much the same holds for the pallid daylight to be met in Hardy's

Wessex as readily as in his Dorset. The sky may be 'a zinc-coloured archivault of immovable cloud' (*Two on a Tower*, Ch. 9), or cast a 'milky, colourless shine' upon the floor of a room (*The Mayor of Casterbridge*, Ch. 27); and as night falls, we are made aware of surroundings 'getting low-toned and dim with the earliest films of night' (*Far from the Madding Crowd*, Ch. 9), or how, as 'the day is turning ghost',

> Further and further from the nooks the twilight's
> stride extends,
> And beamless black impends.
> ('A Commonplace Day')

'Beamless black' of night is fit antiphon to 'Dullest of dull-hued Days'. Elsewhere we find 'a coal-black shadow' and 'each window a dull black blur' and 'the lone frost's black length'. The railway tunnel in *A Laodicean*, I, Ch. 12, has a 'blue-black' mouth. Trees are frequently seen darkly: 'black-stemmed birches' and 'dark-creviced elm' (*Under the Greenwood Tree*, I, Ch. 1); 'the long-armed trees and shrubs of juniper, cedar, and pine varieties, were grayish-black' (*A Pair of Blue Eyes*, Ch. 5); 'the charcoaled stems and trunks out of which the leaves budded' (*The Hand of Ethelberta*, Ch. 27); 'dark-rinded elm and chestnut trees' (*The Trumpet-Major*, Ch. 6). The plantation of firs in *Far from the Madding Crowd*, Ch. 24, has different shades of blackness according to the time of day: 'It was gloomy there at cloudless noontide, twilight in the evening, dark as midnight at dusk, and black as the ninth plague of Egypt at midnight.' In 'To Meet, or Otherwise' the world is a 'brake /Cimmerian / Through which we grope'. Human hair is 'raven black' or 'black as midnight'; eyes are 'sloe-black'; a cloud 'bellies down with black alarms'. Black may be the colour of a sticky bonnet and a jacket as well as of velvets and silks; and black is that 'sooty and grimy' figure that serves the threshing-machine at Flintcomb-Ash Farm 'round whose hot blackness the morning air quivered' (*Tess of the d'Urbervilles*, Ch. 47). Black has for Hardy the familiar funerary associations and connotes grief, and desolation, and suffering. But it also suggests spectral and ghostly apparitions, contrasting light and shadow, strange manifestations and seemings: 'Denser grew the darkness, more developed the wind-voices'; or a Rembrandt-like grouping with sharp chiaroscuro:

All waited in the growing light, their faces and hands as if they were silvered, the remainder of their figures dark, the stones glistening green-gray, the Plain still a mass of shade.

(*Tess of the d'Urbervilles*, Ch. 58)

Hardy's awareness of shades of blackness and degrees of darkness entailed a corresponding sensitiveness to gradations of light and whiteness. In 'Haunting Fingers' the harpsichord says:

> 'My keys' white shine,
> Now sallow, met a hand
> Even whiter . . .'

Elsewhere he speaks of brilliancy of light in one place, of 'intenser brilliancy' in another, of clouds and sky and daylight being 'white', or 'whitish', or 'bleared white'. He distinguishes between 'pink-white' and 'greenish white' and 'bluish white'; between 'zinc-coloured' and 'milk-hued'; between 'misty white' and 'snow-white' and 'lily-white' and even 'waning lily-white'; between 'dead-white' and 'ghost-white'; between 'blanching' and 'bleaching'; between immaculate whiteness and pitiful whiteness; between 'a white shiver' and 'a palpable white squall'. Quite patently, the distinctions rest on the qualifying words and their connotations, straightforward or figurative, but Hardy clearly saw different tints of white, for these are not just stylistic flourishes like those of modern advertisers, but genuine attempts to record visual impressions: a white lane and a white apron and immaculately white curds are all described by the same word, yet they are clearly not of the same colour in the strict sense in which Hardy would use this word; hence his many pains-taking painterly endeavours to specify whenever possible. A good example of this verbal precision is the description of the white dresses in the second chapter of *Tess of the d'Urbervilles*:

> Though the whole troop wore white garments, no two whites were alike among them. Some approached pure blanching; some had a bluish pallor; some worn by the older characters (which had possibly lain by folded for many a year) inclined to a cadaverous tint, and to a Georgian style.

The white gowns are 'a gay survival from Old Style days, when cheerfulness and May-time were synonyms', but in the sunlight the different shades of white show up to symbolize the human pilgrimage from the spotless purity of innocence to the pallor of death. As so often in his fiction and in his poems Hardy's chromatic subtleties are made to serve his description of naturalistic detail as well as being made subservient at the same time to their underlying symbolic texture.

Few English writers took so much trouble with one special part of their vocabulary as Hardy did with colours. Joan Grundy, in *Hardy and the Sister Arts*, has analysed Hardy's indebtedness to the painters and paintings he studied so zealously and has drawn persuasive parallels between specific pictures and passages in Hardy's work. But the business of translating what he saw into what he wrote was his own. Not only did he range widely over the colour words to be found in the English language, but he endowed them with connotations deeply rooted in his private vision. Not only scenes and seasons, times and places were coloured, illuminated, darkened, even the days of the week, if we are to believe Elliott Felkin, but men and women were seen in words of shades and tints and hues that delved deeply beyond their outward appearances into their very souls. Thus we find, in one apt phrase, the difference between two men: 'in juxtaposition with Troy, Oak had a melancholy tendency to look like a candle beside gas'; or between two minds: 'she was once a woman whose intellect was to mine like a star to a benzoline lamp'.

There are moments rich in immediate bright colours, like those of the 'georgeous nosegays of feminine beauty, fashionably arrayed in green, pink, blue, and white', by the river at Christminster, or this merry-go-round of colours in 'The High-School Lawn':

> Gray prinked with rose,
> White tipped with blue,
> Shoes with gay hose,
> Sleeves of chrome hue;
> Fluffed frills of white,
> Dark bordered light
> Such shimmerings through
> Trees of emerald green are eyed
> This afternoon, from the road outside.

But mostly there is the constant seeking for the right nuance – and the occasional defeat when the resources even of Hardy's English are exhausted, as in the description of Tess's eyes, or 'that nameless tertiary hue' of the old furmity woman in Casterbridge Town Hall, or Anne Garland's complexion which was of 'that particular tint between blonde and brunette which is inconveniently left without a name'. Such inconvenient moments are rare.

The wealth of Hardy's vocabulary has only been hinted at in this chapter; to do it better justice would require at least a concordance. He knew no compunction in exploring and exploiting all that the English language had to offer, historically, currently, and potentially. For some of his critics this has been a stumbling block; for a writer as undeterred and undeterrable as Hardy was in the pursuit of the right word, there was no other way. And the magnitude of his achievement both as novelist and as poet has proved him right.

# CHAPTER VI

# Tapestries of Rhetoric

𒀭𒀭𒀭𒀭𒀭𒀭

WHEN John Bayley, in *An Essay on Hardy*, p. 10, speaks of 'the kind of helplessness which is immanent in his style', the reader of Hardy, whether of his prose or verse, may well find him or herself somewhat perplexed. There is nothing helpless about a writer's vocabulary, for one thing, which is drawn with such seeming ease from almost a thousand years of English linguistic history, and which clearly suited his purpose, with an enviable disregard of current fashion or pedantic prescriptiveness. Nor is Hardy's syntax 'helpless'. This is not to deny the occasional awkwardnesses or the sometimes laborious attempts to express thoughts that may have lain too deep for Hardy's particular genius. The sharp visual impact of a face or a hedge or an architrave is liable to become blurred when Hardy attempts to speculate upon it. One recalls the philosophical aftermath to Elfride's first kiss or the syntactically needlessly laborious penultimate paragraph of *The Mayor of Casterbridge*.

Yet Hardy was able to play with his sentences as he played with his words, above all honestly, looking for whatever arrangement best accommodated his meaning. One man's accommodation does not necessarily suit another, however, nor do one man's sentences necessarily accord with another's mode of thought or expression. Hence the readiness of critics to carp at what they consider heavy-handed or long-winded or ill-phrased, when closer analysis often reveals patterns and syntactic structures which are neither fortuitous nor helpless.

From the first, there is ample evidence of Hardy's striving to translate architectural concepts into sentence structures – of balance and contrast, for example:

Time had set a mark upon them all since he had last been there. Middle-aged men were a little more round-shouldered, their wives had taken to

spectacles, young people had grown up out of recognition, and old men had passed into second childhood.
(*An Indiscretion in the Life of an Heiress*, II, Ch. 4)

or of progression:

Graye was handsome, frank, and gentle. He had a quality of thought which, exercised on homeliness, was humour; on nature, picturesqueness; on abstractions, poetry. Being, as a rule, broadcast, it was all three.
(*Desperate Remedies*, Ch. 1)

With experience came greater confidence. But the basic patterns are frequently the same, whether in narrative, or description, or in the mouths of Hardy's more articulate characters. There is a purposeful combination of balance, contrast, and progression in these successive sentences in 'The Romantic Adventures of a Milkmaid', also a relatively early work, although eventually included in *A Changed Man*:

Where he trusted he was the most trusting fellow in the world; where he doubted he could be guilty of the slyest strategy. Once suspicious, he became one of those subtle, watchful characters who, without integrity, make good thieves; with a little, good jobbers; with a little more, good diplomatists.

Whether long or short, compound, complex, or simple sentences, such patterns are among Hardy's favourites. They suit his mode of exploring people, characters, temperaments, by balancing, contrasting, summing up:

Hence people who began by beholding him ended by perusing him.
(*The Return of the Native*, II, Ch. 6)

There is an artfulness even in so short a sentence which certainly is not helplessness, for a moment's pause reveals the manner in which the main clause encompasses the relative clause, allowing the latter's verb-structure to anticipate and determine the former's. The balance is pleasing to the ear, just as the contrast tickles the fancy.

Contrast frequently determines the shape of Hardy's sentences, no matter how many structural elements they consist of:

His measured, springless walk was the walk of the skilled countryman as distinct from the desultory shamble of the general labourer.
(*The Mayor of Casterbridge*, Ch. 1)

The woman who looks an unquestionable lady when she's with a polished-up fellow, looks a tawdry imitation article when she's hobbing and nobbing with a homely blade.
(*The Woodlanders*, Ch. 12)

There is in several of the above examples an echo of the enumerative technique of Hardy's catalogues previously encountered. Sequences of sentences, clauses, and phrases are their syntactic equivalents. Both combine an element of display with a tendency to probe, to search, to explore in order to get things just right. This is Hardy's way to suggest deeper meanings, to hint at connotations important to character or scene or event. The sentences here are clearly constructed on architectural principles, word upon word, phrase upon phrase, each contributing to the whole. The context may be relatively trivial, a sideways glance, say, at some aspect of character, like the description of Dare's ring:

He wore a heavy ring, of which the gold seemed fair, the diamond questionable, and the taste indifferent.
(*A Laodicean*, I, Ch. 6)

Or it may be central to the story, like the almost feverish attempt at defining the Well-Beloved:

Essentially she was perhaps of no tangible substance; a spirit, a dream, a frenzy, a conception, an aroma, an epitomized sex, a light of the eye, a parting of the lips . . .

The conclusion of such grasping at shadows is inescapable:

God only knew what she really was: Pierston did not. She was indescribable.
(*The Well-Beloved*, I, Ch. 2)

But Hardy rarely balked at the indescribable; nor did his characters:

'There is a size at which dignity begins', he exclaimed; 'further on there is a size at which grandeur begins; further on there is a size at which solemnity begins; further on, a size at which awfulness begins; further on, a size at which ghastliness begins. That size faintly approaches the size of the stellar universe.'
(*Two on a Tower*, Ch. 4)

St. Cleve is merely doing what his creator does, but in his mouth the rhetorical patterning becomes more obvious. In mid-narrative such a sentence is less conspicuous, while well designed to enhance character or atmosphere. Hardy uses it effectively, for example, to depict Henchard's increasingly tortuous approach to the weather-caster's cottage, where, as so often, the physical world mirrors a state of mind:

> The turnpike-road became a lane, the lane a cart-track, the cart-track a bridle-path, the bridle-path a foot-way, the foot-way overgrown. The solitary walker slipped here and there, and stumbled over the natural springes formed by the brambles, till at length he reached the house . . .
> (*The Mayor of Casterbridge*, Ch. 26)

At its best this method of cumulative sentence patterning is among Hardy's most successful serious stylistic device, as in the description of Giles Winterborne as Autumn's very brother. But even in less exalted moments the architect's tendency to order things methodically achieves the desired result:

> At the end of the first basin the man had risen to serenity; at the second he was jovial; at the third, argumentative; at the fourth, the qualities signified by the shape of his face, the occasional clench of his mouth, and the fiery spark of his dark eye, began to tell in his conduct; he was overbearing – even brilliantly quarrelsome.
> (*Ibid.*, Ch. 1)

The balance is sometimes jolted by a push in an unexpected direction, as when the anticipated 'done' at the end of this sentence does not materialize:

> Nature had done there many things that she ought not to have done, and left undone much that she should have *executed*.
> (*A Laodicean*, I, Ch. 3)

Or when an unexpected variation is introduced into what promises to be a regular syntactic pattern:

> He had a great many draught horses, a great many milch cows, and of sheep a multitude.
> (*Wessex Tales*: 'Interlopers at the Knap', I)

Both these examples illustrate Hardy's debt to scriptural and liturgical syntax, the first more obviously so, the second echoing, perhaps humorously in view of the similarity in sound, the syntax of the biblical 'and of the devout Greeks a great multitude' of Acts, XVII, 4. What Bayley in the same book (p. 79) calls Hardy's 'tones of the pulpit' is frequently a matter of sentence structure, which determines the cadence of his prose, and not infrequently of his verse as well, right up to the 'Hebraic style' of the embodied Spirit of the Years in *The Dynasts*, II. vi. 7, with its heavy verbal artillery and involuted syntax:

> You may not see the impact: ere it come
> The tomb-worm may caress thee; but believe
> Before five more have joined the shotten years
> Whose useless films infest the foggy Past,
> Traced thick with teachings glimpsed unheedingly,
> The rawest Dynast of the group concerned
> Will, for the good or ill of mute mankind,
> Down-topple to the dust like soldier Saul,
> And Europe's mouldy-minded oligarchs
> Be propped anew; while garments roll in blood
> To confused noise, with burning, and fuel of fire.
> Nations shall lose their noblest in the strife,
> And tremble at the tidings of an hour!

The sentence constituting the last two lines has an audible biblical cadence, which can easily be paralleled in Hardy's prose. For instance:

> But these shaggy recesses were at all seasons a familiar surrounding to Olly and Mrs Yeobright; *and the addition of darkness lends no frightfulness to the face of a friend*.
> (*The Return of the Native*, I, Ch. 4)

– 'and darkness was upon the face of the deep' (Genesis I, 2).

There are of course numerous variations in the structure of Hardy's sentences, from the utterly succinct – 'Presently the gurgoyle spat' – to the methodically complex, from the same novel:

> She was conscious of having brought about this situation by a series of actions done as by one in an extravagant dream; of following that idea as to method, which had burst upon her in the hall with glaring obviousness, by gliding to the top of the stairs, assuring herself by listening to the heavy breathing of her maids that they were asleep, gliding down again, turning the handle of the door within which the young girl lay, and deliberately setting herself to do what, if she had anticipated any such undertaking at

night and alone, would have horrified her, but which, when done, was not so dreadful as was the conclusive proof of her husband's conduct which came with knowing beyond doubt the last chapter of Fanny's story.
(*Far from the Madding Crowd*, Ch. 43)

This may well be regarded as a characteristic specimen of a long Hardy sentence. It occupies an entire paragraph, and with the help of its progressive participles leads inexorably to the confirmation of Bathsheba's suspicions. There are grammatical awkwardnesses: 'done as by one', 'following that idea as to method', 'setting herself to do what' followed by a lengthy conditional clause, and the needlessly complicated 'but which, when done, was not so dreadful as was . . .' But the sentence does its job, of jogging the reader relentlessly on, and it does so particularly well when read aloud.

This is the secret of much of Hardy's more complicated prose, of his long complex sentences, like the above, of his often carefully balanced compound sentences, of the sequences of varying sentence patterns, carefully modulated: they should be read aloud. Hardy's was, as we know, a musical ear, and given proper emphases and pauses, a sentence like the above can be heard to flow on with remarkable ease and effectiveness. Again one is tempted to turn to architecture for analogy, to the subsumption of individual parts in the total design, the absorption of single incongruities in the entire edifice. What the eye accommodates in the latter, the ear will as readily accept in Hardy's prose. This is not to overlook or deny the grammatical quirks to be found in Hardy's writings, verse as well as prose. On the contrary, they are, as much as his lexical idiosyn-crasies, the stamp of his individuality. Prominent among them are the liberties which Hardy takes with conventional word order.

Although English word order became increasingly fixed with the loss of older grammatical inflections, there are potential idiomatic nuances in the syntactic arrangement of words in phrases and sentences. To put it differently, some sound more English than others. In verse unusual word order is more common than in prose and more readily accepted by readers or listeners conditioned to make allowances for the sake of metre or rhyme or rhetorical effect. Hardy had no qualms about ending sentences with prepositions or lines of verse with first person pronouns, or varying the position of adverbs any more than he had about splitting infinitives. Here are some typical examples:

> And there, above
> All, shone my Love,
> That nothing matched the image of.
> ('At a Seaside Town in 1869')

In 'I Have Lived with Shades' the fourth line was revised to read:

> I went mankind among,

and another such unidiomatic inversion occurs in the opening stanza of 'The Dead Man Walking':

> They hail me as one living,
> But don't they know
> That I have died of late years,
> Untombed although?

A tension is set up here between the colloquial 'don't they know' and the inversion with which it is made to rhyme, and this the poem sustains with its contrasting diction of poeticisms like 'It iced me' and the almost slangy, yet apposite, 'the corpse-thing'.

Pronouns appear in emphatic positions at the end of lines:

> They know Earth-secrets that know not I.
> ('An August Midnight')

> '. . . Well, all pay the debt that paid he!'
> ('The Memorial Brass: 186–')

> Only acquaintances
> Seem do we.
> ('In the Street')

> On Beechen Cliff self-commune I.
> ('Midnight on Beechen, 187–')

In 'In Tenebris I', the penultimate stanza reads:

> Tempests may scath;
> But love can not make smart
> Again this year his heart
> Who no heart hath.

The unidiomatic last line is poetically effective not only because of its arresting word order, but because its alliterating monosyllables bring the stanza to a threnodic conclusion which anticipates the culminating 'Waits in unhope' of the poem's last line. Hardy may have remembered Milton's collocation of 'Hath scath'd' in *Paradise Lost* I, 613, for *scath* or *scathe* was not a common word in nineteenth-century English, and such echoes are heard throughout his work.

The post-nominal adjective reappears, this time in the comparative degree, in the line:

> But never will *Fates colder-featured*
> Hold sway there again,
> ('At the Wicket-Gate')

and there is an example of the negative particle placed after its verb in:

> 'What's now to be done? We can *disappoint not*
> The king and queen!'
> ('Royal Sponsors')

The poem 'Faintheart in a Railway Train', first printed in 1920, shows Hardy, now in his eightieth year, as ready to use syntactic inversions for metre, or rhyme, or emphasis, as he had been all along. The diction of this short poem is plain, yet it is in some ways, not least in theme, a characteristic Hardy poem:

> At nine in the morning there passed a church,
> At ten there passed me by the sea,
> At twelve a town of smoke and smirch,
> At two a forest of oak and birch,
> And then, on a platform, she:
>
> A radiant stranger, who saw not me.
> I said, 'Get out to her do I dare?'
> But I kept my seat in my search for a plea,
> And the wheels moved on. O could it but be
> That I had alighted there!

The generic resemblances between some of Hardy's major characters have frequently been noted by critics and have even been made the basis for ingenious theorizing about Hardy's art, as in Geoffrey Thurley's *The Psychology of Hardy's Novels*. Such resemblance occasionally expresses itself in similarity of phrasing. As an example, one may cite Wildeve's words to Eustacia: 'I think I drew out you before you drew out me' (*The Return of the Native*, I, Ch. 6), and compare them with Felice Charmond's words to Grace: 'I *cannot* give him up until he chooses to give up me!' (*The Woodlanders*, Ch. 33). The emphatic personal pronoun at the end of these sentences recalls the same device in Hardy's verse, and it may also be found, quite appropriately, in prose narrative:

> The more briskly they walked the more briskly walked she.
> (*Tess of the d'Urbervilles*, Ch. 44)

In Hardy's prose, divergences from idiomatic syntax frequently involve the positioning of adverbs. He puts his adverbs where they are most effective, which may not be where received usage might tend to put them:

> Nor had trouble very roughly handled her.
> (*Two on a Tower*, Ch. 14)

> . . . perhaps stronger than judgement well could regulate.
> (*The Trumpet-Major*, Ch. 12)

> What had grieved her to tears she would not more particularly tell.
> (*The Well-Beloved*, II, Ch. 10)

In dialogue, the adverb may be placed in unidiomatic positions for the sake of emphasis or irony. Stephen Smith's enthusiasm for the profession of journalism is tinged with Hardy's acerbic taste for reviewers in this comment to Elfride, where the final adverb is a deliberately emphatic afterthought:

> 'Why, I can tell you it is a fine thing to be on the staff of *The Present*. Finer than being a novelist *considerably*.'
> (*A Pair of Blue Eyes*, Ch. 7)

Boldwood uses a similar emphatic construction when he says to Bathsheba:

> 'Heavens, you must be *heartless quite*!'
> (*Far from the Madding Crowd*, Ch. 31)

Already in *Desperate Remedies* Hardy had used this device to indicate the particular tone of a given utterance. Cytherea is speaking to Manston:

> 'That's the effect it has upon me; but it does not induce me to be *honest particularly.*'
> (*Desperate Remedies*, Ch. 12)

The effect here is to qualify without being specific; the contrary may be achieved by the same means, the tone now being one of total resignation:

> 'Well, that's just what I am, too', he said. 'I am fearful of life, *spectre-seeing always.*'
> (*Jude the Obscure*, III, Ch. 4)

Hardy does not italicize these phrases, as I have done here, because the positioning of the adverbs sufficiently draws the reader's attention to their particular function in the context of what is being said and implied. The same effect may be obtained by placing the adverb at the beginning of a sentence. Gabriel Oak is, as it were, advertising the benefits to be bestowed upon Bathsheba, were she to marry him. Her responses, whose sincerity is in inverse proportion to their warmth, are nicely scaled from a tepid 'Yes; I should like that', through a more emphatic 'I should like it very much', to an enthusiastic '*Dearly* I should like that!'. Again, the italics are mine, but the exclamation mark, as in Boldwood's outburst, is Hardy's.

In narrative, as in dialogue, Hardy varies the position of adverbs in order to achieve certain effects. His reason may be to enhance the rhythm of a phrase as in the concluding cadence of this sentence:

> The natural expression of his face was somewhat obscured by the bronzing effects of rough weather, but the lines of his mouth showed that affectionate impulses were strong within him – perhaps stronger *than judgment well could regulate.*
> (*The Trumpet-Major*, Ch. 12)

or to sharpen a contrast:

> Moreover, Tess then lost her strange and ethereal beauty; her teeth, lips, and eyes scintillated in the sunbeams, and she was again the dazzlingly fair dairymaid *only.*
> (*Tess of the d'Urbervilles*, Ch. 20)

or to emphasize an ironic point of view:

> The cause of all this gloom, the millwright Halborough, now snoring in the shed, had been a thriving master-machinist, notwithstanding his free and careless disposition, till a taste for a more than adequate quantity of strong liquor took hold of him; since when his habits *had interfered with his business sadly*.
> (*Life's Little Ironies*: 'A Tragedy of Two Ambitions', I)

or to represent a state of mind which in spoken form would be expressed in the same manner, as illustrated earlier:

> His spirits were oozing out of him *quite*.
> (*Far from the Madding Crowd*, Ch. 42)

> *Much* he deplored trifling with her feelings for the sake of a passing desire.
> (*Life's Little Ironies*: 'On the Western Circuit', III)

> Thus, though he might never love a woman of the island race, for lack in her of the desired refinement, *he could not love long a kimberlin*.
> (*The Well-Beloved*, II, Ch. 3)

Hardy matches, with the aid of such turns of phrase, the way his characters think and feel with the way they speak. This is no accident, but a deliberate feature of his style for which he deserves more credit than is generally accorded to him.

This applies also to ending sentences with prepositions, a common enough occurrence in modern English, despite the occasional fulminations of pedants. Lucy Savile, for example, does so in 'Fellow-townsmen' (*Wessex Tales*): 'Still, as modern tastes develop, people require more room to gratify them in.' And Hardy does so, just as readily, in narrative; perhaps in order to cope more easily with two successive relative clauses:

> Fancy seemed uneasy under the infliction of this household moralizing, which might tend to damage the airy-fairy nature that Dick, as maiden shrewdness told her, had accredited her with.
> (*Under the Greenwood Tree*, II, Ch. 6)

Or to avoid yet another relative clause altogether:

> His mind was arrested by the intense and busy energy which must needs belong to an assembly that required such a glare of light to do its religion by.
> (*A Laodicean*, I, Ch. 2)

There is nothing unusual about such constructions in English: they occur in Chaucer and Shakespeare and have been a feature of English ever since. I mention Hardy's usage here in order to stress that it was entirely idiomatic in his day, as indeed it still is in ours.

One type of syntactic arrangement that Hardy favours is that in which the predicate precedes the subject and verb; it is another mode of rhetorical emphasis. At its simplest we find such a sentence as 'Be agonized she must' (*Desperate Remedies*, Ch. 6); and, from the same novel, a more complex example in which part of a verb phrase comes between predicate and subject:

> But very poor food to a lover is intelligence of a mistress filtered through a friend.
> (*Desperate Remedies*, Ch. 1)

In case these are dismissed as youthful experiments in style, here are three later examples:

> Such a situation had less than three months brought forth.
> (*The Return of the Native*, III, Ch. 4)

> Examine Grace as her father might, she would admit nothing.
> (*The Woodlanders*, Ch. 30)

> Apply to him she would not.
> (*Tess of the d'Urbervilles*, Ch. 15)

It even finds its way into dialogue:

> 'Beg you to change how I will, 'tis no use.'
> (*A Pair of Blue Eyes*, Ch. 36)

Such usages may be idiosyncratic, but they are not fortuitous. It is easy to recognize Hardy's shaping hand in the many instances where a cursory first glance detects merely oddity, as in cases like 'the career of our poor only heroine' (*The Mayor of Casterbridge*, Ch. 43), or 'of what depths I have descended to in these few last days' (*The Return of the Native*, V, Ch. 6). We might have expected 'only poor' and 'last few', as being more idiomatically familiar; but *only* is an adjective here, and in both examples the positioning is a deliberate indication of the emphasis to be placed on the second of each pair of adjectives.

It is important to stress the deliberateness of such phrasing, in order to check the critical tendency which concentrates upon the gaucheries of Hardy's style at the expense of its distinctive achievements. Robert B. Heilman's analysis of Hardy's style in *The Mayor of Casterbridge* concludes that 'the cumbersome, at least in its impact, somewhat outweighs the fluent and well-ordered', and the implication is yet again that Hardy was 'careless', 'bumbling', or 'insouciant', to quote some of Heilman's epithets. Insouciant, that is unconcerned, Hardy was not, and the whole notion of an uncaring, careless writer is contradicted, if by nothing else, at least by Hardy's persistent concern for his text, as evinced by his ceaseless emendations and revisions. The syntactic features so far considered, like the enumerative sentence patterns, often quite complex, or the syntactic inversions, serve definite purposes, which for the alert reader of novel or poem are more important than a momentary awareness of some linguistic singularity. The point of critical concern is not so much that such singularity is to be found in Hardy's English, but why it occurs.

As an example, we may take the prevalence of absolute constructions in Hardy's syntax, as in this sentence:

> There being no knocker, she knocked by means of a short stick which was laid against the post for that purpose; but nobody attending, she entered the passage, and tried an inner door.
> (*The Trumpet-Major*, Ch. 6)

Both parts of this sentence are introduced by absolute constructions: 'There being no knocker . . . but nobody attending'. The parallelism is immediately apparent; so is the succinctness of the two phrases, in place of longer subordinate clauses. In both cases the economy of phrasing leads more immediately to the following active verbs – 'she knocked', 'she entered' – with obvious narrative gain. Already in his early fiction Hardy was aware of the value of such syntactic compression:

> The decision come to, his impatience could scarcely preserve him from rushing to Tollamore House that very daybreak . . .
> (*An Indiscretion in the Life of an Heiress*, I, Ch. 4)

In this instance, the succinct opening phrase defines both the moment reached and the mental activity leading up to it; in the previous example, 'nobody attending' describes an event, whereas 'there being no knocker' describes a continuing state. The latter has obvious descriptive possibilities, of which Hardy is well aware. For example:

> He instantly made towards the latter object. The village was quite still, it being that motionless hour of rustic daily life which fills the interval between the departure of the field-labourers to their work, and the rising of their wives and daughters to prepare the breakfast for their return.
> (*The Mayor of Casterbridge*, Ch. 2)

Here the absolute construction, contrasting vividly with the short sentence beginning 'He instantly . . .', takes up the notion of 'the village was quite still' in a leisurely, unhurried parenthetical explanation. The whole sentence has a distinctive cadence with appropriate stresses on the important words – 'quite still', 'motionless hour', 'rustic daily life' – which makes nonsense of Heilman's niggling comment that *it* 'seems a slight vessel for the freight it is asked to carry'.

Another syntactic shortcoming pounced on by Hardy's critics is that traditionally known as the dangling participle, where the subject of the main clause is not that implied by the participial phrase, as in this instance:

> Having breakfasted at eight that morning, and having been much in the open air afterwards, the Adonis-astronomer's appetite assumed grand proportions.
> (*Two on a Tower*, Ch. 7)

or this:

> While leaning thus upon the parapet his listless attention was awakened by sounds of an unaccustomed kind.
> (*The Mayor of Casterbridge*, Ch. 38)

Hardy's use of such participial phrases suggests that he treated them as if they were absolute constructions. In strict traditional grammar these are solecisms, as they are in Shakespeare, but the gain in conciseness, without obscuring the meaning, amply justifies such 'infringement'.

The use of passives is not necessarily ungrammatical, yet it has also been adduced as one of Hardy's less desirable practices. The passive voice raises considerations of point of view: to be acted upon is often the fate of Hardy's characters, and the use of the passive can either leave the agent unnamed or relegate him to a subordinate role.

> And war was waged anew
> By great Napoléon
> ('The Peasant's Confession')

is a form of indirect statement that shifts the emphasis from Napoléon to war itself. Similarly, in the Dumb Show in *The Dynasts*, II. ii. 7, as Harold Orel noted in *Thomas Hardy's Epic-Drama: A Study of the Dynasts*, p. 94, the passive construction is used 'to good effect', because it diverts attention from individuals to the general anonymity of the battlefield:

> The battle *is begun* with alternate moves that match each other like those of a chess opening . . . A dust *is raised* by this ado, and moans of men and shrieks of horses *are heard* . . . The see-saw *is continued* . . .

In his prose, Hardy's use of passives represents one way of involving himself and his reader in the action. As the agent remains frequently unstated, the reader is forced into more active participation in the drama. At its most patent, this mode of involvement is at work where author and reader join a fictional character in one of those characteristic Hardy glimpses through a door or window. We first meet Marty South thus in *The Woodlanders*, Ch. 2, where Mr. Percomb's eyes 'were fixed' upon her, but she is also 'before us'. It is as if we are all standing beside one another, looking in. Chapter 4 of *A Pair of Blue Eyes* opens with a lengthy paragraph describing the view which Stephen Smith sees from his bedroom window. At the end of the description Smith is not mentioned; instead we are told that 'five minutes after this casual survey *was made* his bedroom was empty'. This time it is as if we had all been looking out at the scene together and, on turning back into the room, find that 'its occupant had vanished quietly from the house'. The passive construction helps to create such impressions.

It also helps, at a more sophisticated level of involvement, to draw the reader into the emotional experiences of Hardy's people. In a scene of great inner turmoil involving Yeobright and Eustacia, the passive voice relieves Hardy of the task of closer psychological analysis while inviting the reader to discover for himself or herself the nature of Eustacia's emotional processes:

The superstratum of timidity which often overlies those who are daring and defiant at heart *had been passed through*, and the mettlesome substance of the woman *was reached*.
(*The Return of the Native*, V, Ch. 3)

Such instances are not uncommon, but no less frequently Hardy is content to use the passive to indicate the anonymity of an action in order to stress its effect, even at the expense of occasional awkwardness:

Worm *was got rid* of by sending him to measure the height of the tower.
(*A Pair of Blue Eyes*, Ch. 4)

Targan Bay – which had the merit of *being easily got at* –*was next visited*.
(*Ibid.*, Ch. 5)

That day *she was seen little of*. By the evening she had come to a resolution, and acted upon it.
(*Ibid.*, Ch. 20)

The awning *was set up again*; the band *was called out* from its shelter, *and ordered* to begin, and where the tables had stood a place *was cleared* for dancing.
(*The Mayor of Casterbridge*, Ch. 16)

The shed *was reached*, and she pointed out the spars.
(*The Woodlanders*, Ch. 3)

Now *could be beheld* that change from the handsome to the curious which the features of a wood undergo at the ingress of the winter months.
(*Ibid.*, Ch. 7)

Such actions are deliberately depersonalized, as if to suggest that there are forces at work which direct what people do, forces of the kind which play their part in the cosmology of *The Dynasts* and which, as we shall note later, appear in Hardy's writings under a variety of names. In the last passage cited from *The Woodlanders* such an impression is reinforced by Hardy's subsequent reference to 'Nature's canvas' in the description of the changing woodland: the Spinner of the Years also functions as the Painter of the Woods. The same directing force seems to be at work in those instances where people appear to be passively propelled from one place to another, as in 'The shed *was reached*', quoted above, or 'Trendle's house *was reached* at last', or at that poignant moment in *Far from the Madding Crowd* where superhuman willpower and a stray dog combine to

drag Fanny Robin finally to the Casterbridge Union-house: 'Thus
the town *was passed*, and the goal *was reached*.'

Such examples demonstrate how effective can be the 'bumbling'
Hardy is sometimes charged with. Inevitably the shaping influences
within him – architectural form, musical movement, the commixture
of inchoate or half-baked ideas nudging one another – were sometimes at odds and hard to discipline. But his sense of rhythm, in prose
as well as in verse, rarely failed him, and when it does, he probably
heard it, just as his reader can hear it. When Hardy struggles with
abstraction, when he attempts to generalize from the particular
incident or experience, he is most liable to flounder. A comparison of
the two following sentences will illustrate this. The first is not
particularly elegant, but it makes its point about Elfride's growing
maturity. By contrast, the second sentence is a feeble appendage with
its awkward concluding verbal cluster:

> A mere season in London with her practised stepmother had so advanced
> Elfride's perceptions, that her courtship by Stephen seemed emotionally
> meagre, and to have drifted back several years into a childish past. In
> regarding our mental experiences, as in visual observation, our own
> progress reads like a dwindling of that we progress from.
> (*A Pair of Blue Eyes*, Ch. 16)

Hardy seems in fact to be making the same point: the further he
departs from visual observation, the less clearly defined is the object
he had been contemplating. Very often such a sentence needs to
be read a second time before it is properly understood, and this
is usually an indication of Hardy philosophizing rather than
noticing things. What may strike some readers as grammatical
oddities may, however, reflect uncertainties of usage in which
tradition, grammatical purism, and colloquial speech may be at odds.
The fluctuations in the use of *who* and *whom* to express objective
function illustrate this. Like many other English writers Shakespeare
had no qualms about using *who* where traditional grammar requires
*whom*: 'Who didst thou leave to tend his majesty?' asks the Bastard in
*King John*; and Shaw somewhere has this telling exchange:

> 'It does not matter who you marry.'
> 'Whom, not who.'
> 'Oh, speak English!'

According to this view, many of Hardy's characters 'speak English' in such utterances as Cytherea Graye's 'Who – is he engaged to?', Bathsheba's 'Who are you speaking of?', Anne Garland's 'And who is he going to marry?', Tess's 'Who to?', and Arabella's 'You know, I suppose, who I married?' Not only women use this form, however, and it was certainly common in Hardy's dialect. In *The Dynasts*, I. v. 4, Nelson asks 'Who have we lost on board here?' In our own time, as Randolph Quirk has pointed out in *The Use of English*, 'an invariable *who* (especially interrogative *who*) is acceptable colloquially'. Twenty years after this was written, it appears to be no less acceptable in more formal English.

A classic case of Hardy's struggling with a pronoun is the sentence in *Desperate Remedies*, Ch. 2: 'Young women have a habit, not noticeable in men, of putting on at a moment's notice the drama of *whosoever's* life they choose.' This first appeared as 'whomsoever's', which the anonymous reviewer in *The Athenaeum* of 1 April 1871 described as 'an odd formation'. Hardy then changed it to 'whose-soever's', an even odder formation, and eventually, in the Wessex Novels edition of 1896, to 'whosoever's'.

Other pronouns have their inconveniences too. The phrase in 'In the Nuptial Chamber', 'And it's he I embrace while embracing you', may be regarded as a poeticism, but Ethelberta's 'Then it was he I saw far away on the road' or Dare's 'That was he' preserve older English usage when most nineteenth-century writers were using the oblique forms, like Emily Brontë's 'If I were her' or Swinburne's 'That's her'. Hardy has the best of both worlds when he writes, in *Jude the Obscure*, III, Ch. 4: 'Her very helplessness seemed to make *her* so much stronger than *he*.' Old Derriman's emphatic 'No, faith. 'Tis nothing to I' (*The Trumpet-Major*, Ch. 6) conforms exactly to William Barnes's explanation in his *Glossary* that 'when a pronoun in an objective case is emphatical, it is given in its nominative shape instead of its objective case'. An unnecessary pronoun is occasionally permitted to appear in a sentence along a stated subject, as a deliberate colloquialism or for emphasis. Rhoda Brook's little boy reports: 'Mr Lodge, he seemed pleased, and his waistcoat stuck out . . .' (*Wessex Tales*: 'The Withered Arm', 2), which effectively catches the cadence of the youngster's speech. In 'Julie-Jane', the line 'Soon, soon that lover he came' deliberately carries on the sing-song repetitions of the three preceding stanzas, which explains the super-fluous *he*. A redundant personal pronoun may creep into a sentence, referring to an antecedent relative pronoun, where the construction is loose. The Crimson Maltster's opening paragraph of 'Squire

Petrick's Lady' in *A Group of Noble Dames* contains this sentence:

> It is said that a relative of his, a very deep thinker, who afterwards had the misfortune to be transported for life for mistaken notions on the signing of a will, taught him considerable legal lore, *which* he creditably resolved never to throw away for the benefit of other people, but to reserve *it* entirely for his own.

Such instances of informal syntax are relatively infrequent. Their effect is to match the colloquial register of Hardy's vocabulary by, to use David Crystal's terms for informality, a more 'intimate' or 'familiar' syntax. Rarely do they impede understanding. The restriction of the words *either* or *neither*, for example, to two antecedents is standard English usage, as *either* means 'one or the other of two' or 'each one of two', of which *neither* is the negative. Hardy's use of these words to refer to more than two alternatives, although again 'strictly' ungrammatical according to traditional usage, is occasionally to be found in earlier writers and certainly avoids more elaborate, possibly cumbersome, constructions. Thus he writes:

> 'Then Sunday?' he said.
> 'Not Sunday', said she.
> 'Then Monday – Tuesday – Wednesday, surely?' he went on experimentally.
> She answered that she should probably not see him on either day.
> (*The Trumpet-Major*, Ch. 7)

Or:

> . . . the waggon rose sideways . . . and out rolled the three maidens into the road in a heap . . .
> When Tony came up, frightened and breathless, he was relieved enough to see that neither of his darlings was hurt.
> (*Life's Little Ironies*: 'Tony Kytes, the Arch-Deceiver')

That Hardy thought such usage perfectly acceptable is obvious from its occurrence in his correspondence, as when he writes to Hermann Lea on 10 October 1899: 'If you would accept either of my novels . . .', meaning any one of them.

The so-called group genitive also involves at least two antecedents, and here too Hardy allows himself some freedom of manipulation. Thus we find in *Jude the Obscure* 'since his wife and furniture's uncompromising disappearance' (II, Ch. 1) and 'Sue and Jude's private minds, (V, Ch. 6). In another phrase involving a genitive, 'all a developed man's unorthodox opinion' (*Desperate Remedies*, Ch. 11), Hardy is anticipating the complex premodified noun phrases which are a common feature of twentieth-century English. Less euphonious but equally convenient is the phrase 'one of the longest chronicled families about here' in 'The Waiting Supper' (*A Changed Man*). Such phrases would require a good deal of circumlocution to make them less of a mouthful.

The same is true of Hardy's preference for succinct adverbial constructions which combine precision of image with economy of diction, for which the occasional sense of unfamiliarity is a small price to pay. Examples occur in all Hardy's work and elsewhere in Victorian English, and in some cases are of venerable ancestry; those in the comparative degree tend to be used by Hardy in verse rather than in his prose. Here are some characteristic examples, first of positives:

> And stately husbands and wives, side by side
>      as they *anciently* slept.
>      ('In Sherborne Abbey')

At the same time the present visitor, even *exteriorly*, was not altogether commonplace.
   (*A Laodicean*, I, Ch. 1)

A light was burning, and each damsel was sitting up *whitely* in her bed, awaiting Tess, the whole like a row of avenging ghosts.
   (*Tess of the d'Urbervilles*, Ch. 31)

And of comparatives:

> . . . we creep and grope
> *Sadlier* than those who wept in Babylon.
>      ('God's Funeral')

> He *closelier* looked; then looked again.
>      ('The Abbey Mason')

> To get their dingy greatness *deeplier* dingied.
>      ('The Obliterate Tomb')

> Truly, or *liker* falsely.
>      ('A Victorian Rehearsal')

> None sees that written *largelier* than himself.
>      (*The Dynasts*, II. i. 1)

Hardy's readiness to shift words from one grammatical category to another, noted in the preceding chapter, allows him a good deal of grammatical freedom. Here again he is often merely following tradition, although by no means averse to innovations. He plays, for example, with the word *forward*:

> 'The road lies all its length the same,
>     *Forwardly* as at rear.'
> ('The Absolute Explains')

Somehow we did not get any *forwarder* in the matter.
  (Preface to *The Mayor of Casterbridge*)

'You see we wasn't aware till this morning that you were going to move, or we could have been *forwarder*.'
  (*The Mayor of Casterbridge*, Ch. 29)

'Why, if I'd wanted you I shouldn't have run after you like this; 'twould have been the *forwardest* thing!'
  (*Far from the Madding Crowd*, Ch. 4; Hardy's italics)

The superlative degree of the adjective *forward* in the last quotation is paralleled by others, some of which are in common use, others not; for example, *awfullest, divinest, formidablest, idlest, illest, purplest, raggedest, yellowest*. In such cases it is important to distinguish the various registers to which such words belong. There is pure comedy in Mrs. Day's 'The parishioners about here . . . are the *laziest, gossipest, poachest, jailest* set of any ever I came among' in *Under the Greenwood Tree*, II, Ch. 6, whereas authorial emphasis is represented in 'The younger woman felt the *awfullest* sense of responsibility at her Vandalism in having undertaken to demolish so imposing a pile' (*Desperate Remedies*, Ch. 5), which at the same time voices Cytherea's feelings by using a word considered appropriate to the emotional utterances of young ladies of that period. On the other hand, there is an undercurrent of irony in the authorial 'Seven hundred and fifty pounds in the *divinest* form that money can wear', which follows immediately upon Oak's mental calculation of the value of Bathsheba's ricks in *Far from the Madding Crowd*, Ch. 36. Could Hardy here be remembering Leigh Hunt's well-known use of this superlative –

> The two divinest things this world has got,
> A lovely woman in a rural spot!

in *The Story of Rimini*? Perhaps, although references to Hunt in the *Life* are purely anecdotal. *Formidablest* and *illest* are poetical usages, the former attributed to Napoléon in *The Dynasts*, II. i. 4, the latter to Tristram in the line 'Your father dealt me *illest* turn in this' in *The Famous Tragedy of the Queen of Cornwall*, scene xiv. There is irony again in the catalogue of superlatives to describe the objects of Barbara's charity in 'Barbara of the House of Grebe' in *A Group of Noble Dames*, where Hardy was not quite game to continue the list in the same morphemic manner in which he begins it: 'the *raggedest*, *idlest*, most drunken, hypocritical, and worthless tramps in Christendom'. The superlatives of light and colour which Hardy occasionally employs are indicative as much of mood as of visual impact; scenery for him is too much part of animate experience to be viewed in isolation:

> One of the *brightest* mornings of late summer shone upon her. The heather was at its *purplest*, the furze at its *yellowest*, the grasshoppers chirped loud enough for birds, the snakes hissed like little engines, and Elfride at first felt lively.
> (*A Pair of Blue Eyes*, Ch. 11)

It does not of course require superlatives to add an emotional dimension to a landscape description; comparatives also serve: '*Darker* grew the evenings, *tearfuller* the moonlights, and *heavier* the dews' (*Two on a Tower*, Ch. 15), where *tearfuller* has a poetic ring that puts it in the same category as similar words in Hardy's poems, like 'a *Powerfuller* than I' ('Hap') or 'But his face, if regarded, is woefully *wanner*, and drier' ('At Madame Tussaud's in Victorian Years').

Hardy's use of prepositions has been described as 'cumbersome', and there are certainly moments of awkwardness while he or his characters are negotiating some of 'the inconveniences of syntax', as he calls them in 'A Mere Interlude' (*A Changed Man*). Heilman points to two examples of what he calls 'Hardy's ungainly handling of subordination [which] appears even in prepositional phrases', both from *The Mayor of Casterbridge*: 'The position of the queer old door and the odd presence of the leering mask suggested one thing above all others as *appertaining to* the mansion's past history' (Ch. 21), and 'The barn . . . was closed *save as to* one of the usual pair of doors facing them' (Ch. 29). With the latter we might compare Sue's 'It is an ignorant place, *except as to* the townspeople, artizans, drunkards, and paupers' (*Jude the Obscure*, III, Ch. 4). These are indeed 'ungainly' and reminiscent of the kind of jargon Hardy is occasionally prone to. But they are relatively infrequent, and the modern reader is more likely to be flummoxed by nineteenth-century prepositional constructions which have not survived. These include such phrases as 'remember *about*', 'visited *at* a country-house', 'to play *at* games', 'to live *away at* Shottsford', 'perseverance . . . was irresistible *by* womankind', 'as was his habit *of* a morning', 'to judge either *of* her age or appearance', 'a tap came *to* the door', 'having arrived over the hills *to* Castle Boterel', 'Father and mother kept Berta *to* school', 'every penny of your property shall remain *to* your personal use', '*under* the belief that', 'I shall be glad *with* them' – all in Hardy's prose. In verse, too, there are some unfamiliar uses of prepositions, as in the opening line of 'The Night of the Dance' – 'The cold moon hangs *to* the sky by its horn,' which is as uncommon as it is felicitous. Contrariwise, prepositions are sometimes omitted where we might expect them: 'He sat *next Fancy*'; 'I will *play you* for nothing', that is, play to you; 'Mighty me, *what a scholar you've grown!*' The transitive use of certain verbs had become obsolete by Hardy's time, but he happily revived it; for example, in

> We *clamoured thee* that thou would'st please
> Inflict on us thine agonies –
>     ('I said to Love')

Hardy's use here of the verb *clamour* with a direct object is found in the seventeenth century but not current thereafter. He uses *commiserate* in the same manner, another common seventeenth-century usage which did, however, survive into the nineteenth. It is found in several Hardy novels, for instance in *A Laodicean* III, Ch. 3: 'Paula instantly gave him audience, *commiserated him*, and commissioned him to carry out a first section of the buildings.' That the parallelism of the two juxtaposed verbs, with their similarity of sound and phrasing appealed to Hardy is evident from his tendency to favour such effects.

Other verbs used transitively include *meditate* in the sense 'to reflect upon, to ponder', which was rare in the later nineteenth century; to *promenade* a place, as in 'The new arrival followed his guide through a little door in a wall, and then promenaded a scullery and a kitchen' (*A Pair of Blue Eyes*, Ch. 2); and similarly *walk*: 'I feel as if I were almost ashamed to be seen *walking such a world*'

(*Desperate Remedies*, Ch. 12), both of which usages are found in other nineteenth-century writers. So is *wait* in the sense of 'await', although it was becoming rare in the latter half of the century. Hardy uses it in both prose and verse:

> Somerset in front had *waited the fall of the curtain* with those sick and sorry feelings . . .
> (*A Laodicean*, III, Ch. 9)

> And when you come to me
> To show you true,
> Doubt not I shall infallibly
> Be *waiting you*.
> ('When Dead')

An idiosyncratic usage is Hardy's *learn* with a personal name as object in the sense of 'to get to know someone':

> Elfride, *learning Knight* more thoroughly, perceived that . . . he had no idea that she had ever been wooed before by anybody.
> (*A Pair of Blue Eyes*, Ch. 27)

On the other hand, the absolute use of *send*, as in the following example, is found in other nineteenth-century writers, although it is now no longer current:

> 'We'll drive to *The Present* office, and get one directly; shall we, papa?'
> 'If you are so anxious, dear, we will, *or send*.'
> (*Ibid*., Ch. 14)

A distinctive feature of Hardy's syntax is the retention of reflexive pronouns where these are now generally omitted. In his verse their inclusion may often be prosodic:

> That one I loved vainly in nonage
> Had *ceased her* to be.
> ('My Cicely')

> Bold Poniatowski *plunged him* in
> Never to re-emerge.
> ('Leipzig')

> Yet while here and there they *thrid them*
> In their zest to sell and buy,

> Let me *sit me* down amid them
>> And behold those thousands die . . .
>> ('The Bridge of Lodi')

'Fear-filled, I *stayed me* till summer-tide,'
> ('Postponement')

where the reflexive construction is an afterthought, the original manuscript version having read 'Stricken, I stayed till the summertide'. Other instances occur in *The Dynasts*; for example:

> When his hired army and his chosen general
> *Surrendered them* at Ulm a month ago . . .
>> (*The Dynasts*, I. v. 5)

In prose, the use of reflexive pronouns permitted considerable latitude in the nineteenth century. Hardy tended towards archaic usage in this as in other respects because its longer survival in dialect reinforced yet again the timelessness enshrined in his vision of Wessex. Thus he uses phrases like 'he *leant himself* against the fork of an apple-tree', 'a bramble that had *intruded itself* there', 'Poor Abel, as he was called, had an inveterate habit of *over-sleeping himself*', and 'she *puzzled herself* till her head ached'. It is worth noting that in all these examples the reflexive pronoun *-self* is used, whereas the personal pronoun tends to be used by itself in Hardy's verse, as in the examples quoted. We might here also note the rare form *selfward*, meaning 'to myself' in the poem 'I Looked Back', a usage more American than British.

Hardy's archaizing tendency includes older and for the most part obsolete forms of verbs, both preterites and past participles. These are not confined to verse – where one would expect them among Victorian poets – and include forms like *clave*, *glode*, *shined*, *trode*, *upclomb*, *updrave*, *vext*, *weeted*, *wist*, and *witted*. In prose, Hardy revives the early modern English preterite form *snapt*, used by Miss Aldclyffe in *Desperate Remedies*, and the analogical preterite *sprung*, in narrative (as in 'the wind sprung up stronger' in *The Hand of Ethelberta*, Ch. 43). The preterite form *eat* 'ate' survived from Middle English into the nineteenth century and is used by Hardy (as in 'She obediently eat some supper' in *Jude the Obscure*, VI, Ch. 5). Another traditional form is *withholden*, which became obsolescent in the course of the seventeenth century and is revived, for example, in *The Return of the Native*, II, Ch. 3, where it is the last word in the chapter, providing a suitable concluding cadence:

> But Providence is nothing if not coquettish; and no sooner had Eustacia formed this resolve than the opportunity came which, while sought, had been entirely withholden.

A now obsolete verbal construction which Hardy retains in occasional use is the expanded tense in a passive sense, as Jespersen called it in *A Modern English Grammar*, III, p. 351, found commonly in eighteenth-century and early nineteenth-century writers like Fielding, Jane Austen, and Dickens. For example:

> The entrance-gate was open now, and under the archway the outer ward was visible, a great part of it being laid out as a flower-garden. *This was in process of clearing* from weeds and rubbish by a set of gardeners.
> (*A Laodicean*, I, Ch. 3)

> ' 'Tis a very strange thing that whenever one of Egdon folk goes to church some rum job or other *is sure to be doing*.'
> (*The Return of the Native*, III, Ch. 2)

> In the kitchen dinner *was preparing*.
> (*The Woodlanders*, Ch. 6)

Another construction involving the verb *to be* which differs from present-day usage is its use to form the perfect and pluperfect tenses of verbs of motion. This goes back to Old English, gradually changed in Middle English, and by the beginning of the nineteenth century had, as K.C. Phillipps notes in *Jane Austen's English*, 'a period flavour'. Hardy normally uses *have*, but occasionally his characters use the older form, among them Boldwood and Grace Melbury and Paula Power, and so does the narrator: 'When the boy *was gone* to bed, Rhoda sat a long time over the turf ashes that she had raked out in front of her' (*Wessex Tales*: 'The Withered Arm', 3).

In his use, or non-use, of the auxiliary verb *to do* Hardy allows himself the same freedom of choice between older and modern usage, both in interrogative sentences as in Christopher's '*How came you* to know?' (*The Hand of Ethelberta*, Ch. 8), and in negation: 'However, *she cared not* for it, if Somerset would but look back!' (*A Laodicean*, VI, Ch. 1). Even when he uses *do* in a question, it can have an archaic ring:

'You are Mrs Jethway, I think. *What do you do here*? And why do you talk so wildly?'
(*A Pair of Blue Eyes*, Ch. 25)

The use of the subjunctive, where it occurs, now imparts a similarly old-fashioned flavour to dialogue or narrative, since the twentieth century has largely dispensed with the subjunctive in English, as it appears to be doing in some other European languages. In the nineteenth century it was often a matter of personal preference, sometimes one of social class, whether or not to use a subjunctive in conditional or optative clauses, and the two could appear side by side, as in Robert Louis Stevenson's story 'Markheim': 'If I *were* dying of thirst, and it *was* your hand that put the pitcher to my lips, I should find the courage to refuse.' In his day-to-day prose Hardy normally uses the indicative in *if*-clauses, but there are occasional subjunctives: 'Time will show if this *be* true or not' (Letter to Gosse, 12 January 1900); 'as if it *were* a game of chess' (Letter to Florence Henniker, 25 February 1900). The same applies to Hardy's fiction in such conditional clauses as these:

'You'll speak to Bob, won't you, honey?' said the miller . . .
'*If he wish me to*', she replied.
(*The Trumpet-Major*, Ch. 39)

The acting was for the benefit of such and such an excellent charity – nobody cared what, *provided the play were played*.
('A Changed Man', II)

On the other hand, here is Tess *en famille*:

'. . . and *if I was quite sure* how it would be living there, I would go any-when.'
(*Tess of the d'Urbervilles*, Ch. 6)

Hardy's treatment of nouns shows fewer divergences from present-day English than is the case with other parts of speech. He has an occasional plural form, like *peaces* in the poem 'Under the Waterfall', which may jolt the modern reader unaware of the fact that some abstract nouns once had plural forms which would now be inadmissible. He preserves the uninflected plural after numerals, as in '*nine couple* of dancers' in prose or 'And *forty couple* walked' in verse, but may use the inflected plural on another occasion: 'He was not more than *five-feet-eight* or nine.' He uses, perhaps for the sake of euphony, the same plural form for a series of compound nouns where we would now differentiate: 'Such men as *Governor-Generals* and *Lord-Lieutenants* . . . *Chief-Justices* and *Lord-Chancellors*', and he may now and then use a singular verb with a plural noun in a construction of colloquial compactness rather than grammatical 'correctness': 'the ensuing *ten minutes was* one of disquietude', where *one* has no other antecedent (*The Trumpet-Major*, Ch. 8).

The pervading impression of Hardy's grammar is his willingness to freely admit archaic usages into the current English of his time; a lifetime, as we need again to remind ourselves, that spans little short of the almost one hundred years separating the appearance of *Nicholas Nickleby* in 1839 and that of *To the Lighthouse* in 1927. He was of course not the only writer of that period in whose work traditional and modern usages co-exist, but more than most he cultivated the former in order to give verbal expression to his sense of the continuing presence of the past in the Wessex of his novels and the personal landscape of his poems.

Hardy's punctuation has only just begun to be an object of critical interest, and it will require more analyses of the kind recently under-taken by Simon Gatrell and Juliet Grindle* to distinguish properly between Hardy's own punctuation and that of his publishers and printers. Gatrell's conclusions are necessarily tentative as they are based on an examination of only two novels, but they suggest that while Hardy's system of punctuation may be inconsistent and at times inadequate, it is 'alive' and 'sensitive to tone and the dynamics of speech and narrative'. This bears out the impression recorded in the preceding pages that Hardy's English is generally shaped by his ear and comes most into its own when read aloud. It is the cadences of his phrasing that determine the reader's response rather than the sometimes unauthentic punctuation in the texts at present before us.

Certain idiosyncrasies of punctuation are detectable in Hardy's poetry with the help of James Gibson's Variorum Edition of *The Complete Poems*. One such, perhaps the most conspicuous, is Hardy's insistent use of exclamation marks. There is, for example, an average of three exclamation marks per poem in *Wessex Poems* and of

---

* Simon Gatrell, 'A Critical Edition of Thomas Hardy's Novel *Under the Greenwood Tree*', Oxford University thesis, 1973, in the Bodleian Library, and 'Hardy, House-Style, and the Aesthetics of Punctuation' in *The Novels of Thomas Hardy*, ed. Anne Smith, pp. 169–92; Juliet Grindle, 'A Critical Edition of *Tess of the d'Urbervilles*', Oxford University thesis, 1974, in the Bodleian Library.

its fifty-one poems only four are without any. Twenty-two poems end with exclamation marks. In his revisions, as indicated by variant readings, Hardy tended to increase the number of exclamation marks considerably; rarely did he withdraw one.

Such statistics can tell us what his habit was, but they cannot reveal its reasons. An exclamation mark, by definition, concludes an exclamatory or emphatic statement. Its frequent use in Hardy's verse suggests a form of assertiveness, as if nothing more can or need be said on the subject. In 'Her Death and After', for example, the full stop of the manuscript was replaced by an exclamation mark in this instance:

> 'My father who's not my own, sends word
> I'm to stay here, sir, where I belong!'

There was no gainsaying such a demand: the child *did* stay.

The same passage illustrates, in the absence of a comma after 'father', Hardy's tendency to try to be faithful to the sound of an utterance rather than follow conventions of punctuation. Only in the version printed in *Selected Poems* is there a comma after 'father' to mark off the relative clause. But what is intended by the poet is the child's uttering the whole phrase in one breath as if all the words were linked by hyphens, because, you see, the-father-is-not-the-father.

Exclamation marks may also be hortatory or imperative, and they may serve prosodic functions, emphasizing rhyming words or refrains. Rhetorical questions may end in exclamation marks, as in 'Channel Firing'. Occasionally they also seem to play a syntactic role, filling in, as it were, some incomplete phrase or clause:

> 'It's her satin dress, no doubt –
> That shine you see –
> My own corpse to me!'
> ('At a Fashionable Dinner')

The same poem ends a rhetorical question with an exclamation mark, uses the same mark several times for emphasis, and plays a typically Hardyan variation on the cadences of the refrain word *Lavine*: a question mark after the first stanza, a full stop after the second, and an exclamation mark after the third and final stanza. Such usages can be multiplied from the entire range of Hardy's poetry.

Another characteristic Hardy usage is that of the dash, frequently used to indicate parenthesis, often of an explanatory or antithetical kind, occasionally alongside brackets:

> 'Our life was June – (September
> It was then); . . .'
> ('The Noble Lady's Tale')

where the brackets were omitted in the two periodical printings but appear in *Time's Laughingstocks*. The dash is a more abrupt form of parenthesis than the bracket, and is also used frequently by Hardy to indicate transitions of whatever kind, as in the movement from narrative to speech: in 'The Mother Mourns' the opening narrative concludes at the end of the fifth stanza with a series of dots, which are followed by a dash at the beginning of the next stanza introducing Nature's 'plaint'. Elsewhere, for example in 'The Superseded', a single explanatory dash may be similarly placed at the beginning of a line; and sometimes there is a dash at the end of a line and another at the head of the next:

> 'War ends, and he's returning
> Early; yea,
> The evening next to-morrow's!' –
> – This I say
> To her, whom I suspiciously survey,
>
> Holding my husband's letter
> To her view. –
> ('A Wife and Another')

The punctuation here is both syntactical, indicating a pause at the end of the opening lines of the poem in direct speech, reinforcing the quotation mark, and rhetorical, indicating a parenthesis explaining the situation of the two women face to face. Later in the poem there is a briefer explanatory parenthesis:

> He came – my husband – as she knew he would.

And in the next but one stanza following, the sequence of dashes in combination with a series of dots is typical of Hardy's way of indicating the dramatic nature of abrupt speech uttered under emotional stress:

'Madam, forgive me!' said she,
   Sorrow bent,
'A child – I soon shall bear him . . .
   Yes – I meant
To tell you – that he won me ere he went.'

Such parenthetical, explanatory, or dramatic, uses of the dash are characteristic of Hardy's punctuation in his poems.

One of the few problems of reading Hardy's handwriting, as James Gibson points out in his Introduction to the Variorum Edition (p. xxiii), is occasional confusion between colons and semi-colons. But the confusion is not entirely the reader's: Hardy himself vacillated and the compositors did not always help. In 'The Dead Quire', for example, there are instances of variant punctuations between the manuscript, the version published in *The Graphic*, and other versions, including *Time's Laughingstocks*, *Selected Poems*, and *Chosen Poems*. These variants involve interchanges between commas and semi-colons, semi-colons and colons, commas and full stops, commas and colons, as well as exclamation marks and dashes. Such variations are not untypical, and where they are authentic changes by Hardy himself they are probably continuing attempts at aural refinement.

The colon is a particularly sensitive mark of punctuation. As Eric Partridge wrote in his *Notes on Punctuation*: 'The colon announces, but it also concludes; it explains and defines; it poises and parallels; it sets in apposition; it accumulates, yet it may indicate opposition or antithesis; it is compensatory or after-thoughted.' Hardy was aware of such nuances, and of the parallel and complementary roles played by the semi-colon:

Ache deep; but make no moans:
Smile out; but stilly suffer:
The paths of love are rougher
   Than thoroughfares of stones.
   ('The End of the Episode')

Here the semi-colons are pauses of contrast, while the colons are pauses inviting both continuity and definition. A similar purpose is served by the two colons following each other in the final stanza of 'The Christening':

'But chained and doomed for life
   To slovening
As vulgar man and wife,
He says, is another thing:
Yea: sweet Love's sepulchring!'

But the precise significance Hardy may have attached to colons and semi-colons, and other marks for that matter, may often elude the reader, although in his finest poems especially they clearly play their part. In 'Wessex Heights', for instance, there appears to be subtle interplay between several colons and semi-colons, yet I find it hard, in the second stanza, for example, to grasp its full intention:

In the lowlands I have no comrade, not even the
   lone man's friend –
Her who suffereth long and is kind; accepts what
   he is too weak to mend:
Down there they are dubious and askance; there
   nobody thinks as I,
But mind-chains do not clank where one's next
   neighbour is the sky.

All one can really say about this is that the music is absolutely right.

   Without corresponding variorum editions of Hardy's novels and stories, it is not feasible to draw any definite conclusions about his punctuation in prose fiction. The recent appearance, however, of Dale Kramer's critical edition of *The Woodlanders*, now makes readily accessible to students of Hardy, information about Hardy's original manuscript readings and the revisions introduced into succeeding editions of this novel by himself, as well as changes for which compositors were probably responsible. At times it is still impossible to say who initiated a particular change, especially in such matters of 'accidentals' as punctuation or capitalization. As Kramer says: 'Hardy's manuscript pointing is clear and adequate (allowing for occasional omitted full stops and commas). However, it is idio-syncratic and individualistic, and the printers of the first texts, Clay, felt no hesitation in imposing a more orthodox system of pointing upon them. As a result, one of the major tasks of a critical edition of Hardy is to acknowledge his natural, personally felt, punctuation' (pp. 28f). In this task, Dale Kramer has been largely successful; for example, in the restoration of dashes, of which Hardy was no less fond in his prose than in his verse:

Giles's features stiffened a little at the news. 'Indeed: what for? But I won't keep you standing here. Hoi, Robert!' he cried . . .
   (*The Woodlanders*, Ch. 9 New Wessex Edition)

Giles's features stiffened a little at the news. "Indeed – what for? – But I won't keep you standing here. – Hoi, Robert!" he cried . . .
   (*Ibid.*, ed. Kramer)

The return to Hardy's manuscript punctuation in most cases where this differs from later printed versions is much to be welcomed, as it brings us closer to the particular cadences of Hardy's prose. This applies especially to the removal of numerous punctuation marks which appeared in the first printed version of *The Woodlanders*, although this was 'set directly from Hardy's manuscript', as Kramer makes clear (p. 52). When revising the text for the Wessex Edition Hardy 'gave primary attention to the removal of commas, and thus he opens his text to a degree which suggests that the manuscript's relatively economical punctuation represents his preference' (p. 50). An example from the same chapter shows Grace displaying a form of eager intentness as she warms to a topic patently above Giles's head:

"My notion is that Méry's style will suit her best because he writes in that soft emotional luxurious way she has . . ."

This reads much more fluently than the same utterance broken by the commas of the later versions:

'My notion is that Méry's style will suit her best, because he writes in that soft, emotional, luxurious way she has . . .'

What Kramer calls Hardy's 'natural style' of punctuation is evident even in his letters, where dashes are frequently used in place of more conventional signs, especially commas, but even full stops, as following capitals make clear. Such usage in letters suggests informality, or even haste, rather than stylistic purpose, but the informality is not irrelevant to his prose fiction, where dashes are freely used in a manner that invites the reader to hear rather than merely read what is being spoken or narrated. Hence the dash in prose is what it frequently is in verse – dramatic, explanatory, or parenthetical – indicating changes of tone, of direction, or of emphasis. This is true also of the colon, which often functions for Hardy as a brief pause for taking breath, but not long enough to break continuity. In the original version of *Under the Greenwood Tree*, for example, as Simon Gatrell has noted, Hardy's use of colons has a dramatic function in Nat Callcome's calling up to Fancy through the chinks in the floor:

> ' 'Tis all right: Dick's coming on like a wild feller: he'll be here in a minute: the hive o' bees . . . swarmed . . .'
> (*Under the Greenwood Tree*, V, Ch. 1)

This is more dramatic than the version we now have:

> ' 'Tis all right; Dick's coming on like a wild feller; he'll be here in a minute. The hive o' bees . . . swarmed . . .'

It is worth noting that in those of Hardy's prose writings which, like 'Candour in English Fiction' or 'The Dorsetshire Labourer', were intended to be read by the eye rather than heard by the ear, his punctuation is much more that of contemporary convention than it is in his fiction: dashes and colons are hardly in evidence at all.

The available evidence thus suggests that Hardy's idiosyncrasies of language and style, his constant searching for the appropriate word, the right phrase, the distinctive cadence, embrace his punctuation as well. Here was another tool he shaped to his purpose.

The quotation which heads the present chapter occurs early in *The Dynasts* where Fox is speaking of

> all Bills this favoured statesman frames,
> And clothes with tapestries of rhetoric
> Disguising their real web of commonplace.
> (*The Dynasts*, I, i. 3)

Much of Hardy's fiction and a good number of his poems are concerned with disguising the web of commonplace by seeking out what he calls 'the uncommon in human experience' (*Life*, p. 150), and to achieve this he developed a style which is itself uncommon. 'The writer's problem', Hardy continues in the same passage, 'is, how to strike the balance between the uncommon and the ordinary so as on the one hand to give interest, on the other to give reality.' His English reflects his own struggle with the problem, ranging as it does from the familiarity of colloquial idiom, in which Hardy would include dialect speech, to the tapestries of rhetoric combining strands of archaic diction with neologisms and literary borrowings and technicalities drawn from numerous sources.

One obvious method of 'disguising' was to create out of the real world of Dorset and its neighbouring counties the fictional world of Wessex. Although Hardy insisted that the parallels between real places and those of his fiction were often tenuous, and that many of his descriptions, especially of buildings, were composite, there is no doubt that he frequently had specific localities in mind whose identity he disguised under fictitious names. The help which he gave to Hermann Lea, as the latter acknowledges in *Thomas Hardy's Wessex*, is ample proof of this.

Some of the place-names of Hardy's Wessex are unchanged, and some of them occur both in their real form and in some disguise, like Chesil Beach, west of Weymouth, which appears thus in *A Pair of Blue Eyes*, and as Chesil Bank in *The Woodlanders*, both of them authentic names. But it appears also as 'Pebble-bank', in *The Well-Beloved*, a name which illustrates that Hardy's disguisings were for the most part by no means fortuitous: 'Pebble' is a literal rendering of Chesil, which derives from Old English *cisel, ceosel* 'gravel, shingle'. Hardy was aware of the earlier forms and etymologies of some of the local place-names which, like the above, he may have gleaned from historical sources, especially the third edition of John Hutchins's *The History and Antiquities of the County of Dorset*. An interesting example is 'Shottsford (Forum)', Hardy's name for Blandford (Forum). The latter, *pace* the 'authorities' cited by Hutchins, contains Old English *blæge* 'gudgeon', so that Blandford is the 'ford where gudgeons were seen', gudgeon being a small freshwater fish. Hardy's name substitutes *shott*, a west-country word for a species of small trout, so that 'Shottsford' plays a deliberate variation on the real name of the little town. Another example is 'Weydon-Priors', the Wessex equivalent of Weyhill, near Andover, Hampshire, famous for its ancient fair, and in *The Mayor of Casterbridge* the scene of Henchard's sale of his wife and child. Hardy's change is again a relatively minor disguise, but makes etymological sense, for *-don*, Old English *dūn*, also, means 'hill'. Moreover, the addition of 'Priors' reinforces the first element, Old English *wēoh* 'holy place'.

Similar examples are not difficult to recognize: they also replace one element of the genuine place-name by another which is etymologically or semantically akin. In *Desperate Remedies*, Ringstead Bay, east of Weymouth, first appeared as 'Laystead shore', then 'Layning shore', before it was given its final Wessex name 'Ringsworth Shore' in the 1896 edition. It also occurs in 'The Distracted Preacher' (*Wessex Tales*). Hardy here substituted one ancient place-name element *worth*, an Old English word meaning 'an enclosure, a homestead', for another, 'stead', Old English *stede*, 'a place, site, farm'.

In quite a number of cases Hardy's Wessex name represents a deliberate revival of an earlier form of the name, some of them attested in Domesday Book, others earlier still. Examples from pre-Norman records include 'Abbot's Cernel' (Cerne Abbas) which is recorded as *Cernel* by Ælfric in the late tenth century; 'Corvsgate Castle' (Corfe Castle), where Hardy used the early eleventh-century form *Corfgetes* of the name Coryates, which is about twenty miles west of Corfe Castle, and applied it to the latter; 'Durnover' (Fordington) is a revival of the Romano-British name for Dorchester, *Durnovaria*; 'Exonbury' (Exeter) is a variation of the name *Exanceaster* recorded in the *Anglo-Saxon Chronicle* in AD 877, the primary meaning of -*bury*, Old English *burh*, being 'a fortified place', the same as Old English *ceaster*; 'Middleton Abbey' (Milton Abbas) is recorded as *Middletun* in the same source in AD 964; and 'Wintonchester' (Winchester) occurs in Old English records as *Wintanceaster* from the eighth century.

Domesday Book furnishes some other parallels with Hardy's Wessex: The 'Estminster aisle' in the poem 'The Inscription' is a thin disguise for the church at Yetminster, near Yeovil, which is recorded as *Etiminstre* in Domesday Book, spelt *Estminstre* in Hutchins; 'Ingpen Beacon' (Inkpen Beacon) is the *Ingepene* of Domesday Book; 'Ivel, Ivell' (Yeovil) appears as *Givele*, with a soft initial /j/, the same sound as in the Domesday Book form *Givelcestre*, which is recorded in 1157 as *Iuelcestr'*, almost identical with Hardy's name 'Ivel-Chester' for Ilchester, north of Yeovil. Hardy's 'Ivel' is identical with the name of the river Ivel, which is etymologically the same as the river-name Yeo 'forked river', on which Yeovil stands. Other examples are 'Stapleford Park' (Stalbridge Park) which is Hardy's variant of the Domesday *Staplebrige*, and 'Wellbridge' (Wool) which preserves the Domesday form *Welle*. Somewhat later is the thirteenth-century *Chastelboterel*, which became Hardy's 'Castle Boterel' for Boscastle.

Hardy's 'Anglebury' for Wareham is an interesting disguise. The town lies on the river Frome (Hardy's 'Froom', which appears in *Tess of the d'Urbervilles* as 'the river Var or Froom'). Wareham, as the Anglo-Saxon forms of the name make clear, means 'village by the weir', which Hardy changes, with appropriate semantic connection as well as topographical relevance to 'Anglebury', which would mean 'village by the bend of a river', an accurate enough description of the situation of Wareham along the northern side of a great curve of the Frome. Another such river bend, this time of the Hampshire Stour, is at Herne or Hurn or Heron just north of Bournemouth. The name derives from Old English *hyrne* 'corner, angle', but was probably linked by Hardy with herons, which in turn may have led him to call it 'Rookington Park' – a circuitous route perhaps, but not uncharacteristic of him. After all, Hartfoot Lane becomes 'Stagfoot Lane' in *The Woodlanders* and *Tess of the d'Urbervilles*, by a similar route, and there is dialectal punning in Hazelbury Bryan in Blackmoor Vale (also in *Tess of the d'Urbervilles*) becoming 'Nuttlebury': *nuttal* in the dialect of 'Lower Wessex', that is Devon and Cornwall, means 'hazel'. A rather grimmer pun may be intended by 'Marlott' (Marnhull), where Tess's unhappy history begins. 'Quartershot' for Aldershot has obvious military connotations; 'Alfredston' for Wantage historical ones; 'Marygreen' for Fawley has family associations; while 'Shakeforest Towers' for Savernake Forest and 'Stoke-Barehills' for Basingstoke may be suggested by sound in the former and topography in the latter.

A few names are translations, like 'Fountall' for Wells, described in AD 766 as 'quod situm est juxta fontem magnum', or 'Kingsbere' for Bere Regis, where Hardy's form is actually a revival of the older *Kingesbere*, recorded in the thirteenth century, and given as 'King's Bere' in Hutchins. But in many cases Hardy's disguising consists of very simple modification of the real name, possibly just a variant spelling, as in 'Pydel Vale' for the river Piddle, which does in fact appear with *y* in a thirteenth-century Assize Roll. Ballard Point becomes, by an equally simple change, 'Bollard Head'; Maiden Castle becomes 'Mai-Dun Castle', which Hardy, following the derivation favoured by Hutchins, explains as 'The Castle of the Great Hill' in 'A Tryst at an Ancient Earthwork' (*A Changed Man*), a fanciful explanation because this and similar place-names, like Maiden Newton, or Maiden Bradley north-west of Shaftesbury, really are connected with maidens.

Other simple changes hardly suffice to conceal the identity of the original: 'Camelton' (Camelford); 'Creston' (Preston); 'Evershead' (Evershot) represents an approximation to the medieval form *Evershet*; 'Lulwind Cove' (Lulworth Cove); 'Marlbury' (Marlborough); 'Nether-Moynton' (Owermoigne) called 'Nether

Mynton' in *Desperate Remedies* from 1896 on; 'Newland Buckton' (Buckland Newton); 'Pen-zephyr' (Penzance); 'St Launce's' Launceston; 'Silverthorn' (Silverton); 'Tolchurch' (Tolpuddle); 'Tor-upon-Sea' (Torquay); 'Trufal' (Truro).

The same is true of names that are telescoped, like Athelhampton Hall becoming 'Athelhall'; or shortened by omitting the initial letter or letters, like 'Emminster' (Beaminster); 'Idmouth' (Sidmouth); 'Oxwell' (Poxwell); 'Roy-Town' (Troy Town); 'Targan Bay' (Pentargon Bay).

In a number of cases, Hardy had recourse to other place-names, sometimes near by, in order to conceal the place he had in mind: St Juliot is disguised as 'Endelstow', probably based on the village of St Endellion about twelve miles away, named after an unknown saint. Newbury is called 'Kennetbridge' after its river; East Creech near Corfe Castle probably suggested half of 'Kingscreech' (Kingston just south of Corfe Castle according to Pinion; Steeple some three miles west of Corfe Castle according to Kay-Robinson); and 'Knollsea' (Swanage) was probably suggested by Church Knowle, Hutchins's Church Knolle, a few miles to the north-west of Swanage. 'Port-Bredy' (Bridport) is an interesting concoction: Little Bredy and nearby Long Bredy, about half-way between Bridport and Dorchester, supplied the name 'Bredy', derived from the river Bride, while Bridport itself supplied 'Port'. Bridport is literally 'the port belonging to Bredy', in other words 'Port-Bredy', and the river Bride which rises at Bride Head in Little Bredy flows into Lyme Bay about two miles south-east of Bridport, only about one mile from the mouth of the river Brit. Bridport stands on the latter river, about a mile from the coast. It is rather confusing for those who do not know this corner of Dorset; nor does Hutchins help by commenting that one river Bredy 'is sometimes confounded with' the other river Bredy! But Hardy's name 'Port-Bredy' is, as so often, aptly chosen.

'Sherton Abbas' is disguised Sherborne with 'Abbas' derived from one of several place-names with this element in Dorset and neighbouring counties, possibly from Bradford Abbas, which is some three miles south-west of Sherborne. 'Stourcastle' is disguised Sturminster Newton, the river Stour supplying half the name and the *quondam* castle, referred to in the fourteenth century in the phrase 'Sturmunstre juxta Newton Castel' supplying the other half. Taunton lies on the river Tone, whence its Wessex name 'Toneborough'. 'Weatherbury' (Puddletown) derives its name from an ancient earth work, Weatherbury Castle, east-north-east of

Puddletown, whose obelisk partly suggested 'Rings-Hill Speer' in *Two on a Tower*.

Some of Hardy's Wessex names represent local forms or local pronunciations: 'Dundagel' (Tintagel) is said to be the local form, as is 'Pummery', Hutchins's 'Pomery or Poundbury', for Poundbury, and 'Shaston' for Shaftesbury, which Hutchins gives as 'the modern name . . . an abbreviation of Shaftesbury'. 'Tivworthy' for Tiverton may be intended to represent local Devon pronunciation, and 'Yalbury' as well as the more obvious 'Yell'ham' may similarly be intended to represent the local Dorset pronunciation of Yellowham, slightly disguised in the case of 'Yalbury'. More obvious are 'phonetic' spellings like 'Po'sham', characterized by Hutchins as *'Vulgo Possum, or Posham'*, for Portisham; 'Warm'ell' for Warmwell Cross; 'Black'on' for Black Down, between Abbotsbury and Dorchester; and 'Rou'tor' for Rough Tor, south-east of Camelford on Bodmin Moor in Cornwall: the loss of /ʃ/ in 'rough' is not uncommon in Lower Wessex dialects.

Among the most familiar names in Hardy's Wessex are 'Casterbridge', combining the old Roman encampment, *castra*, with the 'bridge' across the Frome; 'Christminster', which derives from Christ Church Cathedral, Oxford; and 'Egdon', which may have been prompted by Eggardon Hill, just over half-way between Dorchester and Beaminster, although this appears in Hardy both as 'Eggar' and as 'Haggardon'. Both the local proverb 'As old as Eggardon hill' and the local pronunciation /ɛgn/ may have influenced Hardy's choice of 'Egdon' for his ancient heath. So, for that matter, may the fanciful derivation from British *Egor-dún* 'the open or wide down or fastness' in Hutchins. 'Melchester' (Salisbury) and 'Mellstock' (Stinsford) with its neighbours 'Upper Mellstock' (Higher Bockhampton, Hardy's birthplace) and 'Lower Mellstock' (Lower Bockhampton) are formed with the element 'Mel(l)-' which Hardy may have taken from the name Melcombe Regis, part of the municipal borough of Weymouth. The name Melcombe goes back to Old English *meoluc-cumb* 'valley where milk was obtained'. In *An Indiscretion in the Life of an Heiress* Weymouth was called 'Melport'. The element 'Mel-' occurs in several place-names in Dorset, Wiltshire, and Hampshire, with varying etymological origins, like Melplash, north of Bridport, which means 'mill pool', or Melchet Park in Hampshire, an old forest name probably of Celtic origin. Also in Hardy's more immediate vicinity were places with such names as Melbury Abbas, Melbury Bubb, Melbury

Osmond, Melbury Sampford, Melcombe Regis, and Melcombe Horsey. Hardy's name 'Lyonnesse' for Cornwall is of venerable medieval ancestry, although spellings vary from Malory's 'Lyones' to Swinburne's 'Lyonesse'.

The methods Hardy adopted in his Wessex nomenclature appear to have been prompted by considerations similar to those which shaped his English in general: above all, a strong sense of communion with the past. Many of the names are either revivals of earlier forms or contain traditional elements to be found in the real names of places in southern and south-western England. In other instances he used various modes of disguise: orthographic or phonetic variants, aphetic forms, substitutions suggested by topography or similarity of meaning, even punning. The point that is worth stressing is the deliberate and informed nature of these changes and the part they play in establishing the character of Hardy's language. The place-names of Wessex are not haphazard; they might be described as an integral part of Hardy's linguistic strategy.

Some of his characters bear names derived from place-names. The village of Chickerel just north-west of Weymouth provided the name of the Chickerel family in *The Hand of Ethelberta*. Jude Fawley's surname is the ancestral village of Fawley in Berkshire which in *Jude the Obscure* becomes 'Marygreen'. Hardy's first choice, 'Head', was the maiden name of his paternal grandmother who lived in Fawley as a girl. Although Hinton is a not uncommon place-name in England, Adelaide Hinton's name in *Desperate Remedies* may have been suggested by the Hinton villages west of Blandford Forum. The Luxellian family name in *A Pair of Blue Eyes* probably derives from Luxulian in Cornwall; that of Manston in *Desperate Remedies* from Manston, Dorset, just north-east of Sturminster Newton; and that of the Melbury family in *The Woodlanders* from the several hamlets of that name in the locale of the novel, south of Yeovil. Two miles north of Cerne Abbas are Minterne Magna and Minterne Parva, which share their name with that of Conjuror Mynterne in *Tess of the d'Urbervilles*, who lived at 'Owlscombe', Hardy's name for the village of Batcombe which lies some two or three miles to the west of the Minternes. Batcombe has nothing to do with bats etymologically, but for Hardy the change from bat to owl was as convenient as that from hart to stag, and the nocturnal connotations are appropriate for a conjuror whose name is rooted in the local countryside, who was, according to tradition, the Squire of Bat-combe and who was buried in the church there, as Hutchins records, half of his tomb projecting beyond the church wall. Hardy mentions Conjuror Mynterne in an anecdote in the *Life* (p. 169).

There are other instances of local place-names entering the nomenclature of Hardy's fictional people. Captain Ogbourne's name in 'What the Shepherd saw' (*A Changed Man*) derives from the several villages of that name north of Marlborough in Wiltshire where the story is located. The Petherwin family name in *The Hand of Ethelberta* was probably suggested by the two villages of South and North Petherwin which lie respectively two miles south and four miles north-west of Launceston. In *Tess of the d'Urbervilles*, Ch. 34, is a brief reference to Angel's godmother, Mrs Pitney, whose name may have come to Hardy from Pitney in Somerset, north-west of Yeovil. Similarly, the name of 'the moderately Reverend Mr Tinkleton, Nonconformist' in *The Hand of Ethelberta*, Ch. 31, may have been suggested by the Dorsetshire village of Tincleton, with an ironic echo of *Isaiah* or *First Corinthians* for good measure. A good Dorsetshire name for a man closely identified with the local countryside is that of Giles Winterborne in *The Woodlanders*: the name is found in places around Dorchester, several of them along the river Winterborne which rises near Winterborne Houghton, north-east of Dorchester, and joins the Stour at Sturminster Marshall.

My intention in enumerating these names is not to provide yet another glossary or dictionary of Hardy's people and places, which F.B. Pinion has done so thoroughly and others have done before and since, but to illustrate this somewhat neglected facet of the interplay between Hardy's language and the countryside from which he sprang and of which he wrote. Place-names are among the oldest and most persistent manifestations of the English language. By using them and adapting them as he did, Hardy was weaving yet another, and a strongly evocative, strand in the tapestry of his rhetoric.

The choice of biblical first names, in which his writings abound, represents another important link with local tradition. In his *Dorsetshire Folk-Lore* Udal refers to it as 'once so common a nomenclature in the West of England'. The sad case of young Cain Ball whose mother confused Cain and Abel at his christening (*Far from the Madding Crowd*, Ch. 10) illustrates the propensity among country folk to give their children biblical names, like Abner, Benjamin, Deborah, Ezekiel, Hannah, Hezekiah, Levi, Rachel, Reuben, and Solomon; or names descriptive of the Christian virtues, like Charity, Faith, Hope, Mercy, Modesty, Soberness, and Temperance. That some of these are applied by Hardy to their respective bearers with a good measure of irony does not disprove the argument: the nineteenth century still favoured such names, especially in the country.

Other now uncommon first names are derived from a variety of sources; those from Old English further reinforce the links with the Anglo-Saxon past of Hardy's Wessex, names like Alfred, Cuthbert, Edred, Ethelberta. Classical names occur, such as Aeneas and Eustacia and Festus. There are names with a more distinctively aristocratic flavour, like Alicia, Caroline, Louis, and those which adorn Hardy's Noble Dames. There are idiosyncratic first names like Car and Gad and that highly suggestive combination Suke Damson, where the first name recalls the Dorset form *honeyzuck*, found in Barnes's poem 'Zummer Evenen Dance':

> There be rwoses an' honeyzucks hangen among
> The bushes.

Fitzpiers's amorous encounter with Suke on old Midsummer Eve in *The Woodlanders*, Ch. 20, suggests distinct parallels with Barnes's summer dance, while the 'tasty' quality of Suke is of course reinforced by her surname, as is her 'hoydenish' nature, for the word 'damson' sounds sufficiently like 'damsel' to evoke some of the latter's less flattering connotations.

Many of Hardy's surnames, especially but not exclusively in the earlier novels, have a Dickensian quality. Writing of Dickens's proper names, G.L. Brook notes that 'Dickens was more willing than most novelists to give his heroes unusual or grotesque names' (*The Language of Dickens*, p. 208), and Hardy was on occasion quite happy to do the same. There are farmers called Bollens, and Buckle, and Kex (a dialect word denoting the dry hollow stalk of plants like the cow parsley; see Chapter 3). There are rustics called by such expressive names as Coney ('rabbit'), Kail ('cabbage'), Twink ('chaffinch'), as well as Biles, Blore, Dollop, Groby, Jinks, Leaf, Paddock, Poorgrass, Sneap, Stubb, Weedy, Worm, and Yopper. There is a coachman called Nobbs, a butcher called Grimmett, an agent called Flooks, a coroner called Floy, a magistrate called Blowbody, an innkeeper called Trencher, and a lady's maid called Menlove.

Hardy's lawyers frequently bear facetious monosyllabic names, like Thorn, Green, Sweet, and Long. His clergymen have symbolic names like Mincing, Thirdly, Toogood, Woodwell, and Glim, which is a dialect word meaning 'a light, candle' also found in urban slang. It is thus used by Sikes in Dickens's *Oliver Twist*. There is a venerable trio of theological doctors called Brown, Smith, and Robinson in *A Pair of Blue Eyes*; a medical Dr. Chestman in *Desperate Remedies*, another called Dr. Bath in *The Mayor of Caster-bridge*, and a dentist called Rootle in *The Trumpet-Major*, whose name inevitably suggests the somewhat uncouth activity of pigs extracting edibles from under the ground. There is a firm of builders called Nockett and Perch in *The Hand of Ethelberta*, a dynasty of pig-killers called Lickpan in *A Pair of Blue Eyes*, and there are three maidens in *Under the Greenwood Tree* with the improbable names of Bet Taller, Vashti Sniff, and Mercy Onmey.

Hardy seems to have enjoyed the business of finding or inventing names for his characters. It taxed his ingenuity rather more as he progressed from the more grotesque names in *Desperate Remedies* and its immediate successors to names which had some linguistic connection with Wessex or embodied a symbolism appropriate to character or story. Thus we have names like Cantle in *The Return of the Native*, a dialect word in 'Outer Wessex' meaning 'a slice of cheese'; or Creedle, that 'swaying collection of old clothes' in *The Woodlanders*, a word from 'Lower Wessex' meaning 'to creep, to crawl'. The pathetic figure of Abel Whittle dragged from his bed without his breeches in *The Mayor of Casterbridge* recalls the Dorset meaning of *whittle* as 'a child's woollen napkin', as Barnes defines it in his *Glossary*.

The symbolic import of names like Boldwood and Troy is as apparent as that of Oak when it is recalled that *wood* means 'mad' and that *Troy-town* is a west-country expression for 'a state of confusion or disorder'. Names like Angel Clare and Sue Bridehead require no comment, and few readers will miss the import of the names of Pierston and Avice Caro in *The Well-Beloved*.

That Hardy took considerable trouble over the names of places and characters is evident from the changes he made in the course of his writing and revising. This is true of his poems as well as his fiction and will become increasingly apparent as more critical editions of the novels and stories are published. The genesis of Tess from Love to Cis to Sue to Rose-Mary to Tess, from Woodrow to Troublefield to Durbeyfield, is one familiar example. That Suke Damson in *The Woodlanders* was originally called Suke Sengreen in the serial version is also of historical interest; but in scrutinizing Hardy's diction what is of importance is that his final choice for the girl's name was that of a juicy fruit rather than a common plant which grows on walls, or on 'a thatch-roofed house' in 'The Inquiry', or 'sprouted from the eaves of the low surrounding buildings', as he describes 'the houseleek or sengreen' in *Far from the Madding Crowd*, Ch. 9. In *The Mayor of Casterbridge*, the Scotsman was originally called Alan Stansbie before being re-named Donald Farfrae, a name, as Pinion notes, that 'indicates the wistfulness of a Scot, "far frae hame" '. It is a particularly suitable name, not only for its wistfulness, but as a constant reminder of Farfrae's Scottish accent.

Similar instances of changed names of people and places punctuate the textual history of Hardy's works. Their occurrence testifies to his constant urge for refinement and perfection or, as Florence Emily Hardy noted (*Life*, p. 451n.) to 'his artistic inability to rest content with anything that he wrote until he had brought the expression as near to his thought as language would allow'. Hardy's revisions were of course not confined to changing proper names, but extended across the entire spectrum of his language – words, phrases, paragraphs, punctuation, and so on. To study the genesis of his works, as is being increasingly done in books like John Paterson's and John Laird's or articles like James Gibson's,* is both fascinating in its own right and important for our understanding of Hardy's creative processes, but for a proper understanding of his *oeuvre* and the language used therein, we can at present but turn to the best texts we have. They represent his last major revision, his final 'expression as near to his thought as language would allow'.

This 'artistic inability to rest content' is, however, by no means purely a matter of revision; it is also a matter of casting about, no less restlessly, for different expressions to denote identical or similar concepts, or to dress up recurrent themes in different language. Such concepts and such themes have been the objects of much critical attention. The concept of a controlling force, or controlling forces, for example, impinging upon and shaping human lives and destinies is one which occupied Hardy's thought from his early poem 'Hap', written in 1866, to the despondent recognition of 'some demonic force' in the penultimate poem of *Winter Words*. His was not, as he reiterated, a systematic or 'harmonious' philosophy, hence the continued struggle with the meanings of words: 'Crass Casualty' and

---

* John Paterson, *The Making of 'The Return of the Native'*, and 'The Genesis of *Jude the Obscure*'; J.T. Laird, *The Shaping of Tess of the d'Urbervilles*; James Gibson, 'Hardy and his Readers' in *Thomas Hardy. The Writer and his Background*, ed. by Norman Page.

'dicing Time' and 'These purblind Doomsters' all occur in successive lines in 'Hap'. It is characteristic of Hardy, even at this early stage in his career as a writer, that among the first attempts to clothe the idea of an indifferent fate in words, he should choose one word that was practically obsolete in this sense, for the modern sense of *casualty*, 'victim of accident or disaster or military action' was already well established, and another, *Doomsters*, which was archaic. The very title of the poem, 'Hap', is an archaism denoting an agency inherently neither good nor bad, as is plain from Shakespeare's practice of using *hap* with qualifying adjectives like 'good' or 'ill'. The sense of what in a later poem ('Doom and She') Hardy described as 'vacant of feeling' was anticipated five hundred years earlier by Chaucer, who defined *hap* in his translation of Boethius's *Consolatio* thus: 'hap is an unwar betydinge of causes assembled in thingis', where the crucial word is *unwar* 'unaware, accidental'.

This unconsciousness or insensibility of fate to human striving and suffering is a persistent theme in Hardy which eventually leads him to express the hope that 'the Great Foresightless' might become sentient and that all manner of things shall then be well. This is the burden of the final auspicious chorus of *The Dynasts*:

> But – a stirring thrills the air
> Like to sounds of joyance there
>   That the rages
>   Of the ages
> Shall be cancelled, and deliverance offered from
>   the darts that were,
> Consciousness the Will informing, till It fashion
>   all things fair!

'The Immanent Will', as Hardy calls it in the opening line of *The Dynasts*, in the poem 'The Convergence of the Twain', and else-where, 'works unconsciously'; it is both *automatic* and *unweeting*, a juxtaposition of two words in successive lines in the Fore Scene of the drama which is characteristic of Hardy's linguistic eclecticism: *automatic* is Greek in origin but essentially a modern word in the sense of mechanical actions carried out with no conscious thought, while *unweeting* is of Germanic origin and was an archaism long before Hardy revived it here or in his reference to the performance of the mummers in *The Return of the Native*, II, Ch. 4. The mechanical, insentient workings of the Will are poignantly expressed in the final chorus of the Spirit Ironic in the After Scene of *The Dynasts*:

> the dreaming, dark, dumb Thing
> That turns the handle of this idle Show!

The impersonality of this *Thing*, always referred to in *The Dynasts* by the neuter pronoun, is variously expressed in the novels, stories, and poems by the use of several neutral words, including *thing* or *things*:

> 'I have been injured and blighted and crushed by *things* beyond my control!'
> (*The Return of the Native*, V, Ch. 7)

> The direct antagonism of *things*.
> (*Jude the Obscure*, VI, Ch. 3)

> The grisly grin of *things* . . .
> ('Four in the Morning')

There is frequent use of the word *circumstance*, both singular and plural, with similar connotations both of an unconscious agency and of the situations it brings about; for example:

> *Circumstance*, as usual, did it all.
> (*A Pair of Blue Eyes*, Ch. 13)

> He sometimes had philosophy enough to appreciate *a satire of circumstance*, because nobody intended it.
> (*The Hand of Ethelberta*, Ch. 13)

Circumstance is given several attributes implying inflexibility, fortuitousness, and pitilessness: 'inexorable circumstance', 'the impishness of circumstance', 'the intractability of circumstances', 'cynic circumstance', and:

> The events that had, as it were, dashed themselves together into one half-hour of this day showed that curious refinement of cruelty in their arrangement which often proceeds from the bosom of the whimsical god at other times known as blind Circumstance.
> (*Wessex Tales*: 'Fellow-townsmen', VIII)

To these attributes others are added: strangeness and whimsy and irony. 'Odd coincidences' first appear in *Desperate Remedies*, they reappear as 'whimsical coincidences' in *Far from the Madding Crowd*, and are stated to be 'common enough in fact, though scarcely credited in chronicles' in *A Laodicean*. Troy's experience with the gurgoyle is a 'singular accident'; John Loveday encounters 'a curious little incident'; Rhoda Brook is confronted by 'the freaks of coincidence'. In addition to 'satires of circumstance', Hardy talks of 'the cruel satires that Fate loves to indulge in', of 'the satire of Heaven', of 'a curious fatefulness', of 'some supernatural legerdemain', of 'impish tricks' of Chance, of 'a cast of the die of destiny' (where the manuscript reads 'Destiny').

Coincidences are chance occurrences happening simultaneously or seemingly connected, and Hardy uses several words to express the notion of events dashing themselves together, as he put it in the above quotation from *Wessex Tales*. The list reads almost like an extract from Roget's *Thesaurus*: 'the unexpected *collision* of incidents'; 'a strange *concurrence* of phenomena'; 'a *conflux* of circumstances'; 'the *conjunction* of incidents' and 'strange *conjunctions* of phenomena' (a late revision for 'of circumstances' in *A Pair of Blue Eyes*); 'the *conjuncture* itself'; 'harrowing *contingencies*'; '*converging* destinies' and 'all the while they were *converging*, under an irresistible law, as surely as two streams in one vale'. A related notion is that of 'the *concatenation* of events', a linking together, which brings into play metaphor and myth in such expressions as the *World-weaver* of the poem 'Doom and She'; The '*Spinner* of the Years' of 'The Convergence of the Twain'; the '*spinners wheel*, onfleeing' in 'According to the Mighty Working'; 'Life's *mad spinning*' in 'End of the Year 1912'; 'the pattern in the great *web* of human doings then *weaving* in both hemispheres' in *The Woodlanders*; and the Will's 'Eternal *artistries in Circumstance*' in *The Dynasts*. In *The Mayor of Casterbridge*, Henchard is up against 'the ingenious *machinery* contrived by the Gods for reducing human possibilities of amelioration to a minimum': the ancient myths of Moirai and Parcae spinning and measuring and cutting, of Germanic Wyrd and Weird Sisters, are here modernized into *machinery*. In the same novel an actual piece of machinery is introduced as metaphor:

> Her triumph was tempered by circumspection; she had still that field-mouse fear of *the coulter of destiny* despite fair promise, which is common among the thoughtful who have suffered early from poverty and oppression.
>
> (*The Mayor of Casterbridge*, Ch. 14)

It is apparent from the examples so far given that the diction of Hardy's cosmology is characteristically eclectic. It must also have become apparent that Hardy draws upon theistic as well as fatalistic terminology to convey the notion of some agency at work in determining human destiny. *Destiny* itself is one such word. Donne personified Destiny into 'the Commissary of God'; in *Paradise Lost* Destiny 'ordained'; in *The Return of the Native*, I, Ch. 7, Hardy speaks of its 'interference'; in *A Laodicean*, V, Ch. 14, de Stancy acknowledges that 'destiny is supreme'; and Jude is said to be *predestinate*, after 'a compelling arm of extraordinary muscular power seized hold of him – something which had nothing in common with the spirits and influence that had moved him hitherto' (*Jude the Obscure*, I, Ch. 7). *Destiny* is not a biblical word, nor are *Fate* and *Fortune*, both of which also appear personified as well as conceptualized in abstract terms. In *The Hand of Ethelberta*, Ch. 13, Hardy speaks of 'the sad buffoonery that fate, fortune, and the guardian angels had been playing with Ethelberta of late', a list somewhat reminiscent of Shelley's 'Fate, Time, Occasion, Chance, and Change' in *Prometheus Unbound*. Fortune is given a feminine *persona*, as befits her traditional image, by Sir William de Stancy as he talks of 'her favour', and is similarly personified by the narrator later in *A Laodicean*: 'Fortune as usual helped him in his dilemma'. The familiar image of the wheel of fortune is invoked at the beginning of Chapter 31 of *The Mayor of Casterbridge* in the description of Henchard's decline, and is alluded to in the poem 'Dream of the City Shopwoman', and elsewhere.

*Fate* is both abstract, and personified as a separate agent in the singular and as a figure of the classical goddesses in the plural: Wildeve uses both concepts in speaking to Eustacia in *The Return of the Native*:

'*Fate* has treated you cruelly.' (IV, Ch. 3)

'*The fates* have not been kind to you.' (IV, Ch. 6)

'Character is Fate' says Hardy in *The Mayor of Casterbridge*, Ch. 17, translating Novalis's word *Schicksal*, which George Eliot had rendered 'destiny', and there is an echo of this in the words of the Spirit of Rumour:

> And of whose kindred other yet may fall
> Ere long, if character indeed be fate.
> (*The Dynasts*, II, vi. 6)

In *The Return of the Native*, III, Ch. 1, 'the waggery of fate' is held responsible for Yeobright's choice of trade. In *The Woodlanders*, Ch. 25, 'the finger of fate' touches Grace Melbury and turns her from maiden into wife, and earlier in the novel we are reminded of the futility of trying to oppose the dictates of fate:

> *Fate*, it seemed, would have it this way, and there was nothing to do but to acquiesce.
> (*The Woodlanders*, Ch. 15)

Echoes of the traditional image of classical mythology, like that evoked by Wildeve, also occur elsewhere; for example:

> She had hoped to be a teacher at the school, but *the fates* seemed to decide otherwise.
> (*Tess of the d'Urbervilles*, Ch. 6)

In his poem 'Paradox' Hardy plays yet another verbal variation by writing of 'men's *fatings*'.

Shelley's 'Time . . . Chance . . . To these / All things are subject but eternal Love' sounds a further echo in the narrator's comment on Susan Henchard:

> When she plodded on in the shade of the hedge, silently thinking, she had the hard, half-apathetic expression of one who deems anything possible at *the hands of Time and Chance* except, perhaps, fair play.
> (*The Mayor of Casterbridge*, Ch. 1)

Throughout the novels and stories the search for the right expression continues: '*Something external* to us' in Sue Bridehead's terminology corresponds to '*a power external* to herself' in the case of Elfride Swancourt. Farfrae acknowledges that 'it's ourselves that are ruled by *the Powers above* us!'; for Jude and Sue 'other *forces and laws* than theirs were in operation', and blame for misfortune attaches to '*the universe*, I suppose – *things in general*, because they are so horrid and cruel!'.

The pessimistic fatalism of such remarks is frequently re-stated by references to human beings as the playthings of superior powers, not only in the famous ending of *Tess of the d'Urbervilles*, which Hardy took considerable pains to mould into its final shape, but in such phrases as 'what a *sport for Heaven* this woman Eustacia was' and 'We are the *sport of fate*'. The cruelty and malignancy of these sportive powers, summed up in one poem ('After the Last Breath') by the phrase 'the Wrongers all', is also expressed in different ways: In 'Destiny and a Blue Cloak' (*Old Mrs Chundle and Other Stories*) Agatha senses that '*a malign influence* seemed to be at work without any visible human agency'; Henchard superstitiously believes in 'the scheme of *some sinister intelligence* bent on punishing him'; Elizabeth-Jane and Jude are subject to '*malignant stars*'; in the tragedy of Tess, Hardy says, 'one may, indeed, admit the possibility of a *retribution* lurking in the present catastrophe'. There is the well-known reference to 'the *Unfulfilled Intention*, which makes life what it is' in the description of the struggling trees and parasites of the ancient woodland where every organism battles for survival, in *The Woodlanders*, Ch. 7, a concept that recurs, using the same phrase, in the argument with the 'Causer' in the poem 'A Philosophical Fantasy'. And there is repeated assertion of *doom*, both in fatalistic terms like 'There seemed to be no help for it; hither she was *doomed* to come', as Tess reaches Flintcomb-Ash; and in Christian terms, as Father Time, shuddering, whispers 'It do seem like *the Judgment Day*', or as the woman's skeleton moulders 'Till the Call shall be . . . / till Doom's-dawn' in 'Not Only I'.

Hardy's Christian upbringing and his thorough knowledge of scriptural and liturgical language inevitably led him to clothe some of these notions of external powers in Christian language specifically, or in theistic terms more generally. The use of the word *Heaven* in this sense is equivocal, especially in phrases like '*Heaven's persistent irony* towards him' or 'the *satire of Heaven*' or 'a *sport for Heaven*' or in Eustacia's passionate outburst:

> 'O, the cruelty of putting me into this ill-conceived world! I was capable of much; but I have been injured and blighted and crushed by things beyond my control! O, how hard it is of *Heaven* to devise such tortures for me, who have done no harm to *Heaven* at all!'
> (*The Return of the Native*, V, Ch. 7)

*Heaven* is used with the same unfavourable connotations as Elizabeth-Jane becomes aware of 'the wreck of each day's wishes' and wonders 'what unwished-for thing *Heaven* might send' next.

*Providence*, although not a biblical word, has strong Christian associations. Hamlet's 'there's a special providence in the fall of a sparrow' with its deterministic 'yet it will come' was no doubt deeply embedded in Hardy's memory as he writes of 'waiters on

Providence', or makes Farfrae exclaim 'It's Providence! Should any one go against it? No . . .!', or adds yet another Shakespearean echo in this sentence:

> 'There is no choice in it – read that', said Paula, handing Havill's letter, as if she felt that *Providence had stepped in to shape ends* that she was too undecided or unpractised to shape for herself.
> (*A Laodicean*, III, Ch. 4)

A direct equation between Providence and God is established as Jude returns from his 'chimerical' trip to Kennetbridge to find Sue's letter asking him to visit her, and thought that this was 'another special intervention of *Providence* to keep him away from temptation. But a growing impatience of faith, which he had noticed in himself more than once of late, made him pass over in ridicule the idea that *God* sent people on fools' errands' (*Jude the Obscure*, III, Ch. 10).

The word *providence* connotes 'foreseeing' as well as 'guidance' and 'ordaining' and is thus in direct antithesis to the concept of 'the Great Foresightless' of *The Dynasts*. Its power to see is given stark expression in Grace's passionate exclamation to Fitzpiers after the incident of the man-trap:

> 'O, Edred, there has been an *Eye watching over us* to-night, and we should be thankful indeed!'
> (*The Woodlanders*, Ch. 47)

But such references to a personal divinity or directly to God are used sparingly in Hardy's fiction. Sue Bridehead, in the throes of religious contrition, understandably speaks of 'the Power above us' and of 'His poor creatures' and concludes that 'It is no use fighting against God!' all in the same breath. But Hardy is more reluctant to be drawn into such direct commitment. He speaks of *the gods*, even *the Gods*, and seems more in sympathy with such a formulation as he attributes to Eustacia:

> Yet, instead of blaming herself for the issue she laid the fault upon the shoulders of *some indistinct, colossal Prince of the World*, who had framed her situation and ruled her lot.
> (*The Return of the Native*, IV, Ch. 8)

The phrasing, the allusions, the capital letters suggest a deliberate personifying, yet without any definite identification with the

Christian deity of the kind we are more liable to meet in Hardy's poems. Here the language is often biblical or liturgical, but tinged with irony in its concern with 'such "questionings" in the exploration of reality', as Hardy speaks of in the 'Apology' to *Late Lyrics and Earlier*. Irony is implicit in such titles as 'God-Forgotten', 'God's Education', and 'God's Funeral', and references to God are frequently couched in ironic language: In 'New Year's Eve' the opening lines set the tone:

> 'I have finished another year', said God,
>     'In grey, green, white, and brown . . .'

where the sense of mechanical action is made obvious in the concluding lines by the familiar figure of 'weaving . . . by rote' and the emphatic, alliterating epithet of the last line:

> He *sank to raptness* as of yore,
>     And opening New Year's Day
> *Wove it by rote* as theretofore,
> And went on working evermore
>     In his *unweeting* way.

The word *God*, when not ironic, is frequently censorious. As early as 'Neutral Tones' 'the sun was white, as though chidden of God' and, in the penultimate line, becomes 'the God-curst sun', while in 'I Travel as a Phantom Now' the poet, in the spectral manner which he describes in the *Life*, p. 210, wonders

>     if Man's consciousness
> Was a mistake of God's.

That an 'unweeting' God, or the 'Unknowing God' of 'The Bedridden Peasant', makes mistakes is patently part of Hardy's belief: in a letter to Gosse of 25 July 1906 Hardy speaks in words that could hardly be plainer of 'a stupid blunder of God Almighty'. Less personal but no less censorious is the phrase 'some Vast Imbecility' in 'Nature's Questioning', a phrase which carries manifold connotations of mental and physical debility – and is no more flattering to the 'Causer' of 'Earth's old glooms and pains' than is its description in the same poem as 'an Automaton / Unconscious of our pains'.

Hardy goes yet further in his ironic use of the diction of Christian scripture and liturgy by echoing their archaic grammar and familiar cadences:

> I towered far, and lo! I stood within
> The presence of the Lord Most High,
> Sent thither by the sons of Earth, to win
> Some answer to their cry.
>
> – 'The Earth, sayest thou? The Human race?
> By Me created? Sad its lot?
> Nay: I have no remembrance of such place:
> Such world I fashioned not.' –
>
> – 'O Lord, forgive me when I say
> Thou spakest the word that made it all.' –
> 'The Earth of men – let me bethink me . . . Yea!
> I dimly do recall' . . .
> ('God-Forgotten')

Despite Hardy's disclaimers of any consistent *Weltanschauung*, his language inescapably draws a picture of 'God' or 'the Lord' as chiding, cursing, blundering, although without any *avowed* evil design, for he is *unknowing*, *unweeting*, *logicless*, and works with a 'too oft unconscious hand'. Such a concept clearly demanded language less fixed and circumscribed than that of established religion, language more suited to poetry where private allusion was less likely to provoke public outcry, as Hardy, having suffered much of the latter, acknowledged in October 1896, a few months before the publication of *The Well-Beloved*:

'Poetry. Perhaps I can express more fully in verse ideas and emotions which run counter to the inert crystallized opinion – hard as a rock – which the vast body of men have vested interests in supporting. To cry out in a passionate poem that (for instance) the Supreme Mover or Movers, the Prime Force or Forces, must be either limited in power, unknowing, or cruel – which is obvious enough, and has been for centuries – will cause them merely a shake of the head; but to put it in argumentative prose will make them sneer, or foam, and set all the literary contortionists jumping upon me, a harmless agnostic, as if I were a clamorous atheist, which in their crass illiteracy they seem to think is the same thing . . . If Galileo had said in verse that the world moved, the Inquisition might have let him alone.'

(*Life*, pp. 284f.)

Yet in his prose fiction, as we have seen, Hardy was not unwilling to be 'argumentative', using language which revealed quite starkly his notions of uncaring, even malignant, forces sporting with human beings and shaping their destinies. In the poems there is not so much a further loosening of restraint as a widening of Hardy's linguistic horizon. Abstract concepts more frequently appear personified, a rhetorical trope long familiar in English poetry:

> And Devotion droops her glance
> To recall
> What bond-servants of Chance
> We are all.
> ('Ditty')

It is worth noting that the manuscript reading 'devotion' in 1870 became 'Devotion' in the 1898 printing of *Wessex Poems*. In 'A Sign-Seeker', from the same collection, 'Nescience mutely muses'; in his poem on the death of Queen Victoria, 'V.R. 1819–1901', Hardy personifies 'the Absolute' and 'the All-One'; and in a later poem speaks of 'the scribe of the Infinite' ('The Masked Face'). *Doom* remains an abstract notion of judgment and retribution in some poems, but is majestically personified in 'The King's Experiment':

> And Nature met King Doom beside a lane.

In 'Fragment' the poet's *persona* asks the souls of the entombed bodies what they are waiting for. The answer anticipates Beckett's *Waiting for Godot* by almost forty years.*

> 'O we are waiting for one called God', said they,
>   '(Though by some the Will, or Force, or Laws;
>   And, vaguely, by some, the Ultimate Cause);
> Waiting for him to see us before we are clay.
>   Yes; waiting, waiting, for God *to know it* . . .'

The expectation is that eventually what Hardy elsewhere calls 'The Great Adjustment' will take place: 'God' or 'the Will', or whatever

---

* In the *Life*, p. 224, Hardy had written: 'I have been looking for God 50 years, and I think that if he had existed I should have discovered him. As an external personality, of course – the only true meaning of the word.'

other word may suit, will realize just what has been happening on 'Earth's bewildering ball':

> 'It is clear he must know some day.'

The sentiment is again that of the concluding Chorus of *The Dynasts*:

> Consciousness the Will informing, till It
> fashion all things fair!

The diction of 'Fragment' also recalls the manner in which the Phantom Intelligences variously refer to the Will in *The Dynasts*. Indeed, the reader of Hardy's poems becomes increasingly aware of the lexical probing taking place in the earlier ones towards the more assured expression of Hardy's *Weltanschauung* attained in *The Dynasts*. The several Spirits, once they are established in his cosmology, return in a few later poems, like 'Honeymoon Time at an Inn', or the Armistice poem 'And There Was a Great Calm' in *Late Lyrics and Earlier* and in another poem from the same collection, 'In a London Flat':

> And the Spirits behind the curtains heard,
> And also laughed, amused at her word,
> And at her light-hearted view of him.
> 'Let's get him made so – just for a whim!'
> Said the Phantom Ironic. ' 'Twould serve her right
> If we coaxed the Will to do it some night.'
> 'O pray not!' pleaded the younger one,
> The Sprite of the Pities. 'She said it in fun!'

With characteristic irony, Hardy does make the husband a widower within the year: the Will is patently amenable to coaxing of such sportive kind.

*The Will* is Hardy's preferred name for whatever it is that runs the universe, but he frequently uses other terms to stress its (or as he would write: Its) active, determining, causative role. *The Ultimate Cause* suggests, presumably deliberately, a creative function, for the word was early familiar to Hardy from its biblical uses – 'He causeth the grass to grow for the cattle, and herb for the service of man' – a function made more explicit by personifying *Cause* to *Causer*, as in that bitter poem 'On the Portrait of a Woman about to be Hanged' or in 'A Philosophical Fantasy', a late poem in which the diction is still that of more serious speculation, but the tone is one of banter; as J.O. Bailey says in *The Poetry of Thomas Hardy*, 'Hardy is playing with profound ideas so familiar that they no longer bother him'.

The Will 'decides' (in 'The Torn Letter'); it 'stirs' and 'urges' and determines (in 'The Convergence of the Twain'); it is 'Moulder of Monarchies' (in 'I Met a Man'); it is 'the Absolute', 'the All-One' (in 'V.R. 1819–1901'); and it is frequently, if not identified, at least in some manner fused with the actions of 'Nature' and 'Time':

> . . . the scheme Nature planned for them.
> ('Horses Aboard')

> Through an unconscienced trick of Time!
> ('The Pedestrian')

> Of Time that builds, of Time that shatters.
> ('Nothing Matters Much')

> . . . Time, the Fair's hard-hitter.
> ('A Forgotten Miniature')

That from this hotchpotch of language some notions of Hardy's emerge with reasonable clarity has long been recognized. Life is a 'lottery', a brief 'blight', 'a show / God ought surely to shut up soon', 'the melancholy marching of the years' in 'a world decaying', tossed about by 'chance and change', subject to 'the Mighty Working'. But the very fact that it *is* a hotchpotch of *personae* and concepts culled from Christianity and paganism, from myth and vague theism, from philosophical speculations and scientific theories, does seem to confirm Hardy's insistence that he is not offering anything like a systematic and comprehensive view of things. His linguistic probings are the reflection of his ' "questionings" in the exploration of reality'. It may be true that these questionings ceased to bother him, but neither did they lose their interest for him, nor did he, as Wordsworth did, give them up in despair. What is of relevance here, however, is that Hardy's linguistic fecundity in voicing his ideas retained its vitality to the end of his life.

There are other concerns in Hardy's work over which he pored with the same resourcefulness of language. One such is the recurring theme of the relationship between the sexes, especially in wedlock, to which Hardy brought not only his personal experience of romantic courtship and a marriage increasingly unhappy for both partners, but his own particular genius for endowing individual words and phrases with a tonal range to suit the emotional range encompassed.

All Hardy's novels and many of the short stories explore the themes of love and marriage to varying depths and from various points of view. According to John Bayley (*An Essay on Hardy*, p. 164) 'an incongruous love-situation in a perculiar setting' is Hardy's 'favourite theme'. In his poetry, however, there is a noticeable shift of interest away from this theme in the later volumes, although Hardy's disillusionment with marriage continues to erupt in telling phrases in some of his later poems. One characteristic feature of Hardy's treatment is to contrast the innocent promise of love with the reality of unhappy wedlock, the focus shifting with increasing bitterness to the latter. Occasionally he treated this theme humorously, keeping the language deliberately impersonal by making use of the passive voice and the neuter pronoun and such nondescript phrases as 'some people':

> It may have been observed that there is no regular path for getting out of love as there is for getting in. Some people look upon marriage as a short cut that way, but it has been known to fail.
> (*Far from the Madding Crowd*, Ch. 5)

In the same novel, Troy utters the ironic commonplace 'All romances end at marriage', a notion which Hardy elaborated in the four stanzas of the poem 'The Conformers', where in characteristic phrases romantic courtship and dreary, even sordid, wedlock are progressively contrasted, as 'stolen trysts', 'choice ecstasies', and 'leapings each to each' are doomed to wane into

> syllables in frigid tone
> Of household speech.

Other poems take up the burden; contrasting the lovers' romantic vision with stark reality, here in language reminiscent of Heine:

> No more will now rate I
> The common rare,
> The midnight drizzle dew,
> The gray hour golden,

The wind a yearning cry,
   The faulty fair,
Things dreamt, of comelier hue
   Than things beholden! . . .
     ('He Abjures Love')

In 'The Fiddler' the language is even simpler, eschewing even
the grammatical inversions or archaic verb forms to which Hardy
inclined. In their place there is but the lively word *prancing* with its
animal connotations and an alliterative lilt that skips through the
whole poem. Here is the second stanza:

> He sees couples join them for dancing,
>    And afterwards joining for life,
> He sees them pay high for their prancing
>    By a welter of wedded strife.

In 'A Church Romance', a poem about Hardy's parents, it is Age
that 'had scared Romance', while in yet another poem from *Time's
Laughingstocks*, 'The Christening', love is not merely paid dearly for
in marriage, or frightened away, but likely to be buried altogether:

> 'But chained and doomed for life
>    To slovening
> As vulgar man and wife,
> He says, is another thing:
> Yea: sweet Love's sepulchring!'

Hardy is following several related trains of thought: the belief
that the reality of marriage is very different from the romantic
expectations of young lovers, which implies that marriage is a risk,
that it is liable to lead to suffering, and that it is degrading (*slovening*
is an uncommon verb remarkably expressive in this context); as well
as the firm conviction that social conventions, far from working
towards happiness in marriage, aggravate its miseries. The phrase
'chained and doomed for life' would be almost as fitting an epigraph
for *Jude the Obscure* as Hardy's choice, 'The letter killeth'.

The riskiness of marriage is expressed in a number of ways.
Bluntly, by using words like *risk* or *venture*: In 'The Bride-Night
Fire' the story concludes with people

Saying Tim and his lodger should *risk*
it, and pair.

In 'The Contretemps' the two strangers accidentally thrown into each other's arms are about to join in 'a *life-long leap*' into the unknown to the accompanying wry comment,

> 'One pairing is as good as another
> Where all is *venture*!'

Both the poem 'The Well-Beloved' and the novel of that name are concerned with matrimonial risk: 'Brides are not what they seem', says the poem; while in the novel Hardy suggests that the risks depend upon the choice of partner:

> She was, in truth, what is called a 'nice' girl; attractive, certainly, but above all things nice – one of the class with whom *the risks of matrimony* approximate most nearly to zero.
> (*The Well-Beloved*, I, ch. 2)

To enter into marriage is to make one's vows in church 'For bale or else for bliss', or to have 'a husband-and-wife-time,/For good or for ill'. There is the figure of exploring unknown ways:

> Note here within
> The bridegroom and the bride,
> Who smile and greet their friends and kin,
> And down my stairs *depart for tracks untried*.
> ('The Two Houses')

The same notion is expressed in prose:

> . . . Elizabeth-Jane seeming to show no ambition to quit her safe and secluded maiden courses for *the speculative path of matrimony*.
> (*The Mayor of Casterbridge*, Ch. 19)

The hazards of matrimony are suggested by the accumulation of such emotive words and phrases as these, from the same novel:

> The *ruin* of good men by bad wives, and, more particularly, the *frustration* of many a promising youth's high aims and hopes and the *extinction* of his energies *by an early imprudent marriage*, was the theme,
> (*Ibid.*, Ch. 1)

or by Elizabeth-Jane's realization 'that marriage was as a rule *no dancing matter*' (Ch. 44), nor a prancing matter either, as we have seen. In the seventh of Hardy's 'Satires of Circumstance in Fifteen Glimpses', the ardent lover is instantly made aware of matrimonial hazard by hearing and seeing his beloved 'rating her mother with eyes aglare': he flees with the comforting thought

> 'My God! – *'tis but narrowly I have escaped.*'
> ('Outside the Window')

Hardy was of course not unaware of the practical side of marriage, the deliberate taking a risk for sound business reasons. Ethelberta and Arabella represent such a point of view: the former would not 'upset a well-considered course on the haste of an impulse', and asks her sister

> 'Why should I be afraid to make a plunge when chance is as trustworthy as calculation?'
> (*The Hand of Ethelberta*, Ch. 43)

And Arabella is coolly 'business-like' about marriage, from her first glimpse of Jude to her re-marriage to him. 'Life with a man is more business-like after it, and money matters work better', she tells Sue, concluding:

> 'I'd advise you to get the business legally done as soon as possible. You'll find it an awful bother later on if you don't.'
> (*Jude the Obscure*, V, Ch. 2)

There are other characters in Hardy's fiction who propound similar arguments: Louis advocating Lady Constantine's marrying the Bishop of Melchester, for example, in *Two on a Tower*, a step which was to prove eminently sensible; or Angel Clare lauding the practical advantages of marrying one who 'understands the duties of farm life as well as a farmer himself', despite his father's 'conviction that a knowledge of a farmer's wife's duties came second to a Pauline view of humanity' (*Tess of the d'Urbervilles*, Ch. 26).

The matrimonial sufferings which Hardy dwells on with great linguistic resourcefulness born out of strong feeling may be explained in part by the combination of a melancholy temperament and an unhappy marriage. The spate of poems Hardy wrote after his first wife's death, which Desmond Hawkins in *Hardy: Novelist and*

*Poet* well described as 'this unique mausoleum of verse for the dead Emma', recalls their romantic love and courtship – 'Summer gave us sweets' – as well as the subsequent estrangement – 'but autumn wrought division'. The poem to which these words belong is entitled 'After a Journey', a word whose matrimonial connotations Hardy continued to explore, as will already have become apparent. Recalling perhaps Fanny Robin's laborious struggle along the milestones on Casterbridge Highway in *Far from the Madding Crowd*, Hardy addressed himself in the 1896 Preface to *A Laodicean* to those of his readers 'to whom marriage is the pilgrim's Eternal City, and not a milestone on the way'. At first the way of marriage is envisaged, as it was for the courting Hardy and his Emma, as 'paths through flowers', and the language is made to evoke again and again the sweetness and colour and youthfulness of romantic love: 'You love her for her pink and white', 'Her form and flesh bloom yet more fair', 'Love is . . . a sweet allure'. But the milestones of matrimony inexorably 'lead up to' wretchedness in Hardy's scheme of things and his language ranges from mild words like *discomfort* – 'buying a month's pleasure with a life's discomfort', says Jude – to extremes of acerbity. Hardy can be quite moderate: 'to grow a little less warm to their respective spouses . . . is the rule of married life' (*Life's Little Ironies*: 'The History of the Hardcomes'). He talks of 'being so sorrily wed', of 'stale familiarity', and then with growing bitterness of 'the antipathetic, recriminatory mood of the average husband and wife of Christendom'. He employs his characteristic enumerative technique to contrast the more positive with the destructive ingredients of marriage:

> They gazed at each other with smiles, and with that unmistakable expression which means so little at the moment, yet so often leads up to passion, heart-ache, union, disunion, devotion, overpopulation, drudgery, content, resignation, despair.
> (*Life's Little Ironies*: 'On the Western Circuit', I)

And he rails against division and agonies and waste by evoking images of traps and ensnarement, as in Eustacia's 'mire of marriage' or Jude's 'devilish domestic gins and springes', or in phrases such as 'this lock' and 'chained to me', or in the revealing change of a line in 'Intra Sepulchrum' from the manuscript reading 'Like other men and their wives' to 'The *tether* of typic minds'. He invokes fate, as he so often does, in such a typical Hardy compound as 'O *weird-wed* man', and in such a no less typical archaic Hardy phrase as 'spousals doomed to nought'.

There is frequent reference to marrying the wrong person, in single words like *mismating* and *mismatch*, the former a nineteenth-century word, the latter a Renaissance coinage; as well as in more expanded wise. In 'Her Death and After', one of Hardy's favourite poems, the wrong choice of mate is the heart of the tragedy; while in 'The Echo-Elf Answers' the message is as unequivocal as the language is succinct:

> And which will my bride be?
> The right or the wrong?
> 'The wrong.'

The poignant word *division* may be made to carry the whole weight of matrimonial unhappiness, as in 'After a Journey'; or it may be reinforced by adjectives: 'our *deep* division', 'divisions *dire and wry*'; or the same idea may be expressed by verbs in the manner dear to Hardy:

> Some heart-bane *moved our souls to sever*.
> ('The Spell of the Rose')

The word *heart-bane* is one of several compounds Hardy coined to enrich his matrimonial vocabulary; another is *heart-outeating*; yet another occurs in 'their wedlock's *aftergrinds*', a word strongly evocative of being ground down, of attrition, and of monotonous toil. In the same poem, 'Honeymoon Time at an Inn', occurs the line

> 'And their loves grow numbed ere death, by
> the cark of care,'

with its metrical suggestion of slow decay and the age-old connotations of burdensome anguish in the phrase 'cark of care', so much more memorable than its blunt equivalent 'both our burdens' uttered by the disillusioned husband in 'I Knew a Lady'.

The 'days of blight' of Hardy's matrimonial nightmare also bring resignation and domestic tedium to their victims. This thought, too, finds varied expression:

> . . . the *stagnation* caused by the *routine* of a practical household and the *gloom* of bearing children to a *commonplace* father.
> (*Life's Little Ironies*: 'An Imaginative Woman')

> Their slumbers have been normal after one day
>     more of formal
> *Matrimonial commonplace* and *household life's*
>     *mechanic gear*.
>         ('The Dawn after the Dance')

In 'A Conversation at Dawn' household routine becomes 'the domestic *groove*', a word not merely denoting 'a rut', but probably known to Hardy also in the Somerset dialect sense of 'a pit, a mine shaft', which re-inforces the notion of matrimonial pitfalls.

Hardy's pre-occupation with the social and legal aspects of wedlock is most strongly voiced in *Jude the Obscure*, but there are occasional statements elsewhere. The telling words here emphasize the incompatibility, as Hardy sees it, between a feeling 'whose essence is its voluntariness' and the demands of a sexually restrictive society. Words with legal connotations abound: *contract*, *laws*, *ordinances*, *decree*, *bonded*, *licensed*, *plightage* – the last of these specially coined by Hardy for Maria Carolina in *The Dynasts* III. v. 4. No wonder that for many of Hardy's characters 'the reality of marriage was startling', as the narrator says in *Tess of the d'Urbervilles*, Ch. 31, and as Jude was increasingly to discover. The following passage, early along Jude's matrimonial journey, shows Hardy constructing a paragraph on this theme in the manner of a syntactic pyramid: a lengthy complex sentence is followed by a shorter one, then by a shorter one still, the whole being capped by a simple sentence of four words which succinctly sums up Jude's predicament:

> There seemed to him, vaguely and dimly, something wrong in a social ritual which made necessary a cancelling of well-formed schemes involving years of thought and labour, of foregoing a man's one opportunity of showing himself superior to the lower animals, and of contributing his units of work to the general progress of his generation, because of a momentary surprise by a new and transitory instinct which had nothing in it of the nature of vice, and could be only at the most called weakness. He was inclined to inquire what he had done, or she lost, for that matter, that he deserved to be caught in a gin which would cripple him, if not her also, for the rest of a lifetime? There was perhaps something fortunate in the fact that the immediate reason of his marriage had proved to be non-existent. But the marriage remained.
> (*Jude the Obscure*, I, Ch. 9)

The same ideas are expressed in the next but one chapter with greater incisiveness in one complex sentence:

> Their lives were ruined, he thought; ruined by the fundamental error of their matrimonial union: that of having based a permanent contract on a temporary feeling which had no necessary connection with affinities that alone render a life-long comradeship tolerable.
> (*Ibid.*, I, Ch. 11)

As the matrimonial problems multiply, so the language takes on a more bitter note. Jude, in love with Sue, thinks of himself as 'a man who was licensed by the laws of his country to love Arabella and none other unto his life's end' (II, Ch. 4). Sue draws a different image when she declares that 'the social moulds civilization fits us into have no more relation to our actual shapes than the conventional shapes of the constellations have to the real star-patterns' (IV, Ch. 1). The figure is still that of a victim being manipulated, a sense which thirty years earlier Hardy had condensed into one poetic compound, *custom-straitened*, in his poem 'Amabel'. But it is in their exchange in the opening chapter of Part Fifth, the most restless of all the books of this novel, that Jude and Sue voice most vehemently and bitterly their feelings about the 'iron contract' that tends to extinguish tenderness, that permits a husband to cherish his wife 'under a Government stamp' and licenses her 'to be loved on the premises'. 'It is foreign to a man's nature', Sue continues, 'to go on loving a person when he is told that he must and shall be that person's lover'. Sue's final 'fanatic prostitution', as she returns and yields herself to Phillotson, is an 'enslavement to forms', a phrase in the penultimate chapter of the novel, that distils the essence of the view of marriage which the book has been presenting.

I have no wish to oversimplify the complexities of *Jude the Obscure* by this brief glance at its 'matrimonial diction', only to illustrate its range and tonal qualities. It is important to remember, however, that, as the example of 'Amabel' illustrates, Hardy was voicing some of the same sentiments in his earliest poems and continued to do so in verse after *Jude the Obscure*. 'At a Bridal', for example, anticipates Jude's phrase 'enslavement to forms' by the line

Should I, too, wed as *slave to Mode's decree* . . .?

This was written in 1866. In 'The Burghers', also printed in *Wessex*

*Poems*, the husband who surprises his wife with her lover, thinks of himself magnanimously as

But *licensed tyrant* to *this bonded pair*,

anticipating the repeated *licensed* to love or be loved of *Jude the Obscure* as well as the notion of the tyrannical constraints of laws and ordinances and iron contracts. And here the bond which unites the pair is one of passionate love, not the 'social ritual' which binds husband and wife.

There is of course a note of irony, often bitter irony, in Hardy's formulations about matrimony. A whole poem, like 'At the Draper's' or 'The Curate's Kindness', may be one extended ironic comment on marriage, or an ironic conclusion may follow upon a tale of matrimonial misery, like the old surgeon's story of 'Barbara of the House of Grebe' in *A Group of Noble Dames*, which ends with a sermon by the Dean of Melchester on 'the folly of indulgence in sensuous love for a handsome form merely'. While Hardy clearly had strong views about the miseries of the married state, he was, however, quite capable of acknowledging that happy marriages were possible on the basis of what he repeatedly called *comradeship*, a word that brings to mind A.E. Housman rather than Hardy. It appears first rather self-consciously French as *camaraderie*, a word Hardy may have picked up in an old copy of *Fraser's Magazine*:

This good-fellowship – *camaraderie* – usually occurring through similarity of pursuits, is unfortunately seldom superadded to love between the sexes, because men and women associate, not in their labours, but in their pleasures merely. Where, however, happy circumstance permits its development, the compounded feeling proves itself to be the only love which is strong as death – . . .
(*Far from the Madding Crowd*, Ch. 56)

As an aside, it is worth noting the similar cadences of the phrases 'for a handsome form merely' and 'but in their pleasures merely', which the final positioning of the adverb, a favourite in Hardy's syntax, helps to bring about. Yet another example will be found a few lines below. The notion of *camaraderie* persists. In *The Woodlanders*, Ch. 28, it is no longer superadded, but fundamental: 'a new foundation was in demand for *an enduring and staunch affection* – a sympathetic interdependence, wherein mutual weaknesses are made the grounds of *a defensive alliance'*. In *Tess of the d'Urbervilles*, Ch. 25, Clare realizes that success in marrying Tess 'would depend upon whether the germs of *staunch comradeship* underlay the temporary emotion, or whether it were a sensuous joy in her form only, with no sub-stratum of everlastingness'. In *Jude the Obscure*, I, Ch. 11, in a passage quoted earlier, Jude is aware of the need to base marriage on 'affinities that alone render *a life-long comradeship* tolerable'. When the word recurs in a late poem, 'The Mound', it is deliberately placed in inverted commas and seems rather to refer to the kind of relationship adumbrated in *Jude the Obscure* between Sue and her undergraduate friend.

*Comradeship*, for all its antique aura, is a nineteenth-century word. Scott used it; so did George Eliot when she made Romola discover a new sensation, 'the sense of comradeship', as Tito smiles on her. The irony of this discovery in Romola's later experience does not invalidate the favourable connotations which the word has in Hardy's fiction. It was left to the twentieth century to give the word *comrade* a new political twist.

For Hardy the word *staunch* goes with 'comradeship', a word whose original concrete meaning of 'water-tight', whence 'firm, well-constructed', is re-inforced by his references to 'foundation' and 'substratum'. Even in his impassioned advocacy of *camaraderie* in *Far from the Madding Crowd* something of the original meaning of *staunchness* is audible, for the passage quoted above goes on as follows:

> . . . that love which many waters cannot quench, nor the floods drown, beside which the passion usually called by the name is evanescent as steam.

A more empirical view of marriage is taken by Ethelberta in weighing up the pros and cons of yielding to the importunities of the infatuated Lord Mountclere, in a series of sentences which display yet again Hardy's architectonic sense of syntactic balance, contrast, and progression:

> 'I have seen marriages where happiness might have been said to be ensured, and they have been all sadness afterwards; and I have seen those in which the prospect was black as night, and they have led on to a time of sweetness and comfort. And I have seen marriages neither joyful nor sorry, that have become either as accident forced them to become, the persons having no voice in it at all.'
> (*The Hand of Ethelberta*, Ch. 43)

For those, women especially, for whom that ideal of sympathetic interdependence is unattainable, Hardy has comfort in the 'mild, placid, durable way – in that way which perhaps, upon the whole, tends most generally to the woman's comfort under the institution of marriage, if not particularly to her ecstasy' (*A Group of Noble Dames*: 'The First Countess of Wessex'). This is a matrimonial compromise between 'sweet allure' and 'heart-bane', and nowhere does it more sadly reflect Hardy's and Emma's own 'division' than in these words from *The Well-Beloved* describing Avice the Second pursuing 'her household courses without interference, initiating that kind of domestic reconciliation which is so calm and durable, having as its chief ingredient neither hate nor love, but an all-embracing indifference' (III, Ch. 1).

Few of Hardy's characters succeeded in finding even this road to matrimonial calm and durability. Even where the knot is tied in most auspicious circumstances, the nightingale may sing a discordant note or there may be shadows from the past or extending all the way from a battlefield in Spain; but let the last word on this topic go to the Widow Edlin:

> 'I don't know what the times be coming to! Matrimony have growed to be that serious in these days that one really do feel afeard to move in it at all. In my time we took it more careless; and I don't know that we was any the worse for it! When I and my poor man were jined in it we kept up the junketing all the week, and drunk the parish dry, and had to borrow half-a-crown to begin housekeeping!'
> (*Jude the Obscure*, VI, Ch. 5)

Mrs Edlin's blunt appraisal of marriage uttered in the language of Wessex folk is a masterstroke of common sense – and humour – coming as it does at the end of a novel which depicts marriage as being rather more of a devilish trap than a blessed sacrament. Hardy had tried a similar method before when describing, in the words of Jan Coggan, the 'most ungodly recipe' used by Bathsheba's father to counteract the feelings of staleness and constraint he experienced when his sweetheart had been 'ticketed as my lawful wife' (*Far from the Madding Crowd*, Ch. 8). The lively, frank, common-sensical speech of local men and women nicely balances the sonorous, often abstruse, character of Hardy's English when he is endeavouring to give voice and form to his seemings and fugitive impressions.

That the same immediacy of language appertains to much of Hardy's figurative diction is another salient factor in maintaining this balance. His rhetoric may be magniloquent at times, but it can also be homespun, most evidently so in the spontaneous recourse to some homely simile in the speech of his rustics. Here is one of Henchard's men uttering such a simile in a sentence deliberately innocent of neat syntactic ordering:

> 'Why, you see, sir, all the women side with Farfrae – being a damn young dand – of the sort that he is – one that creeps into a maid's heart like the giddying worm into a sheep's brain – making crooked seem straight to their eyes!'
> (*The Mayor of Casterbridge*, Ch. 27)

And here is Giles Winterborne, noticing Marty's shorn head:

> 'Why, Marty – whatever has happened to your head? Lord, it has shrunk to nothing – it looks like an apple upon a gate-post!'
> (*The Woodlanders*, Ch. 3)

Both images mirror the concerns of their speakers, the former reinforced by a biblical echo, the latter perhaps harking back in Hardy's characteristic diachronic manner to the bawdy seventeenth-century connotations of 'apple-wife'. It does not of course need the immediate vicinity of Somerset cider to prompt such imagery: when Andrew's face is described in 'Old Andrey's Experience as a Musician' in *Life's Little Ironies* 'as if it were made of rotten apple', Hardy is obviously seeking no further than the nearest orchard, although yet again there may have been the more distant echoes at work in his memory of heads 'crushed like rotten apples' in Shakespeare's *Henry V*. The apple upon a gate-post, however, albeit apposite to Marty's present appearance, has a deeper reality in prefiguring the barrenness of her whole life, of a fruitful ripening going to waste. There is a caution in its sharp visual impact.

Figurative language like that of the creeping giddying worm or the impaled apple bridges the gap between humanity and the external word, co-existing, subject to similar fates, comic and tragic, yet in their essences isolated from each other. Hardy conveys both the separateness and the kinship by drawing much of his metaphorical diction from the natural world as well as by his insistent anthropomorphism to which he confesses in the *Life*: 'In spite of myself I cannot help noticing countenances and tempers in objects of scenery, *e.g.* trees, hills, houses' (p. 285). 'The building gradually crept upwards, and put forth chimneys', he wrote in his twenty-fifth year in 'How I Built Myself a House'; sixty years later an old house addresses a 'smart newcomer' in 'The Two Houses'. Hills have their 'countenances', like Rainbarrow appearing 'but as a wart on an Atlantean brow' in the second chapter of *The Return of the Native*, or like a wood on a hill showing itself 'bisected by the highway, as a head of thick hair is bisected by the white lines of its parting', in the opening scene of the original version of *The Woodlanders*.

This passage was deleted from the later, post-serial versions of the novel, but it expressed what J.O. Bailey calls 'a recurrent memory' with Hardy. He had used the same simile previously:

> Before him stretched the long, laborious road, dry, empty, and white. It was quite open to the heath on each side, and bisected that vast surface *like the parting-line on a head of black hair*, diminishing and bending away on the furthest horizon.
> (*The Return of the Native*, I, Ch. 2)

And it recurs yet again in 'The Roman Road' in *Time's Laughing-stocks*:

> The Roman Road runs straight and bare
> *As the pale parting-line in hair*
> Across the heath.

But it is above all in trees that Hardy notices countenances and tempers and shapes his language accordingly. As we noted in Chapter 4, the sounds of the Hintocks trees in *The Woodlanders* provide unceasing accompaniment to the unfolding story. The trees moreover enter into the story as actors in what John Bayley has called 'a display of pseudo-consciousness'. The diction is deliberately 'humanized', requiring of the reader almost a deliberate effort to recall its metaphorical import. We see trees 'crooking their limbs', 'wrinkled like an old crone's face', 'naked-legged, and as if ashamed' after being barked. We see a bough smiting the roof of Giles's hut 'in the manner of a gigantic hand smiting the mouth of an adversary, to be followed by a trickle of rain, as blood from the wound'. We see trees 'in jackets of lichen and stockings of moss', and we are made aware of their inner life 'when saps are just beginning to heave with the force of hydraulic lifts inside all the trunks of the forest'.

The same anthropomorphism infuses the language of Hardy's poetry. In 'On the Way' the trees 'fret fitfully and twist'; in 'A

Procession of Dead Days' they were 'turning in their sleep / Upon their windy pillows of gray'; in 'Last Week in October',

> The trees are undressing, and fling in many places –
> On the gray road, the roof, the window-sill –
> Their radiant robes and ribbons and yellow laces.

In 'One Who Married Above Him' trees are said to be 'spitting amid the icicled haze'. Birch and beech have 'fingers . . . skeleton-thin'; yew-trees have 'arms, glued hard to the stiff stark air'; pollard willows stand 'like shock-headed urchins, spiny-haired'; pines are 'joyless'. There is a memorable glimpse of a wintry day, with its hint of suffering for the old, in the opening lines of 'The Prospect':

> The twigs of the birch imprint the December sky
> Like branching veins upon a thin old hand.

The death of a tree, like the death of a person, is a majestic tragedy. Hardy's poem 'Throwing a Tree', first printed under the title 'Felling a Tree' shortly before his death, may be a reminiscence of Barnes's poem 'Vellen o' the Tree'. Both poems describe the process of felling and conclude on comparable notes of wistfulness:

> Zoo the girt elem tree out in little hwome-groun',
> Wer a-stannen this mornen, an' now's a-cut down.

> And two hundred years' steady growth has been ended
>     in less than two hours.

Whether or not Hardy's poem was, as Paul Valéry claimed in a note accompanying its first printing in Paris, the last poem he wrote, it stands as an emblem of his life-long preoccupation with trees as symbols of humanity. Already in what remains of his first novel there is the tendency to see people as trees:

> The transplanting of old people is like the transplanting of old trees; a
> twelvemonth usually sees them wither and die away,
>     (*An Indiscretion in the Life of an Heiress*, I, Ch. 3)

– a tendency that soon became a habit: Henchard 'moving like a great tree in a wind', people 'waving backwards and forwards like a forest of pines swayed by a gentle breeze', 'regiments crash like trees at felling-time'.

His metaphorical language imperceptibly leads Hardy on to a complete fusing of the human and the arboreal, as in 'The Wind Blew Words':

> Behold this troubled tree,
> Complaining as it sways and plies;
> It is a limb of thee.

Or to a pairing, as in 'The Felled Elm and She' in which the woman and the tree were, however, unaware 'That your lives formed such a pair'. The *locus classicus* of such parallel destinies is provided by the great elm tree in *The Woodlanders* and its role in the life and death of John South. The dialect word *shrouding*, as Winterborne lops off its boughs, in Chapter 13, has a curiously prognostic connotation in the context.

This may be accidental, although Hardy was alert to such nuances, but much of Hardy's figurative diction involving trees, as well as other natural phenomena, is strongly emotive. This tendency, too, began early in his creative career. In *An Indiscretion in the Life of an Heiress*, I, Ch. 8, 'Old trees seemed to look at him through the gloom, as they rocked *uneasily* to and fro', and even their dead leaves in the ditches 'shifted their position with *a troubled rustle*'. Two novels later such emotive metaphorical diction grows more insistent:

> The trees of the fields and plantations *writhed like miserable men* as the air wound its way swiftly among them: the lowest portions of their trunks, that had hardly ever been known to move, were visibly rocked by the fiercer gusts, *distressing* the mind by its *painful unwontedness*, *as when a strong man is seen to shed tears*.
> (*Under the Greenwood Tree*, IV, Ch. 3)

In *The Hand of Ethelberta*, Ch. 44, the firs 'spoke in those *melancholy moans and sobs* which give to their sound *a solemn sadness* surpassing even that of the sea' – a passage soughing with sibilant alliteration. And in his next novel, Hardy goes further yet in his assault upon his reader's sensibilities:

> The wet young beeches were undergoing *amputations, bruises, cripplings*, and *harsh lacerations*, from which the *wasting sap* would *bleed* for many a day to come, and which would leave *scars* visible till the day of their burning. Each stem was *wrenched* at the root, where it moved like a bone

in its socket, and at every onset of the gale *convulsive* sounds came from the branches, *as if pain were felt*.
    (*The Return of the Native*, III, Ch. 6)

    One could go on, but trees are of course not the only ingredients of his figurative diction to which Hardy paid such close attention. Winds were sufficiently audible and palpable along the Wessex coastline and across its uplands to evoke some forceful language: 'The atmospheric cutlery of the eastern blast'; distress likened to 'cold air from a cave' or to 'a cold blast over a pool'; a storm beginning 'with a heave of the whole atmosphere, like the sigh of a weary strong man on turning to recommence unusual exertion'. The somewhat ponderous phrase is soon followed by a fusillade of verbs, as hailstones are propelled by the wind 'in battalions – rolling, hopping, ricochetting, snapping, clattering down the shelving banks in an undefinable haze of confusion' (*A Changed Man*: 'A Tryst at an Ancient Earthwork'). Winds do many things in Hardy and give him ample scope to display his fondness for verbs: *rasping*, *scraping*, *brooming*, *filliping*, *skipping sportively*, *running along helterskelter*. They can also be delicate zephyrs wafting thistledown touched by a passing hem, another of Hardy's recurrent memories –

> The light dresses of the ladies sweeping over the hot grass and brushing up thistledown which had hitherto lain quiescent, so that it rose in a flight from the skirts of each like a comet's tail.
>     (*The Hand of Ethelberta*, Ch. 31)

And in verse:

>         Do you recall
>         That day in Fall
> When we walked towards Saint Alban's Head,
> On thistledown that summer had shed,
>         Or must I remind you?
>
> Winged thistle-seeds which hitherto
> Had lain as none were there, or few,
> But rose at the brush of your petticoat-seam
> (As ghosts might rise of the recent dead),
> And sailed on the breeze in a nebulous stream
>         Like a comet's tail behind you . . .?
>     ('Days to Recollect')

Not only ghosts but all humanity is finally embraced by the memory of thistledown in tumbling flight:

> We are but thistle-globes on Heaven's high gales,
> And whither blown, or when, or how, or why,
> Can choose us not at all!
> *(The Dynasts*, II. ii. 6)

More graceful even than thistledown is the most exquisite of Hardy's images, enshrined in the phrase 'as delicate as lamp-worm's lucency' in the poem 'In the Seventies'. Wholly characteristic of Hardy's gift for noticing minute objects like grains of corn and dew drops and 'a dead fly's wing on a sheet of spider's web', a 'lamp-worm's lucency', with its inspired neologism, is worthy to be placed alongside a similar figure of a thousand years earlier:

> . . . Shrivel as coal on the hearth,
> Shrink as dirt on the wall,
> And waste away like water in a pail.
> Become as small as a grain of linseed,
> And far smaller than a hand-worm's hip-bone,
> And become even so small that you become
>      nothing at all.

Hardy would have appreciated this Old English charm 'Against a Wen', with its succession of homespun similes, 'smalling' to a hand-worm's hip-bone, first published in 1878 in the *Transactions of the Royal Society of Literature*, whose Gold Medal was awarded to him many years later.

In his metaphorical conjoining of man's inner and outer worlds Hardy harks back, as in so many facets of his language, to the very beginnings of English writing. For him the external world is, like 'all the words in the dictionary', of a piece in its capacity to furnish symbols and images to express his vision. It is a world where men woo in the undertones of purling milk while the sun rests his chin upon the meadows, where women blaze up like furze-faggots while a stream hisses sarcastically, where rhubarb and cabbage plants sleep in the sun like half-closed umbrellas, where lovers leap together like a pair of dewdrops on a leaf. By themselves many of Hardy's figurative phrases are not particularly remarkable; some are trite. What matters is that their insistent appeal to every sense produces for the reader the cumulative effect of touching, seeing, and hearing as Hardy felt, saw, and heard. Smell also enters into this experience of Hardy's world. It may be difficult 'to cage a perfume', as he wrote in *The Well-Beloved*, but there are distinctive evocations of smell in such images as the tranter 'smelling like a summer fog', or William, in 'The Super-stitious Man's Story' in *Life's Little Ironies*, making his presence smelt, so to speak, by 'something clammy in the air, as if a cellar door was opened close by your elbow'. Even the picture of Sue Bridehead, asleep in Jude's coat, 'looking warm as a new bun', suggests an aroma of fresh bakery as well as sensations of sight and feeling.

And over all Hardy's fiction and verse looms his most compelling symbol, the ever-visiting moon, upsidling, hanging to the sky, sheeting the landscape, gazing through windows, shedding its 'hazy mazy' light upon humanity which, from the moon's-eye view of *The Dynasts* is but a collection of busy cheese-mites, of gyrating animal-cula, of animated dots, of dancing house-flies, doomed to finish, in the unappetizing phrase of 'The Levelled Churchyard', as 'mixed to human jam'.

Rhetoric is the art of using language to persuade. Chaucer knew this six hundred years ago; and for Hardy the aim of his prose and verse is to persuade the reader to see things his way. His words, his syntax, his images are deliberately set down to that end, so that he complains with justice when he is misunderstood or is criticized for doing what he set out to do. As he wrote to Gosse on 17 September 1901: 'Can there be anything more paralyzing than to know that features, subjects, forms, & methods, adopted advisedly, will be set down to blundering, lack of information, pedantry, & the rest.' Like all persuaders he sometimes fails; but, as Isobel Grundy writes,* the idiosyncrasies of what she calls the 'harshness' of Hardy's poetic style – to which his prose style is closely akin – 'are perfectly fitted to convey a sense of the anomalous position, in his view, of consciousness in a universe of nescient striving forces'. To gain such understanding – and 'perfectly' is a powerful tribute – would have assured Hardy that his tapestries of rhetoric had not been woven in vain. I would not, however, call his style 'harsh', for it has too much music in it. Nor, for that matter, would I call it helpless.

---

* 'Hardy's Harshness', in *The Poetry of Thomas Hardy* ed. P. Clements and J. Grindle, p. 16.

# CHAPTER VII

# The Technicist

🔊🔊🔊🔊🔊🔊

HARDY thought seriously about his language and his art. His comments on the writing of fiction and poetry and on style are scattered throughout his prefaces and essays, his autobiography and his letters, and there are not a few *obiter dicta* about the English language as well. These comments do not amount to a systematic theory of literature any more than the many notions and words and phrasings gathered in the preceding chapter add up to a consistent philosophy or an acceptable alternative to inherited canons of marriage. They do, however, help to explain the individuality of Hardy's English.

Perhaps he was being rather disingenuous when he wrote in a letter to the Rev. George Bainton, on 11 October 1887, 'A writer's style is according to his temperament, & my impression is that if he has anything to say which is of value, & words to say it with, the style will come of itself'. 1887 was the year of *The Woodlanders*, a novel affected as much as any of his works by his constant urge to revise. It is hard therefore to believe that its style, here manifestly expressing Hardy's art at the height of his creative genius in prose, came 'of itself'. What he meant was conveyed more clearly several years previously when he had been re-reading Addison, Macaulay, and a string of other English writers, not forgetting *Times* leaders, in a study of style, concluding that 'the whole secret of a living style and the difference between it and a dead style, lies in not having too much style – being, in fact, a little careless, or rather seeming to be, here and there. It brings wonderful life into the writing . . .' (*Life*, p. 105).

'Seeming to be a little careless' is easier in verse than in prose; indeed, Hardy continues the above passage by acknowledging that 'it is, of course, simply a carrying into prose the knowledge I have acquired in poetry – that inexact rhymes and rhythms now and then are far more pleasing than correct ones'. There is certainly considerable variety and some 'inexactitude' in Hardy's rhymes and rhythms, as there is in the diction of his verse. His verses can trip or dance, jog or clog, can echo Barnes's Celticisms as in 'The Last Signal', or medieval triolets as in a group of poems in *Poems of the Past and Present*. There are odd rhymes like *old houses: drowses: spouse is*; comic ones, like *Delta: felt a*; eye-rhymes, like *enough: sough: Love*, unless Hardy is here suggesting a west-country pronunciation [sʌf], which should more properly be [zʌf] in that case. But this is unlikely in the context of the poem 'I Need Not Go'. There are triple rhymes sustained through an entire poem, as in 'To Sincerity'; there is an unusual reversed rhyme scheme in 'A Leaving' in which the rhyme words of the first six lines recur in reverse order in the six lines of the second stanza, the first and last lines of the poem being identical. There are internal rhymes in such poems as 'The Dawn after the Dance' and 'To a Lady Playing and Singing in the Morning'. There is a succession of macaronic rhymes, displaying some linguistic ingenuity, in 'After Reading Psalms XXXIX, XL, etc.', for example stanza three:

> At my start by Helicon
>    Love-lore little wist I,
> Worldly less; but footed on;
>    Why? *Me suscepisti*!

And there are comic rhymes, as in that tripping poem 'A Refusal' which begins:

> Said the grave Dean of Westminster:
> Mine is the best minster
> Seen in Great Britain,
> As many have written . . .

and, after making it clear that Byron was *persona non grata* in Poets' Corner, ends thus:

> 'Twill next be expected
> That I get erected
> To Shelley a tablet
> In some niche or gablet.
> Then – what makes my skin burn,
> Yea, forehead to chin burn –
> That I ensconce Swinburne!

A particular, even peculiar, linguistic flair is necessary to produce rhymes ranging from Byronic doggerel (like 'optim. : cupp'd him : stopp'd 'em'; and so on through *Don Juan*) as in Hardy's 'Liddell and Scott' ('Donnegan : con again'; 'ẃwðɳṣ: bodies') to the haunting quatrains of 'The Voice', with that inspired shift of stress from 'víew you, then' to 'knew you thén' in the second stanza to which Leavis drew attention. The doggerel emphasizes that Hardy was certainly not without a sense of humour, despite all the gloom and melancholy which readers encounter in his work.

In his prose fiction Hardy's humour expresses itself not only in comic or absurd situations or in some entertaining quirks of character, but in a good deal of verbal humour involving incongruities of diction, caricatures of speech, amusing imagery, and an occasional playing with words, as in Winterborne's *shrouding* or in some of the names given to his characters, like Whittle or Creedle or Mercy Onmey. There are moments when his lexical idiosyncrasies overreach themselves and produce involuntarily comic results, as in 'The Obliterate Tomb', a poem with a story 'scarcely worth the telling', as Pinion drily remarks, and with such phrasings as 'To get their dingy greatness deeplier dingied' or ' "Ha", they hollowly hackered'.

From such lapses it is a joy to turn to moments of genuine, and intended, verbal humour, especially in Hardy's prose. To Christian Cantle's reporting himself addressed as 'you slack-twisted, slim-looking maphrotight fool' in *The Return of the Native*, I, Ch. 3, or Festus Derriman addressing John Loveday as 'you dirty miller's son, you flour-worm, you smut in the corn!' in *The Trumpet-Major*, Ch. 28. Or to superlative exclamations like Somerset's 'What a heavenly client!' in *A Laodicean*, I, Ch. 9, or Margery's 'How divine – what joy to be here!' in 'The Romantic Adventures of a Milkmaid', V (*A Changed Man*), both of which convey that tinge of irony which one comes to associate with Hardy's use of words with religious connotations. There is a good deal of more direct verbal humour in some of Hardy's allusions to the Christian church and religion. Stephen Smith's architectural success in India, which includes a commission by 'the ruling powers, Christian and Pagan alike', to design 'a large palace, and cathedral' and such other useful buildings as 'fortifications', is appropriately celebrated by a Mayorial address to the St. Launce's 'Every-Man-his-own-Maker Club' (*A Pair of Blue Eyes*, Ch. 36). Cathedrals suggest not only comparisons with railway stations but the image of an 'incongruous sound, as if one should hear of croquet-playing in a cathedral aisle' (*Far from the Madding Crowd*, Ch. 52). The same novel evokes the forbidding atmosphere 'of a Puritan Sunday lasting all the week' (Ch. 14), the opposite of which stern observance is Nat Chapman's 'One hour a week wi' God A'mighty and the rest with the devil' (*Two on a Tower*, Ch. 13). That observance need not be sabbatical is plain from the description of the romantic Margery's future husband, Jim Hayward, as 'a respectable, market-keeping Christen', and that parsons are liable to offend against another of the commandments is gently hinted at in 'Ethelberta breathed a sort of exclamation, not right out, but stealthily, like a parson's damn' (*The Hand of Ethelberta*, Ch. 26). Some of Hardy's pa'sons of course swear rather more lustily, as one of the crusted characters reminds us in *Life's Little Ironies*.

Hardy's biblical and liturgical allusions creep humorously as well as seriously into narrative and dialogue. The prelude to Angel Clare's chivalrous carriage of the church-bent maidens across the flooded lane in *Tess of the d'Urbervilles*, Ch. 23, is spiced with pointed verbal humour, not the least of which is the satanic *thistle-spud* carried by the 'angelic' Clare:

> 'And I do colour up so hot, walking into church late, and all the people staring round', said Marian, 'that I hardly cool down again till we get into the That-it-may-please-Thees'.
>
> While they stood clinging to the bank they heard a splashing round the bend of the road, and presently appeared Angel Clare, advancing along the lane towards them through the water.
>
> Four hearts gave a big throb simultaneously.
>
> His aspect was probably as un-Sabbatarian a one as a dogmatic parson's son often presented; his attire being his dairy clothes, long wading boots, a cabbage-leaf inside his hat to keep his head cool, with a thistle-spud to finish him off.
>
> 'He's not going to church', said Marian.
>
> 'No – I wish he was!' murmured Tess.
>
> Angel, in fact, rightly or wrongly (to adopt the safe phrase of evasive controversialists), preferred sermons in stones to sermons in churches and chapels on fine summer days.

Marian's *That-it-may-please-Thees* have the same concrete presence in time that the weather-caster's *Revelations* have in space: ' 'Twill be more like living in Revelations this autumn than in England' (*The Mayor of Casterbridge*, Ch. 26). For their speakers such usages are not funny; they are simply Litany or Scripture absorbed into the daily vocabulary. The humour rests in the reader's awareness of an element of linguistic incongruity, comparable to some such figurative antithesis as in a priest's locking up his confessional after a five minutes' session 'with another loud click, like a tradesman full of business' (*A Laodicean*, VI, Ch. 2). Elsewhere, too, Hardy sees the business of saving souls as a trade: the painter of texts in *Tess of the d'Urbervilles*, Ch. 12, talks to the troubled girl 'in a trade voice'.

Comic imagery demonstrates Hardy's ability not merely to notice oddities in human behaviour but to convey them as such with the aid of a telling word or phrase or an unexpected comparison. Sometimes the reader may be reminded of Samuel Johnson's description of a metaphysical conceit: 'a combination of dissimilar images, or discovery of occult resemblances in things apparently unlike', yet even if Hardy's ideas are at time heterogeneous, they are not generally yoked 'by violence' together. The comic effect is not so much in the unforeseen as in the often seen but not connected: messengers darting about 'like house-flies dancing their quadrilles' (*The Dynasts*, III. vii. 2); or people crowding in a doorway 'partly covering each other like a hand of cards, yet each showing a large enough piece of himself for identification' (*The Trumpet-Major*, Ch. 14); or an attractive woman appearing in a change of dress 'like a new edition of a delightful volume' (*A Pair of Blue Eyes*, Ch. 7). Not only sight of course is thus conveyed, but sound: rustic throats being cleared making a noise 'as of atmospheric hoes and scrapers' (*Two on a Tower*, Ch. 2); or a man sighing 'like a poet over a ledger' (*The Hand of Ethelberta*, Ch. 39); and touch:

> And Knight laughed, and drew her close and kissed her the second time, which operations he performed with the carefulness of a fruiterer touching a bunch of grapes so as not to disturb their bloom.
> (*A Pair of Blue Eyes*, Ch. 28)

The humorous word or phrase may be a colloquialism: 'Soldiers bain't particular, and she's *a tidy piece o' furniture* still' (*A Changed Man*: 'Enter A Dragoon', I); or it may be dialectal:

> 'Benjy Pennyways were not a true man or an honest baily – as big a betrayer as Joey Iscariot himself. But to think she can carr' on alone! . . . Never *in all my creeping up* – never!'
> (*Far from the Madding Crowd*, Ch. 15)

'There is sommit wrong in my make, your worshipful!' said Abel, 'especially in the inside, whereas my poor dumb brain gets as dead as a clot afore I've said my few *scrags of prayers*.'
   (*The Mayor of Casterbridge*, Ch. 15)

Henery Fray's *creeping up* with its echoes of *mumbudgeting*, unless invented by Hardy for the speaker, appears to be a local Dorset word for 'growing up', for the *English Dialect Dictionary* records no other instance. Abel Whittle's *scrags* of prayers are comically apt for the lean young man who had no chin and regularly overslept and whose hair grew thin for fear of his master. Because 'his gait was shambling', there may also have been in Hardy's mind the Dorset sense of *scrag* as 'a crooked branch of a tree', just as he may have known that in the south-east *joey* was a word for 'a toad' when he put the familiar substitution for 'Judas' in Henery Fray's mouth. There is a touch of comic pomposity in 'Sir' John Durbeyfield's 'it has been just found out by me this present afternoon, p.m.', in the opening chapter of *Tess of the d'Urbervilles*: his new-found dignity demands appropriately stately language.

   Language as a class indicator is but one of the linguistic registers of which Hardy made use. He uses it delightfully in his poem 'The Ruined Maid', whose third stanza is worth repeating here:

– 'At home in the barton you said "thee" and "thou", and "thik oon", and "theäs oon", and "t'other"; but now Your talking quite fits 'ee for high compa-ny!' – 'Some polish is gained with one's ruin', said she.

Such polish is the attribute, or achievement, of those who 'can spaik real language', as Billy Smallbury describes it in *Far from the Madding Crowd*, Ch. 15. It means knowing the right words as well as the right people, as Hardy himself was to discover, in his society crushes, knowledge which he anticipated in his first novel:

'You will come back some day a wondrous man of the world talking of vast Schemes, radical Errors, and saying such words as the "Backbone of Society", the "Tendency of Modern Thought", and other things like that. When papa says to you, "My Lord the Chancellor", you will answer him with "A tall man, with a deep-toned voice – I know him well". When he says, "Such and such were Lord Hatton's words, I think", you will answer, "No, they were Lord Tyrrell's; I was present on the occasion"; and so on in that way. You must get to talk authoritatively about vintages and their dates, and to know all about epicureanism, idleness, and fashion . . .'

   (*An Indiscretion in the Life of an Heiress*, I, Ch. 8)

The comic corollary to knowing the right words and the right people is given to Lady Petherwin to enunciate, in Hardy's 'society novel' *The Hand of Ethelberta*. Lady Petherwin has discovered Ethelberta's authorship of a recently published volume of poems:

> 'But surely you have not written every one of those ribald verses?'
> Ethelberta looked inclined to exclaim most vehemently against this; but what she actually did say was, ' "Ribald" – what do you mean by that? I don't think that you are aware what "ribald" means.'
> 'I am not sure that I am. As regards some words as well as some persons, the less you are acquainted with them the more it is to your credit.'
> (*The Hand of Ethelberta*, Ch. 10)

If Hardy himself entertained any such social leanings in matters of vocabulary, they were fortunately outweighed by his tendency to dip deeply into the vast repository of traditional and regional English. 'Town words', like 'a regular *bore*' in the same novel, had limited scope in Wessex where, as he wrote in *The Woodlanders*, 'the local and better word' regularly came into its own. The contrast is nicely pointed when Grace Melbury speaks to Fitzpiers of Giles as 'my betrothed lover still', to which Fitzpiers responds:

> 'You say your betrothed lover still', he rejoined. 'When, then, were you betrothed to him, or engaged, as we common people say?'
> (*The Woodlanders*, Ch. 46)

*Betrothed* is the older of the two words by far, firmly rooted in medieval English, whereas *engaged* in this sense is no older than the eighteenth century. For Grace, as for Hardy, the local word is the older, long traditional, hence the better word. As Pinion has written in the Introduction to the New Wessex *Two on a Tower*: 'His rustics often utter perennial sense in incomparable language which raises a smile and goes straight to its mark'.

The flight to the mark is sometimes helped along, not only in rustic speech, by those explanatory asides, like Fitzpiers's above, or Mr Day's in 'Netty Sargent's Copyhold' (*Life's Little Ironies*) who, having said *inkhorn* in his 'oldfashioned way', then corrects it to *inkstand*; or Hardy's own authorial annotations, which are not restricted to elucidating dialectal usages. In 'The Melancholy Hussar of the German Legion' (*Wessex Tales*), for example, Hardy sees fit to explain a *buck* by the parenthetical 'as fast and unmarried men were then called', a return to eighteenth-century usage, as in Fielding. On the whole, however, Hardy expected his readers to be conversant with older usages more readily than with some recent accretions to the language, as in this instance from *The Woodlanders* (Ch. 22): 'Fitzpiers when he was present exercised a certain fascination over her – or even more, an almost psychic influence, *as it is called*', a notion still sufficiently novel in the second half of the nineteenth century to qualify for such annotation. Another word singled out for special treatment is *bureaucratic*, also a nineteenth-century coinage, which Oswald and Agatha are unsure about in 'Destiny and a Blue Cloak' (*Old Mrs Chundle and Other Stories*). Both, however, agree that 'it is a very bad thing'! A more knowing explanation, in this case of a jargon word, is offered by John Loveday as he expatiates on his rank to Anne Garland: 'And by the orders of the War Office, I am to exert over them (*that's the government word*) – exert over them full authority' (*The Trumpet-Major*, Ch. 11).

Many recent words are not of course singled out for such commentary from whatever source. In 'An Imaginative Woman', written, or at least 'touched up', in 1893 and at first included in *Wessex Tales* before its transposition to *Life's Little Ironies*, Hardy speaks of *jerry-built* houses without feeling the need to explain a word then still quite young in English. On the other hand, he is aware of semantic changes which may affect a particular usage of a word and comments accordingly:

> He was a youth who might properly have been characterised by a word the judicious chronicler would not readily use in such a connexion, preferring to reserve it for raising images of the opposite sex. Whether because no deep felicity is likely to arise from the condition, or from any other reason, to say in these days that a youth is beautiful is not to award him that amount of credit which the expression would have carried with it if he had lived in the times of the Classical Dictionary.
>
> (*Two on a Tower*, Ch. 1)

The turgid style of this passage might have profited by some editorial advice, but the semantic point it makes is one of which late-twentieth-century speakers of English are constantly reminded when confronted with words like *gay*.

The problem posed by the loss of the word *beautiful* from the catalogue of male attributes is small compared with that faced by Hardy in describing the feelings and experiences of women 'in men's words'. Both in *Desperate Remedies*, where this phrase occurs, and in *Far from the Madding Crowd*, Hardy adverts to it. In the former novel, Cytherea's heart, after her momentary meeting with Edward Springrove on the day of her marriage to Manston,

> was near to breaking with the intensity of the misery which gnawed there. At these times a woman does not faint, or weep, or scream, as she will in the moment of sudden shocks. When lanced by a mental agony of such refined and special torture that it is *indescribable by men's words*, she moves among her acquaintances much as before, and contrives so to cast her actions in the old moulds that she is only considered to be rather duller than usual.
>
> (*Desperate Remedies*, Ch. 13)

In the other novel the same thought is expressed by Bathsheba as she tries to answer Boldwood's probings into her present feelings for him:

> 'I don't know – at least, I cannot tell you. It is difficult for a woman to define her feelings in *language which is chiefly made by men* to express theirs.'
>
> (*Far from the Madding Crowd*, Ch. 51)

Much of Hardy's creative endeavour went into wrestling with this problem, and there are occasions when his reliance upon archaic or local language seems like a deliberate attempt to free contemporary English of its more inhibiting, 'male' associations. In a recent essay Adrian Poole writes: 'Hardy's women are not without a language of their own; they can take over words when they need them'.* The classic example cited is Tess's 'taking over' Angel's word *tremulous*, 'pausing over the new word as if it impressed her'; but Tess is in this respect of all Hardy's women the most impressionable. Twice within the five chapters that frame this passage Hardy emphasizes the fact that Tess had been led by her admiration of Angel 'to pick up his vocabulary', 'had caught his manner and habits, his speech and phrases', as if he were a Hotspur, 'mark and glass, copy and book, / That fashion'd others'. It was the inevitable consequence of her first impression of Angel at the club-walking as of a young man who had spoken 'so nicely'.

It cannot truthfully be averred that Hardy's women have in any important sense a language of their own. Nor, strictly speaking, have his men. The traits that distinguish Hardy's characters cut across

* ' "Men's Words" and Hardy's Women', *Essays in Criticism* 31 (1981), 343.

sexual division; nor is language used by Hardy consistently to create idiolects. There are certain linguistic characteristics, apart from dialect, that mark a few of Hardy's people as in some measure distinctive: De Stancy, as Paula correctly gauges, is 'too full of exclamations and transports'; he and Dare, writes Barbara Hardy, in the New Wessex *A Laodicean*, 'lack inner life. Their language is violent or clamorous, never passionate'. Arabella has a coarse turn of phrase using words with a strongly pictorial, concrete import, like 'cracks your noddle with a poker' or 'the harm you did yourself by dirting your own nest', which deliberately contrasts with the abstract, Shelleyan diction of Sue Bridehead:

> 'Everybody is getting to feel as we do. We are a little beforehand, that's all. In fifty, a hundred, years the descendants of these two will act and feel worse than we. They will see weltering humanity still more vividly than we do now, as
> > Shapes like our own selves hideously multiplied, and
> will be afraid to reproduce them.'
> (*Jude the Obscure*, V, Ch. 4)

Clym Yeobright, plain, high-thinking Clym, favours short simple sentences, and so do those other worthy men, Gabriel Oak and Giles Winterborne. They are, in Geoffrey Thurley's typifying terminology, Hardy's 'statuesque' characters, in contrast to the opposite extreme of the 'nervous' ones – Wildeve, Fanny Robin, Grace Melbury. But, at least in terms of language, and probably from other points of view as well, such typology should not be carried too far. Tess's language, for one, changes from her early 'bilingualism' of home and school to speaking more and more like Angel Clare. Elizabeth-Jane perforce sheds her dialectal proclivities under Henchard's stern tutelage. By contrast, the educated Phillotson slips back into dialect when under stress of emotion, when, as he puts it, he is 'all abroad'. Nor is Grace Melbury's expensive education a safe insurance against similar linguistic retrogression. Contemplating the possibility of her marrying Winterborne, her father says 'Fancy her white hands getting redder every day, and her tongue losing its pretty up-country curl in talking' (*The Woodlanders*, Ch. 11). As it happens, the up-country curl is not lost and to the end of the novel Hardy maintains the contrast between it and Marty South's unaffected dialectal cadences.

There are of course numerous incidents in Hardy's fiction in which his characters briefly reveal some trait of character or social attitude by some chance remark of linguistic import, or have it revealed for them by authorial comment. Fancy Day's sense of 'propriety' causes her to charge her father and the tranter to avoid dialect usages which might offend 'persons of newer taste'. In *A Pair of Blue Eyes*, Mrs Smith's newly acquired awareness of linguistic niceties makes her chide her husband for failing to achieve the same 'politeness' in his speech when he refers to the landlady of the Falcon Hotel rather crudely as 'the public-house woman'. The same point about 'polite' language is made in the story of the Honourable Laura in *A Group of Noble Dames*, where a young waiter is sweeping away the snow 'and talking the local dialect in all its purity, quite oblivious of *the new polite accent* he had learned in the hot weather from the well-behaved visitors'. Henchard, facing the newly genteel Lucetta in her room, on the other hand, is 'conscious that in this room his accents and manner wore a roughness not observable in the street' and that his speech lacks 'the polish of what you've lately learnt to expect for the first time in your life'. As for Lucetta herself, she settles in Casterbridge not merely as a genteel stranger, but determined to conceal her past and preserve her incognito, and 'not the least amusing of her safeguards was *her resolute avoidance of a French word* if one by accident came to her tongue more readily than its English equivalent. She shirked it with the suddenness of the weak Apostle at the accusation, "Thy speech bewrayeth thee!" '. Others are similarly bewrayed. Henry Knight's jottings include the note: 'Generally begins career by actions which are popularly termed showing-off', where *popularly* is a significant pointer to Knight's fastidious discrimination between colloquial speech and its social origins and his own almost pathological respectability. Ethelberta, dropping her customary mask, eschews circumlocution when pressed by her sister into confessing that the visitor she is expecting 'is not a lady . . . He is – I suppose – my lover, *in plain English*', a phrase which appears as Oak's '*in plain British*', somewhat surprisingly, as Hardy did not much care for the word. Mrs Garland regrets her daughter's proneness to pick up dialect words or accents from the neighbours because it lessens her own respectability. In *Two on a Tower* Viviette points to a failing in Swithin when she reproves him for speaking 'so *affectedly*', after Hardy himself had been guilty of the same fault in the opening chapter by explaining the local name Haymoss as 'the encrusted form of the word Amos, *to adopt the phrase of philologists*'. The grimy, satanic 'creature from Tophet' serving the machine at Flintcomb-Ash

is made the more outlandish by speaking in *a strange northern accent*.
Avice the Second has for Pierston a particularly attractive mode of
speaking, upon which Hardy expatiates with a musician's skill:

> She attracted him by the cadences of her voice; she would suddenly drop it
> to a rich whisper of roguishness, when the slight rural monotony of its
> narrative speech disappeared, and soul and heart – or what seemed soul
> and heart – resounded. The charm lay in the intervals, using that word in
> its musical sense. She would say a few syllables in one note, and end her
> sentence in a soft modulation upwards, then downwards, then into her
> own note again. The curve of sound was as artistic as any line of beauty
> ever struck by his pencil – as satisfying as the curves of her who was the
> World's Desire.
> (*The Well-Beloved*, II, Ch. 7)

There is another passage, remarkably beautiful, in which Hardy tries
to analyse a particular mode of speech, but here instead of musical
language there is an imperceptible gliding from what looks at first like
articulatory physiology into sheer poetry:

> Some of the dairy-people, who were also out of doors on the first Sunday
> evening after their engagement, heard her impulsive speeches, ecstasized
> to fragments, though they were too far off to hear the words discoursed;
> noted the spasmodic catch in her remarks, broken into syllables by the
> leapings of her heart, as she walked leaning on his arm; her contented
> pauses, the occasional little laugh upon which her soul seemed to ride – the
> laugh of a woman in company with the man she loves and has won from all
> other women – unlike anything else in nature. They marked the buoyancy
> of her tread, like the skim of a bird which has not quite alighted.
> (*Tess of the d'Urbervilles*, Ch. 31)

Both these passages reveal Hardy's fine auditory perception
and his ability to transpose details of utterance, quality of voice,
and modulations of speech into facets of personality and facts of
experience. Not all his observations on language of course are
intended to be taken at face value or too seriously. In the fourth tale
of *A Group of Noble Dames*, Lady Mottisfont is impressed by the
Anglo-Italian Countess's ability to spice her discourse with Italian
and French words, 'which was considered *a great improvement to
speech* in those days, and, indeed, is by many considered as such in
these'. That things said or thought in private are not always suitable
for public consumption is the point of the nice distinction Hardy
draws between what is permissible in private and what he calls

*company speech*, at the trapped Mr. Miller's outburst in 'Enter a Dragoon' in *A Changed Man*. That a *question of grammar* should become a catalyst in a mother's relationship with her son, as happens in 'The Son's Veto' in *Life's Little Ironies*, is not so much a linguistic observation as a starkly ironic comment on what constitutes true nobility in a man – in this case, doubly ironically, a clergyman.

Hardy's characters include not a few who are by no means averse to the pleasures of strong drink, of which there are particularly notable examples in *Far from the Madding Crowd* and *The Mayor of Casterbridge*, as well as such devotees as that 'three-bottle man', Squire Dornell, in the opening story of *A Group of Noble Dames*. A note of regret creeps into Hardy's 1895 Preface to *Far from the Madding Crowd*, as he records the passing not only of venerable village customs like the shearing-supper and the harvest-home, but of 'much of that love of fuddling to which the village at one time was notoriously prone'. Clearly, there were at one time many folk in Weatherbury and elsewhere in Wessex who would have heartily seconded Pierston's response to the question 'What'll you drink?' : 'Oh! it doesn't matter what, so that it is alcohol in some shape or form.'

Occasionally, Hardy allows himself a hint or two of the effects of such indulgence on speech, as in that of the heroine of the poem 'My Cicely', now the mistress of the Three Lions inn on the western highway, with

> Her liquor-fired face, her thick accents,

– accents spelt out more audibly in the inebriated 'Whash her name?' of a gallant warrior in *The Trumpet-Major*, Ch. 9; or by Arabella hiccuping her way home, after conducting Jude 'through the varieties of spirituous delectation' whose landmarks she knew so well:

> 'I feel I belong to you in Heaven's eye, and to nobody else, till death us do part! It is – hic – never too late – hic – to mend!'
> (*Jude the Obscure*, VI, Ch. 6)

Or by Joseph Poorgrass who suffers not merely from a multiplying eye at the Old Buck's Head, but from a multiplying stammer as well:

> 'I feel too good for England: I ought to have lived in Genesis by rights, like the other men of sacrifice, and then I shouldn't have b-b-been called a d-d-drunkard in such a way!'
> (*Far from the Madding Crowd*, Ch. 42)

Such linguistic slapstick is not the rule, however: Henchard's speech is not audibly – or visibly – affected by liquor, neither in the opening scene in the tent at Weydon Priors nor after he 'have busted out drinking after taking nothing for twenty-one years' at the Three Mariners inn. In these and similar episodes Hardy allows the action to speak for itself and the characters to speak for themselves in whatever 'normal' language he deems appropriate.

There is a small group of words and some phrases which Hardy uses more than once. Some of the latter are interesting because they occur in similar episodes, as W.M. Parker has noted.* In *Under the Greenwood Tree*, II, Ch. 7, Dick and Fancy wash their hands in the same basin, the only basin she possesses:

> Thereupon he plunged in his hands, and they paddled together. It being the first time in his life that he had *touched female fingers under water*, Dick duly registered the sensation as rather a nice one.
>  'Really, I hardly know *which are my own hands and which are yours, they have got so mixed up together*', she said . . .

After almost twenty years, Hardy describes a similar incident, as Tess and Angel arrive at Wellbridge manor-house:

> The place having been rather hastily prepared for them they washed their hands in one basin. Clare *touched hers under the water.*
>  '*Which are my fingers and which are yours?*' he said, looking up. '*They are very much mixed.*'
>  (*Tess of the d'Urbervilles*, Ch. 34)

Another example given by Parker links two similar descriptions:

> 'True', said a smoking gentleman, whose coat had *the fine polish about the collar, elbows, seams, and shoulder-blades that long-continued friction* with grimy surfaces will produce.
>  (*The Mayor of Casterbridge*, Ch. 1)

Several novels later much the same phrasing is used to describe Phillotson when Sue and Jude visit him at Lumsdon:

> . . . a spare and thoughtful personage of five-and-forty, with a thin-lipped, somewhat refined mouth, a slightly stooping habit, and a black

---

* 'Notes on Thomas Hardy', *The Thomas Hardy Year Book* (1971), pp. 88–9.

frock coat, *which from continued frictions shone a little at the shoulder-blades, the middle of the back, and the elbows.*
 (*Jude the Obscure*, II, Ch. 4)

Such repetitions, as well as recurrent images, occur in Hardy's verse also, sometimes linking it with his prose. The poem 'I Look into My Glass' in *Wessex Poems* is epitomized in one sentence in *The Well-Beloved*, II, Ch. 12: 'When was it to end – this curse of his heart not ageing while his frame moved naturally onward?' This is the poem:

> I look into my glass,
> And view my wasting skin,
> And say, 'Would God it came to pass
> My heart had shrunk as thin!'
>
> For then, I, undistrest
> By hearts grown cold to me,
> Could lonely wait my endless rest
> With equanimity.
>
> But Time, to make me grieve,
> Part steals, lets part abide;
> And shakes this fragile frame at eve
> With throbbings of noontide.

Later in the novel the same thought recurs as Pierston by chance looks into a mirror:

What he saw was his own shape. The recognition startled him. The person he appeared was too grievously far, chronologically, in advance of the person he felt himself to be . . . While his soul was what it was, why should he have been encumbered with that withering carcase . . .?
 (*The Well-Beloved*, III, Ch. 4)

There is of course nothing unusual in a person's associating similar experiences with similar turns of phrase when they are put into words. Many a country frock coat in Dorchester must have had a *shining* surface or *polish* derived from continued friction; hands do tend to touch and get *mixed up* together if washed in the one basin; mirrors inexorably reveal signs of senescence, although not everyone by any means can describe so memorably the tension between a young heart and an aging frame as Hardy does in that moving poem.
 The phrase '*throbbings* of noontide' draws attention to one of

Hardy's favourite words. The semantic range of the verb *throb*, embracing both the motion of the heart and the heart as the seat of emotion, symbolizing life as in 'To Shakespeare' and passion as in the poem above, suited Hardy's vision of the passage and ravage of time and the human condition in an uncaring universe. The word tends to be used by Hardy in its full connotative force: 'Ethelberta, though of all women most miserable, was brimming with compassion for *the throbbing girl* so nearly related to her' (*The Hand of Ethelberta*, Ch. 23). The reference is to Picotee whose secret love for Christopher Julian the elder sister had only just discovered. Both the strength and the hopelessness of her passion are powerfully conveyed by *throbbing*.

Other favourite verbs soon become familiar to the reader: *largen*, for example, one of those Victorian poeticisms which Hardy adopted with enthusiasm:

> The yellowing years will not abate
> My *largened* love and truth to you.
> ('A Maiden's Pledge')

And its opposite, as in this stage direction in *The Dynasts*, I. i. 6:

The scene changes. The exterior of the Cathedral takes the place of the interior, and the point of view recedes, the whole fabric *smalling* into distance . . .

There are favourite adverbs like *stilly* and *whitely*, the latter capable of producing such striking effects as this linking of ghostliness and ghastliness:

> And I saw but a thing of flesh and bone
> Speeding on to its cleft in the clay;
> And my dream was scared, and expired on a moan,
> And I *whitely* hastened away.
> ('The Dream-Follower')

Hardy's dialect words include several to which, like *home-along*, he had frequent recourse, but probably the most characteristic of all his favourite words is the adjective *flexuōus*. A Renaissance word derived from Latin *flexuosus*, it was defined by Dr Johnson as 'Winding; full of turns and meanders; tortuous . . . Bending; not

strait, variable; not steady'. Bacon is quoted by Johnson as apply-
ing the word to 'the flexuous burning of flames'. Among Hardy's
contemporaries Oliver Wendell Holmes applied it to the female form
'undulating with flexuous grace'. It would be tempting to seek here
the source of Hardy's inspiration, but when Hardy met Holmes in
1886, he noted (*Life*, p. 180) that he had never read his essays, and by
this time the word was well established in his vocabulary.

Hardy uses *flexuous* to connote sensuousness as well as sinuous-
ness, and there is often a strong element of sensual as well as aesthetic
pleasure in its application. Although by no means restricted to female
forms, it is a word to which Hardy instictively turns when describing
women, particularly women's faces and figures. Describing the
haymakers at work in Bathsheba's fields, he writes: 'They consisted
in about equal proportions of gnarled and *flexuous* forms, the former
being the men, the latter the women' (*Far from the Madding Crowd*,
Ch. 25). The contrast, the choice of words here, are indicative of
Hardy's way of looking at the sexes. Through the eyes of George
Somerset he sees that but for her unfortunate possession of the de
Stancy nose Charlotte's face might have been lent a certain kind of
beauty 'by the *flexuous* contours of the mobile parts' (*A Laodicean*, I,
Ch. 3), an echo of the glimpse of Fanny Robin's face briefly lit by a
passing carriage lamp: 'The face was young in the groundwork, old in
the finish; the general contours were *flexuous* and childlike, but the
finer lineaments had begun to be sharp and thin' (*Far from the
Madding Crowd*, Ch. 40). Hardy sometimes treats the word almost
as if it were a verb, to denote a winding, meandering motion, a sense
close to the Latin that is even more strongly conveyed when it is
describing something actually moving, like water or masses of people
or swirls of mist. In 'A Mere Interlude' (*A Changed Man*), Hardy
contrasts a patch of 'vermiculated and lumpy' looking water with its
*flexuous* appearance elsewhere; in the Dumb Show in *The Dynasts*,
III. iv. 1, slowly moving dark patches in the landscape turn out to be
armies on the move, '*flexuous* and riband-shaped', marching (a few
lines further on) 'in *flexuous* courses of varying direction'; in 'The
Sheep-Boy' an August fog rolls over Egdon Heath

> *Flexuous* and solid, clammy vapour-curls, –

a line that suggests both mass and movement, and represents a closer
approximation to Hardy's vision than the manuscript reading
*opaque*, later replaced by *flexuous*. There is no motion in opaque-

ness. Nor is there, strictly speaking, in the outlines of buildings, yet Hardy's meaning is plain when he talks of the 'weak, *flexuous*, constructional lines' of St Mark's in Venice (*Life*, p. 193); and much the same is true of the undulating shapes – much like those of the downs around Casterbridge – which '*flexuous* changes' produced among the assembled company at the great public dinner at the King's Arms in Chapter 6 of *The Mayor of Casterbridge*, as the diners, overcome by much food and liquor, droop and slump in their seats, leaving only Henchard 'stately and vertical'.

The word satisfied not a few of Hardy's imaginings, yet it is at its most apposite in his description of women. Lucetta Templeman's gait, we are told, 'had a *flexuousness* about it, which seemed to avoid angularity of movement less from choice than from predisposition', and two chapters later she is described as depositing herself on her sofa 'in her former *flexuous* position', one arm thrown above her brow, 'somewhat in the pose of a well-known conception of Titian's' (*The Mayor of Casterbridge*, Ch. 22). There is again movement in all this, her gait, her positioning, the 'throwing' of the arm, as well as sensuousness bordering on sensuality. The comparison with a kitten which the parlour-maid Sophy suggests to the vicar in the opening section of 'The Son's Veto' (*Life's Little Ironies*) further underlines these connotations: 'What a kitten-like, *flexuous*, tender creature she was!' The same image had been in Hardy's mind when he referred to Tess's '*flexuous* and stealthy figure' on her nocturnal walks after her return home from The Slopes, and it lingers into the next chapter (14) where Tess is again described as '*flexuous* and finely-drawn'.

The word takes on yet another layer of meaning when Hardy describes Angel Clare, after Tess's confession, as 'scourged out of all his former pulsating *flexuous* domesticity' (Ch. 36). P.N. Furbank's gloss 'full of natural grace' in the New Wessex edition of *Tess of the d'Urbervilles* does not fully convey the sensuous connotations which Hardy attaches to this word: Clare's domesticity at Talbothays was full of vibrating life as well as rich in its appeal to the senses. The eroticism Hardy sought to convey by *flexuous* is here made manifest by its juxtaposition with *pulsating*, a synonym for *throbbing*.

Hardy's 'cunningly odd and favoured word', as Adrian Poole terms *flexuous*, was never in frequent use in English, nor was it a poetic word. This suited him, in this case as in so many others, because it allowed him a certain amount of semantic leeway without obscuring the basic meaning which any reader could deduce from the word's semantic and morphemic closeness to *flexible* and *sinuous/sensuous*. There is in this approach to language, as Poole's phrase implies, deliberate craftsmanship, cunning in its old sense of 'knowing': it points to Hardy the technician.

But Hardy is also the artist, using his technical skills to express his imaginative vision, and to the combination of these two aspects of the creative personality he gave the name *technicist*. His first use of it, in *A Laodicean* III, Ch. 11, describes Somerset 'as chief technicist working out his designs on the spot', supervising the proposed alterations to Stancy Castle, and the *Oxford English Dictionary* appropriately glosses it as equivalent to *technician*, 'one who has technical knowledge'. But when Hardy used the word again, ten years later, in 'The Science of Fiction', it had clearly enlarged its meaning for him:

> The most devoted apostle of realism, the sheerest naturalist, cannot escape, any more than the withered old gossip over her fire, the exercise of Art in his labour or pleasure of telling a tale. Not until he becomes an automatic reproducer of all impressions whatsoever can he be called purely scientific, or even a manufacturer on scientific principles. If in the exercise of his reason he select or omit, with an eye to being more truthful than truth (the just aim of Art), he transforms himself into a technicist at a move.

The technicist is one who selects or omits *deliberately*, who adopts words and shapes sentences, as Hardy wrote to Gosse, 'advisedly'. Hardy's may often be native woodnotes, but they are not wild. S.F. Johnson in his essay 'Hardy and Burke's "Sublime" ' writes: 'However important *what* he said was to him, it is obvious that he laboured over *how* to say it'. Beyond the undeniable unevenness of his style wherein shortcomings and awkwardnesses impinge on passages of sublimity, there are constant reminders that Hardy not merely 'laboured' over his English, but that he laboured with a purpose.

I do not here mean the immediate, obvious purpose of telling his tale so that its import is clear and its mode pleasing, or of expressing in verse his 'impressions whatsoever' as truthfully as he could contrive; but his purpose so to shape his language that what he wrote was in keeping with his vision of an unbroken heredity of what might be termed linguistic genes. In 'The Pedigree', Hardy sees as in a mirror the long line of his begetters and realizes how firmly his language is rooted in theirs, 'generation and generation':

And then did I divine
That every heave and coil and move I made
Within my brain, and in my mood *and speech*,
   Was in the glass portrayed
As long forestalled by their so making it;
  The first of them, the primest fuglemen of my line,
Being fogged in far antiqueness past surmise and reason's reach.

Such an attitude is more than a response to contemporary philological issues, however hotly debated, as Dennis Taylor thought. It
may have been nurtured, and probably was nourished, by the impact
of nineteenth-century philology on Victorian writers, for this was
the age of discovery in language as much as in biology or geology, the
age of giants like W.W. Skeat and Henry Sweet, F.J. Furnivall and
Richard Trench, of the Philological Society, the English Dialect
Society, and the Early English Text Society, of the *English Dialect
Dictionary*, to which Hardy contributed, and the beginnings of the
*Oxford English Dictionary*.

Hardy no doubt received considerable stimulus from William
Barnes whose philological interests are reflected in his grammars and
in his essays, in the tendency to Saxonize his vocabulary, and in the
dialect, diction, and versification of his poems. But what Hardy
responded to most strongly with all his creative genius was the
recovery – painstaking and methodical on the part of the philologists,
piecemeal but imaginative on his part – of our linguistic past through
reconstruction of the grammar and vocabulary of earlier periods of
English. At its most obvious level, Hardy's response took the form
of imitation, of concocting pieces of narrative or dialogue supposedly
authentic of their period, similar to, but less consistent than, Scott's
use of 'period language'. In 'Master John Horseleigh, Knight' (*A
Changed Man*), for instance, there are such passages of mock-Tudor
English as these: 'Without the gatehouse, paled in, a large square
greene, in which standeth a faire chappell', or 'God wot! How be I
going to face her with the news, and how be I to hold it from her? To
bring this disgrace on my father's honoured name, a double-tongued
knave!'

In *The Famous Tragedy of the Queen of Cornwall*, Hardy peppers
the dialogue with archaic, or 'period', words like *certes* and *plaisance*,
or forms like *forth'd* and *glode*, and occasionally slips into a form of
mock-medieval English:

Dole him his alms in Christ's name, if ye must,
And irk me not while setting to bowse with these.

Although written long after the turn of the twentieth century, this
reads much like a typical Victorian imitation or re-telling of an older
romance or saga. This impression is further enhanced by judicious
use of alliteration, a prosodic device to which Hardy was strongly
attracted. There are lines and half-lines in his poems which satisfy all
the criteria of Sievers's system of scanning Old English verse:

*B*asked by the *b*ank, and *b*ent to the ripple-gleam,

or:

In *w*istful *w*anderings through old *w*astes of thought,
Where bristled *f*ennish *f*ungi, *f*ruiting nought,

or:

And the *f*orms so *f*oreign to *f*ield and tree.

Both the first and the last of these examples are the result of second
thought, deliberate revisions to enhance the alliteration, thus making
it conform more closely to traditional models.

Hardy's use of dialect is, together with his revivifying of obsolete
of archaic words, his principal means of linking the past of the
language with the present. How strongly he felt the past in all
its manifestations to be part of the here and now is evident from
several explicit statements, from the *ghostings* that crowd upon his
consciousness, from descriptions like Egdon Heath whose 'ancient
permanence' dates back to 'the beginning of vegetation' to that of the
old house in 'The Two Houses' holding 'The Presences from afore-
time'. For Hardy, the English language which expresses his art is like
these presences in the house:

'Where such inbe,
A dwelling's character
Takes theirs, and a vague semblancy
to them in all its limbs, and light, and atmosphere.'

Hardy's dialect, as has been said before, is no thorough-going,
complete, or methodical representation of Dorchester speech any
more than Barnes's poems reproduce that of Sturminster on anything

like 'scientific principles'. In both cases what is achieved is a kind of vague semblancy, but both writers are so deeply imbued with the spirit of 'the venerable local language' that they were prepared at times to offend polite sensibilities and even to momentarily court incomprehensibility for the sake of being more truthful than truth.

Hardy's willing recourse to the English of earlier writers – Chaucer, Shakespeare, the Bible, Milton – stems from the same consciousness of the relevance of the language of their day to that of his. How much he drew on others needs no further emphasis here; what is worth repeating is that they not only helped to shape Hardy's English but remained embedded in it as presences from afore-time by a deliberate exercise of his reason. Not only are there direct quotations, but mimetic phrases and images link Hardy's writings with those of predecessors as well as contemporaries in numerous subtle ways. The quartet of early sonnets, 'She, to Him', is unmistakably Shakespearean:

> When you shall see me in the toils of Time,
> My lauded beauties carried off from me,
> My eyes no longer stars as in their prime,
> My name forgot of Maiden Fair and Free . . .
> ('She, To Him, I')

A year later, in the poem entitled '1967', the metaphysical conceit of 'That thy worm should be my worm, Love!' is, as Hardy was well aware, pure Donne. The periphrastic 'hopping casement-comers' in 'The Farm-Woman's Winter' is a poeticism recalling Spenser's 'finny drove'. Milton's 'wakeful Bird / Sings darkling', reverberating through English poetry is heard in Keats's 'Ode to a Nightingale', in Keble and Arnold, and is heard again in Hardy's 'The Darkling Thrush'. And there are resonances of contemporary poets, like Browning or Swinburne, or of that kindred soul A.E. Housman, whose 'Is my team ploughing, / That I was used to drive . . .' was Hardy's favourite in *A Shropshire Lad* and was to inspire the light-hearted canine poem,

> 'Ah, are you digging on my grave,
> My loved one? – planting rue?'
> ('Ah, Are you Digging on my Grave?')

At the same time as their words and phrases became part of

Hardy's English, so did the more general features of their English impress themselves upon Hardy's own linguistic consciousness. Biblical cadences, Chaucerian *un*-words, the linguistic inventiveness of Renaissance writers which Moth in *Love's Labour's Lost* calls 'a great feast of languages', the rich classical vein of Milton, right down to the colloquial turns of Browning – all these not only inspired but justify what may be called Hardy's artistic fusion of the synchronic and the diachronic in his acceptance of the English language as all of a piece.

Virginia Woolf was, I believe, mistaken: it *is* possible to rationalize Hardy's style and the language that constitutes it, as it is possible to rationalize the charm of a muddy country road. The latter's fascination lies in one's recognition that the squelchy tracks underfoot are but the efforts of precursors plodding their weary way towards the same destination; in one's growing awareness of seasonal change from firm footing to precarious exploration; in learning to acknowledge that a hazardous road can call forth some of man's finest attributes – determination and ingenuity among them. Hardy's English, similarly determined and ingenious, makes sense if it is accepted as following in the tracks of his predecessors to the point of treading in their very footsteps; as a means of verbal exploration even at the risk of hostile criticism; above all, as moulded to suit that 'sense of timelessness' which possessed Hardy, as Robert Gittings reminds us in the second chapter of *Young Thomas Hardy*, from early childhood.

Like a muddy road such an approach to language has pitfalls. There are places where one becomes 'mire-bestrowed', like the cavalry on the road to Waterloo which

> With frothy horses floundering to their knees,
> Make wayfaring a moil of miseries!
> (*The Dynasts*, III. vi. 8)

It was inevitable that the salient features of Hardy's English – its eclectic vocabulary, its indebtedness to literary, technical, and regional registers, its readiness to revive, restore, and innovate, and its 'squarely shaped sentences' (to use a phrase of his own) vying with passages of ruptured syntax – should at times produce mismarriages, oddities of grammar, fluctuations in expression from the transparent to the opaque, from lucidity to obscurity. These are the extremes of T.S. Eliot's notorious dictum, but in between there is of course much more 'good' writing than Eliot allows. The faults to which Henry James and Andrew Lang and Vernon Lee and a long line of subsequent critics have drawn attention are not disputed. What may be disputed is their importance.

No doubt, Hardy's English is occasionally mismanaged. There are sentences which expand into shapeless conglomerates of phrases and clauses linked by idiosyncratic punctuation, although Hardy was mercifully free of the involutions of James's later style. Hardy's grammar sometimes offends against the canons of received standard English. His catalogues may suggest lapses of taste. His verses may at times sink to a depressingly pedestrian level because of clichés, tautologies, awkward juxtapositions of the sonorous and the trite, as in:

> While she lifted orbs aggrieved and round
> That scandal should so soon abound,
> (As she had raised them to nine or ten
> Of antecedent nice young men).
> ('The Sweet Hussy')

Humour, if that is what is intended, is no excuse for poor writing.

But the very same features of language that can go wrong can also go right. Hardy's diction is often a triumphant vindication of his eclectic methods; his punctuation – when authentic – is a subtle instrument of modulation; his sentences can snap as well as snarl; his grammar plays the gamut from the crude colloquial to the bookish refined, and when it is least 'correct' it may be a deliberate echo of 'those ungrammatical, unrhythmical and unpoetical songs' in which the Dorset 'fathers and forefathers delighted', in the words of a one-time Secretary of the Dorset Field Club. Even his name-dropping can be astonishingly suggestive. And his verses frequently assemble into memorable poems.

One of the principal impressions created by Thomas Hardy's English is the undeniable honesty of a writer seeking the apt word from no matter how far back in time or how remote in region. W.H. Auden was wrong when he branded Hardy's vocabulary as 'outlandish'; for it is the very opposite – 'inlandish', native to its very roots, both in Hardy's retrieving for contemporary sensibilities the rich heritage of English words, and in his imaginative use of the morphemic resources of the language as living means of further enrichment. On the other hand, Auden was wholly right in claiming

for Hardy that 'here was a "modern" rhetoric which was more fertile
and adaptable to different themes than any of Eliot's gas-works and
rats' feet which one could steal but never make one's own'. Hardy
was not only 'poetical father' to Auden, but Banquo to a line of
twentieth-century poets, begetting what Donald Davie in *Thomas
Hardy and British Poetry* calls 'the Hardyesque tone in so much
British writing'.

The question 'What in the world else could he have written?'
proves to be a rhetorical one. For Hardy there was no other way than
the way he chose to give 'shape and coherence to a series of seemings,
or personal impressions'. Personal impressions require personal
expressions. These take on numberless shapes, in his prose and in his
verse, like the appeal of moonlight to the senses of hearing and
tasting:

> . . . the frail light shed by a slim young moon
> > Fell like a friendly tune.
> > Fell like a liquid ditty.
> ('After a Romantic Day')

Or turning the need for a rhyme into verbalized history, as the inner
precinct of Hampton Court, in 'A Spellbound Palace', becomes
doubly a repository of the past by the choice of the phrase

> As 'twere History's own asile,

for *as 'twere* is as much as *asile* part of that English heritage of
which the palace is the physical embodiment. Or, to give one more
example, putting his personal seal upon a place which has private
connotations beyond the story in which it figures; whence the
description of Portland, Hardy's 'Isle of Slingers', as 'the rocky *coign*
of England' in the Preface to *The Well-Beloved*. The spelling is
archaic, the word obsolete except in its technical, architectural,
sense; it has become Hardy's word for a place in a novel that has
much of Hardy, man and artist, in it.

Another important feature of Hardy's English is the diversity of
tones which it is capable of achieving. This is not to restrict it solely to
its musical qualities, although these inhere in much of his verse
and not a little of his prose. Many of Hardy's poems have been set
to music, most memorably by Benjamin Britten in his song cycle
*Winter Words*, op. 52. Britten's selection of eight poems includes

at least two with distinctive programmatic qualities, namely 'The Choirmaster's Burial' and 'Proud Songsters'; on the other hand, despite their affinities with Heine and the musical associations thereby conjured up, poems like 'Wagtail and Baby' and 'The Little Old Table' do not immediately suggest song. Nor would that characteristically Hardyan travail 'Before Life and After'. Yet all these, as well as the remaining poems selected by Britten ('At Day-Close in November', 'Midnight on the Great Western', and 'At the Railway Station, Upway') are imbued by diction, phrasing, and metre with a distinctive musicality, which Britten was able to develop into powerful compositions.

Prose sentences flow differently; yet in his prose also Hardy's voice is mostly controlled by his ear, so that when we read it aloud we may often wish to ascribe to him the words he addressed to another:

> And in its cadence catch and catch again
> Your nature's essence . . .
> ('To an Actress')

The essence of Hardy's nature may be caught again and again in his descriptions of scenic impressions; while he captures the salient externals of the scene the music of humanity is often-times heard in subtle accompaniment. A phrase may suggest it:

> There was much to contemplate in that peaceful Sunday morning – the windless trees and fields, the shaking sunlight, *the pause in human stir*.
> (*A Changed Man*: 'The Romantic Adventures of a Milkmaid', IX)

or a single word:

> And thus waiting for night's nearer approach, he watched the placid scene, over which the pale luminosity of the west cast a *sorrowful* monochrome, that became slowly embrowned by the dusk.
> (*A Pair of Blue Eyes*, Ch. 25)

Such passages are characteristic of Hardy's modulations of language – the shaking sunlight, the embrowning dusk – and they bear out his own prescript that 'a writer who is not a mere imitator looks upon the world with his personal eyes, and in his peculiar moods'. Eyes and moods animate the voice, a voice different from any other Englishman's; a voice well endowed with varieties of timbre to express varieties of emotion and circumstance. Hardy's English can be rough and gnarled like old trees in *The Woodlanders*, and it can be smooth and polished like the staircase at Enkworth Court, 'so milk-white and delicately moulded'. His language is often business-like as in the titles of his novels, upon which he expended some labour. Yet here, too, there is in several of them a recurrent rhythm, there are layers of meanings in the quotations he used and touches of artifice as in the alliteration of *Two on a Tower*. His English combines the modernity of the twentieth century with the antiquity of the age of Chaucer, as the word *asile* illustrates with its roots in Wyclif's Bible and its branches stretching into the contemporary connotations of political *asylum*. On 20 February 1982 *The Times* provided graphic illustration of this peculiar synchronism by printing a picture of Woolbridge Manor, where Tess and Angel spent their ill-fated honeymoon, as it would appear overshadowed by the proposed Winfrith nuclear power station. Civilization is still the enemy of Egdon. But the intrusion of modern Harwell into ancient Dorset is emblematic of all Hardy's work and of the language which he made so uncompromisingly his own.

# Select
# Bibliography
🖾🖾🖾🖾🖾🖾

### 1. EDITIONS OF HARDY'S WORKS, NOTEBOOKS, AND LETTERS

*The Wessex Novels*, 16 vols., London, 1895–6.

*The Wessex Edition*, 24 vols., London, 1912–31.

*The New Wessex Edition*, ed. P.N. Furbank, 22 vols., London, 1974–7.

*The Woodlanders*, ed. Dale Kramer, Oxford, 1981.

*The Complete Poems*, ed. James Gibson, London, 1976.

*The Complete Poems. Variorum Edition*, ed. James Gibson, London, 1979.

*The Dynasts*, London, 1910.

*An Indiscretion in the Life of an Heiress*, ed. Terry Coleman, London, 1976.

*Our Exploits at West Poley*, with an introduction by R.L. Purdy, Oxford, 1978.

*The Famous Tragedy of the Queen of Cornwall*, London, 1923.

*The Literary Notes of Thomas Hardy*, ed. Lennart A. Björk, 2 vols., Göteborg, 1974.

*The Personal Notebooks of Thomas Hardy*, ed. Richard H. Taylor, New York and London, 1979.

*Thomas Hardy's Personal Writings*, ed. Harold Orel, Lawrence, Kansas, 1966, London, 1967.

*The Architectural Notebook of Thomas Hardy*, ed. C.J.P. Beatty, Dorchester, 1966.

*The Collected Letters of Thomas Hardy*, ed. R.L. Purdy and Michael Millgate, 3 vols. to date, Oxford, 1978–82.

Hardy, Evelyn, and F.B. Pinion, eds., *One Rare Fine Woman: Thomas Hardy's Letters to Florence Henniker, 1893–1922*, London, 1972.

2. OTHER PRIMARY SOURCES

Hardy, Florence Emily, *The Life of Thomas Hardy, 1840–1928*, London, 1962. (The 'Autobiography').
*The Poems of William Barnes*, ed. Bernard Jones, 2 vols., Carbondale, Ill., 1962.
*Select Poems of William Barnes*, chosen and ed. Thomas Hardy, London, 1908.

3. REFERENCE

*The Oxford English Dictionary*, ed. J.A.H. Murray, Henry Bradley, W.A. Craigie, and C.T. Onions. Corrected re-issue, 13 vols., Oxford, 1933, and Supplements, ed. R.W. Burchfield, Oxford, 1972, *et seq.* (*OED*).
*The English Dialect Dictionary*, ed. Joseph Wright, 6 vols., Oxford, 1898–1905. (*EDD*).
Brewer, E.C., *The Dictionary of Phrase and Fable*, London, 1870 *et seq.*
*Collins Dictionary of the English Language*, ed. Patrick Hanks *et al.*, London and Glasgow, 1979.
Ekwall, Eilert, *The Concise Oxford Dictionary of English Place-Names*, 4th ed., Oxford, 1960.
Lewis, C.T., and Charles Short, *A Latin Dictionary*, Oxford, 1870 *et seq.*
Barnes, William, *A Glossary of the Dorset Dialect with a Grammar*, Dorchester and London, 1886; repr. St. Peter Port, Guernsey, 1970.
Crystal, David, *A First Dictionary of Linguistics and Phonetics*, (The Language Library), London, 1980.
Haynes, John, 'A Dorsetshire Vocabulary', ed. John E.T. Loveday, *Notes and Queries* 6th Series VII, 1883, 366, and VIII, 1883, 45.
Hurst, Alan, *Hardy: An Illustrated Dictionary*, London and New York, 1980.
Leeming, Glenda, *Who's Who in Thomas Hardy*, London, 1975.
Maskell, J. 'A Dorsetshire Vocabulary', *Notes and Queries* 6th Series VIII, 1883, 157.
Partridge, Eric, *A Dictionary of Catch Phrases*, London, 1977.
Pinion, F.B., *A Hardy Companion*, London, 1968, rev. 1974.
Purdy, R.L., *Thomas Hardy. A Bibliographical Study*, Oxford, 1954, repr. 1968.
Saxelby, F.O., *A Thomas Hardy Dictionary*, London, 1911.

#### 4. CRITICAL STUDIES

*This section includes works cited in the text and others which proved to be especially helpful.*

*(a) Books and Collections of Essays*
Aliesch, Peter, *Studien zu Thomas Hardys Prosastil*, Bern, 1941.
Archer, William, *Real Conversations*, New York, 1904.
Bailey, J.O., *The Poetry of Thomas Hardy. A Handbook and Commentary*, Chapel Hill, 1970.
——, *Thomas Hardy and the Cosmic Mind: A New Reading of "The Dynasts"*, Chapel Hill, 1956.
Barber, D.F., ed., *Concerning Thomas Hardy: A Composite Portrait from Memory*, London, 1968.
Bayley, John, *An Essay on Hardy*, Cambridge, 1978.
Baugner, Ulla, *A Study on the Use of Dialect in Thomas Hardy's Novels and Short Stories with Special Reference to Phonology and Vocabulary*, (Stockholm Theses in English, 7), Stockholm, 1972.
Blunden, Edmund, *Thomas Hardy*, London 1942.
Brook, G.L., *English Dialects*, (The Language Library), London, 1963.
——, *The Language of Dickens*, (The Language Library), London, 1970.
Brooks, Cleanth, *The Relation of the Alabama-Georgia Dialect to the Provincial Dialects of Great Britain*, Baton Rouge, 1935.
Clements, Patricia, and Juliet Grindle, eds., *The Poetry of Thomas Hardy*, London, 1980.
Collins, Vere H., *Talks with Thomas Hardy at Max Gate*, London, 1928, repr. 1978.
Cox, J.S. and G.S., eds., *Thomas Hardy Year Book*, St. Peter Port, Guernsey, 1970 *et seq*.
Cox, R.G., *Thomas Hardy: The Critical Heritage*, London and New York, 1970.
Davie, Donald, ed., *Agenda: Thomas Hardy Special Issue*, London, 1972.
——, *Thomas Hardy and British Poetry*, London, 1973.
Döll, Martha, *Die Verwendung der Mundart bei Thomas Hardy*, Giessen, 1923.
Drabble, Margaret, ed., *The Genius of Thomas Hardy*, London, 1976.

Select Bibliography

Draper, R.P., ed., *Thomas Hardy: The Tragic Novels*, London, 1975.

Eliot, T.S., *After Strange Gods*, London, 1934.

Elliott, R.W.V., *Hardy: Far From the Madding Crowd*, (Macmillan Critical Commentaries), London, 1966.

Firor, Ruth A., *Folkways in Thomas Hardy*, Philadelphia, 1931.

Gibson, James and Trevor Johnson, eds., *Thomas Hardy: Poems*, (Casebook Series), London, 1979.

Gittings, Robert, *Young Thomas Hardy*, London, 1975.

——, *The Older Hardy*, London, 1978.

——, and Jo Manton, *The Second Mrs Hardy*, London and Seattle, 1979.

Gregor, Ian, *The Great Web: The Form of Hardy's Major Fiction*, London, 1974.

Groom, B., *The Formation and Use of Compound Epithets in English Poetry from 1579*, (S.P.E. Tract XLIX), Oxford, 1937.

Grundy, Joan, *Hardy and the Sister Arts*, London, 1979.

Guerard, Albert J., ed., *Hardy: A Collection of Critical Essays*, (Twentieth Century Views), Englewood Cliffs, N.J., 1963.

Halliday, F.E., *Thomas Hardy: His Life and Work*, Bath, 1972.

Hardy, Evelyn, *Thomas Hardy, a Critical Biography*, London, 1954, re-issued 1970.

Hawkins, Desmond, *Hardy: Novelist and Poet*, Newton Abbot, 1976.

Hickson, Elizabeth, C., *The Versification of Thomas Hardy*, Philadelphia, 1931.

Holloway, John, *The Victorian Sage*, London, 1953.

Hutchins, John, *The History and Antiquities of the County of Dorset*, 4 vols., 3rd ed., Westminster, 1861–70.

Hynes, Samuel, *The Pattern of Hardy's Poetry*, Chapel Hill, 1961.

Jespersen, Otto, *A Modern English Grammar on Historical Principles*, 7 vols., London and Copenhagen, 1909 *et seq.*, repr. 1954.

Johnson, Lionel, *The Art of Thomas Hardy*, New York, 1894, rev. ed. 1923, repr. 1965.

Kay-Robinson, Denys, *The First Mrs Thomas Hardy*, London, 1979.

——, *Hardy's Wessex Reappraised*, Newton Abbot, 1972.

Kramer, Dale, *Thomas Hardy: The Forms of Tragedy*, London and Detroit, 1975.

——, ed., *Critical Approaches to the Fiction of Thomas Hardy*, London, 1979.

Laird, J.T., *The Shaping of Tess of the d'Urbervilles*, Oxford, 1975.

Lawrence, D.H., *Phoenix*, London, 1936.

Lea, Hermann, *Thomas Hardy's Wessex*, London, 1913, repr. 1977.

Lee, Vernon (Violet Paget), *The Handling of Words and Other Studies in Literary Psychology*, London and New York, 1923.

Lerner, Laurence and J. Holmstrom, *Thomas Hardy and his Readers: A Selection of Contemporary Reviews*, London, 1968.

Lodge, David, *The Language of Fiction : Essays in Criticism and Verbal Analysis of the English Novel*, London and New York, 1966.

Marsden, Kenneth, *The Poems of Thomas Hardy: A Critical Introduction*, London, 1969.

Miller, J. Hillis, *Thomas Hardy: Distance and Desire*, Cambridge, Mass., 1970.

Millgate, Michael H., *Thomas Hardy: His Career as a Novelist*, London and New York, 1971.

——, *Thomas Hardy: A Biography*, Oxford, 1982. (This book did not reach me until after the completion of my manuscript.)

Orel, Harold, *Thomas Hardy's Epic Drama: A Study of the Dynasts*, Lawrence, Kansas, 1963.

O'Sullivan, Timothy, *Thomas Hardy: An Illustrated Biography*, London, 1975.

Page, Norman, *Thomas Hardy*, London, 1977.

——, ed., *Thomas Hardy: The Writer and his Background*, London, 1980.

Partridge, Eric, *Notes on Punctuation*, Oxford, 1955.

Paterson, John, *The Making of the Return of the Native*, Berkeley, 1960.

Phillipps, K.C., *Jane Austen's English*, (The Language Library), London, 1970.

——, *Westcountry Words and Ways*, Newton Abbot, 1976.

Pinion, F.B., *A Commentary on the Poems of Thomas Hardy*, London, 1976.

——, *Thomas Hardy: Art and Thought*, London, 1977.

——, ed., *Budmouth Essays on Thomas Hardy*, Dorchester, 1976.

——, ed., *Thomas Hardy and the Modern World*, Dorchester, 1974.

Quirk, Randolph, *The Use of English*, London, 1962.

Rogers, N., *Wessex Dialect*, Bradford-on-Avon, 1979.

Rutland, William, *Thomas Hardy: A Study of his Writings and Their Background*, Oxford, 1938, repr. New York, 1962.

Smith, Anne, ed., *The Novels of Thomas Hardy*, London, 1979.

Southworth, James G., *The Poetry of Thomas Hardy*, New York, 1947.

Stewart, J.I.M., *Thomas Hardy: A Critical Biography*, London, 1971.

Stummer, Peter, *Sprachliche und Stoffliche Ausdrucksformen in den Romanen von Thomas Hardy*, München, 1969.

Thurley, Geoffrey, *The Psychology of Hardy's Novels: The Nervous and the Statuesque*, St. Lucia, Qld., 1975.

Tulloch, Graham, *The Language of Walter Scott. A Study of his Scottish and Period Language*, (The Language Library), London, 1980.

Udal, J.S., *Dorsetshire Folk-Lore*, Hertford, 1922.

Vigar, Penelope, *The Novels of Thomas Hardy: Illusion and Reality*, London, 1974.

Weber, Carl J., *Hardy of Wessex: His Life and Literary Career*, New York, 1940; rev. ed. New York and London, 1965.

Webster, H.C., *On a Darkling Plain: The Art and Thought of Thomas Hardy*, Chicago, 1947, repr. 1964.

Wheeler, Michael, *The Art of Allusion in Victorian Fiction*, London, 1979.

Widén, Bertil, *Studies on the Dorset Dialect*, (Lund Studies in English XVI), Lund, 1949.

Williams, Gordon, *Figures of Thought in Roman Poetry*, New Haven and London, 1980.

Williams, Merryn, *Thomas Hardy and Rural England*, London, 1972.

Wing, George, *Hardy*, (Writers and Critics), Edinburgh and London, 1963.

Wright, Elizabeth Mary, *Rustic Speech and Folklore*, Oxford, 1913.

Zietlow, Paul, *Moments of Vision: The Poetry of Thomas Hardy*, Cambridge, Mass., 1974.

*(b) Articles, Essays and Chapters*

Auden, W.H., 'A Literary Transference', *Southern Review* 6, 1940, 78–86.

Bailey, J.O., 'Hardy's "Mephistophelian Visitants" ', *PMLA* 61, 1946, 1146–84.

Bartlett, Phyllis, 'Hardy's Shelley', *Keats-Shelley Journal* 4, 1955, 15–29.

Beatty, C.J.P., 'Desperate Remedies 1871', *The Thomas Hardy Year Book* 2, 1971, 29–38.

Björk, Lennart A., 'Hardy's Reading', in *Thomas Hardy: The Writer and his Background*, ed. N. Page, 102–27.

Brooks, Cleanth, 'The Language of Poetry: Some Problem Cases', *Archiv für das Studium der Neueren Sprachen and Literaturen* 203, 1967, 401–14.

Carpenter, Richard C., 'The Mirror and the Sword: Imagery in *Far from the Madding Crowd*', *Nineteenth-Century Fiction* 18, 1963–64, 331–45.

Collins, Philip, 'Hardy and Education', in *Thomas Hardy: The Writer and his Background*, ed. N. Page, 41–75.

Davie, Donald, 'Hardy's Virgilian Purples', *Agenda* 10, nos. 2–3, 1972, 138–56.

Doherty, Paul C. and E. Dennis Taylor, 'Syntax in Hardy's "Neutral Tones" ', *Victorian Poetry* 12, 1974, 285–90. |

Eagleton, Terry, 'Thomas Hardy: Nature as Language', *Critical Quarterly* 13, 1971, 155–62.

Felkin, Elliott, 'Days with Thomas Hardy: from a 1918–1919 Diary', *Encounter* 18, 1962, 27–33.

Gallivan, Patricia, 'Science and Art in *Jude the Obscure*', in *The Novels of Thomas Hardy*, ed. A. Smith, 126–44.

Gatrell, Simon, 'Hardy, House-Style, and the Aesthetics of Punctuation', *ibid.*, 169–92.

Gibson, James, 'Hardy and his Readers', in *Thomas Hardy: The Writer and his Background*, ed. N. Page, 192–218.

Goldberg, M.A., 'Hardy's Double-Visioned Universe', *Essays in Criticism* 7, 1957, 374–82.

Goto, Yoshinoshin, 'Thomas Hardy Quoted in O.E.D. and E.D.D.', *Memoirs of Suzuka College of Technology* 1, 1967, 37–42.

Griffith, Philip M., 'The Image of the Trapped Animal in Hardy's Tess of the d'Urbervilles', *Tulane Studies in English* 13, 1963, 85–94.

Gunn, Thom, 'Hardy and the Ballads', *Agenda* 10, nos. 2–3, 1972, 19–46.

Hall, William F., 'Hawthorne, Shakespeare and Tess: Hardy's Use of Allusion and Reference', *English Studies* 52, 1971, 533–42.

Hardy, Evelyn, 'Thomas Hardy and Turner – The Painter's Eye', *London Magazine*, June–July 1975, 17–27.

Heilman, Robert B., 'Hardy's Mayor: Notes on Style', *Nineteenth-Century Fiction* 18, 1963–4, 307–29.

Horsman, E.A., 'The Language of *The Dynasts*', *Durham Uni-*

*versity Journal* n.s. 10, 1949, 11–16.

Hynes, Sam, 'Hardy and Barnes: Notes on Literary Influence', *South Atlantic Quarterly* 58, Winter 1959, 44–54.

Ingham, Patricia, 'Dialect in the Novels of Hardy and George Eliot', in *Literary English since Shakespeare*, ed. George Watson, Oxford, 1970, 347–63.

Jacobus, Mary, 'Tree and Machine: The Woodlanders', in *Critical Approaches to the Fiction of Thomas Hardy*, ed. Dale Kramer, 116–34.

Johnson, S.F., 'Hardy and Burke's "Sublime" ', in *Style in Prose Fiction* (English Institute Essays 1958), ed. Harold C. Martin, New York, 1959, 55–86.

Kramer, Dale, 'Repetition of Imagery in Thomas Hardy', *Victorian Newsletter* (N.Y.) 23, 1963, 26–7.

Laird, J.T., 'New Light on the Evolution of *Tess of the d'Urbervilles*', *Review of English Studies* 31, 1980, 414–35.

Larkin, Philip, 'Wanted: Good Hardy Critic', *Critical Quarterly* 8, 1966, 174–79.

Leavis, F.R., 'Hardy the Poet', *Southern Review* 6, 1940, 87–98.

Lewis, C. Day, 'The Lyrical Poetry of Thomas Hardy' *Proceedings of the British Academy* 37, 1951, 155–74.

Loane, George G., ' "The Dynasts" and the N.E.D.', *The Times Literary Supplement*, 14 February 1929, 118.

——, 'Hardy and N.E.D.', *ibid.*, 21 January 1932, 44.

McDowell, Frederick P.W., 'Hardy's "Seemings or Personal Impressions": The Symbolical Use of Image and Contrast in "Jude the Obscure" ', *Modern Fiction Studies* 6, 1960, 233–50.

May, Charles E., 'Hardy's "Darkling Thrush": the "Nightingale" grown old', *Victorian Poetry* 11, 1973, 62–5.

Morcos, Louis, ' "The Dynasts" and the Bible', *Annual Bulletin of English Studies*, Cairo, 1955, 29–65.

Morgan, William W., 'Syntax in Hardy's "Neutral Tones", Lines Seven to Eight', *Victorian Poetry* 11, 1973, 167–8.

Moynahan, Julian, '*The Mayor of Casterbridge* and the Old Testament's First Book of Samuel: A Study of Some Literary Relationships', *PMLA* 71, 1956, 118-30.

Page, Norman, 'Visual Techniques in Hardy's *Desperate Remedies*', *Ariel* 4, 1973, 65–71.

Paterson, John, 'The "Poetics" of "The Return of the Native" ', *Modern Fiction Studies* 6, 1960, 214–22.

Poole, Adrian, ' "Men's Words" and Hardy's Women', *Essays in*

*Criticism* 31, 1981, 328–345.

Porter, Katherine Anne, 'On a Criticism of Thomas Hardy', *Southern Review* 6, 1940, 150–61; repr. in *The Collected Essays and Occasional Writings of Katherine Anne Porter*, New York, 1970.

Ransom, John Crowe, 'Honey and Gall', *Southern Review* 6, 1940, 2–19.

Salter, C.H., 'Unusual Words beginning with *un*, *en*, *out*, *up* and *on* in Thomas Hardy's Verse', *Victorian Poetry*, 11, 1973, 257–61.

Sankey, Benjamin, 'Hardy's Prose Style', *Twentieth Century Literature* 11, 1965, 3–15; repr. in Sankey, *The Major Novels of Thomas Hardy*, Denver, 1965.

Scott, James F., 'Thomas Hardy's Use of the Gothic: An Examination of Five Representative Works', *Nineteenth-Century Fiction* 17, 1962–63, 363–80.

Sherman, Elna, 'Music in Thomas Hardy's Life and Work', *Musical Quarterly* 26, 1940, 419–45.

Slack, Robert C., 'The Text of Hardy's *Jude the Obscure*', *Nineteenth-Century Fiction* 11, 1957, 261–75.

Smart, Alastair, 'Pictorial Imagery in the Novels of Thomas Hardy', *Review of English Studies*, n.s. 12, 1961, 262–80.

Smith, L.E.W., 'The Impercipient (At a Cathedral Service)', in *Thomas Hardy: Poems*, ed. J. Gibson and T. Johnson, 185–9.

Stallworthy, Jon, 'Read by Moonlight', in *The Poetry of Thomas Hardy*, ed. P. Clements and J. Grindle, 172–88.

Tanner, Tony, 'Colour and Movement in *Tess of the d'Urbervilles*', *Critical Quarterly* 10, 1968, 219–39; repr. in *Hardy: The Tragic Novels*, ed. R.P. Draper, 182–208.

Taylor, Dennis, 'Victorian Philology and Victorian Poetry', *Victorian Newsletter* 53, 1978, 13–16.

Tristram, Philippa, 'Stories in Stone', in *The Novels of Thomas Hardy*, ed. Anne Smith, 145–68.

Vandiver, E.P., Jr., 'Hardy and Shakespeare Again', *Shakespeare Association Bulletin* 13, 1938, 87–95.

Weber, Carl J., 'Twin-Voice of Shakespeare', *Shakespeare Association Bulletin* 9, 1934, 91–7.

——, 'Shakespeare's Twin-Voice Again', *ibid.*, 162–3.

Williams, Raymond, 'Wessex and the Border', extracted from *The Country and the City*, in *The English Novel: Developments in Criticism since Henry James*, ed. Stephen Hazell (Casebook Series), London, 1978, 190–205.

Woolf, Virginia, 'The Novels of Thomas Hardy', in *The Second Common Reader*, London 1932; repr. in *Collected Essays*, vol. I, London, 1966, 256–66.

Zabel, Morton Dauwen, 'Hardy in Defense of his Art: The Aesthetic of Incongruity', *Southern Review* 6, 1940, 125–49.

Zietlow, Paul, 'Thomas Hardy and William Barnes', *PMLA* 74, 1969, 291–303.

# Index of Words

This Index lists those of Hardy's words and phrases which seemed of particular interest or relevance to the discussion. The Index is intended to be used in conjunction with the General Index where additional references will be found under appropriate headings.

zounds, 226,
zwailing, 75,

# General Index

In this Index Hardy's stories are referred to under the title of their collections, poems are referred to by title. For major works only the more important references are listed.

'At Wynyard's Gap', 107,
Auden, W.H., 22, 352f.,
'August Midnight, An', 158, 221, 261,
Austen, Jane, 110, 280,

Bacon, Francis, 345,
Bagehot, Walter, 25, 178,
'Bags of Meat', 223,
Bailey, J.O., 117, 310, 323,
Bainton, Rev. George, 329,
Barnes, William, 20, 26f., 30, Ch.3 *passim*, 138, 174, 190f., 208, 217, 297, 324, 330, 348ff.,
Bastow, H.R., 25, 113,
Baugner, Ulla, 40,
Bayley, John, 255, 259, 311, 323,
Beatty, C.J.P., 144, 146, 153n.,
'Beauty, The', 84,
'Beauty's Soliloquy during Her Honeymoon, A', 223,
Beckett, Samuel, 308,
'Bedridden Peasant, The', 306,
'Beeny Cliff', 247,
'Before and after Summer', 203,
'Before Life and After', 354,
'Before Marching and After', 175,
*Beowulf*, 185, 191,
'Bereft, She Thinks She Dreams', 202,
Bible, Ch.4,
    quotations, verbal echoes from, biblical and liturgical language, 111f., 114, 116f., 259, 304ff., 322, 332f., 350f.,
'Bird-Catcher's Boy, The', 189,
'Birds at Winter Nightfall', 173,
Björk, Lennart A., 24, 224,
Blomfield, Sir Arthur, 23,
Blunden, Edmund, 17, 20, 221,
Boldrewood, Rolf, 39, 65,
'Bride-Night Fire, The', Ch.3 *passim*, 312f.,
'Bridge of Lodi, The', 177, 279,
Britten, Benjamin, 353f.,
'Broken Appointment, A', 176, 183,
Brontë, Emily, 272,
Brook, G.L., 29n., 48, 296,

Brooks, Cleanth, 18, 32, 106, 213,
'Brother, The', 225,
Browne, Sir Thomas, 195,
Browning, Robert, 26, 135, 176, 350f.,
'Budmouth Dears', 215,
'Burghers, The', 318f.,
'By Henstridge Cross at the Year's End', 179,
Byron, Lord, 204, 214, 331,

'Caged Thrush Freed and Home Again, The', 93,
'Candour in English Fiction', 288,
Carlyle, Thomas, 134f., 195,
'Catching Ballet of the Wedding Clothes, The', 212,
Catullus, 128, 130,
Caxton, William, 194,
*Changed Man, A*,
    'The Waiting Supper', 105f., 108, 230, 248,
    'Alicia's Dairy', 149,
    'Enter a Dragoon', 92, 333, 341,
    'A Tryst at an Ancient Earthwork', 140, 326,
    'What the Shepherd Saw', 295,
    'A Committee Man of "The Terror" ', 108,
    'Master John Horseleigh, Knight', 227, 348,
    'A Mere Interlude', 276, 345,
    'The Romantic Adventures of a Milkmaid', 90, 148, 230, 244, 256,
'Channel Firing', 237, 283,
Chaucer, Geoffrey, 63, 170, 195, 214, 266, 299, 350f., 355,
Cheyne, T.K., 140,
'Chimes Play "Life's a Bumper", The', 216,
'Choirmaster's Burial, The', 354,
'Chosen, The', 239,
'Christening, The', 237, 285, 312,
'Christmas Ghost-Story, A', 176,
'Church-Builder, The', 147,
'Church Romance, A', 312,
classics, influence on Hardy's language, 126ff.,

language of men, of women, 336ff.,
received standard, 28ff., 339,
'Eunice', 149, 248f.,
'Every Artemisia', 241,
exclamations, 90, 225ff.,
'Expostulation, An', 135,

'Faded Face, The', 187,
'Faintheart in a Railway Train', 262,
'Family Portraits, 202,
*Famous Tragedy of the Queen of Cornwall, The*, 93, 184f., 227, 229, 248, 276, 348f.,
*Far from the Madding Crowd*, 13f., 111ff., 164f., 270f., 319f., 341,
'Farm-Woman's Winter, The', 46, 350,
Faulkner, William, 20, 32,
Faustus, Dr., 131,
Felkin, Elliott, 253,
'Felled Elm and She, The', 325,
'Fiddler, The', 312,
Fielding, Henry, 135, 280, 335,
'Fight on Durnover Moor, The', 77, 208,
figurative language, Ch. 4 *passim*, 172ff., 321ff., 333,
Firor, Ruth A., 88f.,
'Flirt's Tragedy, The', 211f.,
foreign words, 91f., 167ff.,
'Forgotten Miniature, A', 310,
*Fortnightly Review, The*, 119,
Fourier, F.M.C., 25,
'Four in the Morning', 239, 300,
'Fragment', 308,
*Fraser's Magazine*, 170, 319,
French influence, 233f.,
'Friends Beyond', 191,
Furbank, P.N., 346,
Furnivall, F.J., 348,

Gallivan, Patricia, 140,
Gatrell, Simon, 282, 288,
'Genitrix Laesa', 131, 181,
'Genoa and the Mediterranean', 177, 181ff.,
'Gentleman's Second-Hand Suit, A', 223,

Gibson, James, 204, 282, 285, 298,
Gifford, J.A., 29,
Ginnung Gap, 132,
Gittings, Robert, 113, 119, 160, 171, 351,
'God-Forgotten', 306f.,
'God's Education', 306,
'God's Funeral', 204f., 274, 306,
'Going, The', 183, 248,
Goldberg, M.A., 141,
Gosse, Sir Edmund, 25, 138, 188, 210, 281, 306, 328, 347,
Goto, Yoshinoshin, 171,
grammer, 271ff., 282,
grammatical categories, shifted, 211ff., 275,
*Graphic. The*, 127, 137, 285,
Graves, Robert, 171, 209, 211,
'Graveyard of Dead Creeds, The', 175,
Gray, Thomas, 137, 194,
Greuze, J.B., 111, 154,
Grigson, Geoffrey, 81, 121n.,
Grindle, Juliet, 282,
Groom, B., 173,
Grose, Francis, 224,
group genitive, 273f.,
*Group of Noble Dames, A*,
  'The First Countess of Wessex', 321,
  'Barbara of the House of Grebe', 276, 319,
  'The Marchioness of Stonehenge', 136,
  'Lady Mottisfont', 340,
  'Squire Petrick's Lady', 272f.,
  'The Duchess of Hamptonshire, 206,
  'The Honourable Laura', 153, 191
Grove, Agnes, 148,
Grundy, Isobel, 328,
Grundy, Joan, 157, 253,
Gunn, Thom, 19,

Hales, John, 60,
*Hand of Ethelberta, The*, 139, 145, 221, 320, 335,
'Hap', 10, 192, 276, 298f.,
Hardy, Barbara, 338,

# General Index

'Self-Unconscious', 193,
'Self-Unseeing, The', 193,
sentences,
  structure, 255ff.,
Shakespeare, William, 32, 58, 60,
  117, 120ff., 170, 187, 195, 211,
  213, 215, 217f., 266, 268, 271,
  299, 322, 350f.,
Shaw, G.B., 271,
'She at His Funeral', 187,
'Sheep-Boy, The', 247, 345,
Shelley, Percy Bysshe, 26, 135, 138,
  141, 148f., 170, 215, 302f., 338,
Sherman, Elna, 151n.,
'She to Him, I, II, III, IV, 350,
Shorthouse, J.H., 135,
'Shut Out that Moon', 176,
'Sick Battle-God, The', 181,
Sievers, Eduard, 349,
Sign-seeker, A', 308,
'Singer Asleep, A', 213,
Skeat, Rev. W.W., 348,
Skrymir, 134,
slang, 224f.,
'Sleep-Worker, The', 150,
Smart, Alistair, 154,
Smith, L.E.W., 193,
Smollett, Tobias, 225,
Sophocles, 126,
'Souls of the Slain', 179, 185,
'Sound in the Night, A', 190,
South, Robert, 136,
Southern Review, The, 16f.,
Southworth, J.G., 234, 240,
'So Various', 135,
Spasskaia, Vera, 37,
Spectator, The, 118,
'Spectres that Grieve', 158,
'Spellbound Palace, A', 238, 246,
  353,
'Spell of the Rose, The', 161, 316,
Spencer, Herbert, 135, 160,
Spenser, Edmund, 204, 211, 214,
  350,
'Spot, A', 215,
'Spring Call, The', 104,
'Squire Hooper', 212,
Steele, Sir Richard, 135,
Stephen, Leslie, 135,

Stephens, George, 27,
stereotyped language, 220f.,
Sterne, Laurence, 137,
Stevenson, Robert Louis, 281,
Stewart, J.I.M., 28,
style,
  Hardy's comments on, 329,
subjunctive, see verbs,
suffixes, 203ff.,
'Sunday Morning Tragedy, A', 161,
Sunday Times, The, 156,
'Superseded, The', 284,
'Supplanter, The', 177,
Sweet, Henry, 348,
'Sweet Hussy, The', 352,
Swinburne, Algernon, 135, 175,
  179, 272, 294, 350,
Sydney Mail, The, 127,
syntax, 255ff.,

Tanner, Tony, 155, 237,
Tannhäuser, 131,
Taylor, Dennis, 348,
Taylor, Richard H., 28, 164, 166,
technical language, 158ff.,
'Temporary the All, The', 175,
Tennyson, Alfred Lord, 135, 143,
  176, 195, 211, 215,
Terence, 26, 128,
Tess of the d'Urbervilles, 14, 115f.,
  122f., 127, 151, 154f., 170, 236f.,
  239f., 248, 337, 340,
'Tess's Lament', 192f.,
Thales, 140,
theatre,
  influence on Hardy's language,
  157f.,
Thor, 134,
'Thought in Two Moods, A', 243,
  249,
'Thoughts at Midnight', 203,
'Thoughts of Phena', 200,
Three Wayfarers, The, 157,
'Throwing a Tree', 324,
Thurley, Geoffrey, 263, 338,
Time's Laughingstocks and Other
  Verses, 284f., 312,
Times, The, 25, 138, 193, 329, 355,
'To a Lady Playing and Singing in

385